The Evolving Geography of Productivity and Employment

WORLD BANK LATIN AMERICAN AND CARIBBEAN STUDIES

The Evolving Geography of Productivity and Employment

Ideas for Inclusive Growth through a Territorial Lens in Latin America and the Caribbean

Elena Ianchovichina

Contents

Boxes

Figures

Maps

Tables

Foreword

For too long, lasting solutions to the low economic growth in Latin America and the Caribbean (LAC) have remained elusive. Even more perplexing, the high density of cities in this highly urbanized region has not fueled strong agglomeration economies as it has elsewhere in the world. Not only has this paradox prevented the LAC region from catching up to the standards of living in advanced economies, but it has also posed challenges, making it harder for the region's largely urban workforce to achieve its true potential.

The Evolving Geography of Productivity and Employment seeks to cast fresh light on this paradox with new data sources and methods. The central aim of the report is to examine the challenges through a "territorial" lens and thus gain a deeper, more detailed, and more nuanced understanding of the barriers to inclusive growth in a region known for its high income inequality.

The study dissects the evolving geography of productivity and employment in the LAC region across various territorial categories, from national economies to the provincial, municipal, and local levels. Among the most salient findings is that territorial inequality has declined in most countries since the turn of the century largely because urban productivity growth fell behind the productivity growth in poorer agricultural and mining areas. Many of these areas have thrived thanks to investments made during the commodity boom driven by demand in China.

The study identifies three interlocking factors that have weakened urban productivity. First, as LAC cities deindustrialized over the last three decades, urban employment shifted toward less dynamic, low-productivity nontradable services that tend to benefit less from agglomeration economies, especially in the largest cities, which typically are highly congested. Second, LAC cities are not optimally connected with each other. Poorly planned and inadequate infrastructure is one of the factors that has made it costly to transport goods around and across countries, thereby limiting market access and making it harder for firms to benefit from specialization by relocating to smaller low-cost urban locations. Third, in cities divided into distant low-income parts and affluent areas, agglomeration economies and knowledge spillovers are geographically limited, and the high informality in low-income settlements generates economic inefficiencies.

This report concludes that Latin America can rekindle its stalled inclusive growth only if it rebalances its development model to better leverage the skills and talents of its urban workforce. The report then proposes a range of policies across different territorial levels aimed at improving the productivity of urban economies and the efficiency with which countries transform their vast natural wealth into human capital, infrastructure, and institutions.

For the local level, it highlights the importance of improving the competitiveness, economic dynamism, and livability of cities. Competitive cities tend to have strong local institutions, good intraurban connectivity, enterprise support, access to finance and land, efficient permitting processes, and effective law enforcement. Improvements in air quality, public transportation, public education, and health services can also help urban authorities attract talent and stoke innovation in their municipalities.

At the regional level, a greater effort must be made to enhance the domestic infrastructure to reduce intercity transport costs, while also coordinating with partners in regional trade blocs to improve transnational connectivity. It would also help to abolish regulations that limit competition in the transport sector, as well as accelerate investments in information and communication technology and complementary services.

Finally, to boost nationwide competitiveness, the LAC region's governments must continue to make improvements in a wide range of areas: from macroeconomic management and education to nationwide innovation capabilities and the doing business environment.

No doubt this is a complex, but worthy, policy agenda. If tailored to the needs of individual countries and coordinated across geographic scales, it promises to finally accelerate inclusive growth in Latin America.

William F. Maloney
Chief Economist
Latin America and the Caribbean Region
World Bank

Carlos Felipe Jaramillo
Vice President
Latin America and the Caribbean Region
World Bank

Acknowledgments

The study described in this report was led by Elena Ianchovichina, a lead economist and head of research and analytics in the Jobs cross-cutting solutions group of the World Bank, and was conducted under the general guidance of William F. Maloney, chief economist, Latin America and the Caribbean Region (LCR). During the concept note stage, the report benefited from the guidance of Martin Rama, former LCR chief economist.

The report was written by Elena Ianchovichina, with inputs from a team that included Prottoy Akbar (Aalto University), Karen Barreto (World Bank), Martijn Burger (Erasmus University), Bruno Conte (University of Bologna), Olivia D'Aoust (World Bank), Carolina Diaz Bonilla (World Bank), Juan Carlos Duque (EAFIT University), Virgilio Galdo (World Bank), Gustavo García (EAFIT University), Nicole Gorton (University of California, Los Angeles), Federico Haslop (George Washington University), Anton Heil (London School of Economics and Political Science), Remi Jedwab (George Washington University), Nancy Lozano-Gracia (World Bank), Ruth Montanes (World Bank), Juan Ospina (EAFIT University), Jorge Patino (EAFIT University), Rafael Prieto Curiel (EAFIT University), Luis Quintero (Johns Hopkins University), Diana Sanchez (World Bank), Pedro Ferreira de Souza (Institute of Applied Economic Research, Brazil), Roy van der Weide (World Bank), Hernan Winkler (World Bank), and Roman Zarate (World Bank).

The team was fortunate to receive support from many experts and colleagues. Javier Morales (World Bank) provided useful suggestions on road networks data. Klaus Desmet (Southern Methodist University), Pablo Fajgelbaum (University of California, Los Angeles), David Nagy (Barcelona School of Economics), Esteban Rossi-Hansberg (University of Chicago), and Edouard Schaal (Barcelona School of Economics) shared their modeling codes. Prottoy Akbar, Victor Couture (University of British Colombia), Gilles Duranton (University of Pennsylvania), and Adam Storeygard (Tufts University) shared their mobility data.

Several distinguished peer reviewers provided excellent advice. Lorenzo Caliendo (Yale University), Klaus Desmet, Somik Lall (World Bank), and Mark Roberts (World Bank) offered insightful comments during the concept note stage, and at the World Bank Carlos Rodríguez Castelán, Luc Christiaensen, and Mathilde Lebrand provided valuable comments on the final draft. Appreciation is extended to Klaus Desmet and Esteban Rossi-Hansberg for their guidance during the initial stages of this work and to Matias Herrera Dappe, Doerte Doemeland, Imad Fakhoury, He He, Michel Kerf, Nancy Lozano-Gracia, Ayah Mahgoub, Carolina Monsalve, Sally Murray, Kristin Panier, Nicolas Peltier, Maria Marcela Silva, David Sislen, Dmitry Sivaev, Ayat Soliman, Maria Vagliasindi, and Anna Wellenstein—all at the World Bank—for their useful comments on the decision draft.

In addition, the study benefited from the comments of Erhan Artuc (World Bank), Sam Asher (Imperial College London), Martina Kirchberger (Trinity College Dublin), Somik Lall, Mathilde Lebrand, Eduardo Lora (Harvard Growth Lab), Nancy Lozano-Gracia, Bob Rijkers (World Bank), Adam Storeygard, and Frank van Oort (Erasmus University). All served as discussants of the background papers and notes prepared for the report and presented at an authors' workshop in June 2021. Luis Andrés (World Bank), Marek Hanusch (World Bank), William F. Maloney, Javier Morales, Martin Rama, Kavita Sethi (World Bank), Aiga Stokenberga (World Bank), and seminar audiences at Purdue University and the Urban Economics Association meetings also offered helpful comments on early drafts of the background work.

During its final stages, the study benefited from the comments of participants in two World Bank seminars organized by the LCR's Sustainable Development and Infrastructure Practices and from excellent policy advice and inputs by Nancy Lozano-Gracia, Dmitry Sivaev, and Aiga Stokenberga.

Publication of the report was overseen and carried out by Patricia Katayama (acquisitions editor), Stephen Pazdan (production editor), Sabra Ledent (copy editor), and Gwenda Larsen (proofreader) of the World Bank's formal publishing program. Bruno Bonansea and Brenan Gabriel Andre, information officers in the Cartography unit of the World Bank, prepared the final versions of some of the maps featured in the book. The translation of the overview into Spanish was reviewed by José Andrée Camarena Fonseca (World Bank) and into Portuguese by Rafael Vilarouca Nunes (World Bank). Finally, Jacqueline Larrabure Rivero provided excellent administrative support.

Although their guidance was valuable, any remaining errors, omissions, or interpretations should not be attributed to the reviewers, advisers, or discussants of this report.

About the Author

Elena Ianchovichina is a lead economist and head of research and analytics in the Jobs cross-cutting solutions group of the World Bank. Previously, she was deputy chief economist and lead economist for the Latin America and the Caribbean and the Middle East and North Africa Regions. Her work focuses on policies for inclusive growth—a concept she helped define and link to productive employment in 2009. Since then, she has led research and diagnostic studies on various dimensions of inclusive growth, such as the geography of urban employment, inequality, subjective well-being, migration and trade frictions, middle-class dynamics, infrastructure and job creation, foreign direct investment, political risk, polarization and conflict, and ways to boost female employment. Prior to 2009, she worked in the World Bank's Trade Research Group, the East Asia and Pacific Region, and the Economic Policy and Debt Department, where she focused on policies for economic growth, fiscal sustainability, and trade. Her research has been published in books and scholarly journals, such as the *Journal of Development Economics*, *Journal of International Business Studies*, *Review of Income and Wealth*, and *World Bank Economic Review*. She holds a PhD from Purdue University, which named her a Distinguished Woman Scholar in 2022.

Main Messages

- *The Evolving Geography of Productivity and Employment* uses a "territorial" lens to analyze the perennial problem of low growth in Latin America and the Caribbean (LAC). It employs new data sources and methods to dissect how productivity and employment evolved in different geographic locations and sheds light on the region's urban productivity paradox of cities that are dense but not particularly productive.
- A key finding is that a striking convergence in labor and place productivity within countries reduced territorial inequality between the early 2000s and the late 2010s throughout the LAC region. Poor, predominantly rural regions began catching up due to improvements in agricultural productivity and investment in mining activities. However, urban productivity growth remained relatively weak.
- Convergence narrowed the income disparities with leading metropolitan areas in the LAC region, including the gaps that could be exploited by migrating to these top locations—these areas deindustrialized but continued to attract migrants. Among residents in the bottom 40 percent of the income distribution, these gaps became negligible in most LAC countries except Bolivia, Brazil, Panama, and Peru, where regional inequality remained high.
- This report identifies three intertwined factors that have weakened the benefits of agglomeration economies, thereby providing an explanation for the LAC region's urban productivity paradox: (1) the deindustrialization of cities, (2) connectivity issues, and (3) divisions within cities.
  - With the deindustrialization of LAC cities over the last three decades, urban employment has shifted toward less dynamic, low-productivity, nontradable services, such as retail trade and personal and other services. These activities offer lower wages and returns to experience, have more limited potential for catch-up through dynamic productivity gains, and benefit less from internal returns to scale than urban tradables, such as manufacturing and tradables services. The shift constrains the growth in nationwide productivity because the region's workforce is mostly urban. It also limits urban place productivity because firms

offering nontradable products and services benefit less from co-location than firms offering urban tradables, and their agglomeration benefits are reduced more rapidly with increases in congestion, which is a major problem in the LAC region's largest cities.

- Connectivity issues negatively affect the performance of the LAC region's network of cities by limiting market access, knowledge spillovers, and the ability of firms to specialize by relocating to smaller urban areas. High intercity transport costs reflect to different degrees in different countries a host of issues, including low and badly allocated investments in road improvements, backhaul problems, imperfect competition, government regulations, and information frictions. Digital technologies can be leveraged to overcome transport infrastructure deficiencies, but the LAC region's progress in expanding access to affordable high-speed internet services, especially among poor and rural communities, has been slow.

- Reinforced by long and costly commutes, divisions within cities, especially in some of the region's leading metropolitan areas, have hurt urban productivity by limiting the geographic span of agglomeration economies to central business districts. Divisions also generate spatial misallocation stemming from the informality traps in low-income neighborhoods, often located in the urban periphery. Moreover, deficiencies in basic infrastructure and public services in these low-income areas erode the employability, productivity, and resilience of less affluent urbanites through greater exposure to climate shocks, disease, and crime.

• The findings in the report reveal that during the Golden Decade (2003–13), the LAC region's commodity-driven model of development delivered convergence in territorial productivity and living standards but achieved only a short-lived spurt in economic growth. To accelerate growth in a sustainable, inclusive way, the region needs to blend its resource-driven model of development with one that better leverages the skills and labor of its urban workforce. To develop such a two-pronged development model, countries in the region will have to improve the productivity and competitiveness of their urban economy and enhance the efficiency with which they transform natural wealth into human capital, infrastructure, and institutions.

• Firing up the engine of urban growth requires implementing policies on three territorial scales: national, regional, and local.

- At the national level, countries must boost nationwide competitiveness to stimulate the growth of urban tradables and thus the potential of these sectors to generate high-productivity jobs. Improvements are needed in a wide range of areas: from macroeconomic management and education to nationwide innovation capabilities, competition policy, and the "doing business" environment. Making regulations simpler and more predictable, increasing the transparency of legal frameworks and property protection, strengthening competition policy, improving access to finance, enforcing the rule of law, facilitating trade and investment, and harmonizing behind-the-border regulations will attract foreign investment and stimulate export growth. The weak rise in the share of employment in tradable services over the last three decades suggests that the LAC region also needs to implement comprehensive reforms that speed up competition and innovation in these sectors, in addition to closing skill gaps that limit the supply of talent to these sectors. Progress in these areas should go hand in hand with efforts to strengthen national institutions for the management of resource rents and their efficient spending.

- At the regional level, a greater effort is needed toward enhancing domestic infrastructure to reduce intercity transport costs, while also coordinating with regional trading partners to improve transnational transport connectivity. Abolishing regulations that limit competition in the transport sector and accelerating investments in digital connectivity and complementary services would also be helpful. In this context, it is important to improve the efficiency of subnational spending and the ability of regional governments to mobilize their own resources.

  - At the local level, it is important to improve the competitiveness, economic dynamism, and livability of cities. To turn around the fortunes of their cities, local governments must invest in local institutions and enterprise support, as well as improve access to finance and land, the efficiency of permitting processes, and the effectiveness of law enforcement. Investing in basic urban infrastructure, affordable housing, and improvements in air quality, public transportation, education, health services, and other urban amenities could also help attract talent and stoke innovation in their municipalities.

- The complex policy agenda just outlined must be tailored to the needs of individual countries and coordinated across different territorial scales through enhanced intergovernmental collaboration. If implemented well, these policies promise to finally lift inclusive growth in Latin America above the disappointing levels of the past decades.

Executive Summary

Geographical factors have largely been ignored by those trying to explain the record of persistently low economic growth in Latin America and the Caribbean (LAC). The study described in this report has attempted to rectify that oversight. Relying on the core concepts of economic geography, state-of-the-art techniques, and new data sources, the study adopts a "territorial" lens to identify the geographical factors that constrain inclusive growth in the region. An analytical framework that embraces all spatial scales offers insights that cannot be gained by focusing separately on each spatial level or by conducting a country-level analysis that overlooks the spatial unevenness of economic activity and its persistence over time.

The report begins with a broad view of territorial productivity differences across various locations—from predominantly urban to mostly rural areas—and their evolution between the early 2000s and the late 2010s in many LAC countries. It then explores the frictions that limit the mobility of goods and people within and across countries in the region and quantifies the extent to which those frictions hamper economic growth and welfare. Next, urban areas come under the lens. The analysis traces the evolution of the composition of urban employment by city size and the factors that weaken urban productivity growth, such as mobility and congestion issues. Finally, the lens shifts toward economic activity within cities, shedding light on socioeconomic differences across neighborhoods in some of the LAC region's largest cities and their productivity implications.

The study finds that three factors undermine the economic advantages of cities and merit special attention: (1) the deindustrialization of cities, which has sapped them of their dynamism and shifted economic activity toward low-productivity, nontradable services; (2) the costs of distance between cities, which hamper economic integration, specialization, and knowledge spillovers—and therefore productivity growth; and (3) the divisions of cities into disconnected poor and affluent areas, which limit the geographic span of agglomeration economies, obstruct information flows, and generate resource misallocation because of the prevalence of informality in low-income neighborhoods.

Territorial productivity and employment trends

Until the early 2000s, the territorial differences in labor income in the LAC countries were large and persistent, or they were declining at a relatively slow pace. By the early 2000s, however, many LAC countries had begun to diverge from the path of other low- and middle-income countries where industrialization through export-led growth had powered the growth of cities. This report documents a dramatic convergence in labor and place productivity at the regional level in most Latin American countries and at the municipal level in all of them. This convergence reduced regional inequality in most countries in the first two decades of the twenty-first century. Within countries, the income disparities between the leading metropolitan and other areas also declined from the early 2000s to the late 2010s, reflecting improvements in the endowments of households living outside the largest cities and, in many cases, smaller differences in the returns from education. Thus by the end of the 2010s, the potential benefits of migration to the top metropolitan localities had become relatively small (especially among the bottom 40 percent of the income distribution) in all countries except Bolivia, Brazil, Panama, and Peru, where residents of the poorest subnational regions still face high barriers to migration.

Meanwhile, many rural areas prospered following years of high commodity prices stemming from the growing demand for resources and farm products by China and other fast-growing economies. During the commodity boom of the Golden Decade (2003–13), investments and incomes in rural areas increased, but the Dutch Disease effects from the commodity windfall—and, in some countries, remittances—also boosted spending on imported goods and services, weakening the competitiveness of urban tradable goods and services. At the same time, steep foreign competition, especially from China after it joined the World Trade Organization in 2001, along with advances in labor-saving technologies as machines replaced workers, further depressed manufacturing employment.

These developments continued a deindustrialization trend that had begun years earlier. Faced by mounting economic problems, many countries in Latin America abandoned the costly, inefficient import substitution policies that helped them to industrialize, but they did little to create globally competitive manufacturing sectors. Instead, countries leaned on sectors of comparative advantage: agriculture, mining, and the processing of food and natural resources. Ample endowments of fertile soil and natural resources and the growing use of capital and fertilizers improved labor productivity in agriculture and other commodity sectors between 1980 and 2013 and fueled the expansion of commodity exports.

An unbalanced development model

In response, the region's development model gradually became unbalanced. Rural and mining economies turned into powerful engines of economic growth, but cities gradually lost their dynamism. After most Latin American countries sharply reduced tariffs and other trade restrictions in the late 1980s or early 1990s, layoffs in the formal manufacturing sector followed, especially in the largest cities, where laid-off workers switched to informal, lower-quality jobs in the nontradable sector.

The deindustrialization of cities did not lead to deurbanization because agricultural expansion did not require more labor. Although employment in urban tradable services rose, including in finance, insurance, and real estate, the increase began from a low level and was not sufficiently strong to offset the decline in manufacturing employment. Agglomeration forces made it difficult to launch new tradable activities elsewhere as deindustrialization shifted the employment profile of cities of all sizes away from urban tradables. Thus urban employment shifted toward less dynamic and less productive urban nontradables, such as retail trade, personal services, and construction. This happened to varying degrees in different countries, but in nearly all, deindustrialization was most pronounced in the largest metropolitan areas.

By the start of the new millennium, Latin America had a deficit of so-called production cities with a disproportionately large share of employment in urban tradables. None of the production cities were large or globally significant. And yet the cities continued to attract those who wanted to learn from the skilled workers already living there, as well as benefit from better and more diverse consumer amenities and access to political power. The concentration of skills generated benefits, but the net returns of agglomeration economies were not significant in most Latin American countries because cities failed to generate benefits from co-location and market access. On average, the place productivity premia in predominantly urban localities were only slightly higher than those in mostly rural ones in the late 2010s.

Explaining the LAC region's urban productivity paradox

The urban productivity paradox of dense but relatively unproductive cities presents a major growth challenge, not least because of the heavily urbanized nature of Latin America's workforce and the high concentration of workers in large, dense cities. Factors that *increase* the costs of density—including those associated with congestion, crime, competition from informal firms, and real estate prices—are key reasons for the weak net agglomeration economies in Latin America. Those costs escalate when urban policy, planning, and management, as well as improvements in transport, communication, and basic infrastructure, fail to keep up with increases in density. Urban productivity can be further restrained by issues such as the size and shape of cities and inner-city connectedness. This study points to three additional interconnected explanations for weak net agglomeration economies in Latin America. All three center on factors that *reduce* the agglomeration benefits.

First, *deindustrialization* has constrained both labor and place productivity growth in the region's urban areas. In deindustrialized cities where employment is tilted toward low-productivity, nontradable services, agglomeration benefits are weaker because such activities benefit less from being provided in dense cities. Nontradable activities tend to employ unskilled labor, account for a large share of activity in an economy, and are unlikely to exhibit increasing returns to scale if they agglomerate. With increases in congestion, the benefits of agglomeration tend to decline more quickly for nontradables than for tradables. Although the markets for nontradables are potentially larger in bigger and denser cities, traffic congestion and competition can considerably reduce market size because nontradable services are often provided in person during peak business hours. Manufacturing firms can better cope with congestion by using storage and transporting inputs and final goods during off-peak traffic hours. Unfortunately, congestion is a serious problem in Latin America's largest cities, which are some of the most congested in the world.

The employment shift toward nontradables has also reduced the potential for dynamic productivity gains in Latin America's urban areas. Studies have shown that returns to education and work experience vary across urban sectors and are higher in urban tradables. In countries where the share of urban workers in tradables is low, human capital is employed in less productive urban sectors, and, overall, the returns to experience are lower. Productivity growth is also slower in countries with disproportionately high employment in urban nontradables because these activities do not benefit from endogenous innovation and dynamic gains from trade.

Second, the costs of distance are high both within cities and between cities. *Connectivity* issues within cities reduce the agglomeration benefits for firms, especially those in the nontradable sectors. Even without congestion and regardless of city size, moving around within Latin American cities takes longer than in comparable cities in the rest of the world. Uncongested urban mobility also declines much faster as cities in Latin America become denser, suggesting deficiencies in urban planning and infrastructure. Meanwhile, intercity connectivity issues undermine the performance of the region's network of cities by limiting interurban market access and the ability of manufacturing firms to specialize and gain from internal economies of scale by relocating to smaller urban areas, which in the LAC region also struggle with the provision of infrastructure, basic consumer amenities, and local public goods and services.

Interurban transport costs are higher in the LAC region than in the European Union and East Asia because the region has underinvested in transport infrastructure, especially along segments connecting the region's more populous and most productive urban areas. The losses from this misallocation in terms of aggregate output and welfare are considerable in Argentina and Brazil. But they can be fully offset with additional investments along routes that have received insufficient investments in the past. Improved transnational intercity road connectivity can also stimulate regional trade and unlock much-needed efficiency gains, as demonstrated in the cases of MERCOSUR and the Andean Community.

In the meantime, investments in digital infrastructure and high-speed internet services can reduce the costs of distance and allow people to collaborate virtually. Estimates suggest that workers in Latin America rely on telecommuting much less than those in member countries of the Organisation for Economic Co-operation and Development. Territorial differences in the prevalence of telecommuting to work are also large, reflecting differences in the availability of jobs suitable for telecommuting, differences in digital infrastructure, and the affordability of internet services. In addition, there are significant urban deficits in internet access in several Latin American countries. The percentage of urban workers with jobs suitable for telecommuting but without internet access in their homes is largest in Bolivia, Colombia, Guatemala, Mexico, and Nicaragua.

Third, cities in Latin America and the Caribbean are both unequal and divided into geographically distant poor and affluent parts. Using examples from Colombia and Mexico, the report shows that such divisions weaken agglomeration economies and generate economic inefficiencies. *Urban divisions*—reinforced by intraurban connectivity issues—lower the returns to density by limiting their geographic scope. In divided cities, the large gains from sharing, matching, and learning are limited to neighborhoods in central business districts where formal firms operate, consumer amenities are abundant, and residents enjoy better-quality basic infrastructure and public services. The opposite is found in low-income neighborhoods, where residents often face multiple deprivations in terms of access to basic infrastructure and public services. Typically, in the urban periphery firms and workers in low-income neighborhoods are mostly informal, and basic infrastructure and public services are often deficient, exposing residents to the risks of flooding, mudslides, disease, and crime. The existence of a dual urban economy—a formal one in central business districts and a low-productivity one in low-income neighborhoods where residents find themselves in an informality trap—generates spatial misallocation because informal firms do not pay taxes. The occurrence of such misallocation in the region's largest cities could significantly undermine aggregate output growth.

Policy road map

The spatial analysis presented in this report has several important implications for economic policy. Over the last two decades, Latin America's resource-driven model of development delivered convergence in territorial productivity and living standards, but only a short-lived spurt in economic growth during the Golden Decade. To accelerate growth in a sustainable, inclusive way, the region needs to blend its resource-driven model of development with one that better leverages the skills and labor of its urban workforce. Developing such a two-pronged development model will require improving the productivity and competitiveness of the urban economy and enhancing the efficiency with which countries transform natural wealth into human capital, infrastructure, and institutions. If the LAC region succeeds in these tasks, two engines of growth—urban and rural—will power economic growth beyond the low levels of the past and generate much-needed high-productivity jobs in urban areas. However, the transition to a two-pronged model of development depends on whether countries can overcome multidimensional development challenges on all geographic scales—national, regional, and local—recognizing that the mix of issues varies in importance across countries.

At the national level, countries must tackle *nationwide competitiveness weaknesses* that limit inclusive growth, especially that of urban tradables and the potential of these sectors to generate high-productivity jobs. Governments must protect macroeconomic stability, improve the quality of and access to public education, boost nationwide innovation capabilities, and simplify and reduce policy and regulatory distortions. Attracting quality private investment in the urban tradable sectors requires making the regulatory environment more predictable, increasing the transparency of legal frameworks and property protection, strengthening competition policy and the rule of law, improving access to finance, facilitating trade and investment, and harmonizing local regulations with international standards. Improving the state of international connectivity infrastructure and logistics (such as ports and roads) will also help to strengthen export competitiveness and allow Latin American firms to take advantage of global shifts in production such as those linked to green growth, 3D printing, and efforts to increase the importance of services in manufacturing. The weak rise in the share of employment in tradable services over the last three decades suggests that the region also needs to implement comprehensive reforms that speed up competition and innovation in the tradable services sectors, in addition to closing skill gaps that limit the supply of talent to these sectors. Progress in these areas should go hand in hand with strengthening national institutions for managing resource rents and improving intergovernmental fiscal systems.

At the regional level, the report shows that improvements in domestic and transnational transport infrastructure can reduce intercity transport costs and significantly boost economic growth in the region. These investments will have to be complemented with investments in environmental services to address issues associated with flooding and other disaster-related challenges. In parallel, governments should work on abolishing regulations that limit competition in the transport sector and inflate prices along certain routes and on fast-tracking investments in digital connectivity. Closing education, knowledge, and information gaps with the leading metropolitan areas will contribute to technological diffusion and increase the employability of residents in lagging regions and their potential to benefit from migration and employment in regional and national urban centers.

At the local level, authorities should provide a fertile environment for private sector growth and productive job creation. Although there are no recipes for becoming a successful competitive city, studies have identified a set of prerequisites that can help cities reinvent themselves and become competitive. They include good local institutions, enterprise support and finance, skills and innovation, infrastructure and access to land, and good coordination to successfully overcome fragmentation issues that might block progress or increase service provision costs. Local authorities need to improve their efforts to provide infrastructure that enhances intraurban mobility, which is low in cities of all sizes, and implement policies that tackle congestion. City authorities can meet the demand for urban mobility at relatively low infrastructure cost through integrated land use and transport planning; a greater reliance on integrated public transport systems, including mass transit such as metros and bus rapid transit; and policies that increase rail occupancy, discourage private transport, and improve traffic management. The latter includes (1) congestion pricing; (2) high-occupancy vehicle (HOV) restrictions; (3) parking management; (4) improved access to affordable, fast, and reliable internet infrastructure and digital services; and (5) reductions in fuel subsidies. More also needs to be done to improve basic urban infrastructure, the supply of affordable quality housing, and access to public services, especially in poor neighborhoods.

Individual countries must adapt this strategy to their own circumstances and coordinate policies across different territorial scales. This is an ambitious and complex undertaking, but, if implemented well, Latin America could finally enter a new era of higher and more inclusive economic growth.

Abbreviations

BRT	bus rapid transit
CEDLAS	Center for Distributive, Labor and Social Studies (Argentina)
CEPAL	Economic Commission for Latin America and the Caribbean
CES	constant elasticity of substitution
COVID-19	coronavirus disease 2019
DANE	National Administrative Department of Statistics (Colombia)
DENUE	National Statistical Directory of Economic Units (Mexico)
ERCN	Economy-Regions-Cities-Neighborhoods (conceptual framework)
FIRE	finance, insurance, and real estate
FUA	functional urban area
G7	Group of 7
GDP	gross domestic product
GHSL	Global Human Settlement Layer
GPW	Gridded Population of the World
GRIP	Global Roads Inventory Project (World Bank)
GWP	Gallup World Poll
ICT	information and communication technology
IDB	Inter-American Development Bank
INEGI	National Institute of Statistics and Geography (Mexico)
IPUMS	Integrated Public Use Microdata Series
LAC	Latin America and the Caribbean
LCR	Latin America and the Caribbean Region
LISA	local indicators of spatial association
NAFTA	North American Free Trade Agreement
OECD	Organisation for Economic Co-operation and Development
PPP	purchasing power parity
SEDAC	Socioeconomic Data and Applications Center
SEDLAC	Socio-Economic Database for Latin America and the Caribbean
SWB	subjective well-being

Overview

Why does the Latin America and the Caribbean (LAC) region[1] suffer from persistently low economic growth? Repeated attempts by economists to answer this question[2] have rarely focused on geographical factors—that is, those that limit the movement of goods and workers from one area to another and those that weaken urban productivity. Yet these factors may play a key role in keeping the region's economic growth low.

Three issues merit special attention: (1) the deindustrialization of cities, which has sapped cities of their dynamism but has not stopped their growth; (2) the poor connectivity between and within cities, which hampers economic integration, specialization, and agglomeration economies; and (3) the divisions of cities into poor and affluent areas, which limit the geographic scope of agglomeration economies and generate inefficiencies. Paradoxically, although many rural areas have prospered following years of high commodity prices, the region's cities have not performed as well, despite their great density. Indeed, Latin American cities have become bigger, but not better. A costly disconnect between the region's urban and rural economies—as well as between cities and between poor and affluent areas within cities—may be one of the biggest bottlenecks to inclusive growth in Latin America today.

More than four centuries ago, Francis Bacon, the father of empiricism, identified the importance of connectivity *and* urban dynamism. He highlighted "the easy conveyance of men and goods from place to place" and "busy workshops" as two of three factors that make nations great (the other being "fertile soil"). This crucial insight was more recently echoed in the World Bank's 2009 *World Development Report*, which argued that both the concentration of industrial production in urban areas and the institutions that help living standards to converge are essential components of any successful economy (World Bank 2009).

This study explores how labor incomes and productivity evolved in various geographic locations—from dense cities to remote areas—within most Latin American countries between the early 2000s and the late 2010s.[3] It then assesses the extent of limited mobility by looking at transport and migration costs, and then the degree to which limited mobility leads to the misallocation of resources and constrains national output and welfare growth. Last but not least, this study highlights how some structural and geographical features of the LAC countries, such as deindustrialization and residential segregation, undermine the productivity of cities.

Using the core concepts of economic geography, state-of-the-art techniques, and a wide variety of data sources, this report adopts a "territorial" lens to study the key constraints to specialization, migration, and agglomeration and their impact on long-run economic growth in Latin America. It also explores the geography of urban employment and the evolution of its composition by city size over the last few decades. The territorial approach offers insights on the evolution of labor *and* place productivity in different locations within countries and the implications of these developments for inclusive growth.

Forces of deindustrialization

Until the early 2000s, the territorial differences in labor income within Latin American countries were large and persistent, or they were declining at a relatively slow pace,[4] as in most other low- and middle-income countries where industrialization through export-led growth had powered the growth of cities. Stark contrasts were found between lagging and leading territories in Mexico's north and south,[5] Colombia's peripheral and core regions,[6] Brazil's northeast and south,[7] and Peru's coastal and inland areas.[8] Meanwhile, territorial income convergence was either not observed[9] or occurring at a very slow pace.[10]

In the 2000s, however, Latin America started behaving differently from other emerging economies. The urban wage premium began to decline, plummeting rapidly between 2003 and 2008 and stagnating afterward (Rodríguez-Castelán et al. 2022), leading to a decline in inequality between urban and rural areas. This reversal of fortune was driven in part by the rise in commodity rents from the growing demand for resources and farm products by China and other fast-growing economies. During the commodity boom of the Golden Decade (2003–13), investments and incomes in rural areas increased, but the Dutch Disease[11] effects from the commodity windfall—and in some countries remittances—also boosted spending on imported goods and services, weakening the competitiveness of urban tradable activities[12] (Venables 2017). At the same time, steep foreign competition, especially from China after it joined the World Trade Organization in 2001, along with advances in labor-saving technologies as machines replaced workers, further depressed manufacturing employment. With deindustrialization, the composition of urban employment shifted toward mostly low-productivity, nontradable services such as retail, construction, and personal services (Jedwab, Ianchovichina, and Haslop 2022), thereby depressing labor productivity growth in urban areas.[13] Although rural areas were benefiting from the changes taking place, cities were not. Cities continued to grow, but they did not become more efficient. They simply became more crowded and congested.

The deindustrialization of Latin American cities actually began years earlier (Beylis et al. 2020). Faced by mounting economic problems, many countries in Latin America abandoned the costly and inefficient import substitution policies that helped them to industrialize, but did little to create globally competitive manufacturing sectors. Instead, countries leaned on sectors of comparative advantage: agriculture, mining, and the processing of food and natural resources. Ample endowments of fertile soil and natural resources and the growing use of capital and fertilizers improved labor productivity in agriculture (Nin Pratt et al. 2015) and other commodity sectors (Adão 2015) between 1980 and 2012 and fueled the expansion of commodity exports. This expansion eventually enabled the region to become the largest agricultural exporter in the world and the third-largest exporter of fuel and mining outputs (Jedwab, Ianchovichina, and Haslop 2022).

In response, the region's development model became increasingly unbalanced. As rural economies became powerful engines of economic growth, Latin American cities were gradually losing their dynamism. After most Latin American countries sharply reduced tariffs and other trade restrictions in the late 1980s or early 1990s (Bellon 2018; Dix-Carneiro and Kovak 2023; Terra 2003),[14] layoffs in the formal manufacturing sector followed,[15] especially in the largest cities, where laid-off workers switched to jobs in the nontradable sector, which were often informal and of lower quality (Dix-Carneiro and Kovak 2017; Jedwab, Ianchovichina, and Haslop 2022).

Deindustrialization did not lead to deurbanization in the region because the agricultural expansion did not require more labor. Thus as depicted in figure O.1, especially in the largest cities, the employment share of urban tradables declined and urban employment shifted toward less dynamic urban nontradables (Jedwab, Ianchovichina, and Haslop 2022).[16] By about 2000, the LAC region had a deficit of so-called "production cities" with a disproportionately large employment share of urban tradables, and none of them was large or globally significant (map O.1). Instead, city dwellers in the region mostly crowded into large "neutral cities" (such as Buenos Aires and Mexico City), where the employment share of urban tradables was neither too low nor too high, or "consumption cities" (such as Bogotá and Rio de Janeiro), where the employment share of urban tradables was disproportionately low. The concentration in these leading business centers was also driven by access to political power, public services, and consumer amenities.

FIGURE O.1   Evolution of share of employment in tradables by city size and decade: LAC region, 1980 or earlier to circa 2010

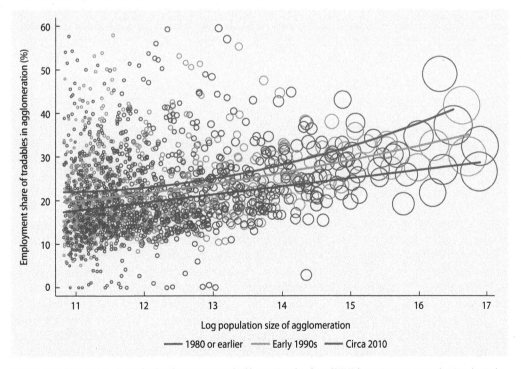

Source: Jedwab, Ianchovichina, and Haslop (2022), using Integrated Public Use Microdata Series (IPUMS, https://www.ipums.org/) census data and the Global Human Settlement Layer database (https://ghsl.jrc.ec.europa.eu/download.php).
Note: The graph shows the downward shift over time in the trend line, linking the employment share of tradables, which include manufacturing and tradable services such as finance, insurance, and real estate services, and the size of functional urban areas (FUAs), proxied with the log of the number of inhabitants of the FUA.

MAP O.1   **Global distribution of consumption, production, and neutral cities, circa 2000**

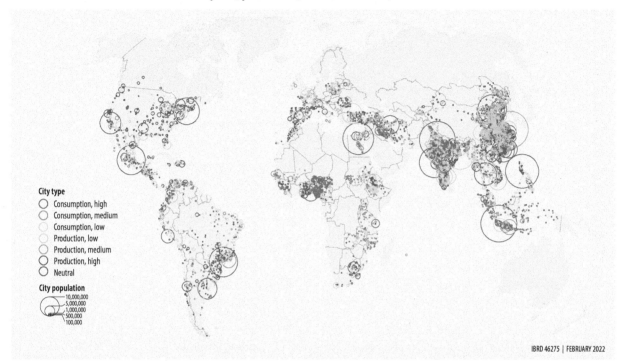

Source: Jedwab, Ianchovichina, and Haslop (2022), using Integrated Public Use Microdata Series (IPUMS, https://www.ipums.org/) census data and the Global Human Settlement Layer database (https://ghsl.jrc.ec.europa.eu/download.php).
Note: An urban area is classified as a *consumption city* (with a disproportionately low employment share of urban tradables), a *production city* (with a disproportionately high employment share of urban tradables), or a *neutral city* (in which the share of employment in tradables is neither too low nor too high). Paler shades of each color indicate lower values for the extent to which a city can be classified as each specific type.

Mapping out the analysis

The Economy-Regions-Cities-Neighborhoods (ERCN) framework in figure O.2 organizes the country-level investigations in this study using territorial scales from highest to lowest: (1) national economy, (2) subnational regions, (3) cities, and (4) neighborhoods. The ERCN framework allows starting with a broad view of territorial productivity differences across first- and second-level administrative regions and their evolution between the early 2000s and the late 2010s in 14 Latin American countries. The first-level administrative regions are administrative units below the national level: states, provinces, or departments, depending on the country. The second-level administrative units are municipalities (such as in Brazil, Colombia, the Dominican Republic, Honduras, and Mexico), provinces (such as in Peru), cantons (such as in Costa Rica and Ecuador), and communes (such as in Chile), which can be large or small predominantly rural, urban, or metropolitan localities.[17]

This framework allows gradual refinement of the focus of the analysis by narrowing the spatial lens to better identify resource misallocation and productivity differences across locations of descending size. Using advanced econometric techniques and general equilibrium models, this study builds a narrative based on a rich set of empirical sources and recently released harmonized household surveys and census data, which are used across each of the four spatial scales whenever possible. This approach yields insights that cannot be obtained by focusing separately on issues at each spatial scale. It also enables detection

FIGURE O.2   Economy-Regions-Cities-Neighborhoods (ERCN) framework for analysis of a country's spatial development

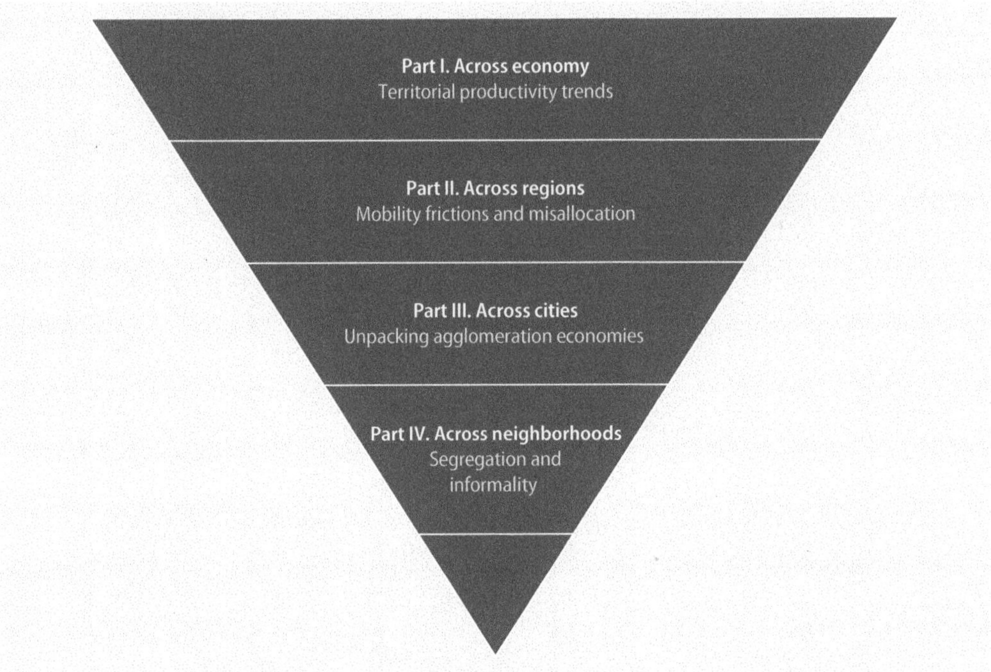

Part I. Across economy
Territorial productivity trends

Part II. Across regions
Mobility frictions and misallocation

Part III. Across cities
Unpacking agglomeration economies

Part IV. Across neighborhoods
Segregation and informality

Source: Original figure for this publication.

of problems that cannot be easily uncovered or studied at the aggregate level, as such an approach ignores the spatial unevenness of economic activity and its persistence over time.[18]

Convergence

Over the last two decades, greater integration into the global economy increased the spatial inequality in many advanced and developing countries. Rural-urban wage gaps grew in China, Ethiopia, and India,[19] where industrialization through export-led growth powered the expansion of urban areas. By contrast, in Latin America the concentration of people and businesses in cities did not stand in the way of income convergence. The Golden Decade ushered in a period of absolute convergence in labor and place productivity at the regional level in most countries (figure O.3) and at the municipal level in all of them (see chapter 2). The commodity boom fueled investments in often remote rural and mining localities, including in some relatively poor rural regions.[20] In many countries, the highest growth in per capita labor incomes was registered in mostly rural areas (D'Aoust, Galdo, and Ianchovichina 2023).

At the same time, urban labor productivity growth decelerated as deindustrialization shifted the composition of urban employment toward low-productivity nontradables.[21] Although employment in urban tradable services rose, including in finance, insurance, and real estate (figure O.4), the rise began from a low level and was not sufficiently strong to offset the decline in manufacturing employment. Thus the leveling up in Latin America reflected both improvements in relatively poor localities and the slowdown in productivity growth in the largest and relatively affluent urban municipalities.[22]

FIGURE O.3   Absolute convergence in per capita labor incomes by first-level administrative region, selected countries, LAC region

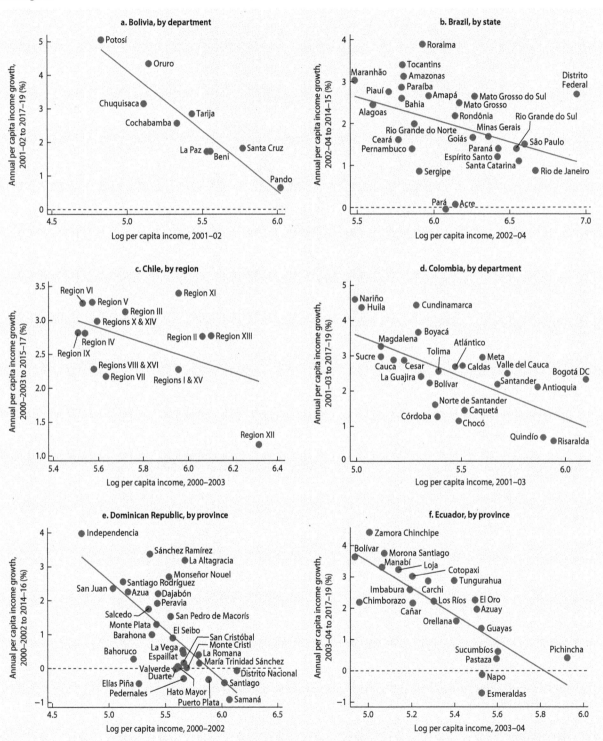

(Continued on next page)

FIGURE O.3   **Absolute convergence in per capita labor incomes by first-level administrative region, selected countries, LAC region** *(continued)*

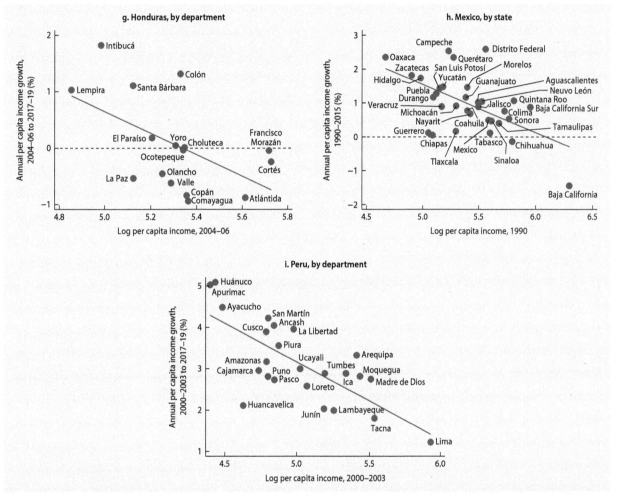

Source: D'Aoust, Galdo, and Ianchovichina 2023.
Note: To ensure comparability within and across countries, the per capita household labor earnings are deflated to adjust incomes for cost-of-living differences across space and time. In 2018 Chile renamed its first-level administrative regions: Region I became Tarapacá; Region II, Antofagasta; Region III, Aracama; Region IV, Coquimbo; Region V, Valparaiso; Region VI, O'Higgins; Region VII, Maule; Region VIII, Biobío; Region IX, Araucanía; Region X, Los Lagos; Region XI, Aysén; Region XII, Magallanes; RM (Region XIII), Metropolitan; Region XIV, Los Ríos; Region XV, Arica and Parinacota; Region XVI, Ñuble.

Income disparities relative to leading metropolitan areas also declined between the early 2000s and the late 2010s (figure O.5). These developments reflected both improvements in the endowments of households living outside the largest cities and smaller differences in the returns from education due to relatively mobile labor and lower returns to employment in deindustrializing leading areas (figure O.5). Thus by the end of the 2010s, the potential benefits of migration to the top metropolitan localities had become relatively small (especially among the bottom 40 percent of the income distribution) in all countries except Bolivia, Brazil, Panama, and Peru.

FIGURE O.4   Evolution of share of employment in manufacturing and tradable services by city size and decade: Latin America, 1980 or earlier to circa 2010

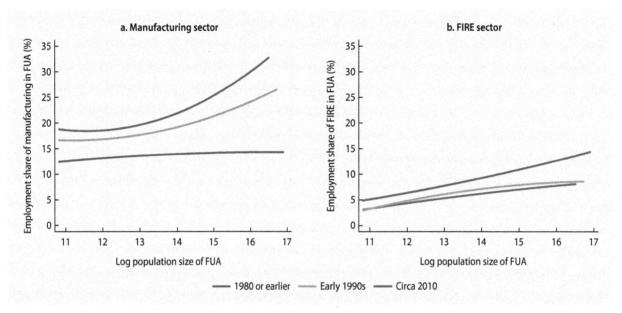

Source: Jedwab, Ianchovichina, and Haslop (2022), using Integrated Public Use Microdata Series (IPUMS, https://www.ipums.org/) survey microdata.
Note: FIRE = finance, insurance, and real estate; FUA = functional urban area. FIRE is a proxy for tradable services. Manufacturing and tradable services jointly account for all urban tradables. All other urban activities are nontradables. A FUA is composed of a city and its commuting zone. The graphs show how the average shares of employment in manufacturing and FIRE for FUAs of different sizes evolved between circa 1980 and circa 2010.

FIGURE O.5   Labor income gap between the leading metropolitan area and the rest of a country's localities and its decomposition by country and period, LAC region

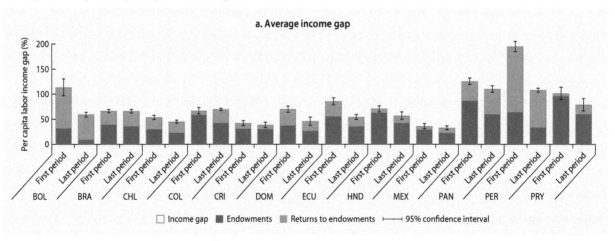

(Continued on next page)

FIGURE O.5   Labor income gap between the leading metropolitan area and the rest of a country's localities and its decomposition by country and period, LAC region *(continued)*

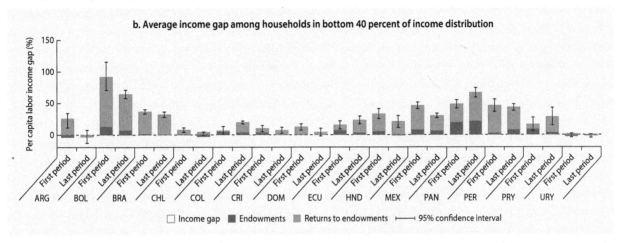

b. Average income gap among households in bottom 40 percent of income distribution

Source: D'Aoust, Galdo, and Ianchovichina 2023.

Note: The income gap is decomposed into an endowment component, capturing differences between the nongeographic household characteristics, such as education, demographics, and employment, in the leading metropolitan and other areas, and a returns-to-endowments component, capturing differences between the returns to these characteristics in the leading and other areas. The figure also shows the 95% confidence interval. To ensure comparability within and across countries, the per capita household labor earnings are deflated to adjust incomes for cost-of-living differences across space and time. Argentina and Uruguay are not included in panel a because the surveys in these countries cover only and mostly urban areas, respectively. The leading metropolitan areas and the respective first and last periods are as follows: Argentina (ARG): Buenos Aires, 2003–05, 2017–19; Bolivia (BOL): Santa Cruz, 2001–02, 2015–19; Brazil (BRA): Belo Horizonte, Rio de Janeiro, and São Paulo, 2012–14, 2017–19; Chile (CHL): Santiago, 2000 and 2003, 2015 and 2017; Colombia (COL): Bogotá, 2001–03, 2017–19; Costa Rica (CRI): urban Central Valley region (includes San José and other main cities), 2001–03, 2008–09; the Dominican Republic (DOM): city of Santo Domingo, 2000–2002, 2014–16; Ecuador (ECU): Quito (urban Pichincha), 2003–04, 2017–19; Honduras (HND): urban Tegucigalpa (Francisco Morazán), 2004–06, 2017–19; Mexico (MEX): Mexico City metropolitan area, 2000, 2002, and 2004; 2016 and 2018; Panama (PAN): urban Panama province, 2001–03, 2017–19; Paraguay (PRY): Asunción, 2002–04, 2017–19; Peru (PER): Lima, 2000–2003, 2017–19; Uruguay (URY): Montevideo, 2000–2002, 2017–19.

The urban productivity paradox

Cities in Latin America are denser than cities in the rest of the world,[23] but they are not particularly productive. The *place productivity premium*[24] in large and dense leading cities, shown in shades of green in panel b of map O.2, is much lower than the average labor productivity, shown in dark blue in panel a. Per capita incomes are high in the largest and densest leading urban areas, mostly because productive and skilled workers are attracted by the opportunities to learn from the skilled workers already living there (Quintero and Roberts 2018)[25] and by the better and more diverse consumer amenities.[26] But the net returns of this concentration are insignificant in most Latin American countries (Ferreyra and Roberts 2018; Quintero and Roberts 2018). On average, the place productivity premia in predominantly urban localities are only slightly higher than those in mostly rural ones (figure O.6).[27]

Although cities in Latin America benefit significantly from a concentration of *skills*, they fail to capture the broader benefits that cities can provide through co-location and market access (Ferreyra and Roberts 2018). The costs of density—including those associated with congestion, crime, and competition from informal firms (Burger, Ianchovichina, and Akbar 2022), as well as the impact on real estate in central urban locations (Duranton and Puga 2020; Lall, Shalizi, and Deichmann 2004)—can substantially reduce or completely offset the agglomeration benefits enjoyed by workers and firms in low- and middle-income countries (Grover and Maloney 2022), giving rise to "sterile" agglomeration economies (Grover, Lall, and Maloney 2022). Indeed, explanations for the Latin American urban paradox emphasize the high costs of density (Ferreyra and Roberts 2018). Those costs escalate when urban policy, planning, and management, as well as improvements in transport,

MAP O.2   Labor and place productivity premia: Latin America, end of the 2010s

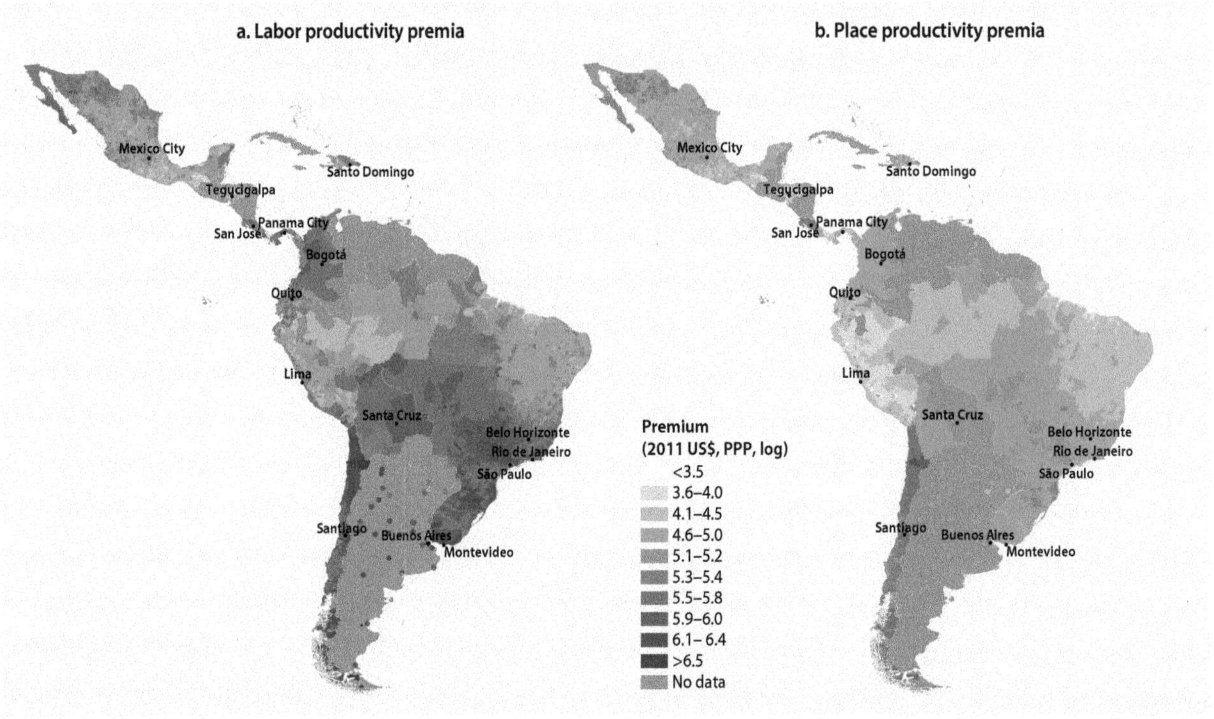

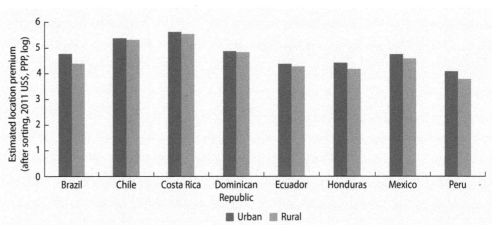

a. Labor productivity premia

b. Place productivity premia

Premium
(2011 US$, PPP, log)
<3.5
3.6–4.0
4.1–4.5
4.6–5.0
5.1–5.2
5.3–5.4
5.5–5.8
5.9–6.0
6.1– 6.4
>6.5
No data

Source: D'Aoust, Galdo, and Ianchovichina 2023.
Note: Labor productivity is proxied with per capita labor income net of the effect of any exogenous shocks that affect all localities in a country at a given time. The place productivity premium is the fraction of per capita household labor income that cannot be accounted for by observable, nongeographic (portable) household characteristics and the effects of exogenous time-variant factors. To ensure comparability within and across countries, per capita household labor earnings are deflated to adjust incomes for cost-of-living differences across space and time. The latest available period is 2008–09 for Costa Rica; 2010 for Brazil; 2014–16 for the Dominican Republic; 2015 for Mexico; 2015–17 for Chile; and 2017–19 for Argentina, Bolivia, Colombia, Ecuador, Honduras, Panama, Peru, and Uruguay. For Bolivia, Colombia, Panama, and Uruguay, these estimates are at the first administrative level (such as states). For Argentina, the estimates are at the level of the urban agglomeration (represented by dots on the maps). For the remaining countries, the estimates are at the second administrative level (such as municipalities). PPP = purchasing power parity.

FIGURE O.6   Average place productivity premia by type of municipality and country: Selected LAC countries, late 2010s

Source: D'Aoust, Galdo, and Ianchovichina 2023.
Note: The place productivity premium is the fraction of per capita household labor income that cannot be accounted for by observable, nongeographic (portable) household characteristics and the effects of exogenous time-variant factors. To ensure comparability within and across countries, the per capita household labor earnings are deflated to adjust incomes for cost-of-living differences across space and time. PPP = purchasing power parity.

communication, and basic infrastructure, fail to keep up with increases in density. Urban productivity can be further restrained by issues such as the size and shape of cities and inner-city connectedness (Duque, Lozano-Gracia, Patiño, et al. 2022).

Latin American cities face productivity challenges restricting economic growth, which has indeed declined over the last half-century. Because four out of five Latin Americans live in urban areas, economic growth depends heavily on the productivity of the urban workforce. Large urban areas are particularly important for economic growth in the region because nearly 40 percent of the population lives in cities with a million or more residents (United Nations 2016). In about a third of the countries in South America, 40 percent of the population is concentrated in just one city. Unfortunately, the large cities in the region are not dynamic production centers.

Three explanations

This study proposes three additional, interconnected explanations for the Latin American urban productivity paradox that have not been previously highlighted. All three center on factors that reduce agglomeration benefits. First, in *deindustrialized* cities where employment is tilted toward low-productivity, nontradable services, agglomeration benefits may be weaker because such activities benefit less from being provided in dense cities (Burger, Ianchovichina, and Akbar 2022; Venables 2017). They also have much less upside potential through dynamic productivity gains than urban tradables (Duarte and Restuccia 2010). Deindustrialization has therefore constrained both labor and place productivity growth in the region's urban areas.

Second, *connectivity* issues within cities reduce the agglomeration benefits for firms, especially those in nontradable sectors (Burger, Ianchovichina, and Akbar 2022). Meanwhile, intercity connectivity issues undermine the performance of the LAC region's network of cities by limiting market access and the ability of manufacturing firms to specialize and gain from internal economies of scale by relocating to smaller urban areas.[28]

Third, agglomeration benefits may be smaller in poorly connected and residentially segregated cities. *Urban divisions*—reinforced by intraurban connectivity issues—weaken agglomeration economies by limiting their geographic scope. In divided cities, the large gains from sharing, matching, and learning are limited to neighborhoods in central business districts where formal firms operate, consumer amenities are abundant, and residents enjoy better-quality basic infrastructure and public services. The opposite is found in low-income neighborhoods. Typically, in the urban periphery firms and workers in these neighborhoods are mostly informal, consumer amenities are scarce, and basic infrastructure and public services are often deficient, exposing residents to the risk of flooding, mudslides, disease, and crime. The existence of a dual urban economy—a modern, formal one in central business districts and a low-productivity one in low-income neighborhoods where residents find themselves in an informality trap—gives rise to spatial misallocation because informal firms do not pay taxes (Hsieh and Klenow 2009). The occurrence of such misallocation in the region's largest cities could significantly undermine aggregate output growth.

Deindustrialization

In recent decades, agglomeration forces failed to power the growth of internationally competitive and globally significant Latin American production cities (map O.1). Instead, they made it difficult to launch new tradable activities elsewhere (Venables 2020) because deindustrialization shifted the employment profile of cities of all sizes away from urban tradable goods and services and toward urban nontradable services (figure O.1). This happened to varying degrees in different countries, but, in nearly all, deindustrialization was most pronounced in the largest metropolitan areas. Thus of the 15 largest cities in Latin America, none are production cities, five (Belo Horizonte, Bogotá, Fortaleza, Recife, and Rio de Janeiro) are consumption cities with a disproportionately low share of employment in urban tradable services, and the rest are neutral cities with a more balanced employment mix between tradables and nontradable activities (map O.1). Most large and globally significant production cities are in China, parts of Europe, India, and Viet Nam, whereas in Latin America only Brazil, Mexico, and Central America have production cities, which are relatively small.

The shift toward employment in urban nontradables has weakened urban labor productivity, making it harder for Latin America to escape the middle-income trap—that is, the situation in which a country is unable to make progress after reaching middle-income level. Returns to education and work experience vary across urban sectors and are higher in urban tradables (Jedwab, Ianchovichina, and Haslop 2022). In countries where the share of urban workers in tradables is low, human capital is employed in less productive urban sectors, and, overall, the returns to experience are lower (Jedwab, Ianchovichina, and Haslop 2022). Productivity growth is also slower in countries with disproportionately high employment in urban nontradables because productivity in manufacturing varies little across countries (Duarte and Restuccia 2010),[29] and international trade stimulates endogenous innovation and growth through market access, comparative advantage, competition, and knowledge spillovers (Melitz and Redding 2021). Each of these four channels has the potential to generate dynamic gains from trade in the long run. According to Duarte and Restuccia (2010), in manufacturing the productivity catch-up explains about half of the gains in aggregate productivity across countries, while in services low productivity and a failure to catch up explain all slowdowns, stagnation, and declines observed across countries.

Firms in nontradable sectors also benefit less from being close to other firms than firms in tradables, especially those using more intensively skilled labor. Nontradable activities (such as retail and wholesale trade, construction, and personal services) tend to employ unskilled labor, account for a large share of activity in an economy, and are unlikely to exhibit increasing returns to scale if they agglomerate (Venables 2017). Smaller firms in nontradable sectors are also exposed to intense competition in larger and denser urban markets. Indeed, Burger, Ianchovichina, and Akbar (2022) have estimated differing returns to urban density. As revealed in chapter 5, returns are higher for formal manufacturing establishments (especially export and foreign-owned enterprises) than for firms supplying services in the local market. The latter are often smaller, less experienced, and younger (figure O.7).

Connectivity issues and the curse of distance
The economic benefits of agglomeration are lost through congestion (Burger, Ianchovichina, and Akbar 2022), which is a serious problem in Latin America's largest cities. A systematic comparison of urban traffic patterns in the region with those in the rest of the world[30] suggests that some of the most congested cities in the world are large Latin American cities (figure O.8).[31] Bogotá leads the ranking, and Mexico City, Guatemala City, and Panama City are among the top 20 most congested cities worldwide (table O.1). Congestion is especially harmful to agglomeration economies in mega consumption cities, where nontradables play a disproportionately large role. Although the markets for nontradables are potentially larger in bigger and denser cities, traffic congestion and competition can considerably reduce their size because nontradable services are often provided in person during

FIGURE O.7 **Heterogeneous "pure" agglomeration economies**

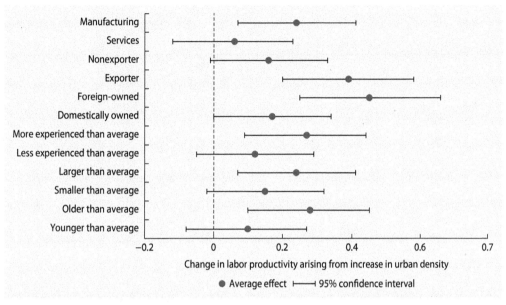

Change in labor productivity arising from increase in urban density

● Average effect ├──────┤ 95% confidence interval

Source: Burger, Ianchovichina, and Akbar 2022.
Note: The figure shows "pure" agglomeration effects by type of firm—that is, the estimated change in labor productivity, measured as the natural logarithm of sales per worker arising from an increase in urban density after controlling for firm characteristics, firm-level and metropolitan-level agglomeration diseconomies, metropolitan-level averages of firm-level variables, and industry, country, and year fixed effects—based on geocoded, firm-level data on 38,526 establishments in 356 metropolitan areas in 80 developing economies. A coefficient of 0.1 means that if urban density doubles, labor productivity increases by 10 percent. Services include firms involved in either tradable or nontradable activities.

FIGURE O.8 **Urban mobility and congestion in cities, LAC region and rest of the world**

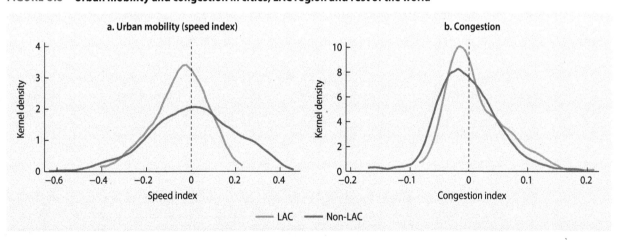

─── LAC ━━━ Non-LAC

Source: Data from Akbar et al. 2022.
Note: The Latin America and the Caribbean (LAC) region includes Argentina, Bolivia, Brazil, Colombia, Costa Rica, the Dominican Republic, Ecuador, El Salvador, Guatemala, Honduras, Jamaica, Mexico, Nicaragua, Paraguay, Peru, Trinidad and Tobago, Uruguay, and República Bolivariana de Venezuela. The y-axis of the graphs are kernel density estimates using Stata's kdensity function (https://www.stata.com/manuals/rkdensity.pdf).

peak business hours. Manufacturing firms can better cope with congestion by using storage and transporting inputs and final goods during off-peak traffic hours. Indeed, this study finds that although traffic congestion reduces agglomeration benefits for all firms, this effect is much stronger for firms in services and for smaller, less experienced, locally owned firms that serve the domestic market (figure O.9).

TABLE O.1   World ranking: 10 slowest and 10 most congested cities in the LAC region

	Slowest				Most congested		
World ranking	City	Country	Index	World ranking	City	Country	Index
19	Lima	Peru	−0.41	1	Bogotá	Colombia	0.21
25	Bogotá	Colombia	−0.40	10	Mexico City	Mexico	0.15
33	Mexico City	Mexico	−0.36	15	Guatemala City	Guatemala	0.14
38	La Paz	Bolivia	−0.36	19	Panama City	Panama	0.13
63	São Paulo	Brazil	−0.30	22	Santo Domingo	Dominican Republic	0.13
67	Huancayo	Peru	−0.30	24	Medellín	Colombia	0.12
69	Guatemala City	Guatemala	−0.29	25	Rio de Janeiro	Brazil	0.12
73	Cusco	Peru	−0.29	32	São Paulo	Brazil	0.12
75	Oaxaca de Juárez	Mexico	−0.28	38	San José	Costa Rica	0.11
85	Medellín	Colombia	−0.27	41	Recife	Brazil	0.11

Source: Akbar (2022), using data from Akbar et al. (2022).

FIGURE O.9   The moderating effect of congestion on "pure" agglomeration economies by sector and firm type

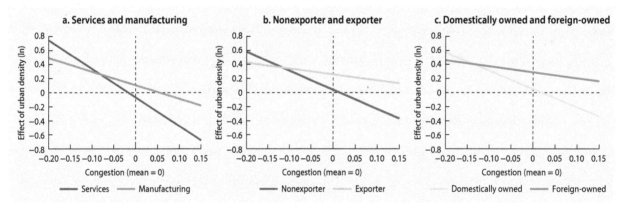

Source: Burger, Ianchovichina, and Akbar (2022), using geocoded, firm-level data on 38,526 formal establishments in 356 metropolitan areas in 80 developing economies from the World Bank's Enterprise Surveys (https://www.enterprisesurveys.org/en/enterprisesurveys) and a new global database on city-level mobility and congestion (Akbar et al. 2022).
Note: The difference in the slope indicates the difference in the speed with which increases in congestion reduce the returns to density for the respective types of firms.

In both Latin America and the Caribbean (LAC) and the rest of the world, urban mobility decreases as cities become denser, mainly because of poor mobility even when there is no congestion (Akbar 2022). This is because in denser cities roads are narrower, and these roads have more intersections, which limits the speed of vehicles. However, this situation also shortens trips and improves market access. Yet even without congestion, in cities of all sizes in the LAC region it takes longer to get around than in comparable cities in the rest of the world (chapter 5), and urban uncongested mobility in the LAC region declines much faster as cities become denser (figure O.10). This finding suggests that urban planning and infrastructure issues are factors that need to be considered when addressing the region's intraurban connectivity issues.

High interregional transport costs, together with barriers to labor mobility, affect the spatial distribution of economic activity and people and thus the productivity differences

FIGURE O.10 **How urban mobility, congestion, and uncongested mobility change with density, world and LAC region**

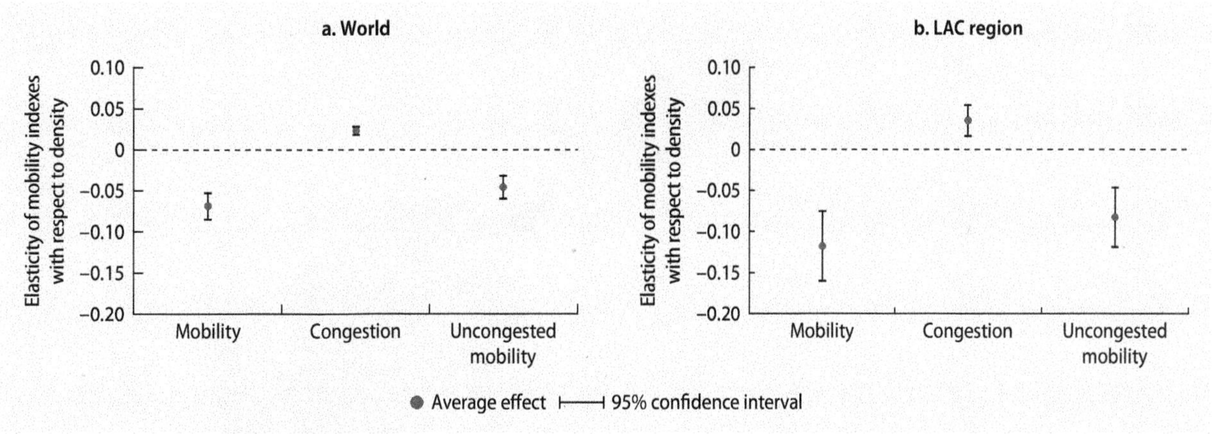

Source: Akbar (2022), using data from Akbar et al. (2022).
Note: The figures show the average effect of density on mobility, as well as the 95% confidence interval. Construction of mobility indexes allows derivation of the elasticity of mobility with respect to density by subtracting the elasticity of congestion from the elasticity of uncongested mobility. This approach reveals that the bulk of the density effects on mobility are driven by their effects on uncongested mobility rather than congestion. The Latin America and the Caribbean (LAC) region includes Argentina, Bolivia, Brazil, Colombia, Costa Rica, the Dominican Republic, Ecuador, El Salvador, Guatemala, Honduras, Jamaica, Mexico, Nicaragua, Paraguay, Peru, Trinidad and Tobago, Uruguay, and República Bolivariana de Venezuela.

within and across countries and their changes over time. Limited and expensive transport services and inadequate or poorly maintained road infrastructure erect barriers to both trade and migration. A host of other factors can also prevent people from moving. Limited information about economic opportunities, an insufficient supply of land, unavailability of affordable formal housing and consumer amenities, legal migration restrictions, discriminatory practices, and social or cultural factors can deter the mobility of socioeconomic groups to varying degrees (Bryan and Morten 2019) and thus constrain inclusive growth.

Entry migration barriers represent the average cost of entering a location, which include the cost of overcoming immigration restrictions, the cost of travel to the location, information and psychological costs, and restrictions stemming from the shortage of housing. These barriers vary within and across the countries in the LAC region (map O.3). Estimated entry migration costs are lowest in the low-income countries of Central America and in Bolivia and Peru[32] and highest in the higher-income countries such as Argentina, Brazil, Costa Rica, Mexico, and Panama, as well as in some remote areas where living conditions are harsh (map O.3). They also tend to be high in some of the region's densely populated urban areas. However, the efficiency losses associated with dispersion of these barriers within countries are small. Analysis suggests that reducing the average entry migration barriers in the larger LAC urban areas to the level of barriers in the bottom quartile of the respective country's entry cost distribution is not expected to lead to gains in the region's real per capita income (Conte and Ianchovichina 2022). This finding implies that entry migration barriers, including those stemming from land regulations and supply of housing, are not major constraints to aggregate economic growth.[33]

Yet, residents of the poorest subnational regions, which are often remote, face significantly higher barriers to migration (see chapter 3).[34] Distance matters for mobility for at least two reasons. First, the strength of migrant networks—which are particularly important to the poorest residents—tends to diminish with distance. Location preferences and discrimination may also discourage migration. Afro-descendants and indigenous workers in Brazil's north and northeast are significantly less likely to migrate out of their states than

MAP O.3   Calibrated entry migration costs by finely disaggregated locations: LAC region, circa 2000

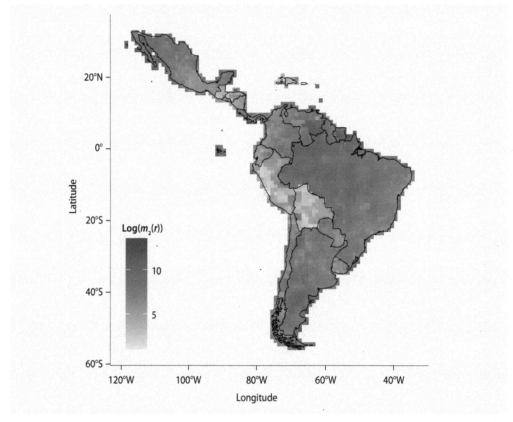

Source: Conte and Ianchovichina 2022.
Note: Conte and Ianchovichina (2022) calibrate the entry migration costs using the dynamic spatial general equilibrium model in Desmet, Nagy, and Rossi-Hansberg (2018), geocoded data from Latinobarómetro and the Gallup World Poll, and finely disaggregated data on population and value added by grid cell (typically, a 1-arc degree cell) from G-Econ data for 2000 (Nordhaus et al. 2006). The LAC region includes Mexico, all countries in Central and South America, and the Dominican Republic and Haiti in the Caribbean.

white residents with similar levels of education (D'Aoust, Galdo, and Ianchovichina 2023). Second, the cost of travel rises with distance and is high in larger countries, where air travel is often the only way to reach remote destinations.

Indeed, many South American countries have large territories and unique topographies. Road networks in the region are less dense than those in other middle-income regions (World Bank 2009), while railway networks remain underdeveloped (Fay et al. 2017).[35] In Brazil, Chile, Colombia, Mexico, and Peru—which together account for more than two-thirds of the region's exports—80 percent of cargo was transported by trucks in the early 2010s (Mesquita Moreira et al. 2013). Prices of transport services are high due to a host of other issues, including government regulations,[36] inefficiencies,[37] imperfect competition,[38] backhaul problems, congestion delays, and information frictions. Yet because of the region's advanced urbanization in which its population is concentrated in large urban areas, high transport costs may not be as problematic in the LAC region as they are in other regions with more dispersed populations. Exports in some LAC countries are also concentrated in relatively few well-connected municipalities (Mesquita Moreira et al. 2013).

Nevertheless, a comparison of transport costs between equidistant pairs of top urban locations in the LAC region, the European Union, and Southeast Asia shows that there are many more pairs of such locations for which transport costs are high in the LAC region than in the European Union and Southeast Asia (figure O.11, panel a). Similarly, the comparison shows that there are more pairs of top urban locations for which transport costs are high in Brazil than in the United States and China (figure O.11, panel b). This is a problem because good intercity connectivity is essential for reducing the dispersion in city productivity within countries and improving the ability of firms to specialize and gain from economies of scale in smaller, well-connected cities. Secondary urban areas have the potential to become competitive cities where firms create productive jobs and raise incomes (Kilroy et al. 2015; Rodríguez-Pose and Griffiths 2021).[39] But in the LAC region, in addition to connectivity issues, smaller cities struggle with the provision of infrastructure, basic consumer amenities, and local public goods and services.

One reason for the high intercity transport costs in the LAC region is its underinvestment in transport infrastructure. Since 1990, the region has spent about 3 percent of its gross domestic product (GDP) on public investment—that is, far less than the spending in East Asia and most other developing regions. The region has also misallocated the little investment it has made in roads (see chapter 4).[40] It has underinvested in road improvements along segments connecting Latin America's more populous and productive urban areas, highlighted in green in map O.4. At the same time, it has overinvested in roads connecting peripheral regions, shown in red in map O.4.[41] The overinvestment in rural roads perhaps reflects the need to transport commodities produced in remote regions to ports for export to China and other countries. However, it also may be a sign of making infrastructure investments based on equity considerations[42] or political priorities rather than efficiency.

FIGURE O.11   Distribution of transport costs between pairs of top urban locations by region and country

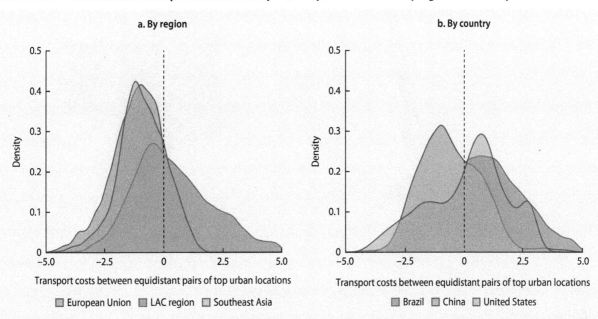

Source: Conte and Ianchovichina (2022), based on the least-cost-route approach in Allen and Arkolakis (2014) and the methodology in Desmet, Nagy, and Rossi-Hansberg (2018).
Note: The cost between any pair of locations reflects the geography of and the distance between the locations, the availability of different types of connectivity infrastructure, and the relative costs of using different modes of ground transportation. Panels a and b compare the costs between equidistant pairs of top urban locations in each region. Top urban locations in a country or a region are the locations whose populations and productivity are higher than the median and top quartile, respectively. The LAC region includes Mexico, all countries in Central and South America, and the Dominican Republic and Haiti in the Caribbean.

MAP O.4   Overinvestment and underinvestment in roads, selected countries, Latin America

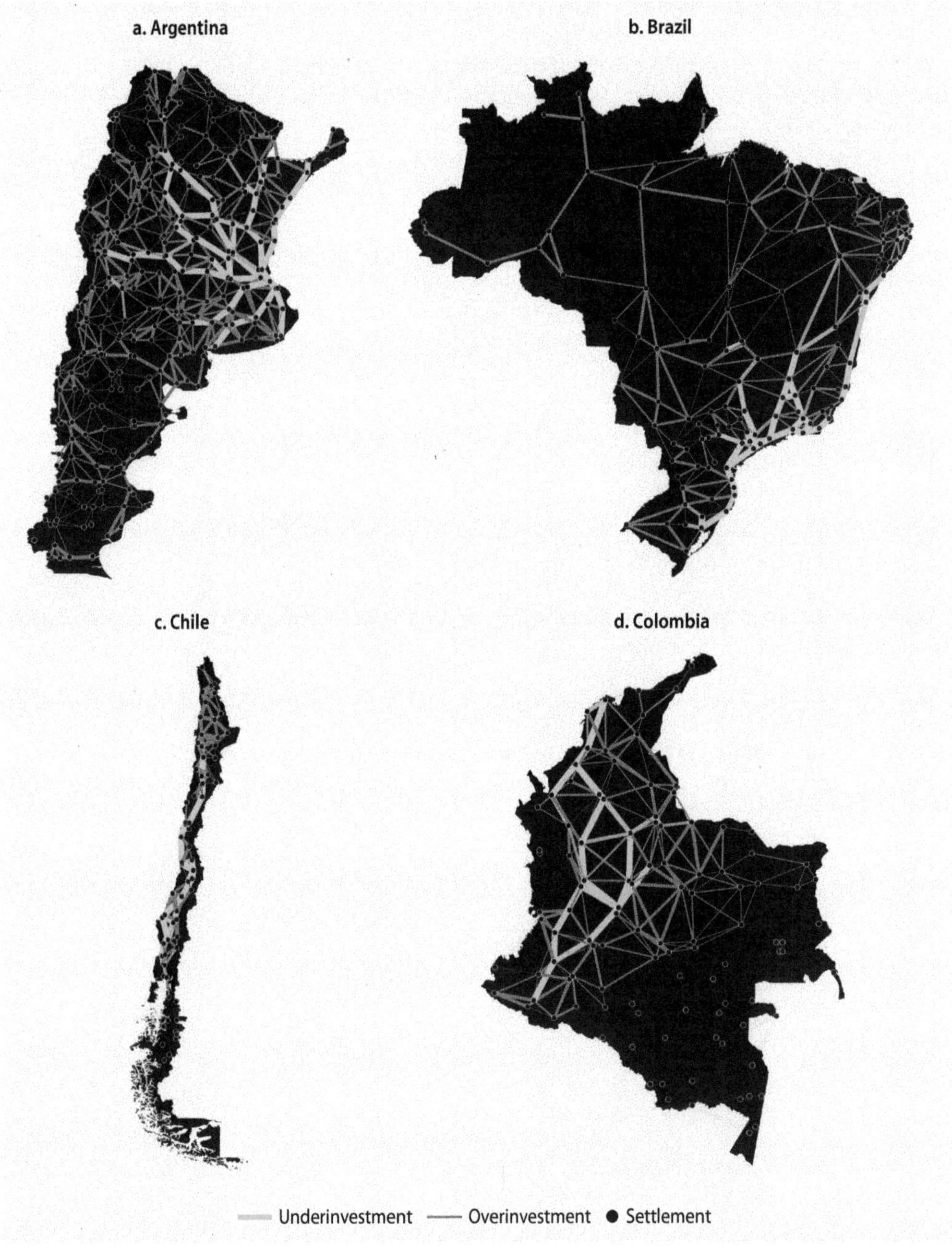

a. Argentina

b. Brazil

c. Chile

d. Colombia

Underinvestment ———— Overinvestment ● Settlement

(Continued on next page)

MAP O.4   Overinvestment and underinvestment in roads, selected countries, Latin America *(continued)*

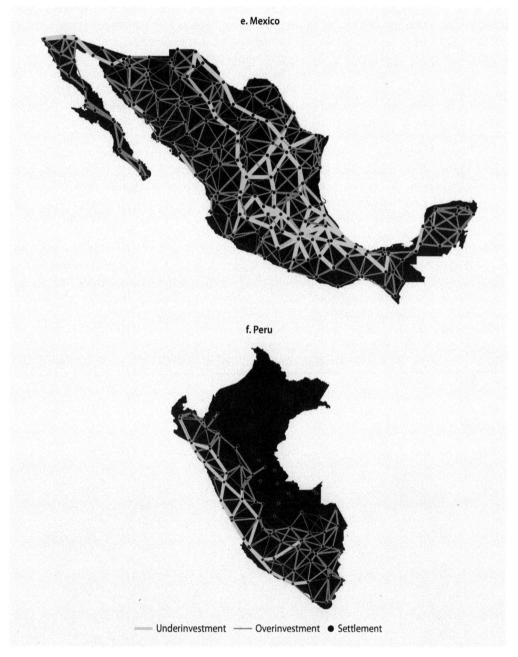

e. Mexico

f. Peru

Underinvestment ——— Overinvestment ● Settlement

Source: Gorton and Ianchovichina 2021.
Note: Green indicates underinvestment, whereas red indicates overinvestment. Thicker segments represent links with larger deviations from the efficient levels of investment. The nodes represent settlements.

The annual welfare losses from the misallocation of road infrastructure investments vary across Latin American countries. They are estimated to be largest in Argentina and Brazil, averaging 2.4 and 2.1 percent of national consumption, respectively, whereas they are negligible in Central America and Uruguay (Gorton and Ianchovichina 2021).[43] The welfare losses can be compensated with improvements in intercity roads,[44] which have received insufficient investments in the past. In the short run, these improvements enhance equity because they benefit regions on the periphery of these investments (map O.5) through better access to bigger cities. Evidence from India suggests that these improvements can stimulate economic development in districts along highways, especially those with better access to education and finance (Das et al. 2019; Ghani, Grover, and Kerr 2013).

In the long run, the dynamic effects of these strategic improvements are considerably larger because they capture economic gains from improved conditions for specialization and agglomeration of economic activity in areas with better market access and greater technological diffusion into neighboring areas (map O.6). By 2100, improved intercity connectivity is expected to boost the present discounted values of the regional real per capita income by 15 percent and welfare by 53 percent, relative to a business-as-usual scenario (Conte and Ianchovichina 2022).[45] The projected welfare gain is higher than the rise in output because migration allows people to relocate to areas with better amenities. These investments also enable the small, relatively low-income countries (such as those in Central America) to retain residents who might otherwise migrate to other countries. Over time, this outcome leads to a virtuous cycle of growth and productivity gains.

Improved transnational intercity road connectivity can also stimulate regional trade and unlock much needed efficiency gains because most countries in South America trade less than they could with their regional partners (Beaton et al. 2017). Within MERCOSUR,[46]

MAP O.5 **Spatial distribution of welfare effects from optimal road improvements, Argentina and Brazil**

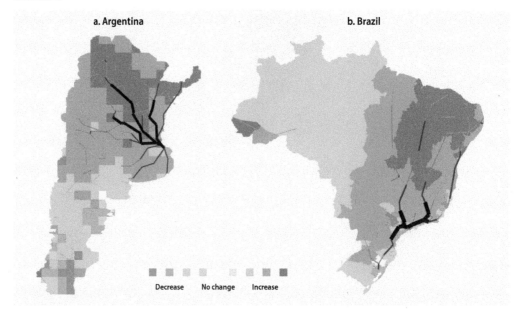

a. Argentina   b. Brazil

Decrease   No change   Increase

Source: Gorton and Ianchovichina 2021.
Note: Green shades identify the cells with welfare increases, whereas orange shades identify cells with welfare declines. The darker the shade, the larger is the increase or decline. Black and grey lines identify road links that receive additional infrastructure investments for road improvements. The darker and thicker the line, the larger are the investments.

MAP O.6   Effects of cuts in intercity transport costs in 2100 by location, LAC region

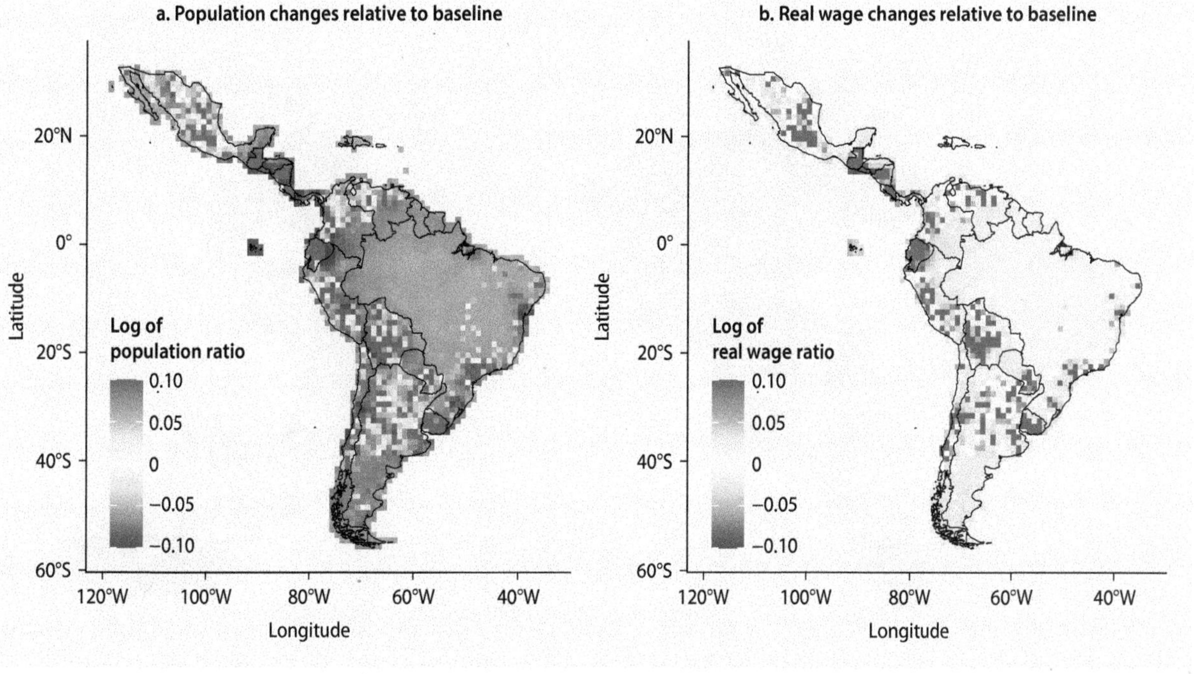

a. Population changes relative to baseline

b. Real wage changes relative to baseline

Source: Conte and Ianchovichina (2022), using the dynamic spatial general equilibrium model in Desmet, Nagy, and Rossi-Hansberg (2018) and the optimal reductions in trade costs from Gorton and Ianchovichina (2021).
Note: The maps show the log ratio between the grid cell level of population (or real wages) in the simulation with optimal cuts in trade costs and the baseline with no cuts. Values larger than zero indicate higher outcomes, and values smaller than zero indicate lower outcomes in the simulation with lower trade frictions.

the need for highway improvements is greatest in Brazil, which accounts for 71 percent of the total additional optimal investments in the bloc, followed by Argentina (22 percent), Uruguay (7 percent), and Paraguay (7 percent)—see map O.7. Within the Andean Community,[47] additional investments are needed along roads from La Paz in Bolivia, north along the coast of Peru to Lima, and then through Quito to Medellín, Colombia. Half of the infrastructure growth needs are in Colombia, a quarter in Peru, slightly less than a quarter in Ecuador, and the remainder in Bolivia. Fortunately, in the countries making the bulk of the investments—Brazil, Colombia, and Peru—the improvements optimally enhance both transnational and domestic road connectivity (Gorton and Ianchovichina 2021). Thus there is an alignment between domestic and regional needs for improved intercity road connectivity.[48] The benefits from the additional optimal investments are largest in Bolivia and Paraguay, the landlocked members of the two trade blocs.

High-speed internet services and digital technologies for data sharing and collaboration have made it possible to telecommute and do virtually many jobs that previously required face-to-face interactions. They were especially useful for helping people cope with mobility restrictions during the COVID-19 pandemic. In turn, telecommuting has dramatically diminished the need for both inter- and intracity travel, including during peak business hours, thereby reducing congestion and allowing telecommuters to avoid long and costly journeys to work. New estimates, presented in chapter 4, suggest that residents of the LAC region relied on this coping mechanism much less than those of member economies of the Organisation for Economic Co-operation and Development (OECD). In the OECD economies, before the pandemic between 15 and 38 percent of workers had jobs suitable for telecommuting, whereas in the LAC region this rate was below 14 percent (Montañés et al. 2021).

MAP O.7   Optimal improvements in transnational road networks, MERCOSUR and Andean Community

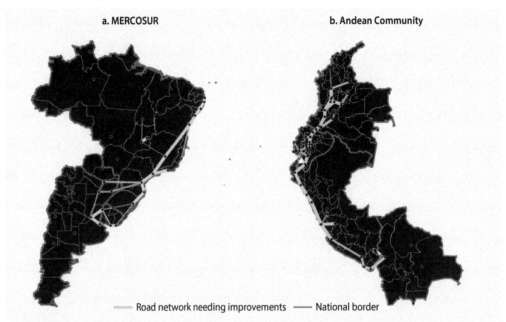

a. MERCOSUR   b. Andean Community

——— Road network needing improvements   ——— National border

Source: Gorton and Ianchovichina (2021), using the spatial general equilibrium model of Fajgelbaum and Schaal (2020).
Note: MERCOSUR is a South American trade bloc. Its full members are Argentina, Brazil, Paraguay, and Uruguay. The Andean Community is a free trade area that includes Bolivia, Colombia, Ecuador, and Peru. Road network segments identified in green need improvements. The thicker and brighter the line, the larger are the investments.

Territorial differences in the prevalence of telecommuting to work are also large, reflecting differences in the availability of jobs suitable for telecommuting, as well as digital and information and communication technology (ICT) infrastructure and the affordability of internet services. In addition to the unaffordability of internet services in many poor and rural communities, they are the least likely to have jobs suitable for telecommuting because of skill deficits and the relatively low prevalence of such jobs in the rural economy and small urban areas. There are also significant urban deficits in internet access in several Latin American countries. The percentage of urban workers with jobs suitable for telecommuting but without internet access in their homes is largest in Bolivia, Colombia, Guatemala, Mexico, and Nicaragua (figure O.12).

Urban divisions

Cities in Latin America and the Caribbean are both unequal[49] and divided[50] into geographically distant poor and affluent parts (map O.8). Where people live in cities reflects the preferences of higher-skilled workers for better amenities in affluent neighborhoods (figure O.13) and their ability to pay for a higher cost of living.[51] Yet as shown in the literature on advanced economies, residential segregation has well-known negative effects on schooling (Baum-Snow and Lutz 2011; Katz, Kling, and Liebman 2001), health (Acevedo-García et al. 2003; Alexander and Currie 2017), equality of opportunity (OECD 2018), intergenerational mobility (Chetty, Hendren, and Katz 2016), information flows (Glaeser 1994), and social capital (Chetty et al. 2022; Granovetter 1973). Strong ties with friends and neighbors are of little use if there are no resources to share or good jobs available (Granovetter 1973). By contrast, having strong ties with a diverse set of friends during the formative stages of life can help to improve the socioeconomic status of individuals during adulthood (Chetty et al. 2022).

FIGURE O.12   Rural and urban workers with jobs suitable for telecommuting but who have no internet access at home, LAC region

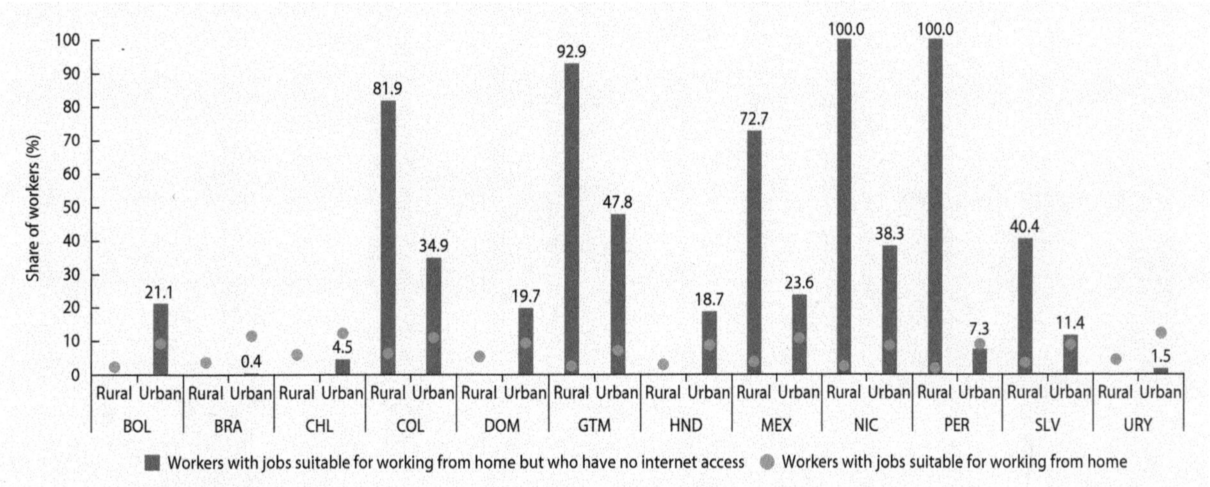

Source: Montañés et al. (2021), based on Socio-Economic Database for Latin America and the Caribbean (CEDLAS and the World Bank, https://www.cedlas.econo.unlp.edu.ar/wp/en /estadisticas/sedlac/) household survey data.
Note: For Bolivia, the Dominican Republic, and Honduras, the zeros in terms of the percentage of workers with jobs suitable for working from home (WFH) but who have no internet access at home indicate the absence of individuals with jobs suitable for telecommuting. For Brazil, Chile, and Uruguay, the zeros indicate that all workers with WFH-amenable jobs have internet access at home. For country abbreviations, see International Organization for Standardization (ISO), https://www.iso.org/obp/ui/#search.

Less well understood are such divisions and their effects on urban productivity in Latin America. Based on newly available data from population censuses and city surveys, chapter 6 analyzes the socioeconomic inequalities and residential segregation in the largest LAC cities and the degree to which they restrict the geographic reach of urban agglomeration economies and lead to misallocation exacerbated by informality.

This study provides evidence that poor Latin American city dwellers often face multiple deprivations in terms of access to basic infrastructure and public services in their neighborhoods. In both Colombia and Mexico, limited access to decent housing is the main source of socioeconomic vulnerability, which is worsened by inadequate education services in Colombia and poor labor market conditions in Mexico. Geographic patterns also reveal overlapping vulnerabilities. For example, in Bogotá, households that are vulnerable in terms of education, housing, and labor market conditions are concentrated in the south of the city, while more affluent households are in the north (map O.8, panel b). In Mexico's major cities, socioeconomic vulnerability is typically low in the city center and high in the outskirts (map O.8, panel c).

In divided cities, place productivity premia vary across neighborhoods within cities. In Bogotá, neighborhood productivity premia are positive only in or near the central business district where the larger, better-established firms are located. Meanwhile, they are negative in the city's poor south, where firms tend to be small, informal, family-owned establishments (map O.9). This result is consistent with other empirical evidence presented in this study showing that large, experienced firms benefit relatively more from agglomeration economies than small, less well-established firms (figure O.7). Although the TransMilenio bus system has eased connectivity problems since 2000, Bogotá remains the most congested city in the world (table O.1). Long and costly commutes limit the access of workers living in poorly connected, low-income neighborhoods to productive jobs downtown. Deficiencies in basic infrastructure and public services in slums also raise the risk of disease, crime,

MAP O.8 **Poverty and socioeconomic vulnerability at the neighborhood level in the largest metropolitan areas, Brazil, Colombia, and Mexico**

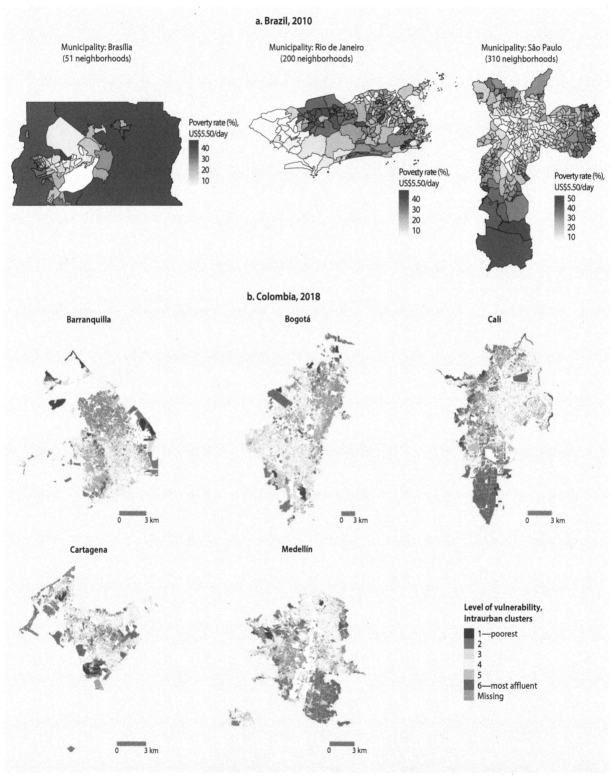

a. Brazil, 2010

Municipality: Brasília
(51 neighborhoods)

Municipality: Rio de Janeiro
(200 neighborhoods)

Municipality: São Paulo
(310 neighborhoods)

Poverty rate (%),
US$5.50/day
40
30
20
10

Poverty rate (%),
US$5.50/day
40
30
20
10

Poverty rate (%),
US$5.50/day
50
40
30
20
10

b. Colombia, 2018

Barranquilla

Bogotá

Cali

0   3 km

0   3 km

0   3 km

Cartagena

Medellín

Level of vulnerability,
intraurban clusters

■ 1—poorest
2
3
4
5
■ 6—most affluent
Missing

0   3 km

0   3 km

(Continued on next page)

MAP O.8   Poverty and socioeconomic vulnerability at the neighborhood level in the largest metropolitan areas: Brazil, Colombia, and Mexico *(continued)*

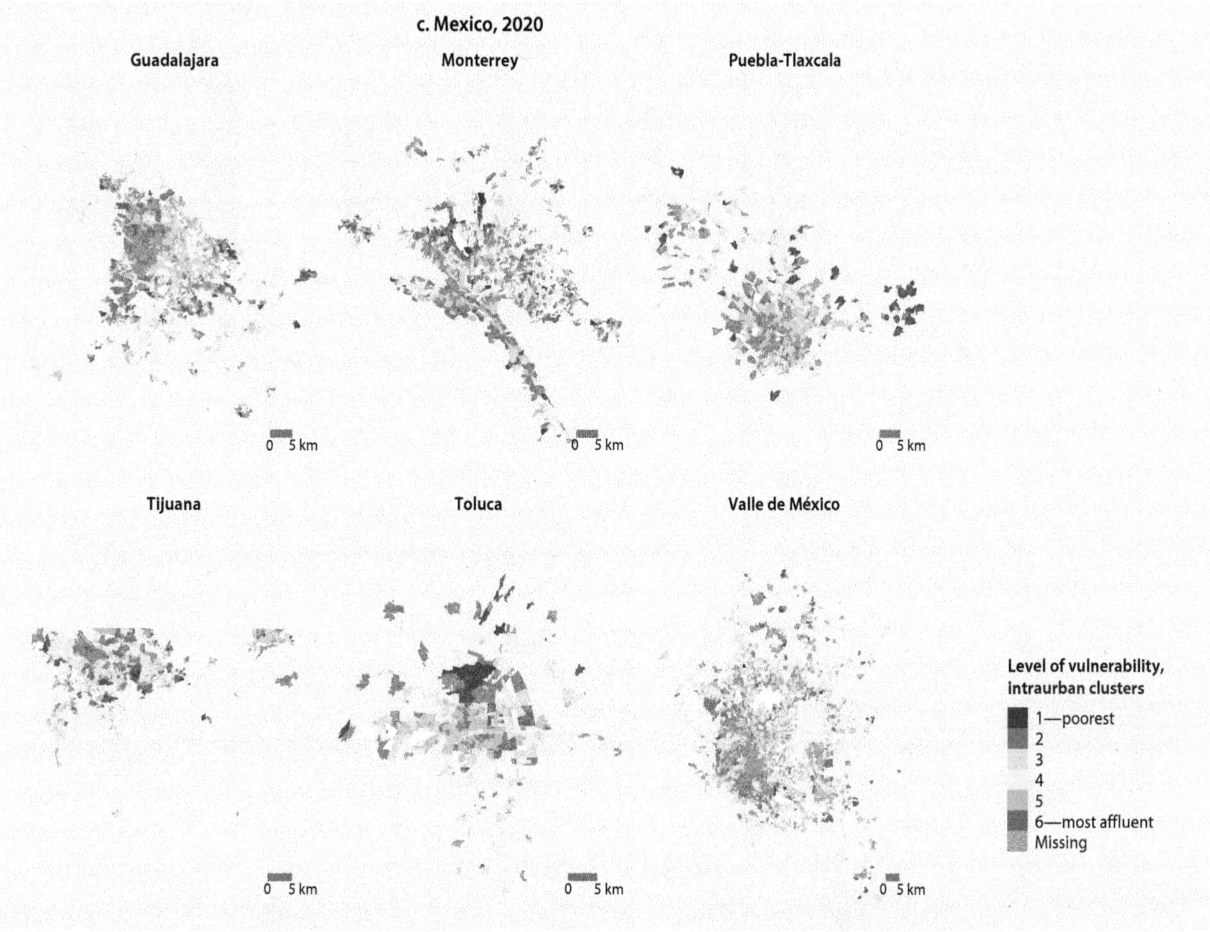

c. Mexico, 2020

Guadalajara   Monterrey   Puebla-Tlaxcala

Tijuana   Toluca   Valle de México

Level of vulnerability,
intraurban clusters

1—poorest
2
3
4
5
6—most affluent
Missing

Sources: Panel a: Van der Weide, Ferreira de Souza, and Barbosa 2020; panel b: Duque et al. 2021; panel c: Duque, Lozano-Gracia, García, et al. 2022.

and damage from natural disasters and so reduce the employability and productivity of Bogotá's low-income residents.

In a poorly connected city, residential segregation may give rise to labor market segregation if a large share of the population can access only a fraction of all jobs in the city within a reasonable commuting time and cost.[52] If low-income residents in peripheral areas choose to work informally close to their homes (Suárez, Murata, and Campos 2015) and shop in local informal stores (Bachas, Gadenne, and Anders 2020), residential labor market segregation may also result in spatial misallocation due to informality traps.[53] Divisions also erect informational barriers between the formal and informal economy, further reducing a city's productivity potential (Glaeser 1994).

Mexico City illustrates this pattern of segregation. Low-income workers in the city live and work mainly on the periphery, where most jobs are informal, while upper-middle- and high-income workers live and work in central locations, where the formal economy dominates (map O.10). Low-income workers also travel mostly to destinations on the periphery, and more affluent residents tend to travel to destinations in the center (map O.11). The division of the city into a formal core and informal periphery gives rise

FIGURE O.13   Association between the number of workers in a location and the share of streets with different amenities in the location by skill level, Mexico City

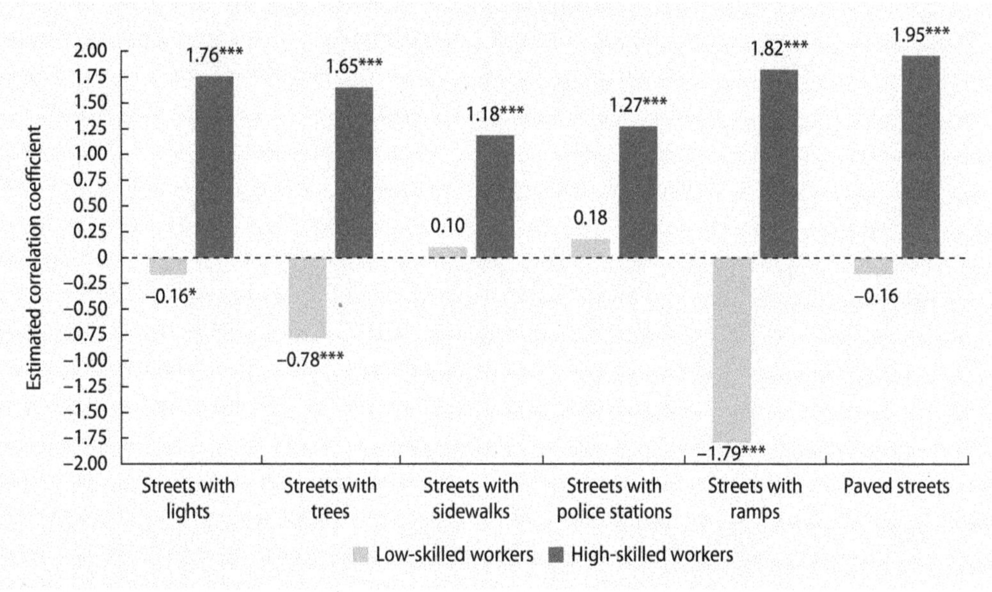

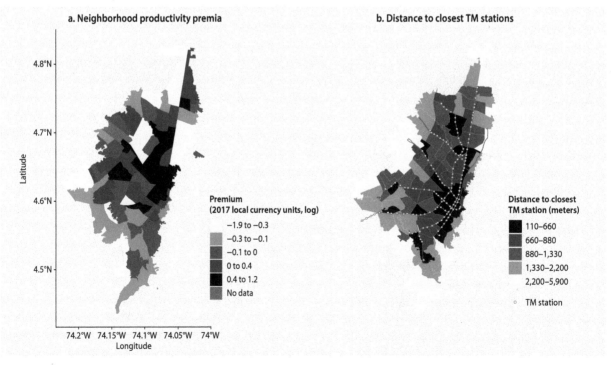

Source: Ianchovichina and Zárate 2021.

Note: The figure shows that the locations where many low-skilled workers live tend to have a low share of streets with amenities, such as lights, trees, and ramps. By contrast, the locations where many high-skilled workers live have a high share of streets with various amenities. The number of workers is calculated at the census level, and the share of streets with a specific amenity is calculated at the borough level.
Significance level: * = 10 percent, *** = 1 percent.

MAP O.9   Neighborhood productivity premia and distance to closest TransMilenio (TM) bus stations, Bogotá

a. Neighborhood productivity premia

b. Distance to closest TM stations

Premium
(2017 local currency units, log)
- −1.9 to −0.3
- −0.3 to −0.1
- −0.1 to 0
- 0 to 0.4
- 0.4 to 1.2
- No data

Distance to closest
TM station (meters)
- 110–660
- 660–880
- 880–1,330
- 1,330–2,200
- 2,200–5,900
- ○ TM station

Source: Heil, Ianchovichina, and Quintero (2022), based on the 2017 Encuesta Multipropósito (EM, Generalities Multipurpose Survey, https://www.sdp.gov.co/gestion-estudios -estrategicos/estudios-macro/encuesta-multiproposito).
Note: Each Unidad de Planeamiento Zonal (UPZ) or neighborhood has an average area of 4.5 square kilometers. UPZ-level productivity premia are the fraction of hourly wages that cannot be accounted for by observable, nongeographic (portable) individual characteristics.

MAP O.10   Spatial divisions in Mexico City: A modern core and an informal periphery

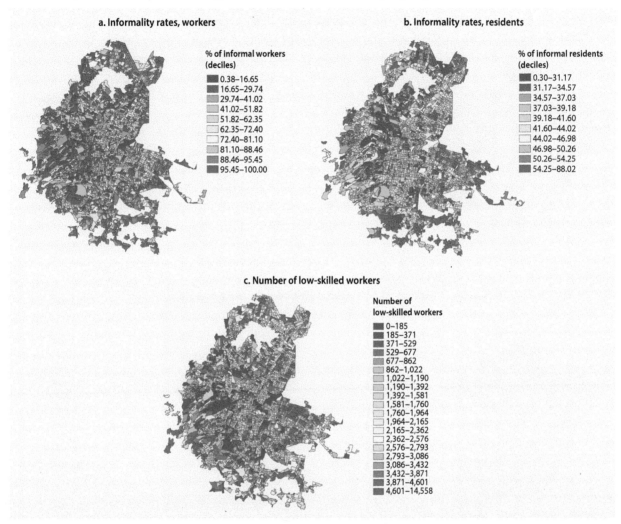

a. Informality rates, workers

% of informal workers (deciles)
- 0.38–16.65
- 16.65–29.74
- 29.74–41.02
- 41.02–51.82
- 51.82–62.35
- 62.35–72.40
- 72.40–81.10
- 81.10–88.46
- 88.46–95.45
- 95.45–100.00

b. Informality rates, residents

% of informal residents (deciles)
- 0.30–31.17
- 31.17–34.57
- 34.57–37.03
- 37.03–39.18
- 39.18–41.60
- 41.60–44.02
- 44.02–46.98
- 46.98–50.26
- 50.26–54.25
- 54.25–88.02

c. Number of low-skilled workers

Number of low-skilled workers
- 0–185
- 185–371
- 371–529
- 529–677
- 677–862
- 862–1,022
- 1,022–1,190
- 1,190–1,392
- 1,392–1,581
- 1,581–1,760
- 1,760–1,964
- 1,964–2,165
- 2,165–2,362
- 2,362–2,576
- 2,576–2,793
- 2,793–3,086
- 3,086–3,432
- 3,432–3,871
- 3,871–4,601
- 4,601–14,558

Sources: Panels a and b: Zárate 2022; panel c: Ianchovichina and Zárate 2021.
Note: The maps show the informality rates of workers and residents and number of low-skilled workers in each census tract.

to resource misallocation. The resulting efficiency losses can be reduced through improvements in connectivity from the city center to its periphery. It is estimated that a new subway line connecting Mexico City's peripheral neighborhoods with central locations would improve aggregate welfare by 1.3 percent and reduce aggregate informality by 4 percentage points (Zárate 2022). The improved connectivity to the low-income areas would compensate for any displacement effects caused by increases in housing prices and rents near newly opened metro stations.[54] Meanwhile, a 15 percent increase in affordable housing for low-income workers in Mexico City's central locations could boost aggregate welfare by 1.6 percent and reduce aggregate informality by 1.5 percentage points (Ianchovichina and Zárate 2021). And yet these measures may be insufficient to address the problem posed by the dual urban economy. Affordable housing projects in Mexico City's central business district such as Bando 2 have proven difficult to implement. Efforts to address crime and resolve long-standing deficiencies in basic infrastructure and public services may also be needed. Furthermore, proximity to jobs may not be enough to improve livelihoods.

MAP O.11   Trip destinations by income group, Mexico City

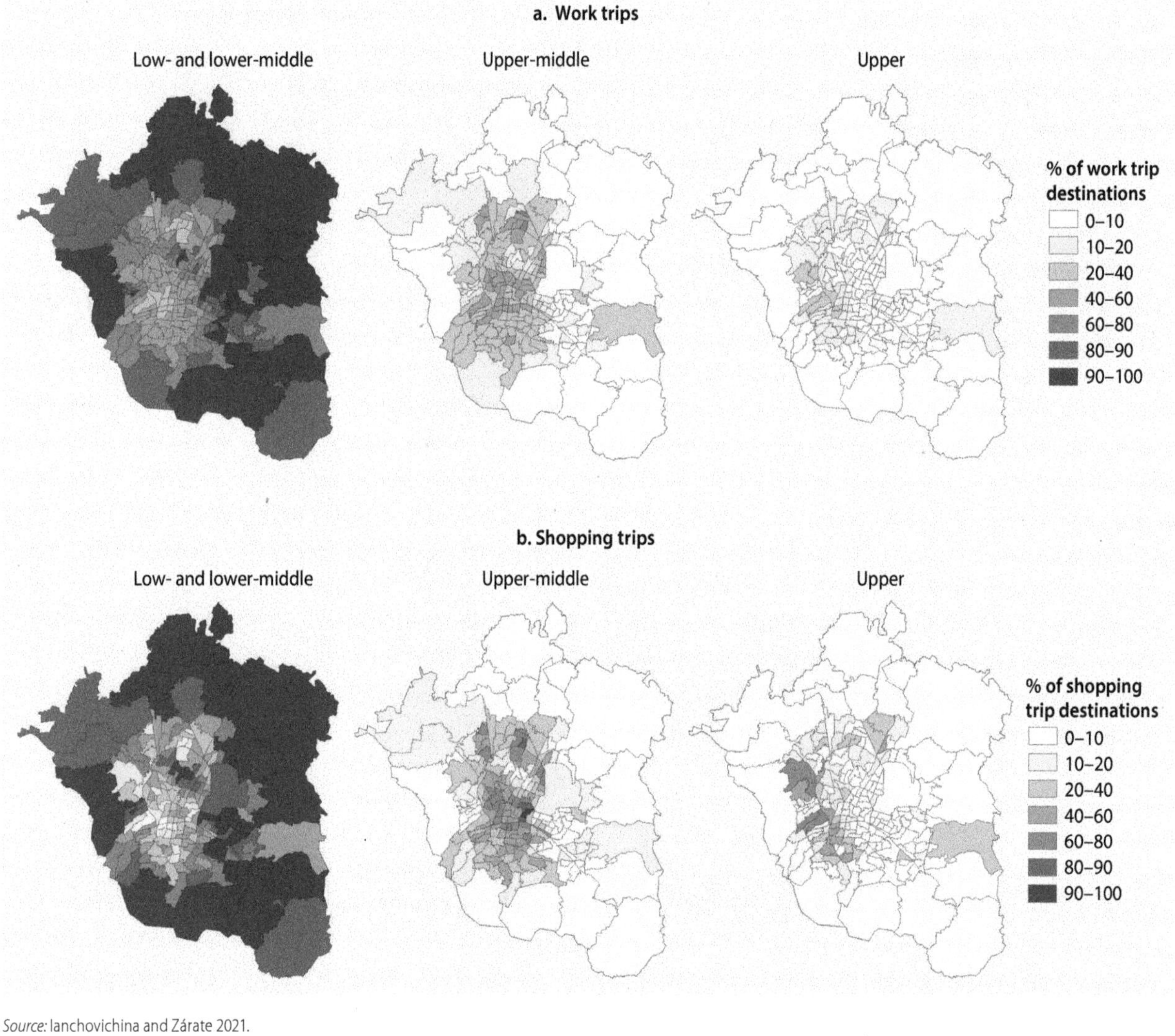

a. Work trips

Low- and lower-middle   Upper-middle   Upper

% of work trip destinations
- 0–10
- 10–20
- 20–40
- 40–60
- 60–80
- 80–90
- 90–100

b. Shopping trips

Low- and lower-middle   Upper-middle   Upper

% of shopping trip destinations
- 0–10
- 10–20
- 20–40
- 40–60
- 60–80
- 80–90
- 90–100

Source: Ianchovichina and Zárate 2021.
Note: Income is proxied with the status of three sociodemographic groups: low- and lower-middle, upper-middle, and upper.

Emerging evidence from Argentina indicates that labor market intermediation combined with improvements in living standards are required to help slum residents find better jobs.

Policy road map

This study identifies three spatial productivity challenges that constrain economic growth in Latin America: (1) the deindustrialization of cities, (2) intercity and intracity connectivity issues, and (3) divisions within cities. It also presents several key analytical findings.

Between the early 2000s and the late 2010s, a dramatic convergence in labor incomes and place productivity within countries reduced regional inequality.[55] This decline comes with good news and bad news. The good news is that relatively poor, predominantly rural regions started catching up due to improvements in agricultural productivity and investments in mining during the commodity boom of the 2000s. The bad news is that urban productivity growth was relatively weak in many urban areas.

Convergence has narrowed the income disparities with the leading metropolitan areas, including the gaps that could be exploited by migrating to these top locations, which deindustrialized but continued to attract migrants. Among the bottom 40 percent in the income distribution, these gaps have become negligible in most Latin American countries, except Bolivia, Brazil, Panama, and Peru, where regional disparities remain large.

Deindustrialization has constrained inclusive growth by shifting urban employment toward less dynamic, low-productivity, nontradable activities. The shift has limited the nationwide growth in labor productivity because the region's workforce is mostly urban. It has also limited urban place productivity because nontradables tend to benefit less from agglomeration economies than urban tradables, and their agglomeration benefits are reduced more quickly with increases in congestion, which is a major problem in the region's largest cities.

Poor interurban connectivity has slowed both urban and nationwide productivity growth by restricting market access, specialization, knowledge spillovers, and agglomeration economies. The relatively high intercity transport costs reflect a host of issues, including low and badly allocated investments in road improvements, backhaul problems, imperfect competition, government regulations, and information frictions. Digital technologies can be leveraged to overcome transport infrastructure deficiencies, but the region's progress in expanding access to affordable high-speed internet services, especially among the bottom 40 percent and rural communities, has been slow.

Divisions within some of Latin America's leading metropolitan areas—reinforced by long and costly commutes—hurt urban productivity by limiting the geographic reach of agglomeration economies and generate misallocation due to informality traps in the low-income, often peripheral, parts of cities. Deficiencies in basic infrastructure and public services in low-income neighborhoods also reduce the employability, productivity, and resilience of workers residing in these areas through greater exposure to climate shocks, disease, and crime.

The spatial analysis presented in this study has several important implications for economic policy. Latin America's resource-driven model of development delivered convergence in territorial productivity and living standards but accomplished only a short-lived spurt in economic growth during the Golden Decade. To accelerate growth in a sustainable, inclusive way and escape the middle-income trap, the region needs to blend its resource-driven model of development with one that better harnesses the skills and labor of its urban workers. Developing such a two-pronged development model will require improving the productivity and competitiveness of the urban economy and enhancing the efficiency with which countries transform natural wealth into human capital, infrastructure, and institutions. If the region succeeds at these tasks, two engines of growth—urban and rural—will power economic growth beyond the low levels of the past without a territorial divergence in living standards. However, the transition to a two-pronged model of development depends on whether countries can overcome multidimensional development challenges at all geographic scales—local, regional, and national—with the mix of issues varying in importance across countries.

Nationwide competitiveness priorities

Countries must tackle *nationwide competitiveness weaknesses* that limit the growth of urban tradables. Governments must protect macroeconomic stability,[56] improve the quality of and access to public education,[57] address skill gaps,[58] boost nationwide innovation capabilities,[59] and reduce policy and regulatory distortions. Quality investments can be attracted and export growth stimulated by making regulations simpler and more predictable, increasing the transparency of legal frameworks and property protection, strengthening competition policy, improving access to finance, strengthening the rule of law, facilitating trade and investment, and harmonizing local regulations with international standards.[60] Improving the state of international connectivity infrastructure and logistics (such as ports and roads) will also help to strengthen the competitiveness of the region's exports,[61] allowing Latin American firms to take advantage of global shifts in production such as those linked to green growth,[62] 3D printing, and efforts to increase the importance of services in manufacturing.[63] The weak rise in the share of employment in tradable services over the last three decades suggests that the region also needs to implement comprehensive reforms that speed up competition and innovation in the tradable services sectors, in addition to closing skill gaps that limit the supply of talent to these sectors.

Progress in these areas should go hand in hand with strengthening national institutions that can help to manage the volatility of commodity rents, following the example of Chile, which has developed high-quality institutions for this purpose, delivering social services and regulating the private sector (Gill et al. 2014). In the context of limited fiscal space and competing priorities, the efficient use of resource rents is crucial for countries' abilities to finance the region's infrastructure needs, estimated at 3.4 percent of the region's GDP per year over the period 2015–30 (Rozenberg and Fay 2019).

Improving intergovernmental fiscal systems is another priority. A report by the Inter-American Development Bank (IDB) and the Economic Commission for Latin America and the Caribbean (CEPAL) (2022) points out that subnational participation in the LAC region's aggregate public spending doubled between 1985 and 2010, stabilizing at 26 percent in 2019. But subnational governments have limited tax powers and remain highly dependent on central government transfers to fund education, health, transport, security, and many other essential community services. It is therefore essential not only to improve the efficiency of subnational spending and the ability of regional and local governments to mobilize their own resources, but also to enhance intergovernmental coordination, clarify the responsibilities of different levels of government, and strengthen fiscal responsibility frameworks in a way that protects subnational public investment and allows responsible access of subnational governments to financial markets.

Regional integration priorities

Improvements in domestic transport infrastructure can reduce intercity transport costs, generating substantial income and welfare gains (Conte and Ianchovichina 2022; Gorton and Ianchovichina 2021). Coordinating the domestic improvements with regional partners could enhance transnational connectivity, generating additional output gains without significantly increasing the costs incurred by individual countries. The benefits from such improvements are expected to be significant, but the estimated investment costs are also sizable (Rozenberg and Fay 2019). Many countries will have to complement these investments in transport infrastructure with investments in environmental services to address, for example, issues associated with flooding.

Because infrastructure projects progress slowly and require significant financial resources that are often insufficient given competing priorities, governments should abolish regulations that limit competition in the transport sector and keep prices high along certain routes. They should also encourage complementary investments in local public goods and services. For example, in India the gains in economic activity associated with the construction of the Golden Quadrilateral highway are larger in districts along the highway with better access to education and financial services (Das et al. 2019; Ghani, Grover, and Kerr 2013). In Argentina, such complementary investments have increased the welfare effects of road investments along the corridors linking Buenos Aires with the Northwest and Mesopotamia by an estimated 45 percent and 65 percent, respectively (World Bank 2020). In addition, investments in ICT connectivity should be fast-tracked. Closing education, knowledge, and information gaps with leading metropolitan areas will contribute to technological diffusion and increase the employability of residents in lagging regions and their potential to benefit from migration and employment in regional and national urban centers.

Local productivity priorities

How can LAC cities fuel nationwide productivity growth? The relatively small average urban productivity premia in the region (figure O.6) and its advanced stage of urbanization imply limited national productivity growth from rural–urban migration except in some of the lower-income LAC countries where agriculture still employs a large segment of the population. To enhance the urban contribution to productivity growth, more LAC urban areas must become production cities, where tradable activities thrive and generate positive productivity and employment effects. Two examples of US cities that have successfully raised their productivity over the years are Boston and Pittsburgh. In Boston, different kinds of human capital and a diversified industrial base have helped the city to become more prosperous and resilient over the last three and a half centuries (Glaeser 2003). Pittsburgh has shown that deindustrialized cities can bounce back by shifting into urban tradable services and improving their livability (King and Crommelin 2021).

A World Bank report identifies 750 "competitive" cities that have provided a fertile environment for private sector growth and productive employment creation (Kilroy et al. 2015). In lower-middle-income and upper-middle-income countries, these competitive cities are mostly production cities specializing in manufacturing and tradable services. Between 2005 and 2010, many competitive cities outperformed their national averages in terms of job growth (73 percent), but fewer managed to do so in terms of productivity (42 percent) and output growth (50 percent), and a much smaller share of supercompetitive cities surpassed national averages in all three areas (18 percent), pointing to trade-offs between these areas. No such trade-off was observed between job growth in tradables and nontradables (Kilroy et al. 2015).[64] Cities in which employment growth in tradables was fastest also recorded high employment growth in nontradables. In less competitive cities, job growth was low in both tradables and nontradables (Kilroy et al. 2015).

Although there are no recipes for becoming a successful competitive city, Kilroy et al. (2015) point to a set of prerequisites that can help cities reinvent themselves and become competitive. They include good local institutions, enterprise support and finance, skills and innovation, and infrastructure and access to land. Local governments in competitive cities facilitate and expedite permitting; ensure public safety and law enforcement, as well as access to essential services, such as water, sanitation, feeder roads, and electricity; provide inexpensive land and office space, good logistics services, and skill training; and successfully overcome fragmentation issues that might block progress or increase service provision costs.

Local authorities need to increase the provision of infrastructure that enhances intra-urban mobility, which is low in cities of all sizes in the LAC region, and implement policies that tackle congestion. According to Rozenberg and Fay (2019), city authorities can meet the demand for urban mobility at a relatively low infrastructure cost of about 0.45 percent of the region's GDP through integrated land use and transport planning; greater reliance on integrated public transport systems, including mass transit such as metros and bus rapid transit; and policies that increase rail occupancy, discourage private transport, and improve traffic management. The latter include (1) congestion pricing; (2) high-occupancy vehicle (HOV) restrictions; (3) parking management; (4) improved access to affordable, fast, and reliable internet infrastructure and digital services; and (5) reductions in fuel subsidies.

Local governments must also do more to improve basic urban infrastructure and access to public services, especially in poor neighborhoods, where services are deficient or lacking. Improving the livability of LAC cities will generate growth dividends because more livable cities attract talented and skilled workers (Glaeser and Xiong 2017). Investments in consumer amenities related to clean air, public transportation, public education, and health services have been found to stimulate innovation activity in Chinese cities (Zhang, Partridge, and Song 2020), while investments in human capital and public goods and services play an important role in patenting activity across US metropolitan areas, especially in areas with limited natural advantages (Mulligan 2020).

Last but not least, although the entry costs associated with housing do not appear to generate substantial aggregate efficiency losses in the LAC region, local governments must do more to improve the supply of affordable quality housing, which is in short supply in low-income neighborhoods. At the same time, they should address long-standing land management issues and put in place institutions that ensure the fluidity of land markets. Michaels et al. (2021) find that the division of land on the outskirts of cities into plots linked to roads and water mains enables the growth of neighborhoods with larger and better laid out buildings and better-quality housing than similar areas that did not receive basic infrastructure investments. However, the debate about the respective merits of upgrading and starting anew in existing low-income neighborhoods (Duranton and Venables 2020) is ongoing, which suggests that urban land use and management practices in the LAC region remain areas for further exploration.

This study identifies the policy priorities that need attention at the national, regional, and local levels to varying degrees in all LAC countries. Because the number of proposed desirable reforms and investments is large, countries will need to prioritize and design strategies that factor in their initial conditions and specific circumstances. This study does not discuss the how and who of these strategies. A recent study by Grover, Lall, and Maloney (2022) provides guidance on the steps governments should follow to evaluate the merit of spatially targeted policies and the key stakeholders they must work with to make progress and increase the chance that packages of reforms promote both spatial inclusion and economic transformation. The report by Kilroy et al. (2015) does that at the city level, detailing the stakeholders and the steps that local authorities need to take for cities to become more competitive.

Notes

1. Latin America includes Mexico and the countries of Central and South America. Throughout the report, the composition of countries in regional aggregates varies, depending on data availability. In some cases, the report features countries in the Caribbean, in which case they are included in reported regional aggregates.
2. Examples include analyses focusing on the role of external shocks and macroeconomic mismanagement (Goyal and Sahay 2007; Vegh et al. 2018); sectoral resource misallocation (Beylis et al. 2020); high inequality (UNDP 2021); high informality (Perry et al. 2007); and firms' weak innovation efforts (Dutz, Almeida, and Packard 2018; Lederman et al. 2014; Maloney and Rodríguez-Clare 2007).
3. The period ends in 2019 before the onset of the COVID-19 (coronavirus disease 2019) pandemic.

4. See Acemoglu and Dell (2010).
5. See Aroca, Bosch, and Maloney (2005); González Rivas (2007).
6. See Burger, Hendriks, and Ianchovichina (2022); Galvis and Meisel Roca (2010).
7. See Ferreira Filho and Horridge (2006).
8. See Escobal and Ponce (2011).
9. See Aroca, Bosch, and Maloney (2005); Bosch et al. (2003).
10. See Serra et al. (2006); Soto and Torche (2004).
11. Dutch Disease can arise from real exchange appreciation, inequality in the distribution of natural resources rents, or political instability, which discourages investments in tradable manufacturing and services (Ianchovichina and Onder 2017).
12. Urban tradables include manufacturing and tradable services, such as finance, insurance, and information technology (IT) services. All other urban activities are nontradables. Tradables include both urban tradables and rural tradables (such as agricultural and mining commodities). Services include both tradable and nontradable services.
13. In line with the efficient nature of Latin America's agriculture, the commodity boom did not lead to deurbanization; it only slowed the pace of rural to urban migration (Rodríguez-Vignoli and Rowe 2018).
14. Only Chile liberalized in the late 1970s (1976).
15. In Brazil, the tariff cuts in the manufacturing sectors resulted in large, long-lasting declines in formal employment (Dix-Carneiro and Kovak 2017).
16. According to Dix-Carneiro and Kovak (2019), the Brazilian regions hardest hit by trade liberalization initially experienced increases in both nonemployment and informality, but a decade and a half later there was no effect on nonemployment and a large positive effect on informal employment, mainly in the nontradable sector, which acted as a buffer, absorbing those displaced by the trade shock. These results are substantiated by Ponczek and Ulyssea (2022).
17. Rural localities are localities in which 50 percent or more of residents are rural. Thus some predominantly rural localities may have a minority share of urban residents.
18. See Maloney and Caicedo (2016).
19. For China, see Baum-Snow et al. (2017); Ethiopia, Grover (2019); and India, Dasgupta and Grover (2022).
20. Adão (2015) documents an increase of 8–16 percent in the commodity wage premium in Brazil stemming from the rise in world commodity prices from 1991 to 2010.
21. Dix-Carneiro and Kovak (2017) explain this long-lasting erosion in labor productivity by pointing to lost agglomeration economies and the slow reallocation of capital away from deindustrializing areas due to slow capital depreciation and the flow of new investment to other areas.
22. Costa, Garred, and Pessoa (2016) find that strong productivity growth in China led to fierce import competition in Brazil's manufacturing sectors, but it also created greater demand for exports of Brazilian commodities, implying that commodity-producing regions benefited from Chinese competition, while major manufacturing urban centers experienced declines. Determining the extent to which individual drivers of deindustrialization have contributed to reductions in territorial inequality in the LAC region is beyond the scope of this study. The effects of these forces are both context- and time horizon–specific and require an in-depth look at countries' institutions, economic structure, and market organization (Dix-Carneiro and Kovak 2023; Goldberg 2015).
23. Regionwide, more than 70 percent of urban areas have population densities above the global median (Roberts 2018).
24. The *place productivity premium* is the fraction of per capita household labor income that cannot be accounted for by observable, nongeographic (portable) household characteristics and the effects of exogenous time-variant factors. In this study, the following terms are used interchangeably: location premia after sorting, location premia, and place productivity.
25. Static productivity gains stem from agglomeration economies, whereas dynamic productivity gains come from learning by working. De La Roca and Puga (2017) provide evidence that the additional value of experience gained in bigger cities persists after leaving the city. Diamond (2016) finds that changes in the local labor demand are the primary reason for

the increased skill sorting, but in the United States from 1980 to 2000 amenities were also adjusted to reinforce this effect.

26. Glaeser, Kolko, and Saiz (2001) argue that consumption amenities, such as restaurants, stores, and public services, are important for attracting firms and skilled workers, who tend to earn higher incomes and to place greater value on the quality and variety of amenities. Big cities supply a greater variety and quality of amenities because they are bigger markets.

27. On average, as shown in chapter 2, urban place productivity is much lower than urban labor productivity.

28. A host of other issues undermine the performance of smaller (secondary or intermediate) cities. It is beyond the scope of this study to assess the differences in the constraints to productivity growth in secondary and primary cities in the region or to provide a comprehensive list of the factors undermining the growth of urban tradables.

29. Duarte and Restuccia (2010) find large productivity differences across countries in agriculture and services and smaller differences in manufacturing.

30. Such a comparison cannot be made for intraurban market access because no data are available on urban accessibility in a large set of cities in developing countries.

31. Chapter 5 shows the distribution of uncongested mobility and congestion by city size for the LAC region and the rest of the world.

32. Entry barriers are lower in the lower-income LAC countries mainly because it is easier to obtain entry documents for these countries than for the higher-income LAC countries.

33. And yet the welfare increase associated with this reduction is larger (19 percent) because it allows some people to relocate to areas with better amenities and derive higher utility.

34. Skoufias and López-Acevedo (2009) and Bryan and Morten (2019) reach similar conclusions.

35. Only 22 percent of land freight is transported by rail in Latin America, compared with 35–45 percent in North America, Europe, and East Asia (Ferreyra and Roberts 2018).

36. In Colombia, the government requires shippers in most sectors other than agriculture and beer to contract trucking companies through intermediaries and sets minimum prices for trucking services along the most important routes in the country, which are binding along some routes, as shown in Cantillo and Hernández (2022).

37. Except in Brazil and Mexico, the firms providing these services are low-productivity, small-scale establishments with aging fleets (World Bank 2021).

38. Allen et al. (2022) and Osborne, Pachón, and Araya (2014) provide evidence of imperfect competition in Colombia and Central America, respectively.

39. In Brazil, as many people moved out of metropolitan areas as moved into them, and those who moved out relocated in intermediate (secondary) cities, increasing their real wages. Only low-skilled domestic migrants lost in nominal terms (Egger 2021).

40. The model used to identify the misallocation considers only the layout of road networks because road transport is the dominant mode of transport in the LAC region. Development of alternative modes of transport (such as river and rail) along routes that have received insufficient investments in road infrastructure improvements may be warranted based on other priorities (such as climate) or when other modes of transport are economically viable.

41. The results for the full set of 16 LAC countries are presented in chapter 4.

42. Road transport is the most efficient mode of transport in low-density locations. People in these areas may be reluctant to move elsewhere because of their preferences and barriers to migration. In agricultural areas, rural roads also offer last-mile access to secondary urban areas where processing activities add value to agricultural value chains.

43. The scenario assumes that as transport costs decline, road congestion increases. Without an increase in congestion, the welfare effects are much larger (Gorton and Ianchovichina 2021).

44. The model does not distinguish between different types of road improvements, such as maintenance, rehabilitation projects, projects that improve the road surface (for example, upgrades of dirt roads to paved ones or the resurfacing of degraded paved roads), projects that broaden existing roads by adding new lanes, or projects that improve the flow of traffic such as bridges and interchanges.

45. When investments in transportation infrastructure are made in an optimal way, the gains of locations that become denser and more productive outweigh any congestion costs and the losses of locations that experience outmigration.

46. MERCOSUR is a South American trade bloc established by the Treaty of Asunción in 1991. Its full members are Argentina, Brazil, Paraguay, and Uruguay. República Bolivariana de Venezuela has been suspended indefinitely since December 2016.

47. The Andean Community is a free trade area that includes Bolivia, Colombia, Ecuador, and Peru.

48. In all cases except Argentina and Peru, the welfare gains from improvements in transnational road networks are comparable to or bigger than those associated with improvements in domestic road networks.

49. According to Acemoglu and Dell (2010), 80 percent of income inequality is explained by within-municipality income differences.

50. Duque et al. (2021) and Duque, Lozano-Gracia, García, et al. (2022) provide evidence of socioeconomic inequality and segregation in many Colombian and Mexican cities, respectively.

51. Recent evidence shows that once the fixed effects of transport modes are included, in Mexico City the differences between high- and low-income workers are associated with differences in neighborhood choices based on amenities rather than sensitivity to travel times (Ianchovichina and Zárate 2021).

52. If the commuter market access of all socioeconomic groups is comparable, a city may be spatially *segmented* but not *segregated*.

53. Because informal firms do not pay taxes, there is heterogeneity in the marginal product of labor across establishments located in central versus peripheral city neighborhoods that generates misallocation (Hsieh and Klenow 2009).

54. According to Pfutze, Rodríguez-Castelan, and Valderrama-Gonzalez (2018), such a displacement occurred near newly opened bus rapid transit (BRT) stations in Barranquilla, Colombia. Tsivanidis (2019) found the same near the BRT system in Bogotá, where high-skilled workers moved into high-amenity, expensive neighborhoods in the north of the city, while low-skilled workers relocated to poor neighborhoods in the south.

55. The convergence reflects trends in labor income net of social transfers and other sources such as remittances.

56. The Commission on Growth and Development (2008) has identified macroeconomic stability as a key ingredient in a successful strategy for sustaining high growth rates over more than two decades.

57. The World Bank (2022) offers strategies for closing the learning gaps that opened during the COVID-19 pandemic.

58. Ferreyra et al. (2021) provide an in-depth discussion of the LAC region's short-cycle programs. These programs offer a way to respond to the needs of the local economy by equipping individuals with skills over a shorter time and at a lower cost than four-year university programs.

59. Ferreyra et al. (2017) document the expansion of the LAC region's higher education and provide policy suggestions for improving its quality.

60. These issues are presented in depth in Rocha and Ruta (2022).

61. Although a discussion of international logistics is beyond the scope of this study, a recent Inter-American Development Bank report by Calatayud and Montes (2021) finds a significant lag in the LAC region's logistics performance relative to that of other regions.

62. A forthcoming World Bank report will explore opportunities for green growth in the region.

63. Nayyar, Hallward-Driemeier, and Davies (2021) discuss the prospects for service-led development.

64. In LAC, examples of successful "competitive cities" that outperformed their national economies in terms of both jobs and output are Saltillo in Mexico and Bucaramanga in Colombia.

References

Acemoglu, D., and M. Dell. 2010. "Productivity Differences between and within Countries." *American Economic Journal: Macroeconomics* 2 (1): 16988.

Acevedo-García, D., K. Lochner, T. Osypuk, and S. Subramanian. 2003. "Future Directions in Residential Segregation and Health Research: A Multilevel Approach." *American Journal of Public Health* 93 (2): 215–21.

Adão, R. 2015. "Worker Heterogeneity, Wage Inequality, and International Trade: Theory and Evidence from Brazil." Massachusetts Institute of Technology, Cambridge, MA. https://economics.yale.edu/sites/default/files/adao_jmp_2015.pdf.

Akbar, P. 2022. "Mobility and Congestion in Urban Areas in Latin America and the Caribbean." Background paper prepared for this report, World Bank, Washington, DC.

Akbar, P., V. Couture, G. Duranton, and A. Storeygard. 2022. "The Fast, the Slow, and the Congested: Urban Transportation in Rich and Poor Countries." CEPR Press Discussion Paper No. 18401, Centre for Economic Policy Research, London. https://cepr.org/publications/dp18401.

Alexander, D., and J. Currie. 2017. "Is It Who You Are or Where You Live? Residential Segregation and Racial Gaps in Childhood Asthma." *Journal of Health Economics* 55: 186–200.

Allen, T., and C. Arkolakis. 2014. "Trade and the Topography of the Spatial Economy." *Quarterly Journal of Economics* 129 (3): 1085–140.

Allen, T., D. Atkin, S. C. Cantillo, and C. Hernández. 2022. "Trucks." https://sites.google.com/site/treballen/research.

Aroca, P., M. Bosch, and W. F. Maloney. 2005. "Spatial Dimensions of Trade Liberalization and Economic Convergence: Mexico 1985–2002." Policy Research Working Paper 3744, World Bank, Washington, DC.

Bachas, P., L. Gadenne, and J. Anders. 2020. "Informality, Consumption Taxes and Redistribution." Policy Research Working Paper 9267, World Bank, Washington, DC.

Baum-Snow, N., L. Brandt, J. V. Henderson, M. A. Turner, and Q. Zhang. 2017. "Roads, Railroads and Decentralization of Chinese Cities." *Review of Economics and Statistics* 99 (3): 435–48.

Baum-Snow, N., and B. Lutz. 2011. "School Desegregation, School Choice, and Changes in Residential Location Patterns by Race." *American Economic Review* 101: 3019–46.

Beaton, K., A. Cebotari, X. Ding, and A. Komaromi. 2017. "Trade Integration in Latin America: A Network Perspective." IMF Working Paper WP/17/148, International Monetary Fund, Washington, DC.

Bellon, M. 2018. "Trade Liberalization and Inequality: A Dynamic Model with Firm and Worker Heterogeneity." https://matthieubellon.com/docs/TradeLiberalizationInequalityDynamics2018.pdf.

Beylis, G., R. Fattal-Jaef, R. Sinha, M. Morris, and A. Sebastian. 2020. *Going Viral: COVID-19 and the Accelerated Transformation of Jobs in Latin America and the Caribbean.* World Bank Latin American and Caribbean Studies. World Bank, Washington, DC.

Bosch, M., P. Aroca, I. J. Fernández, and C. R. Azzoni. 2003. "Growth Dynamics and Space in Brazil." *International Regional Science Review* 26 (3): 393–418.

Bryan, G., and M. Morten. 2019. "The Aggregate Productivity Effects of Internal Migration: Evidence from Indonesia." *Journal of Political Economy* 127 (5): 2229–68.

Burger, M., M. Hendriks, and E. Ianchovichina. 2022. "Happy but Unequal: Differences in Subjective Well-Being across Individuals and Space in Colombia." *Applied Research in Quality of Life* 17 (3): 1343–87.

Burger, M., E. Ianchovichina, and P. Akbar. 2022. "Heterogenous Agglomeration Economies in the Developing Countries: The Roles of Firm Characteristics, Sector Tradability, and Urban Mobility." Policy Research Working Paper 9954, World Bank, Washington, DC.

Calatayud, A., and L. Montes. 2021. *Logistics in Latin America and the Caribbean: Opportunities, Challenges and Courses of Action.* Washington, DC: Inter-American Development Bank.

Cantillo, S. C., and C. Hernández. 2022. "A Toolkit for Setting and Evaluating Price Floors." Social Science Research Network. https://doi.org/10.2139/ssrn.4207884.

Chetty, R., N. Hendren, and L. F. Katz. 2016. "The Effects of Exposure to Better Neighborhoods on Children: New Evidence from the Moving to Opportunity Project." *American Economic Review* 106 (4): 855–902.

Chetty, R., M. O. Jackson, T. Kuchler, J. Stroebel, N. Hendren, R. B. Fluegge, S. Gong, et al. 2022. "Social Capital I: Measurement and Associations with Economic Mobility." *Nature* 608: 108–21.

Commission on Growth and Development. 2008. *The Growth Report: Strategies for Sustained Growth and Inclusive Development.* Washington, DC: World Bank.

Conte, B., and E. Ianchovichina. 2022. "Spatial Development and Mobility Frictions in Latin America: Theory-Based Empirical Evidence." Policy Research Working Paper 10071, World Bank, Washington, DC.

Costa, F., J. Garred, and J. P. Pessoa. 2016. "Winners and Losers from a Commodities-for-Manufactures Trade Boom." *Journal of International Economics* 102: 50–69.

D'Aoust, O., V. Galdo, and E. Ianchovichina. 2023. "Territorial Productivity Differences and Dynamics within Latin American Countries." Policy Research Working Paper 10480, World Bank, Washington, DC.

Das, A., E. Ghani, A. Grover, W. Kerr, and R. Nanda. 2019. "Infrastructure and Finance: Evidence from India's GQ Highway Network." Working Paper No. 19-121, Harvard Business School, Boston, MA.

Dasgupta, K., and A. Grover. 2022. "Trade, Transport, and Territorial Development." Policy Research Working Paper 10066, World Bank, Washington, DC.

De La Roca, J., and D. Puga. 2017. "Learning by Working in Big Cities." *Review of Economic Studies* 84: 106–42.

Desmet, K., D. Nagy, and E. Rossi-Hansberg. 2018. "The Geography of Development." *Journal of Political Economy* 126 (3): 903–83.

Diamond, R. 2016. "The Determinants and Welfare Implications of US Workers' Diverging Location Choices by Skill: 1980–2000." *American Economic Review* 106 (3): 479–524.

Dix-Carneiro, R., and B. Kovak. 2017. "Trade Liberalization and Regional Dynamics." *American Economic Review* 107 (10): 2908–46.

Dix-Carneiro, R., and B. Kovak. 2019. "Margins of Labor Market Adjustment to Trade." *Journal of International Economics* 117: 125–42.

Dix-Carneiro, R., and B. Kovak. 2023. "Globalization and Inequality in Latin America." Inter-American Development Bank, Washington, DC.

Duarte, M., and D. Restuccia. 2010. "The Role of the Structural Transformation in Aggregate Productivity." *Quarterly Journal of Economics* 125 (1): 129–73.

Duque, J. C., N. Lozano-Gracia, G. García, J. Ospina, J. Patiño, and R. Curiel. 2022. "Intraurban Inequality in Mexican Cities." Background paper prepared for this report, Universidad EAFIT, Medellín, Colombia.

Duque, J. C., N. Lozano-Gracia, J. Patiño, and P. Restrepo. 2022. "Urban Form and Productivity: What Shapes Are Latin-American Cities?" *Urban Analytics and City Science* 49 (1): 131–50.

Duque, J. C., N. Lozano-Gracia, M. Quiñones, G. García, J. Ospina, J. Patiño, and K. Montoya. 2021. "Intraurban Inequality in Colombian Cities." Unpublished manuscript, Universidad EAFIT, Medellín, Colombia.

Duranton, G., and D. Puga. 2020. "The Economics of Urban Density." *Journal of Economic Perspectives* 34 (3): 3–26.

Duranton, G., and A. Venables. 2020. "Place-Based Policies for Development." In *Handbook of Regional Science*, edited by M. Fisher and P. Nijkamp. Berlin: Springer.

Dutz, M., R. Almeida, and T. Packard. 2018. *The Jobs of Tomorrow: Technology, Productivity, and Prosperity in Latin America and the Caribbean.* Directions in Development Series, Communication and Information Technologies. Washington, DC: World Bank.

Egger, E.-M. 2021. "Migrating Out of Mega-Cities: Evidence from Brazil." *IZA Journal of Development and Migration* 12 (1): 1–35.

Escobal, J., and C. Ponce. 2011. "Access to Public Infrastructure, Institutional Thickness and Pro-Poor Growth in Rural Peru." *Journal of International Development* 23 (3): 358–79.

Fajgelbaum, P., and E. Schaal. 2020. "Optimal Transport Networks in Spatial Equilibrium." *Econometrica* 88 (4): 1411–52.

Fay, M., L. Andres, C. Fox, U. Narloch, S. Straub, and M. Slawson. 2017. *Rethinking Infrastructure in Latin America and the Caribbean: Spending Better to Achieve More.* Washington, DC: World Bank.

Ferreira Filho, J., and M. Horridge. 2006. "Economic Integration, Poverty and Regional Inequality in Brazil." *Revista Brasileira de Economia* 60 (4): 363–87.

Ferreyra, M. M., C. Avitabile, J. Botero Álvarez, F. Haimovich Paz, and S. Urzúa. 2017. *At a Crossroads: Higher Education in Latin America and the Caribbean.* Washington, DC: World Bank.

Ferreyra, M. M., L. Dinarte, S. Urzúa, and M. Bassi. 2021. *The Fast Track to New Skills: Short-Cycle Higher Education Programs in Latin America and the Caribbean.* Washington, DC: World Bank.

Ferreyra, M. M., and M. Roberts, eds. 2018. *Raising the Bar for Productive Cities in Latin America and the Caribbean.* Washington, DC: World Bank.

Galvis, L. A., and A. Meisel Roca. 2010. "Persistencia de las desigualdades regionales en Colombia: Un análisis espacial." Documento de trabajo sobre economía regional no. 120, Banco de la República, Colombia.

Ghani, E., A. Grover, and W. Kerr. 2013. "Highway to Success in India: The Impact of the Golden Quadrilateral Project for the Location and Performance of Manufacturing." Policy Research Working Paper 6320, World Bank, Washington, DC.

Gill, I., I. Izvorski, W. van Eeghen, and D. De Rosa. 2014. *Diversified Development: Making the Most of Natural Resources in Eurasia.* Washington, DC: World Bank.

Glaeser, E. 1994. "Cities, Information, and Economic Growth." *Cityscape* 1 (1): 9–47.

Glaeser, E. 2003. "Reinventing Boston: 1640–2003." NBER Working Paper 10166, National Bureau of Economic Research, Cambridge, MA.

Glaeser, E., J. Kolko, and A. Saiz. 2001. "Consumer City." *Journal of Economic Geography* 1 (1): 27–50.

Glaeser, E., and W. Xiong. 2017. "Urban Productivity in the Developing World." NBER Working Paper 23279, National Bureau of Economic Research, Cambridge, MA.

Goldberg, P. 2015. *Trade and Inequality.* Edward Elgar Research Collections. Cheltenham, UK: Edward Elgar.

González Rivas, M. 2007. "The Effects of Trade Openness on Regional Inequality in Mexico." *Annals of Regional Science* 41: 545–61.

Gorton, N., and E. Ianchovichina. 2021. "Trade Networks in Latin America: Spatial Inefficiencies and Optimal Expansions." Policy Research Working Paper 9843, World Bank, Washington, DC.

Goyal, R., and R. Sahay. 2007. "Volatility and Growth in Latin America: An Episodic Approach." IMF Working Paper 06/287, International Monetary Fund, Washington, DC.

Granovetter, M. 1973. "The Strength of Weak Ties Theory." *American Journal of Sociology* 78 (6): 1360–80.

Grover, A. 2019. "Firms Far Up: Productivity, Agglomeration, and High-Growth Firms in Ethiopia." Policy Research Working Paper 9099, World Bank, Washington, DC.

Grover, A., S. Lall, and W. F. Maloney. 2022. *Place, Productivity, and Prosperity: Revisiting Spatially Targeted Policies for Regional Development.* Washington, DC: World Bank.

Grover, A., and W. F. Maloney. 2022. "Proximity without Productivity: Agglomeration Effects with Plant-Level Output and Price Data." Policy Research Working Paper 9977, World Bank, Washington, DC.

Heil, A., E. Ianchovichina, and L. Quintero. 2022. "Spatial Variations in Income and Wealth in a Segregated City: Evidence from Bogotá." Background paper prepared for this report, World Bank, Washington, DC.

Hsieh, C.-T., and P. Klenow. 2009. "Misallocation and Manufacturing TFP in China and India." *Quarterly Journal of Economics* 124 (4): 1403–48.

Ianchovichina, E., and H. Onder. 2017. "Dutch Disease: An Economic Illness Easy to Catch, Difficult to Cure." *Future Development* (blog). https://www.brookings.edu/tags/future-development/.

Ianchovichina, E., and R. Zárate. 2021. "Segregation, Informality, and Misallocation." Background paper prepared for this report, World Bank, Washington, DC.

IDB (Inter-American Development Bank) and CEPAL (Economic Commission for Latin America and the Caribbean). 2022. *Panorama de las relaciones fiscales entre niveles de gobierno de países de America Latina y el Caribe.* Washington, DC: IDB and CEPAL.

Jedwab, R., E. Ianchovichina, and F. Haslop. 2022. "Consumption Cities versus Production Cities: New Considerations and Evidence." Policy Research Working Paper 10105, World Bank, Washington, DC.

Katz, L., J. Kling, and J. Liebman. 2001. "Moving to Opportunities in Boston: Early Results of a Randomized Mobility Experiment." *Quarterly Journal of Economics* 116 (2): 607–54.

Kilroy, A., L. Francis, M. Mukim, and S. Negri. 2015. *Competitive Cities for Jobs and Growth: What, Who, and How.* Washington, DC: World Bank.

King, C., and L. Crommelin. 2021. "A Different Perspective on Post-Industrial Labor Market Restructuring in Detroit and Pittsburgh." *Journal of Urban Affairs* 43 (7): 975–94.

Lall, S., Z. Shalizi, and U. Deichmann. 2004. "Agglomeration Economies and Productivity in Indian Industry." *Journal of Development Economics* 73 (2): 643–73.

Lederman, D., J. Messina, S. Pienknagura, and R. Jamele. 2014. *Latin American Entrepreneurs: Many Firms but Little Innovation.* World Bank Latin American and Caribbean Studies. Washington, DC: World Bank.

Maloney, W., and A. Rodríguez-Clare. 2007. "Innovation Shortfalls." *Review of Development Economics* 11 (4): 665–84.

Maloney, W., and F. V. Caicedo. 2016. "The Persistence of (Subnational) Fortune." *Economic Journal* 126 (598): 2363–401.

Melitz, M., and S. Redding. 2021. "Trade and Innovation." NBER Working Paper 28945, National Bureau of Economic Research, Cambridge, MA.

Mesquita Moreira, M., J. Blyde, C. Volpe, and D. Molina. 2013. *Too Far to Export: Domestic Transport Costs and Regional Export Disparities in Latin America and the Caribbean.* Washington, DC: Inter-American Development Bank.

Michaels, G., D. Nigmatulina, F. Rauch, T. Regan, N. Baruah, and A. Dahlstrand. 2021. "Planning Ahead for Better Neighborhoods: Long-Run Evidence from Tanzania." *Journal of Political Economy* 129 (7): 2112–156.

Montañés, R., J. Barreto, C. Bonilla, D. Sánchez, and H. Winkler. 2021. "Working from Home in Latin America and the Caribbean: Enabling Factors and Inequality Implications." Background paper prepared for this report, World Bank, Washington, DC.

Mulligan, G. 2020. "Revisiting Patent Generation in US Metropolitan Areas: 1990–2015." *Applied Spatial Analysis and Policy* 14: 473–96.

Nayyar, G., M. Hallward-Driemeier, and E. Davies. 2021. *At Your Service? The Promise of Services-Led Development.* Washington, DC: World Bank.

Nin Pratt, A., C. Falconi, C. Ludena, and P. Martel. 2015. "Productivity and the Performance of Agriculture in Latin America and the Caribbean: From the Lost Decade to the Commodity Boom." IDB Working Paper No. 608, Inter-American Development Bank, Washington, DC.

Nordhaus, W., Q. Azam, D. Novoa, K. Hood, N. Victor, M. Mohammed, A. Miltner, and J. Weiss. 2006. "The G-Econ Database on Gridded Output: Methods and Data." Working paper, Yale University, New Haven, CT.

OECD (Organisation for Economic Co-operation and Development). 2018 *Divided Cities: Understanding Intra-urban Inequalities.* Paris: OECD.

Osborne, T., M. Pachón, and G. Araya. 2014. "What Drives the High Price of Road Freight Transport in Central America?" Policy Research Working Paper 6844, World Bank, Washington, DC.

Perry, G., W. Maloney, O. Arias, P. Gajnzylber, A. Mason, and J. Saavedra-Chanduvi. 2007. *Informality: Exit and Exclusion.* World Bank Latin American and Caribbean Studies. Washington, DC: World Bank.

Pfutze, T., C. Rodríguez-Castelan, and D. Valderrama-Gonzalez. 2018. "Urban Transport Infrastructure and Household Welfare: Evidence from Colombia." Policy Research Working Paper 8341, World Bank, Washington, DC.

Ponczek, V., and G. Ulyssea. 2022. "Enforcement of Labour Regulation and the Labour Market Effects of Trade: Evidence from Brazil." *Economic Journal* 132 (641): 361–90.

Quintero, L., and M. Roberts. 2018. "Explaining Spatial Variations in Productivity: Evidence from Latin America and the Caribbean." Policy Research Working Paper 8560, World Bank, Washington, DC.

Roberts, M. 2018. "The Many Dimensions of Urbanization and the Productivity of Cities in Latin America and the Caribbean." In *Raising the Bar for Productive Cities in Latin America and the Caribbean*, edited by M. M. Ferreyra and M. Roberts. Washington, DC: World Bank.

Rocha, N., and M. Ruta, eds. 2022. *Deep Trade Agreements: Anchoring Global Value Chains in Latin America and the Caribbean*. Washington, DC: World Bank.

Rodríguez-Castelán, C., L. López-Calva, N. Lustig, and D. Valderrama. 2022. "Wage Inequality in the Developing World: Evidence from Latin America." *Review of Development Economics* 26 (4): 1944–970.

Rodríguez-Pose, A., and J. Griffiths. 2021. "Developing Intermediate Cities." *Regional Science Policy and Practice* 13 (3): 441–56.

Rodríguez-Vignoli, J., and F. Rowe. 2018. "How Is Internal Migration Reshaping Metropolitan Populations in Latin America? A New Method and New Evidence." *Population Studies* 72 (2): 253–73.

Rozenberg, J., and M. Fay, eds. 2019. *Beyond the Gap: How Countries Can Afford the Infrastructure They Need while Protecting the Planet*. Sustainable Infrastructure Series. Washington, DC: World Bank.

Serra, M. I., M. F. Pazmino, G. Lindow, B. Sutton, and G. Ramírez. 2006. "Regional Convergence in Latin America." IMF Working Paper WP/06/125, International Monetary Fund, Washington, DC.

Skoufias, E., and G. López-Acevedo. 2009. *Determinants of Regional Welfare Disparities within Latin American Countries*, Vol. 1, *Synthesis*. Washington, DC: World Bank.

Soto, R., and A. Torche. 2004. "Spatial Inequality, Migration, and Economic Growth in Chile." *Latin American Journal of Economics* 41: 401–24.

Suárez, M., M. Murata, and J. Campos. 2015. "Why Do the Poor Travel Less? Urban Structure, Commuting and Economic Informality in Mexico City." *Urban Studies* 53 (12): 2548–66.

Terra, M. 2003. "Trade Liberalization in Latin American Countries and the Agreement on Textiles and Clothing in the WTO." *Économie Internationale* 94-93: 137–54.

Tsivanidis, N. 2019. "Evaluating the Impact of Urban Transit Infrastructure: Evidence from Bogota's TransMilenio." University of California, Berkeley.

UNDP (United Nations Development Programme). 2021. *Trapped: High Inequality and Low Growth in Latin America and the Caribbean*. Regional Human Development Report. New York: UNDP.

United Nations. 2016. *The World Cities Data Booklet*. New York: United Nations.

Van der Weide, R., P. Ferreira de Souza, and R. Barbosa. 2020. "Intergenerational Mobility in Education in Brazil." Unpublished manuscript, World Bank, Washington, DC.

Vegh, C., G. Vuletin, D. Riera-Crichton, J. P. Medina, D. Friedheim, L. Morano, and L. Venturo. 2018. *From Known Unknowns to Black Swans: How to Manage Risk in Latin America and the Caribbean*. LAC Semiannual Report, October 2018. Washington, DC: World Bank.

Venables, A. 2017. "Breaking into Tradables: Urban Form and Urban Function in a Developing City." *Journal of Urban Economics* 98 (C): 88–97.

Venables, A. 2020. "Winners and Losers in the Urban System." In *Urban Empire: Cities as Global Rulers in the New Urban World*, edited by E. Glaeser, K. Kourtit, and P. Nijkamp. New York: Routledge.

World Bank. 2009. *World Development Report 2009: Reshaping Economic Geography*. Washington, DC: World Bank.

World Bank. 2020. *Territorial Development in Argentina: Diagnosing Key Bottlenecks as the First Step toward Effective Policy.* Washington, DC: World Bank.

World Bank. 2021. "Regulation and Performance of Logistics Services Markets in Latin America." Background paper, *Productive Competition in Latin America and the Caribbean.* World Bank, Washington, DC.

World Bank. 2022. *Two Years After: Saving a Generation.* Washington, DC: World Bank.

Zárate, R. 2022. "Spatial Misallocation, Informality, and Transit Improvements: Evidence from Mexico City." Policy Research Working Paper 9990, World Bank, Washington, DC.

Zhang, M., M. Partridge, and H. Song. 2020. "Amenities and the Geography of Innovation: Evidence from Chinese Cities." *Annals of Regional Science* 65 (1): 105–45.

Introduction | 1

There be three things that make a nation great and strong: a fertile soil, busy workshops, and the easy conveyance of men and goods from place to place.

Francis Bacon, English philosopher and statesman (1561–1626)

More than four centuries ago, Francis Bacon, the father of empiricism, recognized the crucial importance of economic integration and industrial dynamism to the ability of countries to withstand shocks and prosper. His wisdom has endured the test of time. The World Bank's 2009 *World Development Report* echoes the ideas of Francis Bacon with a twist (World Bank 2009). It points out that successful countries benefit from a concentration of industrial production in urban areas through economic integration and institutions that ensure the convergence in living standards within countries.

Recalling these ideas can provide insight into the low-growth predicament in Latin America and the Caribbean (LAC),[1] where, except for the commodity-driven growth acceleration during the Golden Decade (2003–13), incomes grew, on average, at half the rate recorded in emerging Asia. Without sustained, strong growth, the region has remained stuck in a middle-income trap (a situation in which countries are unable to make progress after reaching middle-income level), while standards of living have slipped further behind those in the Group of 7 (G7) countries.[2] In the LAC region in the early 1980s, average per capita incomes in purchasing power parity (PPP) terms were close to half those in the G7 countries, but by 2020 they were just a third. Weak growth has also made it harder to reduce informality, underemployment, and unemployment; effectively respond to economic crises and natural disasters; and adequately invest in human capital and infrastructure that can modernize the economy and lay the foundations for green, resilient, and inclusive development.

Motivation

The LAC region's low growth predicament has puzzled economists for decades. Numerous explanations have emerged over the years, including macroeconomic volatility and mismanagement (Goyal and Sahay 2007; Vegh et al. 2018); sectoral resource misallocation (Beylis et al. 2020); high inequality (UNDP 2021); high informality (Perry et al. 2007); and firms' weak innovation efforts (Dutz, Almeida, and Packard 2018; Lederman et al. 2014; Maloney and Rodríguez-Clare 2007). And yet few have focused on the role of mobility frictions that limit economic integration across regions and generate spatial inefficiencies, or the structural and spatial factors that weaken urban productivity.

This study documents the evolution of territorial differences in labor incomes and place productivity within most Latin American countries between the early 2000s and the late 2010s. It then assesses the size of mobility frictions in the form of transport and migration costs and the extent to which they generate misallocation and reduce aggregate output growth. The study also explores the geography of urban employment and the evolution of its composition by city size over the last few decades. Last but not least, the report reveals how some structural and spatial features of Latin American economies have weakened the returns to density and therefore urban productivity. Using the core concepts of economic geography, state-of-the-art techniques, and various data sources in a nuanced, deliberative way, this study adopts a so-called territorial lens to investigate the key spatial constraints to specialization, migration, and agglomeration and thus long-run economic growth in Latin America.

Looking at productivity issues through a territorial lens is important for understanding the spatial changes in productive employment during economic transitions and their implications for territorial productivity and inclusive growth. In recent years, large spatial income disparities have become a prominent policy and political challenge in countries at all income levels. In the Middle East and North Africa, they were associated with political violence following the Arab Spring uprisings (Ianchovichina 2018). In advanced economies, they have been linked to growing political and social polarization. In the United Kingdom, one of the most spatially unequal advanced economies (Davenport and Zaranko 2020),[3] support for Brexit was strongest in the country's lagging regions (Rodríguez-Pose 2017).

In Latin America, territorial differences in labor income within countries were large and persistent or declining at a relatively slow pace prior to the mid-2000s. In the first half of the 2000s, cross-municipal differences in labor income within countries were, on average, twice the size of cross-country differences in labor income in the region (Acemoglu and Dell 2010). Several studies document the stark contrasts between lagging and leading territories, including Brazil's northeast and south (Ferreira-Filho and Horridge 2006); Colombia's peripheral and core regions (Burger, Hendriks, and Ianchovichina 2022; Galvis and Meisel Roca 2010, 2012); Mexico's north and south (Aroca, Bosch, and Maloney 2005; González Rivas 2007); and Peru's coastal and internal areas (Escobal and Ponce 2011a, 2011b). Studies conducted in the first half of the 2000s also question the notion of territorial income convergence in the region (Aroca, Bosch, and Maloney 2005; Bosch et al. 2003) or argue that convergence has occurred at a very slow pace (Serra et al. 2006; Soto and Torche 2004).

During the 2000s, however, the urban wage premium started to decline, rapidly plummeting between 2003 and 2008 and stagnating afterward (Rodríguez-Castelán et al. 2022). This reversal of fortune was driven in part by the increase in commodity rents from the rising demand for resources and farm products by China and other fast-growing economies (Costa, Garred, and Pessoa 2016). During the commodity boom years of the Golden Decade (2003–13), investments and incomes in rural areas increased, but the Dutch Disease[4] effects from the commodity windfall (and in some countries remittances) also increased spending on imported goods and services, weakening the competitiveness of urban tradables[5] (Venables 2017). At the same time, intense foreign competition, mainly from China, which joined the World Trade Organization in 2001 and sharply increased its exports (the "China Shock"), along with advances in labor-saving technologies, further depressed employment in manufacturing. With deindustrialization (Costa, Garred, and Pessoa 2016), the employment share of urban tradables declined (figure 1.1), and the composition of urban employment shifted toward low-productivity nontradables, such as retail trade, construction, and personal services (Jedwab, Ianchovichina, and Haslop 2022), depressing labor productivity growth in urban areas.[6]

The deindustrialization of Latin American cities actually began years earlier (Beylis et al. 2020). Facing escalating economic and debt problems, many Latin American countries abandoned the costly import substitution policies that helped them to industrialize but not to establish competitive manufacturing sectors. Countries instead leaned on their sectors of comparative advantage: agriculture, food and resource processing, and mining. Between 1980 and 2012, increased use of capital and fertilizers, combined with ample endowments of land and natural resources, improved labor productivity in agriculture (Nin Pratt et al. 2015) and other commodity sectors (Adão 2015) and fueled the expansion of resource and food exports. However, during the same period Latin American cities were gradually losing their dynamism. After most countries sharply reduced tariffs and other trade restrictions in the late 1980s or early 1990s (Bellon 2018; Dix-Carneiro and Kovak 2023; Terra 2003),[7] layoffs from manufacturing firms followed, especially in the largest cities, where laid-off workers switched to informal, lower-quality jobs in the nontradable sector (Dix-Carneiro and Kovak 2017). In Brazil, informal employment in the nontradable sector remained substantially elevated a decade and a half after the initial opening to trade (Dix-Carneiro and Kovak 2019; Ponczek and Ulyssea 2022).[8]

FIGURE 1.1 **Evolution of share of employment in tradables by city size and decade: LAC region, 1980 or earlier to circa 2010**

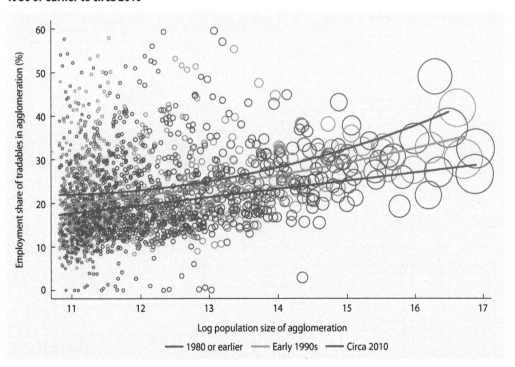

Source: Jedwab, Ianchovichina, and Haslop (2022), using Integrated Public Use Microdata Series (IPUMS, https://www.ipums.org/) census data and the Global Human Settlement Layer database (https://ghsl.jrc.ec.europa.eu/download.php).
Note: The graph shows the downward shift over time in the trend line, linking the employment share of tradables, which include manufacturing and tradable services such as finance, insurance, and real estate services, and the size of functional urban areas (FUAs), proxied with the log of the number of inhabitants of the FUA.

Deindustrialization did not lead to deurbanization because the agricultural expansion did not increase demand for labor; it simply increased the region's dependence on commodity exports (Rocha and Ruta 2022)[9] and shifted the composition of urban employment, especially in the largest cities, toward less dynamic and relatively unproductive nontradable activities (figure 1:1). Thus by circa 2000, the LAC region had a deficit of so-called "production" cities with a disproportionately high share of employment in urban tradables and no large and globally significant production cities (map 1.1). Most large production cities were concentrated in East Asia and Europe. The region had only large "neutral" cities (such as Buenos Aires and Mexico City) with an employment share of urban tradables that was neither too low nor too high, or large "consumption" cities (such as Bogotá and Rio de Janeiro) with a disproportionately low share of urban tradables. The concentration in these urban areas was also driven by access to political power, public services, and consumer amenities. Smaller production cities could be found mainly in Mexico, which became the only exporter of advanced manufacturing products and services in the region, and in Central America and Brazil, which exported mainly products classified as limited manufacturing.

Latin America's weakness may reflect the absence of cities with Francis Bacon's "busy workshops." Indeed, with four out of every five Latin Americans living in urban areas, economic growth in the region, which has declined over the last half-century, depends mostly on the productivity of the region's urban workforce. Large urban areas, in particular, are *systemically* important for Latin America's growth outcomes because nearly 40 percent of the population lives in cities with 1 million or more residents (United Nations 2016).

MAP 1.1   Global distribution of consumption, production, and neutral cities, circa 2000

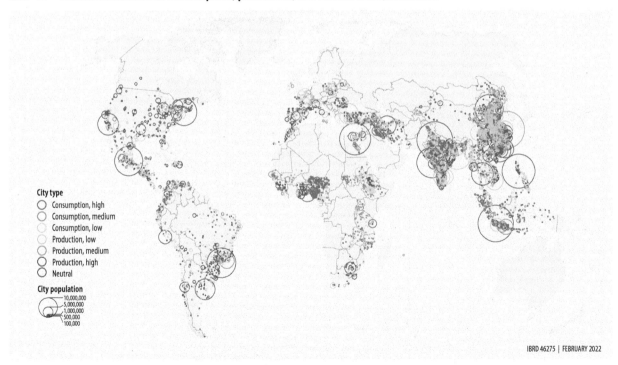

City type
○ Consumption, high
○ Consumption, medium
○ Consumption, low
○ Production, low
○ Production, medium
○ Production, high
○ Neutral

City population
10,000,000
5,000,000
1,000,000
500,000
100,000

IBRD 46275 | FEBRUARY 2022

Source: Jedwab, Ianchovichina, and Haslop (2022), using Integrated Public Use Microdata Series (IPUMS, https://www.ipums.org/) census data and the Global Human Settlement Layer database (https://ghsl.jrc.ec.europa.eu/download.php).
Note: An urban area is classified as a *consumption city* (with a disproportionately low employment share of urban tradables), a *production city* (with a disproportionately high employment share of urban tradables), or a *neutral city* (in which the share of employment in tradables is neither too low nor too high). Paler shades of each color indicate lower values for the extent to which a city can be classified as each specific type.

Although Latin American cities are also denser than cities in other parts of the world,[10] evidence suggests that these cities are not particularly productive. They benefit from strong positive *skill-related* agglomeration externalities, but they fail to capture the broader benefits of agglomeration through co-location and market access (Ferreyra and Roberts 2018). The costs of density, including those associated with congestion, crime, and competition from informal firms (Burger, Ianchovichina, and Akbar 2022) and of real estate in central urban locations (Duranton and Puga 2020; Lall, Shalizi, and Deichmann 2004) can substantially reduce or completely offset the agglomeration benefits (Grover and Maloney 2022), giving rise to "sterile" agglomeration economies (Grover, Lall, and Maloney 2022). Indeed, explanations for the Latin American urban paradox emphasize the high costs of density (Ferreyra and Roberts 2018), which escalate when improvements in transport, communication, basic infrastructure, and urban policy, planning, and management fail to keep pace with increases in density.[11]

This study provides three additional, interconnected reasons for the Latin American urban productivity puzzle that have not been highlighted in the literature. All three center on factors that reduce the "pure" agglomeration benefits from co-location. First, in *deindustrialized* cities, where employment is tilted toward low-productivity nontradables, agglomeration benefits may be weaker because nontradables benefit less from density (Burger, Ianchovichina, and Akbar 2022; Venables 2017). They also have much more limited potential than urban tradables for catch-up through dynamic productivity gains (Duarte and Restuccia 2010). Thus deindustrialization has constrained *both* labor and place productivity growth in the region's urban areas.

Second, the "conveyance of men and goods from place to place" may not be as good as needed to generate strong productivity gains through agglomeration economies, market access, specialization, and technological spillovers. Indeed, *connectivity* issues within cities reduce the agglomeration benefits of firms, especially those in the nontradable sectors (Burger, Ianchovichina, and Akbar 2022), while intercity *connectivity issues* undermine the performance of the region's network of cities and aggregate growth (Conte and Ianchovichina 2022; Gorton and Ianchovichina 2021).

Third, agglomeration benefits may be smaller in poorly connected and residentially segregated cities. Because many large metropolitan areas in the LAC region are unequal[12] and divided,[13] opportunities for sharing, matching, and learning are limited to central business areas, where formal firms operate, consumer amenities are abundant, and residents enjoy better-quality basic infrastructure and public services. By contrast, the neighborhood place productivity premia are negative in low-income neighborhoods, typically on the urban periphery, where firms and workers are mostly informal, consumer amenities are scarce, and basic infrastructure and public services are deficient. In addition, the informal nature of the low-income economy gives rise to spatial misallocation because informal firms do not pay taxes (Hsieh and Klenow 2009), while the fact that such misallocation occurs in some of the region's largest metropolitan areas, which are systemically important for growth, implies potentially large negative aggregate growth effects.

Conceptual framework

The Economy-Regions-Cities-Neighborhoods (ERCN) conceptual framework in figure 1.2 organizes the country-level investigations in this study using four spatial scales from highest to lowest: (1) the national economy, (2) subnational regions, (3) cities, and (4) neighborhoods. The framework allows starting with a broad view of territorial productivity trends and dynamics within economies and then gradually refining the focus by narrowing the spatial lens to spatial misallocation across regions, productivity differences

FIGURE 1.2   Economy-Regions-Cities-Neighborhoods (ERCN) framework for analysis of a country's spatial development

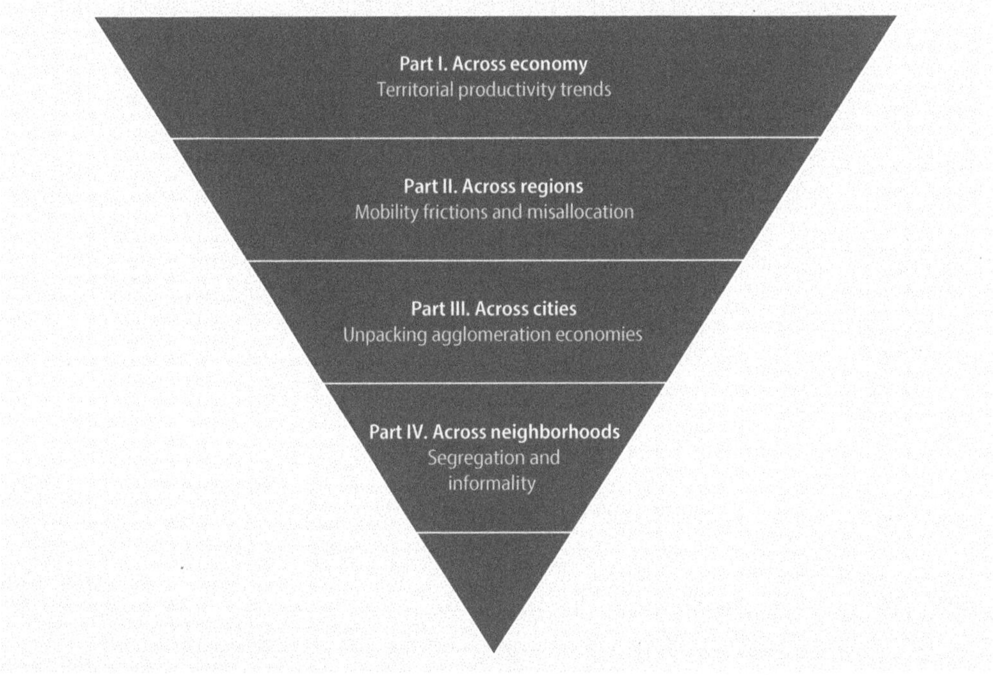

Part I. Across economy
Territorial productivity trends

Part II. Across regions
Mobility frictions and misallocation

Part III. Across cities
Unpacking agglomeration economies

Part IV. Across neighborhoods
Segregation and informality

Source: Original figure for this publication.

across urban areas, and finally productivity differences and misallocation across neighborhoods within cities. Based on both econometric methods and state-of-the-art spatial general equilibrium models, this report builds a narrative based on a rich set of empirical sources and recently released harmonized surveys and census data, which, whenever possible, are used across the four spatial scales. This approach allows the generation of insights that cannot be obtained by focusing separately on issues at each spatial scale.

The ERCN framework is also used to organize the presentation of the analysis and findings in this report into four parts. Part I offers a broad view of territorial labor and place productivity differences and their evolution between the early 2000s and the late 2010s in 14 countries[14] in Latin America and the Caribbean. Chapter 2 presents productivity differences and dynamics across the first- and second-level administrative regions based on empirical evidence in background work by D'Aoust, Galdo, and Ianchovichina (2023) and Jedwab, Ianchovichina, and Haslop (2022). The first-level administrative regions are administrative units just below the national level, which, depending on the country, are states, provinces, or departments. The second-level administrative units are municipalities in Brazil, Colombia, the Dominican Republic, Honduras, and Mexico; provinces in Peru; cantons in Costa Rica and Ecuador; and communes in Chile. They can be large or small predominantly rural, urban, or metropolitan localities.[15]

Drawing on analysis by D'Aoust, Galdo, and Ianchovichina (2023), chapter 3 then focuses on differences in labor income between the leading metropolitan areas and the remaining areas in the country, the evolution of these differences during the period of analysis, and the extent to which these differences reflect gaps in returns to endowments that can potentially be exploited through migration versus differences in endowments that capture the effects of the sorting of more productive workers in the leading metropolitan areas.[16] These areas deserve special attention because they are the main business centers, and they attract migrants, especially skilled workers. In about a third of the South American countries, approximately 40 percent of the population lives in these cities (United Nations 2016). Chapter 3 also presents analysis on the variation in the income gaps with leading metropolitan areas by administrative region, socioeconomic group (that is, rural households, urban households, the skilled), and gender, and the sources of these differences.

Part II explores the extent to which mobility frictions in the form of transportation and migration costs may create barriers to economic integration across regions and generate spatial misallocation. It also evaluates ways to overcome these barriers, drawing on background work by Conte and Ianchovichina (2022), Gorton and Ianchovichina (2021), and Montañés et al. (2021). Chapter 4 assesses the magnitude of mobility frictions at a finely disaggregated geospatial level made possible by advances in measuring transportation costs (Allen and Arkolakis 2014) and migration barriers (Desmet, Nagy, and Rossi-Hansberg 2018). The chapter then evaluates their relative importance for economic growth by employing, in an integrated way, two state-of-the-art general equilibrium frameworks. The static spatial general equilibrium model of Fajgelbaum and Schaal (2020) is used to identify the optimal placement of national (regional) road networks given the existing fundamentals and the reductions in transportation costs stemming from improvements that correct for the identified inefficiencies. The dynamic spatial general equilibrium framework of Desmet, Nagy, and Rossi-Hansberg (2018) is then employed to assess the long-run growth implications of the reductions in transport costs associated with these improvements and of reductions in migration barriers. The chapter ends with a discussion of how the region can overcome the curse of distance by improving its readiness for virtual work.

Parts III and IV focus on structural and spatial factors that weaken agglomeration economies. Drawing on background work by Jedwab, Ianchovichina, and Haslop (2022), chapter 5 in part III discusses the evolution of the employment composition of cities over the last several decades and the implications for urban labor productivity and economic dynamism. It reveals that deindustrialization has weakened both urban labor and place productivity growth in the LAC region. Nontradable activities, which rose in importance with deindustrialization, tend to benefit less from urban density, and these benefits are reduced relatively more by congestion, as shown in background work by Burger, Ianchovichina, and Akbar (2022). Using the novel global data set of Akbar et al. (2022) and analysis by Akbar (2022), the chapter shows that congestion is a particularly serious problem in the leading metropolitan areas of systemic importance to economic growth in the region, while uncongested mobility tends to decline faster with increases in urban density in the LAC region than in the rest of the world.

Chapter 6 in part IV offers evidence on the spatial dimensions of socioeconomic vulnerability and inequality in the largest urban areas in Brazil, Colombia, and Mexico, based on background work by Duque et al. (2021, 2022) and Van der Weide, Ferreira de Souza, and Barbosa (2020); the variation in location premia across neighborhoods in Colombia's capital city, Bogotá, documented by Heil, Ianchovichina, and Quintero (2022); and the spatial misallocation generated by segregation and informality in Mexico's capital district, Mexico City, presented by Zárate (2022) and Ianchovichina and Zárate (2021). Chapter 6 draws on a variety of data sources, including census data, city-level surveys, travel diary surveys, and data on neighborhood amenities. It also relies on a novel spatial general equilibrium model with heterogeneous workers and informality. Finally, chapter 7 summarizes the main messages of the report and ideas on how to leverage spatial development for accelerated and inclusive economic growth in the region.

Contributions to the literature

The study described in this report makes contributions to several literatures. First, it presents new estimates of territorial differences in labor income[17] and local place productivity levels and their evolution between the early 2000s and the late 2010s, using recently released and previously unavailable harmonized censuses and surveys for 14 countries in Latin America and the Caribbean. Previous studies have focused on the period up to the early 2000s; covered one or a limited set of countries; looked at issues of territorial income differences and dynamics separately, mostly at the first administrative level; and relied on disparate data sources—either national accounts or surveys—that do not necessarily provide a complete or consistent picture of territorial income and productivity dynamics. Following the approach of Li and Rama (2015) for India, this report combines analyses of territorial productivity differences and dynamics, differentiating between households and localities in the first- and second-level administrative regions and different types of second-level administrative localities, including small and large predominantly rural areas, small and large predominantly urban areas, and small and large metropolitan areas. To ensure comparability within and across countries, per capita household labor incomes are deflated to address price variations across time and space.

Second, this study considers the main factors underlying territorial income differences with the leading metropolitan areas and the extent to which population groups can benefit from migration to these areas. It assesses the contribution of differences in nongeographic household endowments and returns to these endowments to the gaps in labor income between the leading and other areas by first-level administrative region and by socioeconomic group, differentiating between households based on income (such as those in the bottom 40 percent of the income distribution), skills, location (urban/rural), and gender. Skoufias and López-Acevedo (2009) undertake similar analysis across and within geographic regions for a smaller set of Latin American countries using data only up to the mid-2000s. However, they do not estimate the income gaps with leading areas, nor do they investigate how the income gaps vary across population groups with different skills or by gender. The study described here appears to be the first to estimate gender differences in the labor income gaps within the leading urban areas in a large set of Latin American countries.

Third, this study builds on analytical advances in measuring bilateral trade costs around the world (Allen and Arkolakis 2014) and migration frictions at a finely disaggregated geospatial scale (Desmet, Nagy, and Rossi-Hansberg 2018). The theory-based estimates of migration entry costs in the LAC region are refined through the use of spatially differentiated initial utility measures. In an integrated way, two state-of-the-art spatial general equilibrium models are then used to evaluate the extent to which trade costs matter for aggregate economic growth in the region and the effects of policies aimed at reducing them. Developed by Fajgelbaum and Schaal (2020), the static spatial general equilibrium model with endogenous transportation costs helps to identify the optimal level of investment in national (regional) road networks and the associated cuts in transportation costs along routes that receive additional investments. These cuts then serve as inputs in the dynamic spatial general equilibrium model of Desmet, Nagy, and Rossi-Hansberg (2018) to determine their effect on long-run growth.

Fourth, this report presents estimates of the employment composition of 6,865 functional urban areas, drawing on newly available census microdata for 74 countries, including 19 countries in Latin America and the Caribbean, between 1960 and 2015 (Jedwab, Ianchovichina, and Haslop 2022). The selected urban areas are home to

3 billion people and account for three-quarters of the world's urban population. The benchmarking exercise shows that the "origins" of urbanization matter for the largest cities, which are nations' engines of growth. Compared with cities in advanced economies, cities of similar sizes in resource-rich and deindustrializing economies have lower shares of employment in manufacturing, tradable services, and the formal sector, and higher shares of employment in nontradables and the informal sector. In both resource-rich and deindustrializing countries, larger cities have substantially higher shares of nontradables than smaller cities, but for all city sizes these shares are much larger in the deindustrializing countries than in resource-rich countries (Jedwab, Ianchovichina, and Haslop 2022).

Fifth, this report presents new estimates of the effects of urban density on the labor productivity of different types of establishments and describes the degree to which limited mobility and congestion reduce the returns to density for different types of firms. It differentiates between producers of manufacturing and services, exporters and nonexporters, foreign-owned and domestically owned firms, as well as more experienced and less experienced establishments. The estimations employ firm-level data on more than 51,000 establishments in 649 metropolitan areas in 98 developing economies (of which 20 are in the LAC region) from the World Bank's Enterprise Surveys (geocoded specifically for this report) and a new global database on city-level mobility and traffic congestion (Akbar et al. 2022). Relying on information on the sectoral composition of employment along the urban hierarchy and the heterogeneous agglomeration economies by type of establishment, the report discusses the productivity implications of the large size of the nontradable urban economy in the region.

Finally, drawing on census data for Brazil, Colombia, and Mexico, and other data sources, including travel diary surveys and information on amenities in Mexico from the National Statistical Directory of Economic Units (DENUE), the report presents recent comparative evidence on socioeconomic inequality and segregation in metropolitan areas in Colombia and Mexico. Next, it explores the productivity implications of residential labor market segregation, building on detailed information on income in Bogotá and Mexico City from two unique city-level surveys. Using a spatial general equilibrium model with heterogeneous workers and informality, the report then assesses the effects of policies that aim to increase efficiency by reducing segregation and informality in Mexico City.

Scope of the report

To focus the inquiry on a core set of spatial factors that influence long-run economic growth, this report emphasizes some aspects of spatial transformation and urban productivity more than others, and it omits some topics entirely. The report does not discuss the drivers behind the commodity boom in the 2000s and all the competitiveness issues that limit the LAC region's trade with global partners. It is beyond the scope of this study to explore in a comprehensive way the economic performance of cities along the urban hierarchy, including land markets and management, intergovernmental fiscal relations, local government fragmentation, and local institutions responsible for the provision of education and other services. The study also does not examine in detail the country-specific drivers of convergence, the spatial effects of climate shocks, the sectors that could offer opportunities for green growth, and the sectoral impacts of intraurban divisions. Some of these issues are discussed in depth in other reports, while others must receive attention in the future.

Notes

1. Latin America includes Mexico and the countries of Central and South America. Throughout the report, the composition of countries in regional aggregates varies, depending on data availability. When the report features countries in the Caribbean, they are also included in reported regional aggregates, and so there is a reference to the Latin America and the Caribbean (LAC) region.
2. The G7 members are Canada, France, Germany, Italy, Japan, the United Kingdom, and the United States.
3. Davenport and Zaranko (2020) compare the United Kingdom with 26 other developed economies.
4. Dutch Disease can arise from real exchange appreciation, inequality in the distribution of natural resource rents, or political instability, which discourages investments in tradable manufacturing and services (Ianchovichina and Onder 2017).
5. Urban tradables include manufacturing and tradables services, such as finance, insurance, and information technology services. Tradables include both urban tradables and rural tradables (that is, agricultural and mining commodities). Services include both tradable and nontradable services.
6. In line with the efficient nature of Latin America's agriculture, the commodity boom did not lead to deurbanization; it only slowed the pace of rural to urban migration. The net rate of rural to urban migration remained negative during the 2000s (Rodríguez-Vignoli and Rowe 2018).
7. Only Chile liberalized in the late 1970s.
8. The large, persistent deterioration in formal employment was attributed to lost agglomeration economies, slow capital reallocation, and the flow of new investments to other areas (Dix-Carneiro and Kovak 2017).
9. Urban workers are employed in either urban tradables or urban nontradables. Therefore, a decline in the share of urban tradables implies an increase in the share of urban nontradables.
10. Regionwide, more than 70 percent of urban areas have population densities above the global median (Roberts 2018).
11. Urban form and intercity connectedness also affect the productivity of cities in Latin America (Duque et al. 2022). City sprawl has made it harder to cost-effectively extend public transport and other infrastructure services to areas on the urban periphery.
12. In the early 2000s, 80 percent of income inequality in the region was explained by differences in labor income within municipalities (Acemoglu and Dell 2010).
13. Duque et al. (2021, 2022) provide evidence of socioeconomic inequality and segregation in many Colombian and Mexican cities.
14. The countries are Argentina, Bolivia, Brazil, Chile, Colombia, Costa Rica, the Dominican Republic, Ecuador, Honduras, Mexico, Panama, Paraguay, Peru, and Uruguay.
15. Rural localities are localities in which 50 percent or more of residents are rural. Thus some predominantly rural localities may have a minority share of urban residents.
16. Sorting is the process of co-location of workers with certain skills in certain areas.
17. Labor income is typically better reported than total income. It is also a better proxy for labor productivity.

References

Acemoglu, D., and M. Dell. 2010. "Productivity Differences between and within Countries." *American Economic Journal: Macroeconomics* 2 (1): 169–88.

Adão, R. 2015. "Worker Heterogeneity, Wage Inequality, and International Trade: Theory and Evidence from Brazil." Massachusetts Institute of Technology, Cambridge, MA. https://economics.yale.edu/sites/default/files/adao_jmp_2015.pdf.

Akbar, P. 2022. "Mobility and Congestion in Urban Areas in Latin America and the Caribbean." Background paper prepared for this report, World Bank, Washington, DC.

Akbar, P., V. Couture, G. Duranton, and A. Storeygard. 2022. "The Fast, the Slow, and the Congested: Urban Transportation in Rich and Poor Countries." CEPR Press Discussion Paper No. 18401, Centre for Economic Policy Research, London. https://cepr.org/publications /dp18401.

Allen, T., and C. Arkolakis. 2014. "Trade and the Topography of the Spatial Economy." *Quarterly Journal of Economics* 129 (3): 1085–140.

Aroca, P., M. Bosch, and W. F. Maloney. 2005. "Spatial Dimensions of Trade Liberalization and Economic Convergence: Mexico 1985–2002." Policy Research Working Paper 3744, World Bank, Washington, DC.

Bellon, M. 2018. "Trade Liberalization and Inequality: A Dynamic Model with Firm and Worker Heterogeneity." https://matthieubellon.com/docs/TradeLiberalizationInequalityDynamics 2018.pdf.

Beylis, G., R. Fattal-Jaef, R. Sinha, M. Morris, and A. Sebastian. 2020. *Going Viral: COVID-19 and the Accelerated Transformation of Jobs in Latin America and the Caribbean.* World Bank Latin American and Caribbean Studies. Washington, DC: World Bank.

Bosch, M., P. Aroca, I. J. Fernández, and C. R. Azzoni. 2003. "Growth Dynamics and Space in Brazil." *International Regional Science Review* 26 (3): 393–418.

Burger, M., M. Hendriks, and E. Ianchovichina. 2022. "Happy but Unequal: Differences in Subjective Well-Being across Individuals and Space in Colombia." *Applied Research in Quality of Life* 17 (3): 1343–87.

Burger, M., E. Ianchovichina, and P. Akbar. 2022. "Heterogenous Agglomeration Economies in the Developing Countries: The Roles of Firm Characteristics, Sector Tradability, and Urban Mobility." Policy Research Working Paper 9954, World Bank, Washington, DC.

Conte, B., and E. Ianchovichina. 2022. "Spatial Development and Mobility Frictions in Latin America: Theory-Based Empirical Evidence." Policy Research Working Paper 10071, World Bank, Washington, DC.

Costa, F., J. Garred, and J. P. Pessoa. 2016. "Winners and Losers from a Commodities-for-Manufactures Trade Boom." *Journal of International Economics* 102: 50–69.

D'Aoust, O., V. Galdo, and E. Ianchovichina. 2023. "Territorial Productivity Differences and Dynamics within Latin American Countries." Policy Research Working Paper 10480, World Bank, Washington, DC.

Davenport, A., and B. Zaranko. 2020. "Leveling Up: Where and How?" In *IFS Green Budget 2020.* London: Institute for Fiscal Studies.

Desmet, K., D. Nagy, and E. Rossi-Hansberg. 2018. "The Geography of Development." *Journal of Political Economy* 126 (3): 903–83.

Dix-Carneiro, R., and B. Kovak. 2017. "Trade Liberalization and Regional Dynamics." *American Economic Review* 107 (10): 2908–46.

Dix-Carneiro, R., and B. Kovak. 2019. "Margins of Labor Market Adjustment to Trade." *Journal of International Economics* 117: 125–42.

Dix-Carneiro, R., and B. Kovak. 2023. "Globalization and Inequality in Latin America." Inter-American Development Bank, Washington, DC.

Duarte, M., and D. Restuccia. 2010. "The Role of the Structural Transformation in Aggregate Productivity." *Quarterly Journal of Economics* 125 (1): 129–73.

Duque, J. C., N. Lozano-Gracia, G. García, J. Ospina, J. Patiño, and R. Curiel. 2022. "Intraurban Inequality in Mexican Cities." Background paper prepared for this report, Universidad EAFIT, Medellín, Colombia.

Duque, J. C., N. Lozano-Gracia, M. Quiñones, G. García, J. Ospina, J. Patiño, and J. Montoya. 2021. "Intraurban Inequality in Colombian Cities." Unpublished manuscript, Universidad EAFIT, Medellín, Colombia.

Duranton, G., and D. Puga. 2020. "The Economics of Urban Density." *Journal of Economic Perspectives* 34 (3): 3–26.

Dutz, M., R. Almeida, and T. Packard. 2018. *The Jobs of Tomorrow: Technology, Productivity, and Prosperity in Latin America and the Caribbean.* Directions in Development Series, Communication and Information Technologies. Washington, DC: World Bank.

Escobal, J., and C. Ponce. 2011a. "Access to Public Infrastructure, Institutional Thickness and Pro-Poor Growth in Rural Peru." *Journal of International Development* 23 (3): 358–79.

Escobal, J., and C. Ponce. 2011b. "Spatial Patterns of Growth and Poverty Changes in Peru (1993–2005)." Working Paper No. 78, Rural Territorial Dynamics Program, Latin American Center for Rural Development (RIMISP), Santiago, Chile.

Fajgelbaum, P., and E. Schaal. 2020. "Optimal Transport Networks in Spatial Equilibrium." *Econometrica* 88 (4): 1411–52.

Ferreira-Filho, J., and M. Horridge. 2006. "Economic Integration, Poverty and Regional Inequality in Brazil." *Revista Brasileira de Economia* 60 (4): 363–87.

Ferreyra, M. M., and M. Roberts, eds. 2018. *Raising the Bar for Productive Cities in Latin America and the Caribbean*. Washington, DC: World Bank.

Galvis, L. A., and A. Meisel Roca. 2010. "Persistencia de las desigualdades regionales en Colombia: Un análisis espacial." Documento de trabajo sobre economía regional no. 120, Banco de la República, Colombia.

Galvis, L. A., and A. Meisel Roca. 2012. "Convergencia y trampas espaciales de pobreza en Colombia: Evidencia reciente." Documento de trabajo sobre economía regional no. 177, Banco de la República, Colombia.

González Rivas, M. 2007. "The Effects of Trade Openness on Regional Inequality in Mexico." *Annals of Regional Science* 41: 545–61.

Gorton, N., and E. Ianchovichina. 2021. "Trade Networks in Latin America: Spatial Inefficiencies and Optimal Expansions." Policy Research Working Paper 9843, World Bank, Washington, DC.

Goyal, R., and R. Sahay. 2007. "Volatility and Growth in Latin America: An Episodic Approach." IMF Working Paper 06/287, International Monetary Fund, Washington, DC.

Grover, A., S. Lall, and W. F. Maloney. 2022. *Place, Productivity, and Prosperity: Revisiting Spatially Targeted Policies for Regional Development*. Washington, DC: World Bank.

Grover, A., and W. F. Maloney. 2022. "Proximity without Productivity: Agglomeration Effects with Plant-Level Output and Price Data." Policy Research Working Paper 9977, World Bank, Washington, DC.

Heil, A., E. Ianchovichina, and L. Quintero. 2022. "Spatial Variations in Income and Wealth in a Segregated City: Evidence from Bogotá." Background paper prepared for this report, World Bank, Washington, DC.

Hsieh, C.-T., and P. Klenow. 2009. "Misallocation and Manufacturing TFP in China and India." *Quarterly Journal of Economics* 124 (4): 1403–48.

Ianchovichina, E. 2018. *Eruptions of Popular Anger: The Economics of the Arab Spring and Its Aftermath*. Washington, DC: World Bank.

Ianchovichina, E., and H. Onder. 2017. "Dutch Disease: An Economic Illness Easy to Catch, Difficult to Cure." *Future Development* (blog). https://www.brookings.edu/tags/future-development/.

Ianchovichina, E., and R. Zárate. 2021. "Segregation, Informality, and Misallocation." Unpublished manuscript, World Bank, Washington, DC.

Jedwab, R., E. Ianchovichina, and F. Haslop. 2022. "Consumption Cities versus Production Cities: New Considerations and Evidence." Policy Research Working Paper 10105, World Bank, Washington, DC.

Lall, S., Z. Shalizi, and U. Deichmann. 2004. "Agglomeration Economies and Productivity in Indian Industry." *Journal of Development Economics* 73 (2): 643–73.

Lederman, D., J. Messina, S. Pienknagura, and R. Jamele. 2014. *Latin American Entrepreneurs: Many Firms but Little Innovation*. World Bank Latin American and Caribbean Studies. Washington, DC: World Bank.

Li, Y., and M. Rama. 2015. "Households or Locations? Cities, Catchment Areas and Prosperity in India." Policy Research Working Paper 7473, World Bank, Washington, DC.

Maloney, W., and A. Rodríguez-Clare. 2007. "Innovation Shortfalls." *Review of Development Economics* 11 (4): 665–84.

Montañés, R., J. Barreto, C. Bonilla, D. Sánchez, and H. Winkler. 2021. "Working from Home in Latin America and the Caribbean: Enabling Factors and Inequality Implications." Background paper prepared for this report, World Bank, Washington, DC.

Nin Pratt, A., C. Falconi, C. Ludena, and P. Martel. 2015. "Productivity and the Performance of Agriculture in Latin America and the Caribbean: From the Lost Decade to the Commodity Boom." IDB Working Paper No. 608, Inter-American Development Bank, Washington, DC.

Perry, G., W. Maloney, O. Arias, P. Gajnzylber, A. Mason, and J. Saavedra-Chanduvi. 2007. *Informality: Exit and Exclusion*. World Bank Latin American and Caribbean Studies. Washington, DC: World Bank.

Ponczek, V., and G. Ulyssea. 2022. "Enforcement of Labour Regulation and the Labour Market Effects of Trade: Evidence from Brazil." *Economic Journal* 132 (641): 361–90.

Roberts, M. 2018. "The Many Dimensions of Urbanization and the Productivity of Cities in Latin America and the Caribbean." In *Raising the Bar for Productive Cities in Latin America and the Caribbean*, edited by M. M. Ferreyra and M. Roberts. Washington, DC: World Bank.

Rocha, N., and M. Ruta. 2022. *Deep Trade Agreements: Anchoring Global Value Chains in Latin America and the Caribbean*. Washington, DC: World Bank.

Rodríguez-Castelán, C., L.-N. López-Calva, N. Lustig, and D. Valderrama. 2022. "Wage Inequality in the Developing World: Evidence from Latin America." *Review of Development Economics* 26 (4): 1944–70.

Rodríguez-Pose, A. 2017. "The Revenge of the Places that Don't Matter (and What to Do about It)." *Cambridge Journal of Regions, Economy and Society* 11 (1): 189–209.

Rodríguez-Vignoli, J., and F. Rowe. 2018. "How Is Internal Migration Reshaping Metropolitan Populations in Latin America? A New Method and New Evidence." *Population Studies* 72 (2): 253–73.

Serra, M. I., M. F. Pazmino, G. Lindow, B. Sutton, and G. Ramírez. 2006. "Regional Convergence in Latin America." IMF Working Paper WP/06/125, International Monetary Fund, Washington, DC.

Skoufias, E., and G. López-Acevedo. 2009. *Determinants of Regional Welfare Disparities within Latin American Countries*, Vol. 1, *Synthesis*. Washington, DC: World Bank.

Soto, R., and A. Torche. 2004. "Spatial Inequality, Migration, and Economic Growth in Chile." *Latin American Journal of Economics* 41: 401–24.

Terra, M. 2003. "Trade Liberalization in Latin American Countries and the Agreement on Textiles and Clothing in the WTO." *Économie Internationale* 94-93: 137–54.

UNDP (United Nations Development Programme). 2021. *Trapped: High Inequality and Low Growth in Latin America and the Caribbean*. Regional Human Development Report. New York: UNDP.

United Nations. 2016. *The World Cities Data Booklet*. New York: United Nations.

Van der Weide, R., P. Ferreira de Souza, and R. Barbosa. 2020. "Intergenerational Mobility in Education in Brazil." Unpublished manuscript, World Bank, Washington, DC.

Vegh, C., G. Vuletin, D. Riera-Crichton, J. P. Medina, D. Friedheim, L. Morano, and L. Venturo. 2018. *From Known Unknowns to Black Swans: How to Manage Risk in Latin America and the Caribbean*. LAC Semiannual Report, October 2018. Washington, DC: World Bank.

Venables, A. 2017. "Breaking into Tradables: Urban Form and Urban Function in a Developing City." *Journal of Urban Economics* 98 (C): 88–97.

World Bank. 2009. *World Development Report 2009: Reshaping Economic Geography*. Washington, DC: World Bank.

Zárate, R. 2022. "Spatial Misallocation, Informality, and Transit Improvements: Evidence from Mexico City." Policy Research Working Paper 9990, World Bank, Washington, DC.

I

Within-Country Territorial Productivity Trends in the 2000s and 2010s

Territorial differences in labor earnings are motivating much of the work under way on economic growth and development. With fewer barriers to migration and trade, these differences are expected to decline as technology and capital diffuse relatively quickly within countries. However, spatial income inequality may persist because of differences in fundamentals, including resource endowments (Mesquita Moreira et al. 2013) and human capital (Skoufias and López-Acevedo 2009); poverty traps[1] reflecting ongoing differences in institutions (Galvis and Meisel Roca 2012); or high trade and migration costs (Acemoglu and Dell 2010; Skoufias and López-Acevedo 2009). The latter generate efficiency losses and spatial misallocation by making it costly to trade goods, travel, and relocate for work. Spatial convergence may also be slowed or even reversed by market forces promoting agglomeration of workers and firms in urban areas (Duranton and Puga 2020). Agglomeration allows workers and firms in large metropolitan areas to benefit from co-location through sharing, matching, and learning (Duranton and Puga 2004) and proximity to larger markets (Fujita 1988).

When territorial income differences stem mostly from the sorting of more productive workers into urban areas, reduced barriers to migration may not boost economic growth (Bryan and Morten 2019). If people lack the endowments that could enable them to earn higher real wages after relocating to cities, migration may contribute to congestion and therefore lower the local productivity premia in leading cities (Grover, Lall, and Maloney 2022). Stated differently, localities where labor earnings are high need not be high-productivity places. The high labor income may simply reflect the sorting of more productive workers into these areas, and, if so, the exploitable gains from migration may be limited.

To provide clarity about the size of territorial productivity differences within a country and how they have evolved over time, chapter 2 presents new evidence on the size of and trends in territorial labor and place productivity differences in 13 Latin American countries between the early 2000s and the late 2010s, prior to the onset of the COVID-19 (coronavirus disease 2019) pandemic. Chapter 3 then delves deeper into the productivity differences between the leading metropolitan areas and the rest of these countries. The leading metropolitan areas deserve special attention because they are these countries' major business centers. They also attract migrants, especially the skilled, and in about a third of the South American countries, approximately 40 percent of the population lives in these primate cities (United Nations 2016).

Note

1.   In turn, poverty traps may influence territorial growth through greater social fragmentation, underinvestment, and political instability and conflict (Alesina and Perotti 1996).

References

Acemoglu, D., and M. Dell. 2010. "Productivity Differences between and within Countries." *American Economic Journal: Macroeconomics* 2 (1): 169–88.

Alesina, A., and R. Perotti. 1996. "Income Distribution, Political Instability, and Investment." *European Economic Review* 40 (6): 1203–28.

Bryan, G., and M. Morten. 2019. "The Aggregate Productivity Effects of Internal Migration: Evidence from Indonesia." *Journal of Political Economy* 127 (5): 2229–68.

Duranton, G., and D. Puga. 2004. "Micro-Foundations of Urban Agglomeration Economies." In *Handbook of Regional and Urban Economics*, vol. 4, edited by J. V. Henderson, G. Duranton, and W. C. Strange, 2063–117. Amsterdam: Elsevier.

Duranton, G., and D. Puga. 2020. "The Economics of Urban Density." *Journal of Economic Perspectives* 34 (3): 3–26.

Fujita, M. 1988. "A Monopolistic Competition Model of Spatial Agglomeration: Differentiated Product Approach." *Regional Science and Urban Economics* 18 (1): 87–124.

Galvis, L. A., and A. Meisel Roca. 2012. "Convergencia y trampas espaciales de pobreza en Colombia: Evidencia reciente." Documento de trabajo sobre economía regional no. 177, Banco de la República, Colombia.

Grover, A., S. Lall, and W. F. Maloney. 2022. *Place, Productivity, and Prosperity: Revisiting Spatially Targeted Policies for Regional Development.* Washington, DC: World Bank.

Mesquita Moreira, M., J. Blyde, C. Volpe, and D. Molina. 2013. *Too Far to Export: Domestic Transport Costs and Regional Export Disparities in Latin America and the Caribbean.* Washington, DC: Inter-American Development Bank.

Skoufias, E., and G. López-Acevedo. 2009. *Determinants of Regional Welfare Disparities within Latin American Countries*, vol. 1, *Synthesis.* Washington, DC: World Bank.

United Nations. 2016. *The World Cities Data Booklet.* New York: United Nations.

Subnational Productivity Differences and Their Evolution

2

Many factors play a role in a country's territorial development. It is a path-dependent process influenced by initial conditions, including physical geography (Olfert et al. 2014); human capital and the tendency of people to sort spatially in response to the labor market, amenities, cost of living, and cultural considerations; local investments in physical and technological infrastructure; local institutions;[1] and the spatial structure of economic activity, which is shaped by agglomeration forces, proximity to resources and markets, industrial organization, and competition in local markets.

Territorial income differences and dynamics up to the early 2000s

Territorial income inequality posed a serious challenge in the Latin America and the Caribbean (LAC) region prior to the mid-2000s. Acemoglu and Dell (2010) document large cross-municipal differences in labor income within countries in the first half of the 2000s, and many studies describe stark regional contrasts in the larger LAC economies.[2] These territorial differences have been attributed to factors that include resource endowments and topography (Mesquita Moreira et al. 2013), human capital (Acemoglu and Dell 2010; Skoufias and López-Acevedo 2009), migration barriers (Skoufias and López-Acevedo 2009), proximity to good-quality (paved) roads,[3] and local institutions that determine the provision of local public services (Acemoglu and Dell 2010).[4]

Most studies covering the period prior to the mid-2000s look at issues of territorial income differences and dynamics separately, cover one or a limited number of countries, and rely on disparate data sources that do not necessarily provide a complete or consistent regional picture of the size and evolution of territorial income differences. The studies that rely on value added by sector or per capita gross domestic product (GDP) data at the first administrative level in a country find evidence of absolute convergence, albeit at a speed slower than that observed in developed countries, in Brazil (Azzoni 2001; Serra et al. 2006), Chile (Serra et al. 2006), Colombia (Serra et al. 2006), and Peru (Iacovone, Sanchez-Bayardo, and Sharma 2015; Serra et al. 2006), but not in Argentina (Serra et al. 2006) and Mexico (Chiquiar 2005; Sánchez-Reaza and Rodríguez-Pose 2002; Serra et al. 2006).[5]

Iacovone, Sanchez-Bayardo, and Sharma (2015), who use value-added data by sector to explore the effects of sectoral composition on income dynamics in Peru, find absolute convergence in Peruvian manufacturing and mining—but not in services and agriculture—and slower convergence at the aggregate level than within manufacturing in line with the larger employment shares of services and agriculture. They attribute the lack of convergence in poverty rates across departments to the limited reallocation of labor toward the converging sectors, while Sotelo (2020) suggests that lack of convergence could be due to substantial regional differences in farm income. He links these differences to spatial variations in trade costs and land quality and farmers' practice of growing many kinds of crops that differ in land intensity. In Mexico, growth in tourism also has had uneven spatial effects. Faber and Gaubert (2019) find that the local economic effects of tourism are driven in part by significant positive spillovers into manufacturing. However, in the aggregate these local spillovers are mostly offset by reduced agglomeration economies in regions attracting fewer tourists.

A related strand of this literature shows that trade liberalization and strong demand for commodities also affected income convergence within Latin American countries. In Mexico, the North American Free Trade Agreement (NAFTA) did not reverse the pattern of divergence in state per capita GDP between 1985 and 2001. The agreement benefited states endowed with, or able to attract, human capital and infrastructure and hurt the states in the south with less productive agriculture (Chiquiar 2005). In Brazil, trade liberalization in the early 1990s resulted in larger negative effects on earnings and employment in the regions exposed to deeper tariff cuts (Dix-Carneiro and Kovak 2017; Kovak 2013), even 10 years after the initial trade opening. Because the more affluent regions, including the country's leading metropolitan areas, experienced larger tariff cuts, liberalization contributed to a decline in interregional inequality. Similarly, Costa, Garred, and Pessoa (2016) find that strong productivity growth in China reduced regional inequality in Brazil through deindustrialization and a strong demand for commodity exports, especially during the Golden Decade (2003–13). For Peru, Sotelo (2020) concludes that a higher global demand for grain has had uneven rural-urban effects, benefiting farmers but hurting urban consumers.

Several country studies use survey data from the 1990s to the early 2000s to document territorial household income differences and dynamics in nine Latin American economies.[6] The analysis is mostly conducted at the municipal or provincial (such as in Colombia and Peru) level, except in Ecuador, where the data are at the level of the parish, which is a subdivision of a municipality. The synthesis of the results, available in Modrego and Berdegué (2016), broadly indicates slow, absolute convergence of mean household incomes in Brazil (Favareto and Abramovay 2016), Colombia (Fernández et al. 2016), Ecuador (Larrea et al. 2016), Guatemala (Romero and Zapil Ajxup 2009), and Mexico (Yúnez Naude, Arellano González, and Méndez Navarro 2016),[7] but not in Chile (Modrego et al. 2016) and Peru (Escobal and Ponce 2016). These studies confirm the role of human capital in the convergence process and find that the relevance of other factors varies by country. However, the results from these country studies are not directly comparable because of differences in the level of aggregation of territorial units and the definitions used in each country for poverty lines, income, and other indicators. In addition, none of the studies uses regional price indexes to adjust incomes and poverty lines for cost-of-living differences.

Spatial variations in labor and place productivity

D'Aoust, Galdo, and Ianchovichina (2023) document labor and place productivity trends for 13 Latin American countries between the early 2000s and the late 2010s. Differentiating between households and localities, they provide a regionwide assessment of the variation in labor and place productivity premia within and between LAC countries. D'Aoust and her colleagues rely on labor income, $y_{h,l,t}$ of household h in locality l and period t rather than total income or expenditure because labor income is a better proxy for labor productivity and is reported more accurately than total income. Following the approach in the literature (Li and Rama 2015; Quintero and Roberts 2018; Skoufias and López-Acevedo 2009), the labor productivity premium, $\gamma_{l,t}^{bs}$ in locality l and period t (also called the location premium before sorting and denoted with the superscript bs), is estimated as the average per capita household labor income net of the effects of exogenous time-variant shocks, so that

$$ln(y_{h,l,t}) = \gamma_{l,t}^{bs} + \theta_t + \varepsilon_{h,l,t}. \tag{2.1}$$

The place productivity premium,[8] $\gamma_{l,t}^{as}$ in locality l and period t (also referred to as the location premium after sorting and denoted with the superscript as), is the fraction of the average per capita household labor income that cannot be accounted for by a household's observable, nongeographic characteristics, $X_{h,l,t}$, and any exogenous time-variant shocks,[9] so that

$$ln(y_{h,l,t}) = \gamma_{l,t}^{as} + X_{h,l,t}'\psi_t + \theta_t + \varepsilon_{h,l,t}. \tag{2.2}$$

Annex table 2A.1 lists the observable nongeographic characteristics, and box 2.1 discusses the data used in their analysis.

BOX 2.1 Data for estimating territorial productivity differences and trends

The analysis in D'Aoust, Galdo, and Ianchovichina (2023) draws on recently released and previously unavailable harmonized microdata for 13 Latin American countries. For Brazil and Mexico, the investigation also relies on Integrated Public Use Microdata Series (IPUMS) census microdata harmonized by the Institute for Social Research and Data Innovation at the University of Minnesota. In both cases, the census questionnaires include a module on income, in addition to the standard questions on household and individual characteristics. Furthermore, the harmonization protocol ensures the comparability of geographic units across census years. For other countries, D'Aoust, Galdo, and Ianchovichina (2023) use the Socio-Economic Database for Latin America and the Caribbean (SEDLAC). It includes country harmonized household surveys jointly constructed by the Center for Distributive, Labor and Social Studies (CEDLAS) at the Universidad National de La Plata and the World Bank's Poverty Group for the Latin America and the Caribbean region. Most countries have conducted the surveys on an annual basis since 2000, but the frequency varies by country. Only in Colombia does the analysis at the municipal level rely on per capita value-added data for the last 10 years from the National Administrative Department of Statistics (DANE).

The criteria for selecting survey years include availability of information to harmonize geocodes across survey years at the lowest geographical level possible and to maximize the number of surveyed locations across time. In the case of SEDLAC, two to three consecutive surveys are used to ensure coverage, especially in rural areas, within three specific time periods over the last 20 years: the early 2000s, around 2010, and the late 2010s. Thus, the sample includes only countries with enough information to identify subnational geographic units and ensure comparability across space and time. Annex table 2A.2 provides complete details on data sources, and annex box 2A.1 describes the criteria for harmonizing geocodes across survey years and maximizing the number of surveyed locations across time.

(Continued on next page)

> **BOX 2.1   Data for estimating territorial productivity differences and trends** *(continued)*
>
> Finally, to ensure that the results are comparable both within and across countries, D'Aoust, Galdo, and Ianchovichina (2023) use average monthly per capita household labor earnings, which are deflated to adjust for cost-of-living differences across space and time. Labor income was first converted to constant 2011 US dollars, adjusted for purchasing power parity (PPP), and then adjusted to reflect differences across subnational regions and, whenever possible, different types of areas within subnational regions (such as rural versus urban). Annex table 2A.3 lists the deflators used for each country.

MAP 2.1   Labor and place productivity premia: Latin America, end of the 2010s

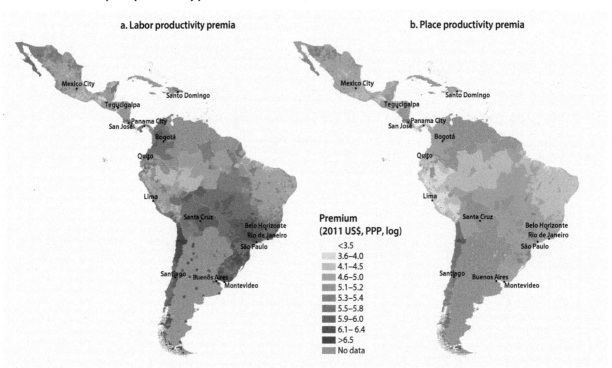

Source: D'Aoust, Galdo, and Ianchovichina 2023.
Note: Labor productivity is proxied with per capita labor income net of the effect of any exogenous shocks that affect all localities in a country at a given time. The place productivity premium is the fraction of per capita household labor income that cannot be accounted for by observable, nongeographic (portable) household characteristics and the effects of exogenous time-variant factors. To ensure comparability within and across countries, per capita household labor earnings are deflated to adjust incomes for cost-of-living differences across space and time. The latest available period is 2008–09 for Costa Rica; 2010 for Brazil; 2014–16 for the Dominican Republic; 2015 for Mexico; 2015–17 for Chile; and 2017–19 for Argentina, Bolivia, Colombia, Ecuador, Honduras, Panama, Peru, and Uruguay. For Bolivia, Colombia, Panama, and Uruguay, these estimates are at the first administrative level (such as states). For Argentina, the estimates are at the level of the urban agglomeration (represented by dots on the maps). For the remaining countries, the estimates are at the second administrative level (such as municipalities). PPP = purchasing power parity.

Map 2.1 displays the labor and place productivity premia by second-level administrative region (such as municipality) for Brazil, Chile, Costa Rica, the Dominican Republic, Ecuador, Honduras, Mexico, and Peru, and by first-level administrative region for Argentina, Bolivia, Colombia, Panama, and Uruguay. Labor productivity premia substantially vary across countries and locations within countries in Latin America.

Labor productivity premia are highest (dark blue) in the resource-rich areas in Chile's north and south; in Argentina's south, the most developed areas in Brazil's south and southeast, and Panama City and surrounding areas; and in a few municipalities in Mexico's north. Labor productivity premia are also relatively high in the leading metropolitan areas (black dots). In all countries, the spatial variation in labor productivity (panel a) is much larger than the spatial variation in place productivity (panel b), indicating that many places, especially the leading areas, are highly productive because productive workers are attracted to them to take advantage of the strong positive learning externalities available in proximity to other skilled workers (Quintero and Roberts 2018)[10] and better consumer amenities.[11]

Declining spatial variation in place productivity since the early 2000s

Throughout Latin America, the territorial variation in labor incomes (net of the effects of exogenous shocks) declined between the early 2000s and the late 2010s—see table 2.1, columns (4) and (5). These declines were largest in Bolivia and Costa Rica, whereas in Brazil and Panama they were relatively small. The variation in place productivity also declined in all countries to various extents during the same period—see table 2.1, columns (6) and (7). The reduction was most noticeable in Bolivia and Mexico and least pronounced in Argentina and Panama. In all countries, the labor productivity premia (the location premia before sorting), shown in columns (4) and (5) of table 2.1, varied across space

TABLE 2.1 Standard deviations and coefficients of variation for labor and place productivity premia, LAC region

Country	Administrative level (1)	Initial period 0 (2)	Last period T (3)	$\sigma_{\gamma_0^{bs}}$ (4)	$\sigma_{\gamma_T^{bs}}$ (5)	$\sigma_{\gamma_0^{as}}$ (6)	$\sigma_{\gamma_T^{as}}$ (7)	$CV_{\gamma_0^{as}}$ (8)	$CV_{\gamma_T^{as}}$ (9)
Argentina	1	2003–05	2017–19	0.31	0.25	0.21	0.20	5.30	4.07
Bolivia	1	2001–02	2017–19	0.44	0.24	0.39	0.18	9.26	3.59
Colombia	1	2001–03	2017–19	0.25	0.19	0.14	0.11	3.43	2.35
Panama	1	2001–03	2017–19	0.65	0.62	0.27	0.27	6.61	5.86
Uruguay	1	2000–02	2017–19	0.22	0.20	0.16	0.13	3.67	2.78
Brazil	2	2000	2014–15	0.57	0.53	0.40	0.36	8.97	4.93
Chile	2	2000–03	2015–17	0.39	0.28	0.24	0.20	5.30	3.78
Costa Rica	2	2001–03	2008–09	0.37	0.18	0.20	0.18	3.87	3.24
Dominican Republic	2	2000–02	2014–16	0.35	0.28	0.27	0.21	5.54	4.24
Ecuador	2	2003–04	2017–19	0.38	0.30	0.27	0.19	7.09	4.47
Honduras	2	2004–06	2017–19	0.50	0.46	0.38	0.35	9.20	8.38
Mexico	2	2000	2015	0.55	0.45	0.46	0.35	10.49	7.62
Peru	2	2000–03	2017–19	0.56	0.43	0.37	0.27	11.24	6.98

Source: D'Aoust, Galdo, and Ianchovichina 2023.

Note: Paraguay is not included in the table because of data limitations. $\sigma_{\gamma^{bs}}$ and $\sigma_{\gamma^{as}}$ are, respectively, the standard deviations of the estimated location premia before sorting (labor productivity premia) and the location premia after sorting (place productivity premia). $CV_{\gamma^{as}}$ is the coefficient of variation in the estimated location premiums after sorting. Column (1) provides the level of regional aggregation by first (1) and second (2) administrative level. Columns (4), (6), and (8) show results for the initial period, specified in column (2). Columns (5), (7), and (9) show results for the last period, specified in column (3). The standard deviation allows comparison of the variation in the productivity variables over time by country, while the coefficient of variation allows cross-country comparisons of the variation in the productivity premia, estimated at the same level of regional aggregation. For Brazil, the indicators for 2014–15 are computed using household data from the Socio-Economic Database for Latin America and the Caribbean (SEDLAC, https://www.cedlas.econo.unlp.edu.ar/wp/en /estadisticas/sedlac/), and those for 2000 using population census data from the Integrated Public Use Microdata Series (IPUMS, https://www.ipums.org/).

a lot more than the place productivity premia (the location premia after sorting), shown in columns (6) and (7) of table 2.1. These results are consistent with those in Quintero and Roberts (2018), who identify sorting of workers as an important factor shaping the variation in place productivity premia across cities.

Sorting did not completely reduce the variation in place productivity premia. In the early 2000s, for the set of countries with municipal-level information, the spatial variation in place productivity—measured with the coefficient of variation to ensure cross-country comparability—was highest in Peru, Mexico, Honduras, and Brazil, while for those with only state or provincial information, it was highest in Bolivia and Panama—see table 2.1, column (8). By the end of the 2010s, the territorial variation in place productivity had declined in all countries, but the change was relatively small in Honduras and Panama—see table 2.1, columns (6) and (7). Consequently, among the countries with information at the second administrative level, opportunities for spatial arbitrage remained most significant in Brazil, Honduras, Mexico, and Peru—see table 2.1, column (9), and figure 2.1.

As expected, median place productivity was considerably higher in higher-income Chile and Costa Rica and relatively low in Honduras and Peru. In all cases, the average place productivity premia in the leading metropolitan areas were in the top quartile of the place productivity premia distribution. Only in Bolivia, Colombia, Panama, and Uruguay was the average place productivity premium in the leading metropolitan area near the maximum location premia observed in the respective countries. This finding suggests that at the end of the 2010s the locations with highest place productivity were not necessarily the leading Latin American metropolitan areas.

FIGURE 2.1 Spatial variations in place productivity premia, Latin America

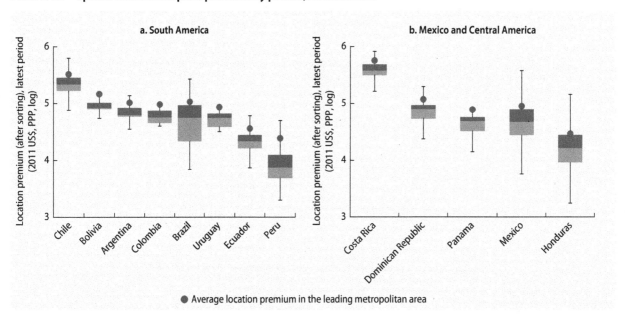

● Average location premium in the leading metropolitan area

Source: D'Aoust, Galdo, and Ianchovichina 2023.
Note: The figure shows the estimated place productivity premia $\gamma_{l,t}^{ss}$ (location premia after sorting) for the last period T in location l. These are premia after controlling for household characteristics (age, age-squared, gender, human capital, marital status, household demographics, and employment characteristics) and survey year fixed effects using the regression model in equation (2.2). The upper and lower ends of the intervals indicate the maximum and minimum estimated premia. The bottom of a bar marks the location premium of the bottom 25 percent of the income distribution. The top of a bar marks the location premium of the top 75 percent. Each bar changes color at the estimated median location premium. PPP = purchasing power parity.

No clear rural-urban divide in place productivity

To explore the variation in productivity across different types of second-level administrative localities (such as municipalities) within countries, D'Aoust, Galdo, and Ianchovichina (2023) define an urban gradient. The granularity of the gradient varies with the size of the country and the territorial coverage of the data, especially in rural areas. For Brazil and Mexico, using the rich information in the Integrated Public Use Microdata Series (IPUMS) population censuses, it is possible to distinguish between six types of localities: (1) large metropolitan areas, (2) small metropolitan areas, (3) large urban areas, (4) small urban areas, (5) large predominantly rural areas, and (6) small predominantly rural areas. Annex table 2B.1 lists the criteria for defining the localities in each country case. For example, in Mexico large metropolitan areas are municipalities with 300,000 or more persons of whom more than 50 percent reside in urban households (as of 2000) and more than 50 percent are metropolitan residents. In Brazil, metropolitan municipalities are defined like those in Mexico, but urban and rural municipalities are considerably larger (annex table 2B.1). In Colombia, official aggregates of value added at the second administrative level are used to define five types of municipalities. Metropolitan municipalities are those designated as such as of 2011. In all other countries, municipalities where the urban population share is above 50 percent (circa 2000) are considered urban, and the rest are classified as rural. Annex table 2B.2 provides details on the number of different types of localities obtained based on the classification in table 2B.1, along with their economic and socioeconomic characteristics. It shows that countries other than Brazil and Chile have more rural than urban or metropolitan municipalities. Brazil has more small urban localities than any other locality type. Chile has more urban than rural municipalities. In all countries, as expected, the shares of residents with a secondary education and wage earners increase with the urban gradient.

Consistent with the steep rise in population density along the urban gradient, LAC metropolitan and urban areas were, on average, more productive than predominantly rural areas in the early 2000s and late 2010s (table 2.2). This finding is in line with the stronger agglomeration economies, better learning externalities, and market access in higher-density localities. However, the rural-urban differences in the average place productivity premia were small in most cases (table 2.2). Rather than a clear rural-urban-metropolitan divide, there is a gradation in labor and place productivity premia by type of locality and an overlap of their distributions, which is present in all cases to different extents (figure 2.2). As shown in figure 2.2, the larger and denser the locality, the further to the right is its location premia distribution. In Mexico, the highest place productivity premia are not observed in the largest metropolitan areas. Instead, they are found in a few smaller metropolitan areas, large urban centers, and even some predominantly rural municipalities (figure 2.2, right-hand panel). Nevertheless, because the dispersion in the place productivity premia in larger metropolitan areas is smaller, on average the place productivity premia in the denser municipalities are higher than those in rural areas. In Brazil, the overlap of the rural and urban distributions is much less pronounced (figure 2.2). The double-hump rural-urban pattern of productivity indicates that most rural municipalities have lower productivity premia than most urban or metropolitan municipalities. In Colombia, the overlap in place productivity premia by type of municipality is akin to the one observed in Mexico.[12] In Chile and the Dominican Republic, except for a few urban localities where the location premia are highest, the rural and urban distributions almost completely overlap, indicating relatively high place productivity in rural areas (table 2.2). In Ecuador and Peru, the least productive localities are rural areas, while the most productive ones are urban areas. Only in Costa Rica and Honduras the least and most productive localities are rural areas (figure 2.2, right-hand panel).

TABLE 2.2   Productivity premia by type of locality: LAC region, early 2000s and late 2010s

2011 US$, PPP, log

a. Rural versus urban average productivity premia

| | Labor productivity premia | | | | Place productivity premia | | | |
| | Early 2000s | | Late 2010s | | Early 2000s | | Late 2010s | |
Country	Urban	Rural	Urban	Rural	Urban	Rural	Urban	Rural
Brazil	5.37	4.72	5.62	5.01	4.52	4.10	4.77	4.39
Chile	5.22	4.91	5.91	5.74	4.52	4.42	5.38	5.31
Costa Rica	5.78	5.38	5.62	5.54	5.16	5.01	5.62	5.54
Dominican Republic	5.32	5.15	5.36	5.29	4.96	4.88	4.87	4.83
Ecuador	4.87	4.56	5.44	5.18	4.05	4.00	4.38	4.28
Honduras	4.91	4.47	5.02	4.61	4.29	4.11	4.42	4.18
Mexico	4.79	4.45	4.97	4.68	4.54	4.30	4.75	4.58
Peru	4.71	3.97	5.26	4.69	3.58	3.17	4.09	3.78

b. Average productivity premia by type of municipality

| | Labor productivity premia, early 2000s | | | | | | Place productivity premia, early 2000s | | | | | |
Country	Metro-large	Metro-small	Urban-large	Urban-small	Rural-large	Rural-small	Metro-large	Metro-small	Urban-large	Urban-small	Rural-large	Rural-small
Brazil	5.83	5.59	5.41	5.28	4.70	4.75	4.70	4.68	4.53	4.46	4.09	4.12
Mexico	5.43	5.17	4.91	4.58	4.54	4.38	4.89	4.76	4.63	4.39	4.40	4.23

| | Labor productivity premia, late 2010s | | | | | | Place productivity premia, late 2010s | | | | | |
Country	Metro-large	Metro-small	Urban-large	Urban-small	Rural-large	Rural-small	Metro-large	Metro-small	Urban-large	Urban-small	Rural-large	Rural-small
Brazil	5.98	5.79	5.65	5.55	4.99	5.04	4.93	4.91	4.78	4.73	4.37	4.41
Mexico	5.41	5.28	5.05	4.82	4.69	4.67	5.00	4.93	4.81	4.65	4.58	4.58

Source: D'Aoust, Galdo, and Ianchovichina 2023.
Note: In panel a, "urban" represents all urban areas, including the metropolitan ones. Annex table 2B.1 defines the urban gradient and different types of localities.
Metro = metropolitan; PPP = purchasing power parity.

FIGURE 2.2   Labor and place productivity premia by type of locality: LAC region, latest available period

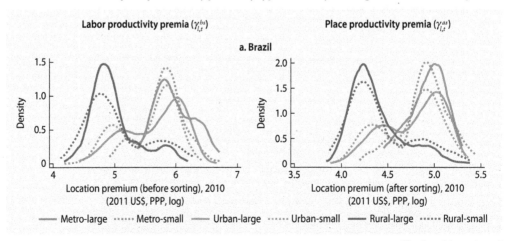

Labor productivity premia $(\gamma_{l,t}^{bs})$

Place productivity premia $(\gamma_{l,t}^{as})$

a. Brazil

Location premium (before sorting), 2010 (2011 US$, PPP, log)

Location premium (after sorting), 2010 (2011 US$, PPP, log)

—— Metro-large   ······ Metro-small   —— Urban-large   ······ Urban-small   —— Rural-large   ······ Rural-small

(Continued on next page)

FIGURE 2.2   **Labor and place productivity premia by type of locality: LAC region, latest available period** *(continued)*

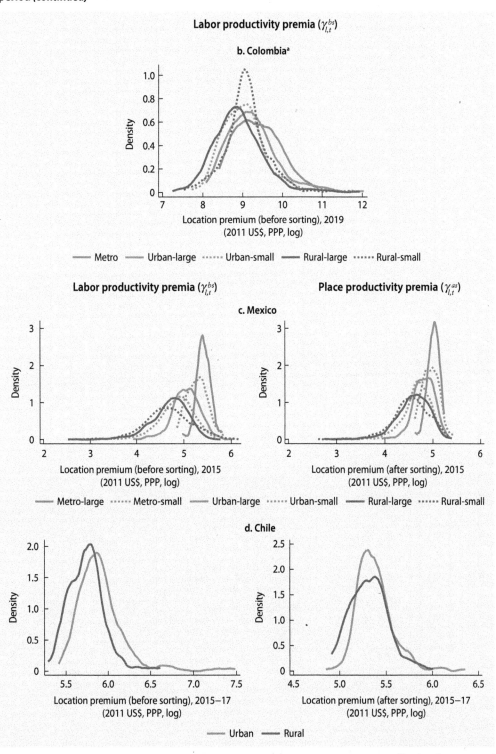

(Continued on next page)

FIGURE 2.2 **Labor and place productivity premia by type of locality: LAC region, latest available period** *(continued)*

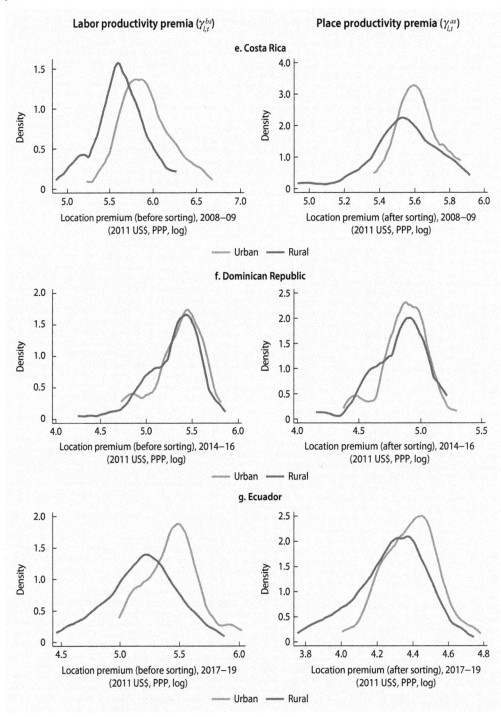

(Continued on next page)

FIGURE 2.2 **Labor and place productivity premia by type of locality: LAC region, latest available period** *(continued)*

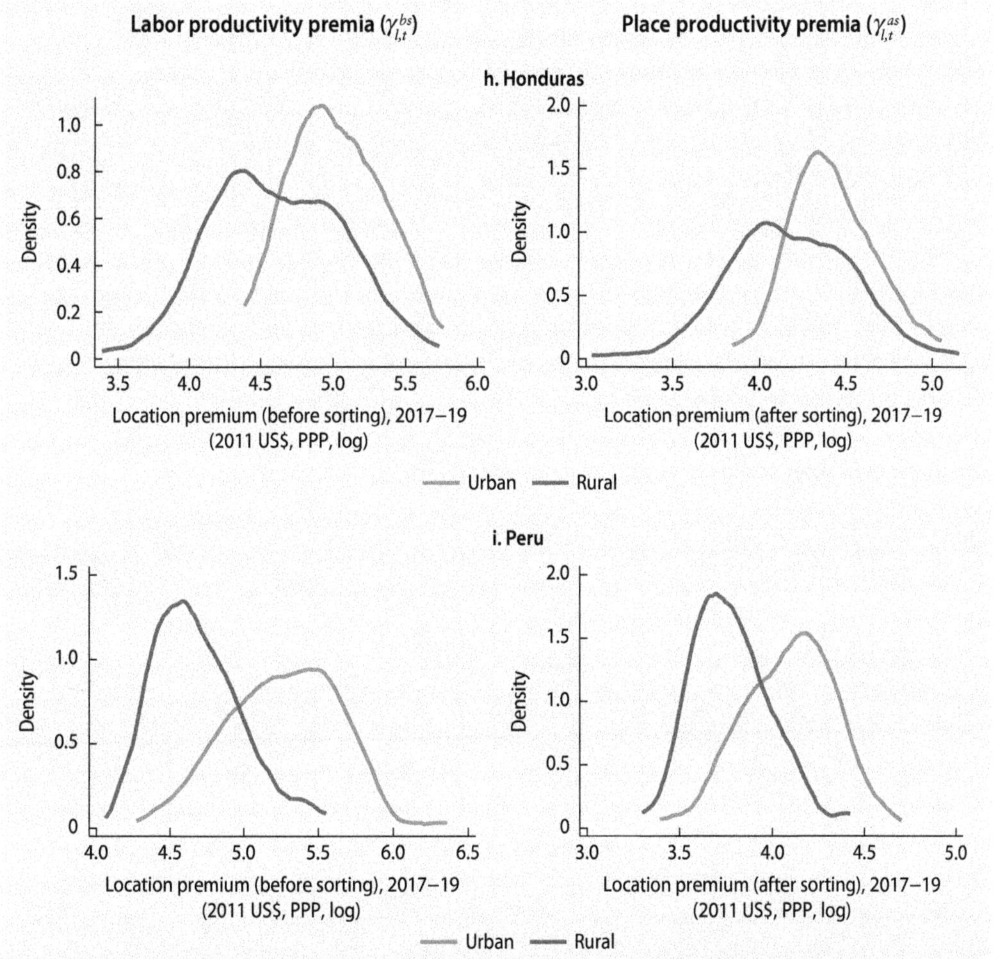

Labor productivity premia ($\gamma_{l,t}^{bs}$) Place productivity premia ($\gamma_{l,t}^{as}$)

h. Honduras

Location premium (before sorting), 2017–19 (2011 US$, PPP, log)

Location premium (after sorting), 2017–19 (2011 US$, PPP, log)

Urban — Rural

i. Peru

Location premium (before sorting), 2017–19 (2011 US$, PPP, log)

Location premium (after sorting), 2017–19 (2011 US$, PPP, log)

Urban — Rural

Source: D'Aoust, Galdo, and Ianchovichina 2023.
Note: The graphs show the density distribution of labor and place productivity premia by type of locality. Metro = metropolitan; PPP = purchasing power parity.
a. Because neither the value-added data source nor the Socio-Economic Database for Latin America and the Caribbean (SEDLAC) provide household information at the second administrative level, it is not possible to estimate place productivity premia in Colombia.

Leveling up in productivity

The assessment of territorial productivity trends relies on the traditional workhorse model in the economic growth literature,

$$g_{l,t,t+T} = \alpha + \beta y_{l,t} + \mu_{l,t}, \tag{2.3}$$

which regresses the average growth in real per capita labor income, $g_{l,t,t+T}$ in location l between period t and $t + T$ on the average real per capita labor income, $y_{l,t}$, in location l at time t. The same model can be used to assess whether there is absolute convergence or divergence in other productivity measures such as the labor productivity premium, proxied with the location premium before sorting ($\gamma_{l,t}^{bs}$), or the place productivity premium, proxied with the location premium after sorting ($\gamma_{l,t}^{as}$). In most cases, the model in equation (2.3) is estimated with data at both the first and second administrative levels, but in a few cases estimates are presented only at the first administrative level because data are not available at the second administrative level.

The results suggest that the years between the early 2000s and the late 2010s were a period of absolute convergence in real per capita household labor incomes (annex table 2C.1) and labor productivity premia in most Latin American countries (figure 2.3). At the first administrative level, income convergence was relatively fast only in Bolivia, Colombia, the Dominican Republic, Ecuador, and Mexico (see the first three columns of annex table 2C.1). In these countries, the rate of convergence surpassed the 2 percent benchmark recorded during past convergence episodes in advanced economies. In Argentina, Brazil, Honduras, Peru, and Uruguay, it fell just below this benchmark. Only in Chile and Panama did convergence occur at a slower pace, and in Costa Rica it was observed only at the second administrative level. In all countries with information at both the first and second administrative levels, absolute convergence was faster at the second administrative level, suggesting that some fast-growing localities are part of relatively affluent first-level administrative regions.

FIGURE 2.3   **Absolute convergence in labor productivity premia by administrative level and country**

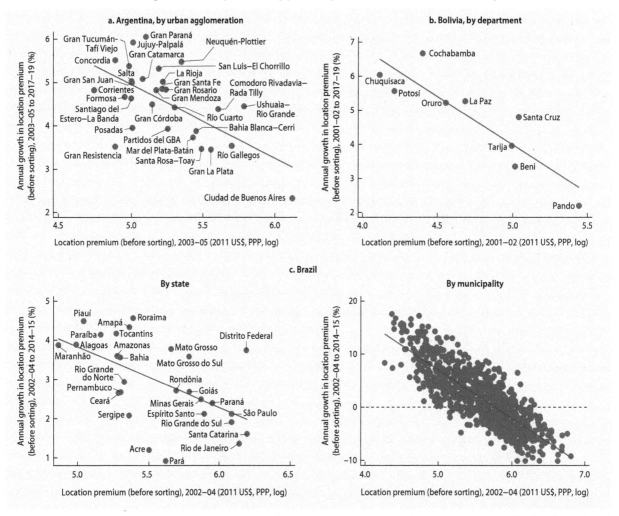

(Continued on next page)

FIGURE 2.3   Absolute convergence in labor productivity premia by administrative level and country *(continued)*

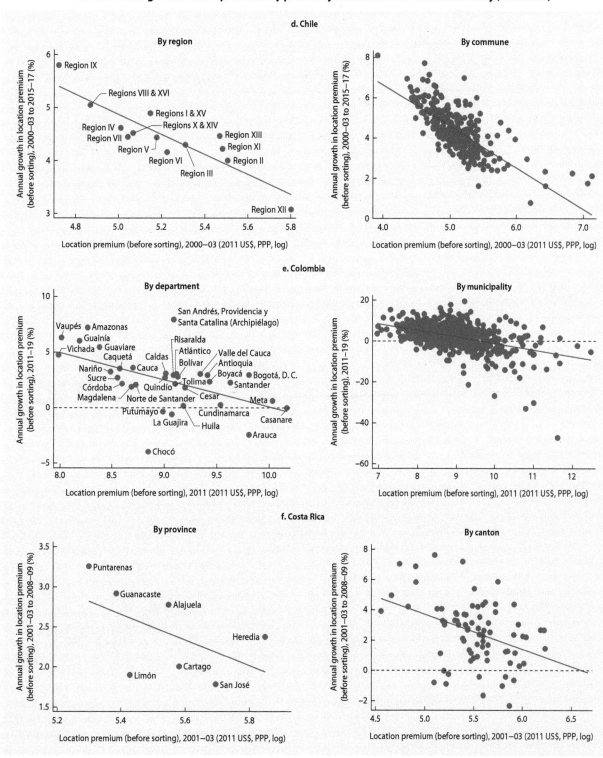

(Continued on next page)

FIGURE 2.3 **Absolute convergence in labor productivity premia by administrative level and country** *(continued)*

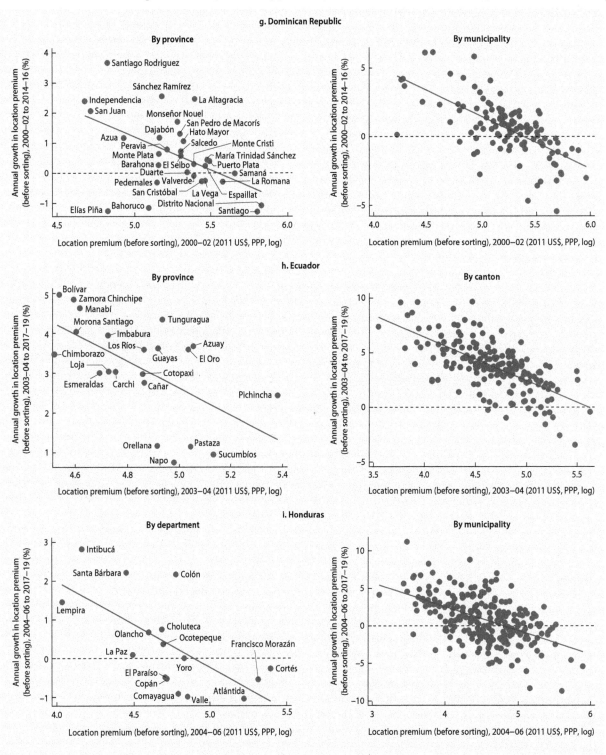

(Continued on next page)

FIGURE 2.3 **Absolute convergence in labor productivity premia by administrative level and country** *(continued)*

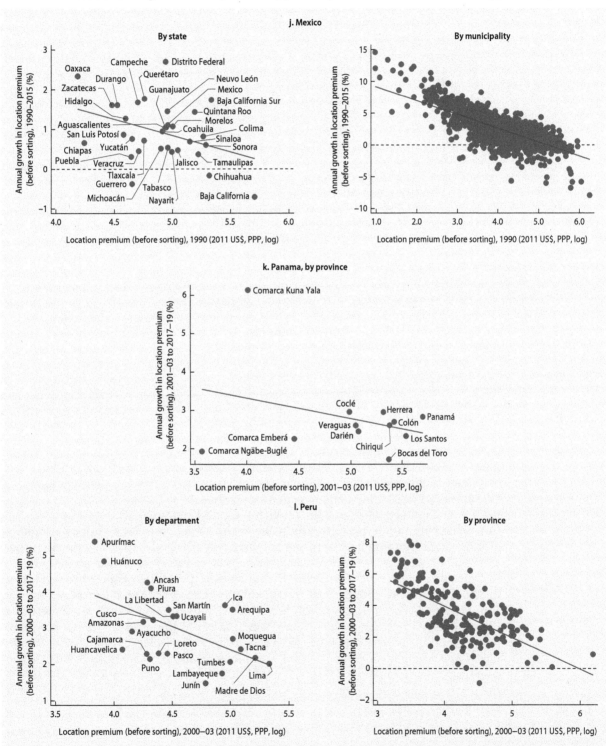

(Continued on next page)

FIGURE 2.3   Absolute convergence in labor productivity premia by administrative level and country *(continued)*

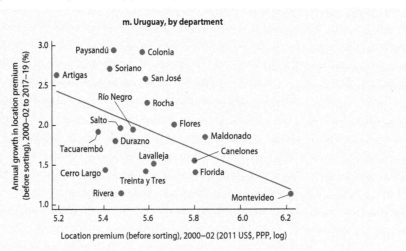

m. Uruguay, by department

Source: D'Aoust, Galdo, and Ianchovichina 2023.
Note: The negative slope of the trend line indicates that productivity growth tended to be slower in more productive subnational regions. Labor productivity premium refers to the location premium before sorting. In 2018 Chile renamed its first-level administrative regions: Region I became Tarapacá; Region II, Antofagasta; Region III, Aracama; Region IV, Coquimbo; Region V, Valparaiso; Region VI, O'Higgins; Region VII, Maule; Region VIII, Biobío; Region IX, Araucanía; Region X, Los Lagos; Region XI, Aysén; Region XII, Magallanes; RM (Region XIII), Metropolitan; Region XIV, Los Ríos; Region XV, Arica and Parinacota; Region XVI, Ñuble. PPP = purchasing power parity.

Convergence can be attributed in part to the commodity boom during the Golden Decade (2003–13). With the rise of commodity rents from the higher demand for resources and agricultural products by China and other fast-growing economies, investments and incomes in rural areas increased (Adão 2015; Rodríguez 2011; Rowe 2014).[13] However, the Dutch Disease effects of the commodity windfall, and in some countries remittances, weakened the competitiveness of the manufacturing sector (Venables 2017), shifting employment away from urban tradables as depicted in figure 1.1 in chapter 1 (Jedwab, Ianchovichina, and Haslop 2022). In addition, steep foreign competition, especially from China, and advances in labor-saving technologies further depressed manufacturing employment, especially in the largest cities (figure 2.4), where laid-off workers switched mostly to informal, lower-quality jobs in the nontradable sectors (Dix-Carneiro and Kovak 2017, 2019; Ponczek and Ulyssea 2022). The share of employment in tradable services rose from a low base, but not sufficiently to offset the steep decline in the share of employment in manufacturing (figure 2.4). Altogether these developments improved the productivity in predominantly rural areas relatively more than the productivity in large urban areas, resulting in absolute convergence in labor and place productivity premia in most Latin American countries (annex tables 2C.2 and 2C.3).[14] Only in Costa Rica and Panama there was no absolute convergence in labor and place productivity premia at the first administrative level.

FIGURE 2.4 **Evolution of share of employment in manufacturing and tradable services by city size and decade: Latin America, 1980 or earlier to circa 2010**

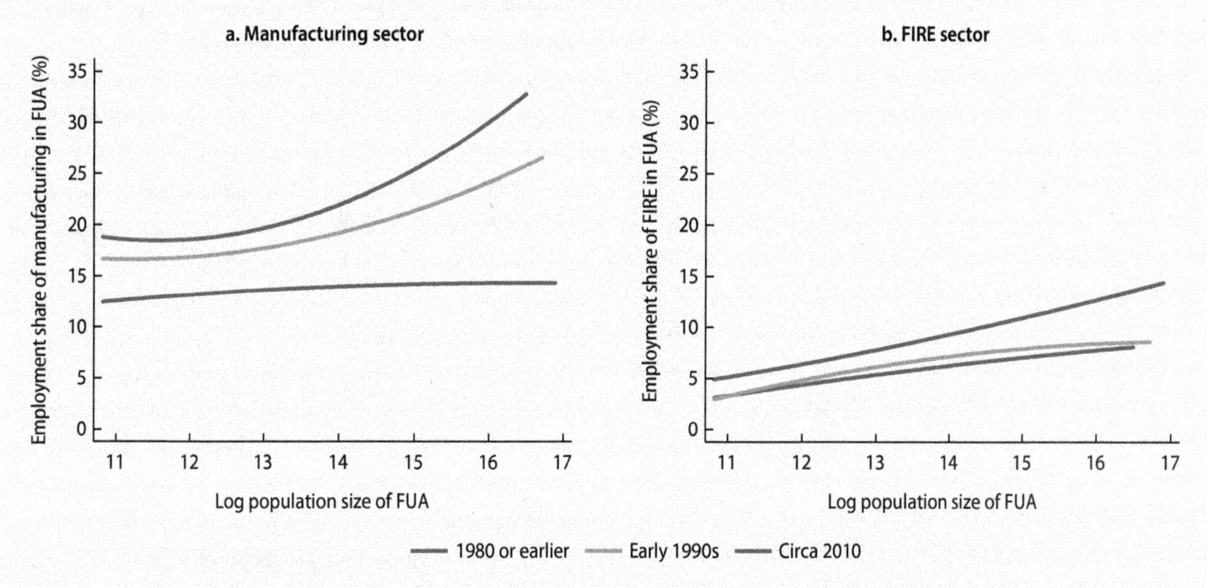

Source: Jedwab, Ianchovichina, and Haslop (2022), using Integrated Public Use Microdata Series (IPUMS, https://www.ipums.org/) survey microdata.
Note: FIRE = finance, insurance, and real estate; FUA = functional urban area. FIRE is a proxy for tradable services. Manufacturing and tradable services jointly account for all urban tradables. All other urban activities are nontradables. A FUA is composed of a city and its commuting zone. The graphs show how the average shares of employment in manufacturing and FIRE for FUAs of different sizes evolved between circa 1980 and circa 2010.

Convergence by type of locality

Abstracting from density, among localities of each type relatively poor ones caught up with their more affluent counterparts during the past couple of decades (see table 2.3), but convergence occurred at different speeds. In Mexico, convergence was fastest across metropolitan areas and slowest across large predominantly rural municipalities. In Brazil, convergence in labor productivity premia was fastest across the large urban and metropolitan areas, while convergence in place productivity premia was fastest across mostly rural areas, especially larger ones. Convergence was faster across rural municipalities in Chile, Colombia, the Dominican Republic, and Peru and urban ones in Costa Rica and Honduras (table 2.3). Place productivity premia converged at similar rates across rural and urban areas in Ecuador. Thus in Costa Rica, Honduras, and Mexico, convergence in place productivity premia was mainly driven by the urbanization process, while in Brazil, Chile, Colombia, the Dominican Republic, and Peru the commodity boom rather than the urbanization process was behind it. In Ecuador, both forces appear to have played an important role.

In line with the results on absolute convergence at the municipal level, in almost all countries productivity growth was highest in rural municipalities (figure 2.5). Yet the dispersion in growth outcomes was also much higher across rural than across urban areas, signaling that economic growth in some rural localities was quite low. Overall, the growth distributions of different types of localities overlap substantially, especially for place productivity (as shown in the right-hand panels of figure 2.5).

TABLE 2.3 Absolute convergence in labor productivity premia by locality type, LAC region

Country and variables	Metro-large	Metro-small	Urban-large	Urban-small	Rural-large	Rural-small
Brazil	Annual labor productivity premium growth, 2000–2010					
γ_0^{bs}	−0.0110***	−0.0110***	−0.0120***	−0.00951***	−0.00920***	−0.00325
	(0.00352)	(0.00153)	(0.000962)	(0.000824)	(0.00194)	(0.00239)
Obs.	46	176	434	842	317	225
R-squared	0.181	0.229	0.264	0.137	0.067	0.008
	Annual place productivity premium growth, 2000–2010					
γ_0^{as}	−0.0110**	−0.00809***	−0.0151***	−0.0152***	−0.0227***	−0.0178***
	(0.00533)	(0.00222)	(0.00137)	(0.00111)	(0.00224)	(0.00272)
Obs.	46	176	434	842	317	225
R-squared	0.088	0.071	0.219	0.183	0.246	0.162
Mexico	Annual labor productivity premium growth, 2000–2015					
γ_0^{bs}	−0.0464***	−0.0313***	−0.0215***	−0.0197***	−0.0170***	−0.0284***
	(0.00531)	(0.00412)	(0.00151)	(0.00137)	(0.00157)	(0.00127)
Obs.	41	72	357	437	586	827
R-squared	0.663	0.451	0.362	0.322	0.166	0.378
	Annual place productivity premium growth, 2000–2015					
γ_0^{as}	−0.0476***	−0.0354***	−0.0254***	−0.0253***	−0.0203***	−0.0311***
	(0.00384)	(0.00375)	(0.00165)	(0.00143)	(0.00154)	(0.00123)
Obs.	41	72	357	437	586	827
R-squared	0.798	0.560	0.399	0.417	0.229	0.437

	Metro	Urban-large	Urban-small	Rural-large	Rural-small
Colombia	Annual labor productivity premium growth, 2011–19				
γ_0^{bs}	−0.0175**	−0.0305***	−0.0341***	−0.0228***	−0.0463***
	(0.00698)	(0.00408)	(0.00529)	(0.00294)	(0.00371)
Obs.	59	168	150	341	404
R-squared	0.099	0.252	0.220	0.151	0.279

	Urban	Rural		Urban	Rural
Chile	Annual location premium growth 2000/03–2015/17 (before sorting)			Annual location premium growth 2000/03–2015/17 (after sorting)	
γ_0^{bs}	−0.0172***	−0.0260***	γ_0^{as}	−0.0140***	−0.0215***
	(0.00144)	(0.00238)		(0.00202)	(0.00282)
Obs.	201	98		201	98
R-squared	0.418	0.553		0.193	0.378

(Continued on next page)

TABLE 2.3   Absolute convergence in labor productivity premia by locality type, LAC region *(continued)*

Country and variables	Urban	Rural		Urban	Rural
Costa Rica	**Annual location premium growth, 2001/03–2008/09 (before sorting)**			**Annual location premium growth, 2001/03–2008/09 (after sorting)**	
γ_0^{bs}	−0.00904 (0.0107)	−0.0245*** (0.00886)	γ_0^{as}	−0.0421*** (0.0129)	−0.0218** (0.0102)
Obs.	30	49		30	49
R-squared	0.025	0.140		0.276	0.088
Dominican Republic	**Annual location premium growth, 2000/02–2014/16 (before sorting)**			**Annual location premium growth, 2000/02–2014/16 (after sorting)**	
γ_0^{bs}	−0.0317*** (0.00499)	−0.0434*** (0.00646)	γ_0^{as}	−0.0349*** (0.00564)	−0.0451*** (0.00553)
Obs.	51	64		51	64
R-squared	0.452	0.421		0.438	0.517
Ecuador	**Annual labor productivity premium growth, 2003/04–2017/19**			**Annual place productivity premium growth, 2003/04–2017/19**	
γ_0^{bs}	−0.0467*** (0.00513)	−0.0448*** (0.00444)	γ_0^{as}	−0.0501*** (0.00489)	−0.0541*** (0.00404)
Obs.	69	122		69	122
R-squared	0.553	0.495		0.610	0.599
Honduras	**Annual location premium growth, 2004/06–2017/19 (before sorting)**			**Annual location premium growth, 2004/06–2017/19 (after sorting)**	
γ_0^{bs}	−0.0400*** (0.00963)	−0.0341*** (0.00370)	γ_0^{as}	−0.0556*** (0.0106)	−0.0421*** (0.00387)
Obs.	33	210		33	210
R-squared	0.357	0.291		0.470	0.363
Peru	**Annual labor productivity premium growth, 2000/03–2017/19**			**Annual place productivity premium growth, 2000/03–2017/19**	
γ_0^{bs}	−0.0158*** (0.00273)	−0.0329*** (0.00303)	γ_0^{as}	−0.0196*** (0.00311)	−0.0394*** (0.00304)
Obs.	71	115		71	115
R-squared	0.326	0.510		0.366	0.597

Source: D'Aoust, Galdo, and Ianchovichina 2023.
Note: The results are estimated based on model (2.3). γ_0^{bs} refers to the initial location premium before sorting (labor productivity premium). These are the estimated location premia without controlling for household characteristics, but they are net of survey year fixed effects as in model (2.2). γ_0^{as} refers to the initial location premium after sorting (place productivity premium). These are the estimated location premia controlling for sorting based on household characteristics (age, age-squared, gender, human capital, marital status, household demographics, and employment characteristics) and net of survey year fixed effects, as in model (2.1). For Mexico, the analysis is based on census data for all periods. For Brazil, census data are used for the period 2000–2010, whereas household data are used for all other periods. For Colombia, official aggregates of value-added data are used, and they include only one category for metropolitan municipalities. For the rest of the countries, the analysis is based on Socio-Economic Database for Latin America and the Caribbean (SEDLAC) harmonized household surveys. Place productivity premia cannot be estimated by type of settlement in Colombia because SEDLAC data do not offer household information below the first administrative level. Metro = metropolitan; obs. = observations.
Significance level: ** = 5 percent, *** = 1 percent.

FIGURE 2.5   Annual growth in productivity premia by locality type, LAC region

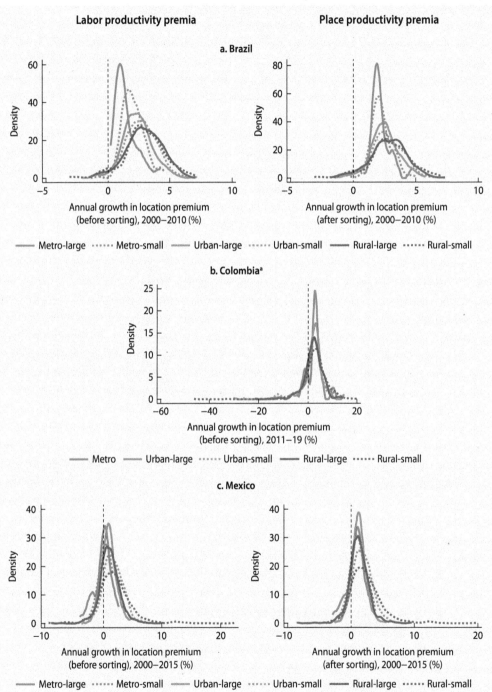

(Continued on next page)

FIGURE 2.5   Annual growth in productivity premia by locality type, LAC region *(continued)*

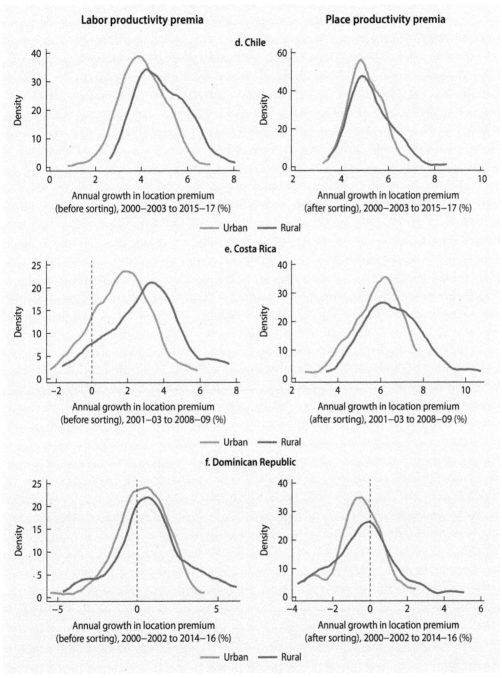

(Continued on next page)

FIGURE 2.5 **Annual growth in productivity premia by locality type, LAC region** *(continued)*

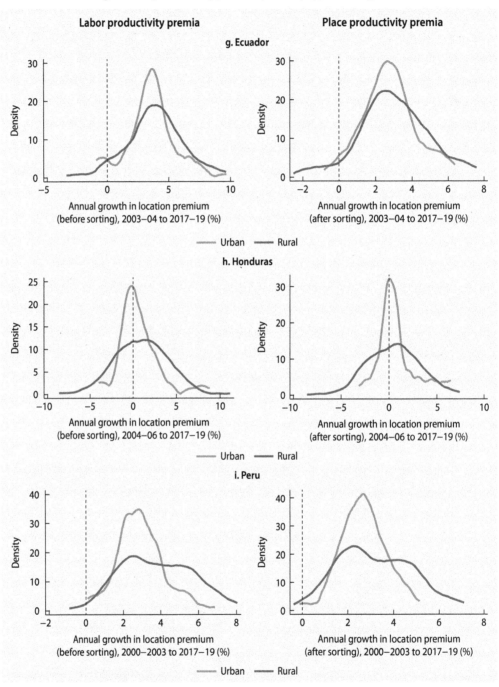

Source: D'Aoust, Galdo, and Ianchovichina 2023.
Note: Metro = metropolitan.
a. Location premia after sorting cannot be estimated by type of settlement in Colombia because Socio-Economic Database for Latin America and the Caribbean (SEDLAC) data do not offer household information below the first administrative level.

In many countries, growth was negative in a sizable share of localities, suggesting that the leveling up reflected both improvements in lagging areas and to different extents a deterioration in previously productive localities. In the Dominican Republic, there was a decline in growth in approximately half of the urban and rural municipalities, whereas in Chile growth was positive in all communes.

In summary, the Golden Decade ushered in a period of absolute convergence in real per capita household labor incomes and labor and place productivity premia at the first and second administrative levels in nearly all Latin American countries. Agglomeration forces did not stand in the way of convergence. The leveling up occurred largely because urban productivity growth fell behind the productivity growth in poorer agricultural and mining municipalities, where investments boosted economic activity in predominantly rural economies.[15]

Yet, at the end of the 2010s, substantial cross-country differences in median place productivity remained. Within countries, opportunities for spatial arbitrage were most significant in Brazil, Honduras, Mexico, and Peru. Instead of a clear rural-urban-metropolitan divide, the productivity distributions of different types of localities overlapped to a great degree. Average urban place productivity was also not much higher than average rural place productivity except in Brazil, Honduras, and Peru (figure 2.6). In many cases, the places with the highest local place productivity were not necessarily the leading metropolitan areas, although in all cases they were among the top 25 percent of most productive places in their respective countries. Chapter 3 explores the extent to which socioeconomic groups can exploit the income gaps with the leading metropolitan areas and the factors that prevent some groups from doing so.

FIGURE 2.6   Average place productivity premia by type of municipality and country: Selected LAC countries, late 2010s

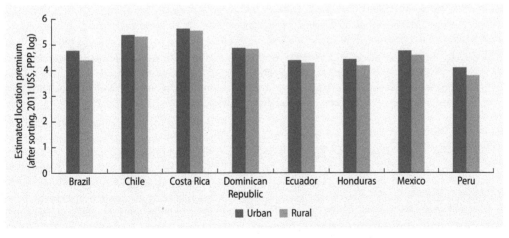

Source: D'Aoust, Galdo, and Ianchovichina 2023.
Note: The place productivity premium is the fraction of per capita household labor income that cannot be accounted for by observable, nongeographic (portable) household characteristics and the effects of time-variant exogenous factors. To ensure comparability within and across countries, the per capita household labor earnings are deflated to adjust incomes for cost-of-living differences across space and time. PPP = purchasing power parity.

Annex 2A Data sources and harmonization criteria

TABLE 2A.1   Variables for portable household characteristics by type of endowment

Type of endowment	Variable
Demographics	Gender Age, age-squared Household size Number of household members under age 2, 3–11, 12–17, 18–59, above 59. All squared values were also included.
Education	Less than completed primary education Less than completed secondary education Less than completed tertiary education Completed tertiary degree Highest attainment in the household
Employment	Employer Salaried worker Self-employed Not salaried Unemployed

Source: D'Aoust, Galdo, and Ianchovichina 2023.
Note: The employment status of a household head may not be fully portable across locations because this is a labor market outcome, and labor market conditions differ across locations. The results are robust to the exclusion of this dimension as in all countries except Bolivia it explains a small share of the income gap with leading cities (see table 3.1 in chapter 3).

BOX 2A.1   Criteria for harmonizing geocodes across survey years

D'Aoust, Galdo, and Ianchovichina (2023) used two criteria to harmonize geocodes across survey years at the lowest geographical level possible and maximize the number of surveyed locations across time:

1. Two to three consecutive surveys were used to ensure coverage for three specific time periods in the last 20 years: the early 2000s, around 2010, and the late 2010s.
2. The surveys had geocodes and location name information that allowed for consistent harmonization of the surveys over the defined time periods.

These considerations were used to decide which Socio-Economic Database for Latin America and the Caribbean (SEDLAC) surveys would not be included in the sample. However, in some instances a particular survey was not used for reasons not mentioned earlier. The 2000 Panama survey was excluded to minimize location recoding. From 2001 up to 2017, Panama's administrative units remained stable. El Salvador was also excluded from the analysis because of potential issues related to the switch in currencies in the early 2000s. Choosing 2005 as the initial period did not help because this resulted in a substantial decline in the number of surveyed locations available in 2005 and in the late 2010s, biasing estimation of the location premia.

TABLE 2A.2   Data sources for the territorial productivity dynamics analysis

Country	Data source	Lowest administrative level	Years
Argentina	SEDLAC-WB	Urban agglomeration	2003, 2004, 2005, 2009, 2010, 2011, 2017, 2018, 2019
Bolivia	SEDLAC-WB	Department	2001, 2002, 2011, 2012, 2013, 2017, 2018, 2019
Brazil	Census-IPUMS	Municipality	2000, 2010
	SEDLAC-WB	Municipality	2002, 2003, 2004, 2009, 2011, 2014, 2015
Chile	SEDLAC-WB	Commune	2000, 2003, 2009, 2011, 2015, 2017
Colombia	VA-DANE	Municipality	2011, 2012, 2013, 2014, 2015, 2016, 2017, 2018, 2019
	SEDLAC-WB	Department	2001, 2002, 2003, 2008, 2009, 2010, 2017, 2018, 2019
Costa Rica	SEDLAC-WB	Canton	2001, 2002, 2003, 2008, 2009
Dominican Republic	SEDLAC-WB	Municipality	2000, 2001, 2002, 2008, 2009, 2010, 2014, 2015, 2016
Ecuador	SEDLAC-WB	Canton	2003, 2004, 2005, 2009, 2010, 2011, 2017, 2018, 2019
Honduras	SEDLAC-WB	Municipality	2004, 2005, 2006, 2009, 2010, 2011, 2017, 2018, 2019 ·
Mexico	Census-IPUMS	Municipality	1990, 2000, 2010, 2015
Panama	SEDLAC-WB	Province	2001, 2002, 2003, 2009, 2010, 2011, 2017, 2018, 2019
Peru	SEDLAC-WB	Province	2000, 2001, 2002, 2003, 2008, 2009, 2010, 2017, 2018, 2019
Uruguay	SEDLAC-WB	Department	2000, 2001, 2002, 2008, 2009, 2010, 2017, 2018, 2019

Source: D'Aoust, Galdo, and Ianchovichina 2023.
Note: DANE = National Administrative Department of Statistics (Colombia, https://www.data4sdgs.org/partner/dane-national-administrative-department-statistics-colombia); IPUMS = Integrated Public Use Microdata Series (https://www.ipums.org/); SEDLAC = Socio-Economic Database for Latin America and the Caribbean (CEDLAS and the World Bank, https://www.cedlas.econo.unlp.edu.ar/wp/en/estadisticas/sedlac/); VA = value added; WB = World Bank. For Brazil, where both IPUMS and SEDLAC surveys are available, the results obtained with the two data sources are similar, with differences being more pronounced for rural administrative areas.

TABLE 2A.3   Data sources for spatially differentiated price deflators by country

Country	Spatial deflators
Argentina	SEDLAC urban poverty lines for six regions by year
Bolivia	SEDLAC poverty lines for each of the nine departments by year and urban and rural area
Brazil	IBGE state GDP deflators and poverty lines for the metropolitan, urban, and rural areas in each state by year
Chile	ECLA poverty lines by year and area of residence
Colombia	DANE spatial deflators at the level of the country's departments by year (An additional correction was made to account for differences across urban and rural areas based on ECLA poverty lines.)
Costa Rica	ECLA poverty lines by year and area of residence
Dominican Republic	ECLA poverty lines until 2016 and SEDLAC from 2017 onward
Ecuador	ECLA poverty lines by year and urban and rural area
El Salvador	SEDLAC poverty lines by year and area of residence; ECLA for 2008 and 2011
Honduras	SEDLAC poverty lines by year and area of residence
Mexico	INEGI state GDP deflators and poverty lines for urban and rural areas in each state
Panama	ECLA poverty lines by year and area of residence
Paraguay	SEDLAC poverty lines by year and area of residence
Peru	INEI spatial deflators at the level of the country's departments by year, including for differences between urban and rural areas
Uruguay	Only urban areas included and no spatial adjustments applied

Source: D'Aoust, Galdo, and Ianchovichina 2023.
Note: DANE = National Administrative Department of Statistics (Colombia); ECLA = United Nations Economic Commission for Latin America (CEPAL in Spanish); GDP = gross domestic product; IBGE = Brazilian Institute of Geography and Statistics; INEGI = National Institute of Statistics and Geography (Mexico); INEI = National Institute of Statistics and Informatics (Peru); SEDLAC = Socio-Economic Database for Latin America and the Caribbean.

Annex 2B Settlement types

TABLE 2B.1   The urban gradient: Definitions of locality types, LAC region

Country and locality type	Population size	Share of urban residents (%)	Share of metropolitan residents (%)
Brazil			
Metro-large	≥300,000	>50	>50
Metro-small	<300,000	>50	>50
Urban-large	≥50,000	>50	≤50
Urban-small	<50,000	>50	≤50
Rural-large	≥30,000	≤50	≤50
Rural-small	<30,000	≤50	≤50
Colombia			
Metro		All designated as metro areas in 2011	
Urban-large	≥20,000	>50	Nonmetro areas
Urban-small	<20,000	>50	Nonmetro areas
Rural-large	≥10,000	≤50	Nonmetro areas
Rural-small	<10,000	≤50	Nonmetro areas
Mexico			
Metro-large	≥300,000	>50	>50
Metro-small	<300,000	>50	>50
Urban-large	≥20,000	>50	≤50
Urban-small	<20,000	>50	≤50
Rural-large	≥10,000	≤50	≤50
Rural-small	<10,000	≤50	≤50
All other LAC countries			
Urban		>50	
Rural		≤50	

Source: D'Aoust, Galdo, and Ianchovichina 2023.
Note: Metro = metropolitan.

TABLE 2B.2   Settlement types: Descriptive statistics, LAC region

Country and locality type	Number	Average growth (%)	Standard deviation, growth	Density (number of people per km²)	Complete secondary (%)	Self-employment share (%)	Wage earners (%)
Brazil		2000–2010			2000		
Metro-large	46	1.1	0.9	3,438	25	24	75
Metro-small	176	1.3	1.4	691	17	24	74
Urban-large	434	1.6	1.5	139	16	31	65
Urban-small	842	1.8	1.9	50	13	31	64
Rural-large	317	2.9	1.7	34	7	44	43
Rural-small	225	2.8	2.4	31	8	44	42
Colombia		2011–19			2000		
Metro	59	2.8	3.3				
Urban-large	168	2.0	4.5				
Urban-small	150	1.6	5.1				
Rural-large	341	2.1	4.0				
Rural-small	404	2.8	5.5				
Mexico		2000–2015			2000		
Metro-large	41	0.3	1.7	1,820	19	22	74
Metro-small	72	1.2	1.8	735	16	24	71
Urban-large	358	1.7	2.1	369	11	27	64
Urban-small	440	3.0	2.7	168	8	33	56
Rural-large	587	3.0	2.9	70	5	35	49
Rural-small	832	4.9	4.4	41	4	43	36
Chile		2000/03–2015/17			2000/03		
Urban	201	3.0	1.6		24	21	69
Rural	98	3.6	1.4		12	29	57
Costa Rica		2001/03–2008/09			2001/03		
Urban	30	1.9	2.2		14	28	63
Rural	63	3.1	2.5		8	32	59
Dominican Republic		2000/02–2014/16			2000/02		
Urban	51	0.7	2.0		11	38	45
Rural	64	1.5	2.8		5	53	30
Ecuador		2003/04–2017/19			2003/04		
Urban	69	2.4	2.5		13	40	52
Rural	122	3.6	2.9		8	53	39
Honduras		2004/06–2017/19			2004/06		
Urban	34	0.5	3.0		9	44	42
Rural	210	0.4	3.8		4	60	28
Peru		2000/03–2017/19			2000/03		
Urban	71	3.0	1.6		24	50	40
Rural	115	4.6	2.1		13	76	18

Source: D'Aoust, Galdo, and Ianchovichina 2023.
Note: Metro = metropolitan.

Annex 2C Additional convergence results

TABLE 2C.1 **Absolute convergence in real per capita household labor income at two administrative levels by country and time period**

Country and variables	Annual per capita growth					
	First administrative level			Second administrative level		
Argentina	2003/05–2017/19	2003/05–2009/11	2009/11–2017/19			
Log Y_0	−0.0181***	−0.0102	−0.0397***			
	(0.00465)	(0.0108)	(0.00965)			
Obs.	29	29	29			
R-squared	0.358	0.032	0.385			
Bolivia	2001/02–2017/19	2001/02–2011/13	2011/13–2017/19			
Log Y_0	−0.0360***	−0.0421***	−0.0590***			
	(0.00500)	(0.0119)	(0.0139)			
Obs.	9	9	9			
R-squared	0.881	0.641	0.719			
Brazil	2002/04– 2014/15	2000–2010	2009/11– 2014/15	2002/04–2014/15	2000–2010	2009/11– 2014/15
Log Y_0	−0.0107**	−0.0189***	−0.00817	−0.0889***	−0.0202***	−0.106***
	(0.00489)	(0.00522)	(0.0114)	(0.00221)	(0.000555)	(0.00921)
Obs.	27	27	27	817	2,040	817
R-squared	0.161	0.345	0.020	0.665	0.394	0.140
Chile	2000/03–2015/17	2000/03–2009/11	2009/11–2015/17	2000/03–2015/17	2000/03–2009/11	2009/11–2015/17
Log Y_0	−0.0111*	−0.0150	−0.0148	−0.0207***	−0.0276***	−0.0385***
	(0.00590)	(0.0116)	(0.0109)	(0.00155)	(0.00259)	(0.00505)
Obs.	13	13	13	299	299	299
R-squared	0.243	0.132	0.142	0.375	0.278	0.164
Colombia	2001/03–2017/19	2001/03–2008/10	2011–19			2011–19
Log Y_0	−0.0238***	−0.0376***	−0.0244***			−0.0319***
	(0.00589)	(0.0113)	(0.00694)			(0.00187)
Obs.	24	24	33			1,122
R-squared	0.425	0.335	0.286			0.206
Costa Rica		2001/03–2008/09			2001/03–2008/09	
Log Y_0		−0.00613			−0.0242***	
		(0.0130)			(0.00642)	
Obs.		7			79	
R-squared		0.043			0.155	
Dominican Republic	2000/02–2014/16	2000/02–2008/10	2008/10–2014/16	2000/02–2014/16	2000/02–2008/10	2008/10–2014/16
Log Y_0	−0.0293***	−0.0313***	−0.0370***	−0.0430***	−0.0647***	−0.0721***
	(0.00601)	(0.00962)	(0.0115)	(0.00395)	(0.00603)	(0.0132)
Obs.	30	30	30	115	115	115
R-squared	0.459	0.274	0.269	0.511	0.505	0.210

(Continued on next page)

TABLE 2C.1   Absolute convergence in real per capita household labor income at two administrative levels by country and time period *(continued)*

Country and variables	Annual per capita growth					
	First administrative level			Second administrative level		
Ecuador	**2003/04–2017/19**	**2003/04–2009/11**	**2009/11–2017/19**	**2003/04–2017/19**	**2003/04–2009/11**	**2009/11–2017/19**
Log Y_0	−0.0428***	−0.0556***	−0.0423**	−0.0464***	−0.0638***	−0.0660***
	(0.00737)	(0.00992)	(0.0184)	(0.00332)	(0.00549)	(0.00799)
Obs.	21	21	21	191	191	191
R-squared	0.639	0.623	0.217	0.508	0.417	0.266
Honduras	**2004/06–2017/19**	**2004/06–2009/11**	**2009/11–2017/19**	**2004/06–2017/19**	**2004/06–2009/11**	**2009/11–2017/19**
Log Y_0	−0.0191**	−0.0328	−0.0408*	−0.0439***	−0.0834***	−0.0872***
	(0.00803)	(0.0193)	(0.0207)	(0.00368)	(0.00776)	(0.00751)
Obs.	16	16	16	243	243	243
R-squared	0.287	0.171	0.216	0.372	0.324	0.359
Mexico	**1990–2015**	**2000–2010**	**2000–2015**	**1990–2015**	**2000–2010**	**2000–2015**
Log Y_0	−0.0142***	−0.0285***	−0.0265***	−0.0243***	−0.0262***	−0.0310***
	(0.00378)	(0.00665)	(0.00476)	(0.000394)	(0.00109)	(0.000609)
Obs.	32	32	32	2,303	2,330	2,320
R-squared	0.319	0.380	0.507	0.624	0.197	0.528
Panama	**2001/03–2017/19**	**2001/03–2009/11**	**2009/11–2017/19**			
Log Y_0	−0.0117**	−0.0131	−0.0218			
	(0.00395)	(0.00780)	(0.0151)			
Obs.	12	12	12			
R-squared	0.465	0.220	0.173			
Peru	**2000/03–2017/19**	**2000/03–2008/10**	**2008/10–2017/19**	**2000/03–2017/19**	**2000/03–2008/10**	**2008/10–2017/19**
Log Y_0	−0.0195***	−0.0224***	−0.0240***	−0.0296***	−0.0308***	−0.0473***
	(0.00370)	(0.00768)	(0.00646)	(0.00168)	(0.00392)	(0.00338)
Obs.	24	24	24	186	186	186
R-squared	0.558	0.278	0.384	0.627	0.252	0.516
Uruguay	**2000/02–2017/19**	**2000/02–2008/10**	**2008/10–2017/19**			
Log Y_0	−0.0177**	−0.0448***	−0.00714			
	(0.00733)	(0.0130)	(0.0175)			
Obs.	19	19	19			
R-squared	0.255	0.410	0.010			

Source: D'Aoust, Galdo, and Ianchovichina 2023.

Note: For Mexico, the analysis is based on census data for all periods, whereas in Brazil it is based on census data only for the period 2000–2010. For the rest of the countries, the analysis is based on Socio-Economic Database for Latin America and the Caribbean (SEDLAC) harmonized household surveys. Only in Colombia (2011–19) the analysis is based on official aggregates of value-added data. Obs. = observations. Y_0 stands for real per capita household labor income. Whenever possible, results are presented for three periods: the longest possible period that extends from the early 2000s (or 1990s in Mexico) to the late 2010s (or mid-2010s in some cases); the period between the early 2000s (or 1990 in Mexico) and the late 2000s; and the period between the early 2010s and the late 2010s (or mid-2010s in some cases).

Significance level: * = 10 percent, ** = 5 percent, *** = 1 percent.

TABLE 2C.2 Absolute convergence in labor productivity premia at two administrative levels by country and time period

Country and variables	Annual labor productivity premium growth					
	First administrative level			Second administrative level		
Argentina	2003/05–2017/19	2003/05–2009/11	2009/11–2017/19			
γ_0^{bs}	−0.0170*** (0.00412)	−0.00892 (0.00728)	−0.0366*** (0.0102)			
Obs.	29	29	29			
R-squared	0.387	0.053	0.325			
Bolivia	2001/02–2017/19	2001/02–2011/13	2011/13–2017/19			
γ_0^{bs}	−0.0283*** (0.00548)	−0.0260* (0.0136)	−0.0594*** (0.0148)			
Obs.	9	9	9			
R-squared	0.792	0.345	0.698			
Brazil	2002/04–2014/15	2000–2010	2009/11–2014/15	2002/04–2014/15	2000–2010	2009/11–2014/15
γ_0^{bs}	−0.0155*** (0.00449)	−0.00506 (0.00477)	−0.0185* (0.00920)	−0.0912*** (0.00219)	−0.00913*** (0.000487)	−0.106*** (0.0104)
Obs.	27	27	27	817	2,040	817
R-squared	0.322	0.043	0.140	0.680	0.147	0.112
Chile	2000/03–2015/17	2000/03–2009/11	2009/11–2015/17	2000/03–2015/17	2000/03–2009/11	2009/11–2015/17
γ_0^{bs}	−0.0189*** (0.00289)	−0.0222*** (0.00491)	−0.0252 (0.0149)	−0.0206*** (0.00116)	−0.0244*** (0.00185)	−0.0311*** (0.00382)
Obs.	13	13	13	299	299	299
R-squared	0.796	0.651	0.206	0.514	0.369	0.183
Colombia	2001/03–2017/19	2001/03–2008/10	2011–19			2011–19
γ_0^{bs}	−0.0341*** (0.00774)	−0.0696*** (0.0163)	−0.0244*** (0.00694)			−0.0319*** (0.00187)
Obs.	24	24	33			1,122
R-squared	0.469	0.453	0.286			0.206
Costa Rica		2001/03–2008/09			2001/03–2008/09	
γ_0^{bs}		−0.0160 (0.0113)			−0.0231*** (0.00580)	
Obs.		7			79	
R-squared		0.288			0.171	
Dominican Republic	2000/02–2014/16	2000/02–2008/10	2008/10–2014/16	2000/02–2014/16	2000/02–2008/10	2008/10–2014/16
γ_0^{bs}	−0.0221*** (0.00685)	−0.0234** (0.00870)	−0.0141 (0.0103)	−0.0380*** (0.00408)	−0.0595*** (0.00631)	−0.0478*** (0.0114)
Obs.	30	30	30	115	115	115
R-squared	0.270	0.205	0.063	0.434	0.440	0.135
Ecuador	2003/04–2017/19	2003/04–2009/11	2009/11–2017/19	2003/04–2017/19	2003/04–2009/11	2009/11–2017/19
γ_0^{bs}	−0.0340*** (0.0107)	−0.0565*** (0.0132)	−0.0158 (0.0244)	−0.0397*** (0.00325)	−0.0453*** (0.00536)	−0.0547*** (0.00667)
Obs.	21	21	21	191	191	191
R-squared	0.348	0.492	0.021	0.442	0.275	0.263

(Continued on next page)

TABLE 2C.2 Absolute convergence in labor productivity premia at two administrative levels by country and time period *(continued)*

Country and variables	Annual labor productivity premium growth					
	First administrative level			**Second administrative level**		
Honduras	2004/06–2017/19	2004/06–2009/11	2009/11–2017/19	2004/06–2017/19	2004/06–2009/11	2009/11–2017/19
γ_0^{bs}	−0.0221***	−0.0351***	−0.0188	−0.0318***	−0.0577***	−0.0513***
	(0.00667)	(0.0114)	(0.0137)	(0.00332)	(0.00593)	(0.00712)
Obs.	16	16	16	243	243	243
R-squared	0.440	0.403	0.119	0.275	0.281	0.177
Mexico	1990–2015	2000–2010	2000–2015	1990–2015	2000–2010	2000–2015
γ_0^{bs}	−0.00817**	−0.0163***	−0.0186***	−0.0217***	−0.0256***	−0.0231***
	(0.00373)	(0.00550)	(0.00467)	(0.000403)	(0.00104)	(0.000671)
Obs.	32	32	32	2,301	2,330	2,320
R-squared	0.138	0.225	0.345	0.558	0.207	0.338
Panama	2001/03–2017/19	2001/03–2009/11	2009/11–2017/19			
γ_0^{bs}	−0.00534	0.00173	−0.0171			
	(0.00517)	(0.00524)	(0.0129)			
Obs.	12	12	12			
R-squared	0.096	0.011	0.151			
Peru	2000/03–2017/19	2000/03–2008/10	2008/10–2017/19	2000/03–2017/19	2000/03–2008/10	2008/10–2017/19
γ_0^{bs}	−0.0129***	−0.0122*	−0.0170**	−0.0199***	−0.0243***	−0.0247***
	(0.00419)	(0.00720)	(0.00679)	(0.00175)	(0.00350)	(0.00299)
Obs.	24	24	24	186	186	186
R-squared	0.301	0.113	0.222	0.413	0.208	0.270
Uruguay	2000/02–2017/19	2000/02–2008/10	2008/10–2017/19			
γ_0^{bs}	−0.0121**	−0.0270***	0.00242			
	(0.00553)	(0.00924)	(0.00885)			
Obs.	19	19	19			
R-squared	0.219	0.334	0.004			

Source: D'Aoust, Galdo, and Ianchovichina 2023.

Note: γ_0^{bs} refers to the initial location premium before sorting or to the labor productivity premium. Location premia before sorting are estimated by regressing $\ln(y_{h,t,t}) = \gamma_i + \theta_t + \varepsilon_{h,i,t}$, where y is per capita income expressed in 2011 purchasing power parity (PPP). For Mexico, the analysis is based on census data for all periods, whereas in Brazil it is based on census data only for the period 2000–2010. For the rest of the countries, the analysis is based on Socio-Economic Database for Latin America and the Caribbean (SEDLAC) harmonized household surveys. Only in Colombia (2011–19) the analysis is based on official aggregates of value-added data. Whenever possible, results are presented for three periods: the longest possible period that extends from the early 2000s (or 1990s in Mexico) to the late 2010s (or mid-2010s in some cases); the period between the early 2000s (or 1990 in Mexico) and the late 2000s; and the period between the early 2010s and the late 2010s (or mid-2010s in some cases). Obs. = observations. Significance level: * = 10 percent, ** = 5 percent, *** = 1 percent.

TABLE 2C.3 Estimations of absolute convergence/divergence in place productivity prèmia at two administrative levels by country and time period

Country and variables	Annual place productivity premium growth					
	First administrative level			Second administrative level		
Argentina	2003/05–2017/19	2003/05–2009/11	2009/11–2017/19			
γ_0^{as}	−0.0125** (0.00598)	−0.00396 (0.00994)	−0.0379*** (0.0135)			
Obs.	29	29	29			
R-squared	0.139	0.006	0.226			
Bolivia	2001/02–2017/19	2001/02–2011/13	2011/13–2017/19			
γ_0^{as}	−0.0327*** (0.00423)	−0.0280** (0.0103)	−0.0704*** (0.0142)			
Obs.	9	9	9			
R-squared	0.895	0.516	0.779			
Brazil	2002/04–2014/15	2000–2010	2009/11–2014/15	2002/04–2014/15	2000–2010	2009/11–2014/15
γ_0^{as}	−0.0178*** (0.00548)	−0.0101 (0.00661)	−0.0207* (0.0120)	−0.0942*** (0.00213)	−0.0142*** (0.000657)	−0.129*** (0.0117)
Obs.	27	27	27	817	2,040	817
R-squared	0.295	0.086	0.106	0.706	0.186	0.129
Chile	2000/03–2015/17	2000/03–2009/11	2009/11–2015/17	2000/03–2015/17	2000/03–2009/11	2009/11–2015/17
γ_0^{as}	−0.0195*** (0.00397)	−0.0138* (0.00747)	−0.0424*** (0.0133)	−0.0173*** (0.00162)	−0.0178*** (0.00251)	−0.0371*** (0.00458)
Obs.	13	13	13	299	299	299
R-squared	0.687	0.236	0.481	0.278	0.145	0.181
Colombia	2001/03–2017/19	2001/03–2008/10	2008/10–2017/19			
γ_0^{as}	−0.0443*** (0.00888)	−0.0775*** (0.0217)	−0.0385*** (0.0112)			
Obs.	24	24	24			
R-squared	0.531	0.367	0.351			
Costa Rica		2001/03–2008/09			2001/03–2008/09 ·	
γ_0^{as}		−0.00782 (0.0215)			−0.0307*** (0.00753)	
Obs.		7			79	
R-squared		0.026			0.177	
Dominican Republic	2000/02–2014/16	2000/02–2008/10	2008/10–2014/16	2000/02–2014/16	2000/02–2008/10	2008/10–2014/16
γ_0^{as}	−0.0239*** (0.00742)	−0.0250** (0.00979)	−0.0214 (0.0132)	−0.0413*** (0.00396)	−0.0609*** (0.00676)	−0.0713*** (0.0113)
Obs.	30	30	30	115	115	115
R-squared	0.270	0.190	0.085	0.491	0.418	0.260
Ecuador	2003/04–2017/19	2003/04–2009/11	2009/11–2017/19	2003/04–2017/19	2003/04–2009/11	2009/11–2017/19
γ_0^{as}	−0.0496*** (0.0100)	−0.0504*** (0.0162)	−0.0695*** (0.0221)	−0.0504*** (0.00309)	−0.0617*** (0.00632)	−0.0809*** (0.00677)
Obs.	21	21	21	191	191	191
R-squared	0.562	0.339	0.342	0.584	0.336	0.431

(Continued on next page)

TABLE 2C.3 **Estimations of absolute convergence/divergence in place productivity premia at two administrative levels by country and time period** *(continued)*

Country and variables	Annual place productivity premium growth					
	First administrative level			Second administrative level		
Honduras	2004/06–2017/19	2004/06–2009/11	2009/11–2017/19	2004/06–2017/19	2004/06–2009/11	2009/11–2017/19
γ_0^{as}	−0.0253**	−0.0326*	−0.0307*	−0.0413***	−0.0669***	−0.0694***
	(0.00944)	(0.0181)	(0.0165)	(0.00364)	(0.00656)	(0.00760)
Obs.	16	16	16	243	243	243
R-squared	0.338	0.188	0.199	0.349	0.301	0.257
Mexico	1990–2015	2000–2010	2000–2015	1990–2015	2000–2010	2000–2015
γ_0^{as}	−0.0145***	−0.0275***	−0.0265***	−0.0263***	−0.0330***	−0.0278***
	(0.00384)	(0.00626)	(0.00540)	(0.000372)	(0.00109)	(0.000687)
Obs.	32	32	32	2,301	2,330	2,320
R-squared	0.323	0.392	0.445	0.686	0.283	0.413
Panama	2001/03–2017/19	2001/03–2009/11	2009/11–2017/19			
γ_0^{as}	−0.0190	0.00568	−0.0515*			
	(0.0133)	(0.0123)	(0.0265)			
Obs.	12	12	12			
R-squared	0.168	0.021	0.274			
Peru	2000/03–2017/19	2000/03–2008/10	2008/10–2017/19	2000/03–2017/19	2000/03–2008/10	2008/10–2017/19
γ_0^{as}	−0.0186***	−0.0122	−0.0286***	−0.0268***	−0.0357***	−0.0317***
	(0.00639)	(0.0124)	(0.00818)	(0.00208)	(0.00427)	(0.00362)
Obs.	24	24	24	186	186	186
R-squared	0.278	0.042	0.356	0.474	0.275	0.294
Uruguay	2000/02–2017/19	2000/02–2008/10	2008/10–2017/19			
γ_0^{as}	−0.0206***	−0.0416***	−0.00549			
	(0.00658)	(0.0110)	(0.0138)			
Obs.	19	19	19			
R-squared	0.364	0.457	0.009			

Source: D'Aoust, Galdo, and Ianchovichina 2023.
Note: γ_0^{as} refers to the place productivity premium, or the location premium after sorting, estimated by regressing $\ln(y_{h,l,t}) = \gamma_l + \psi HC_{h,l,t} + \theta_t + \varepsilon_{h,l,t}$, where y is per capita income expressed in 2011 purchasing power parity (PPP). For Mexico, the analysis is based on census data for all periods, whereas in Brazil it is based on census data only for the period 2000–2010. For the rest of the countries, the analysis is based on the Socio-Economic Database for Latin America and the Caribbean (SEDLAC) harmonized household surveys. Obs. = observations.
Significance level: * = 10 percent, ** = 5 percent, *** = 1 percent.

Notes

1. Institutions change slowly over time, potentially creating conditions for spatial inequality and poverty traps (Galvis and Meisel Roca 2012).
2. See, for example, Aroca, Bosch, and Maloney (2005); Escobal and Ponce (2011); Galvis and Meisel Roca (2010, 2012); González Rivas (2007).
3. Escobal and Torero (2005) empirically connect poor local road infrastructure to higher transaction costs, lower market participation, and reduced household incomes.
4. In countries with federal systems (such as Brazil and Mexico), state and local governments have the authority to change laws (including taxes and administrative charges) and de jure and de facto institutions (such as the degree of enforcement of national laws, the functioning of the judiciary, and the degree of de facto control by local elites). Dell (2010) links the poor outcomes of some communities to the long-run effects of the *mita,* an extensive forced mining labor system in effect in Bolivia and Peru during the colonial era that lowered incomes and access to education and infrastructure. Acemoglu et al. (2007) emphasize the link between political inequality in nineteenth-century Cundinamarca, Colombia, and its current economic outcomes. Similar conclusions are drawn by Naritomi, Soares, and Assunção (2007) for Brazil.
5. In Mexico, convergence was observed up to the mid-1980s but not afterward.
6. The countries are Brazil, Chile, Colombia, Ecuador, El Salvador, Guatemala, Mexico, Nicaragua, and Peru.
7. Davalos et al. (2015) reach a similar conclusion of income convergence using municipality-level income data for Mexico from 1990 to 2010, while López-Calva, Ortiz-Juarez, and Rodriguez-Castelan (2021) find absolute convergence from 1992 to 2014 using a unique five-wave panel data set on municipalities. The convergence process in both cases stemmed from a combination of positive developments in poor municipalities and stagnation or negative growth in richer ones.
8. The terms *place productivity* and *location productivity premia* are used interchangeably throughout this report.
9. Portable characteristics include the gender of the household head, household size, age of the household head and household members along with their squared values, the household head's level of education and employment status, and the highest educational attainment in the household. The inclusion of many observable characteristics addresses issues related to sorting and mitigates to some extent the omission of unobservable nongeographic characteristics such as entrepreneurial spirit and commitment to hard work. Time-fixed effects control for exogenous shocks such as commodity price fluctuations.
10. Static productivity gains stem from agglomeration economies, while dynamic productivity gains derive from learning by working. De La Roca and Puga (2017) provide evidence that the additional value of experience gained in bigger cities persists after leaving the city.
11. Glaeser, Kolko, and Saiz (2001) argue that consumption amenities such as restaurants, stores, and public services are important for attracting firms and skilled workers, who tend to earn higher incomes and place greater value on the quality and variety of amenities. Big cities supply a greater variety and quality of amenities because they are bigger markets. Diamond (2016) finds that in the United States from 1980 to 2000 changes in the local labor demand were the primary reason for the increased skill sorting, but amenities also adjusted to reinforce this effect in the United States from 1980 to 2000.
12. Location premia after sorting cannot be estimated by type of settlement in Colombia because SEDLAC data do not offer household information below the first administrative level.
13. Adão (2015) documents an increase of 8–16 percent in the commodity wage premium (relative to noncommodities) in Brazil due to the rise in world commodity prices from 1991 to 2010.
14. Dix-Carneiro and Kovak (2017) and Costa, Garred, and Pessoa (2016) also show, respectively, that trade liberalization and the "China Shock" reduced regional inequality in Brazil. It is beyond the scope of the report to determine the extent to which individual drivers of deindustrialization have contributed to reductions in territorial inequality in the LAC region. The effects

of these forces are both context- and time horizon–specific and require an in-depth look into countries' institutions, economic structure, and market organization (Dix-Carneiro and Kovak 2023; Goldberg 2015).

15. The results for Mexico presented in this chapter are consistent with those in López-Calva, Ortiz-Juarez, and Rodriguez-Castelan (2021), who find absolute convergence in total incomes and poverty in Mexico from 2000 to 2014. They attribute the convergence to positive developments in the poorest municipalities and the stagnant or deteriorating performance of affluent ones, as well as the role of redistributive programs. D'Aoust, Galdo, and Ianchovichina (2023) find absolute convergence even in the absence of redistributive transfers.

References

Acemoglu, D., M. A. Bautista, P. Querubín, and J. A. Robinson. 2007. "Economic and Political Inequality in Development: The Case of Cundinamarca, Colombia." NBER Working Paper 13208, National Bureau of Economic Research, Cambridge, MA.

Acemoglu, D., and M. Dell. 2010. "Productivity Differences between and within Countries." *American Economic Journal: Macroeconomics* 2 (1): 169–88.

Adão, R. 2015. "Worker Heterogeneity, Wage Inequality, and International Trade: Theory and Evidence from Brazil." Massachusetts Institute of Technology, Cambridge, MA. https://economics.yale.edu/sites/default/files/adao_jmp_2015.pdf.

Aroca, P., M. Bosch, and W. F. Maloney. 2005. "Spatial Dimensions of Trade Liberalization and Economic Convergence: Mexico 1985–2002." Policy Research Working Paper 3744, World Bank, Washington, DC.

Azzoni, C. 2001. "Economic Growth and Regional Income Inequality in Brazil." *Annals of Regional Science* 35: 133–52.

Chiquiar, D. 2005. "Why Mexico's Regional Income Convergence Broke Down." *Journal of Development Economics* 77: 257–75.

Costa, F., J. Garred, and J. P. Pessoa. 2016. "Winners and Losers from a Commodities-for-Manufactures Trade Boom." *Journal of International Economics* 102: 50–69.

D'Aoust, O., V. Galdo, and E. Ianchovichina. 2023. "Territorial Productivity Differences and Dynamics within Latin American Countries." Policy Research Working Paper 10480, World Bank, Washington, DC.

Davalos, M., G. Esquivel, L. F. López-Calva, and C. Rodríguez-Castelán. 2015. "Convergence with Stagnation: Mexico's Growth at the Municipal Level 1990–2010." Working Paper No. 2015-001, Sobre Mexico.

De La Roca, J., and D. Puga. 2017. "Learning by Working in Big Cities." *Review of Economic Studies* 84: 106–42.

Dell, M. 2010. "The Persistent Effects of Peru's Mining *Mita*." *Econometrica* 78 (6): 1863–1903.

Diamond, R. 2016. "The Determinants and Welfare Implications of US Workers' Diverging Location Choices by Skill: 1980–2000." *American Economic Review* 106 (3): 479–524.

Dix-Carneiro, R., and B. Kovak. 2017. "Trade Liberalization and Regional Dynamics." *American Economic Review* 107 (10): 2908–46.

Dix-Carneiro, R., and B. Kovak. 2019. "Margins of Labor Market Adjustment to Trade." *Journal of International Economics* 117: 125–42.

Dix-Carneiro, R., and B. Kovak. 2023. "Globalization and Inequality in Latin America." Inter-American Development Bank, Washington, DC.

Escobal, J., and C. Ponce. 2011. "Access to Public Infrastructure, Institutional Thickness and Pro-poor Growth in Rural Peru." *Journal of International Development* 23 (3): 358–79.

Escobal, J., and C. Ponce. 2016. "Dinámicas provinciales de pobreza en el Perú, 1993–2007." In *Los dilemas territoriales del desarrollo en América Latina,* edited by Modrego Benito and J. A. Berdegué. Bogotá: Ediciones Uniandes.

Escobal, J., and M. Torero. 2005. "Adverse Geography and Differences in Welfare in Peru." In *Spatial Inequality and Development*, edited by Ravi Kanbur and Anthony Venables, 17–122. New York: Oxford University Press.

Faber, B., and C. Gaubert. 2019. "Tourism and Economic Development: Evidence from Mexico's Coastline." *American Economic Review* 109 (6): 2245–93.

Favareto, A., and R. Abramovay. 2016. "Contrastes territoriales de los indicadores de ingreso, pobreza monetaria y desigualdad en el Brasil de los años noventa." In *Los dilemas territoriales del desarrollo en América Latina,* edited by F. Modrego Benito and J. A. Berdegué. Bogotá: Ediciones Uniandes.

Fernández, M., C. Hernández, A. M. Ibáñez, and C. Jaramillo. 2016. "Dinámicas provinciales de pobreza en Colombia 1993–2005." In *Los dilemas territoriales del desarrollo en América Latina*, edited by F. Modrego Benito and J. A. Berdegué. Bogotá: Ediciones Uniandes.

Galvis, L. A., and A. Meisel Roca. 2010. "Persistencia de las desigualdades regionales en Colombia: Un análisis espacial." Documento de trabajo sobre economía regional no. 120, Banco de la República, Colombia.

Galvis, L. A., and A. Meisel Roca. 2012. "Convergencia y trampas espaciales de pobreza en Colombia: Evidencia reciente." Documento de trabajo sobre economía regional no. 177, Banco de la República, Colombia.

Glaeser, E., J. Kolko, and A. Saiz. 2001. "Consumer City." *Journal of Economic Geography* 1 (1): 27–50.

Goldberg, P. 2015. *Trade and Inequality.* Edward Elgar Research Collections. Cheltenham, UK: Edward Elgar.

González Rivas, M. 2007. "The Effects of Trade Openness on Regional Inequality in Mexico." *Annals of Regional Science* 41: 545–61.

Iacovone, L., L. Sanchez-Bayardo, and S. Sharma. 2015. "Regional Productivity Convergence in Peru." Policy Research Working Paper 7499, World Bank, Washington, DC.

Jedwab, R., E. Ianchovichina, and F. Haslop. 2022. "Consumption Cities versus Production Cities: New Considerations and Evidence." Policy Research Working Paper 10105, World Bank, Washington, DC.

Kovak, B. 2013. "Regional Effects of Trade Reform: What Is the Correct Measure of Liberalization?" *American Economic Review* 103: 1960–76.

Larrea, C., R. Landín, A. I. Larrea, A. W. Wrborich, and R. Fraga. 2016. "Mapas de pobreza, consumo per cápita y desigualdad social en Ecuador: 1995–2006." In *Los dilemas territoriales del desarrollo en América Latina,* edited by F. Modrego Benito and J. A. Berdegué. Bogotá: Ediciones Uniandes.

Li, Y., and M. Rama. 2015. "Households or Locations? Cities, Catchment Areas and Prosperity in India." Policy Research Working Paper 7473, World Bank, Washington DC.

López-Calva, L., E. Ortiz-Juarez, and C. Rodriguez-Castelan. 2021. "Within-Country Poverty Convergence: Evidence from Mexico." *Empirical Economics* 62: 2547–86.

Mesquita Moreira, M., J. Blyde, C. Volpe, and D. Molina. 2013. *Too Far to Export: Domestic Transport Costs and Regional Export Disparities in Latin America and the Caribbean.* Washington, DC: Inter-American Development Bank.

Modrego, F., and J. Berdegué. 2016. "Large-Scale Mapping of Territorial Development Dynamics in Latin America." *World Development* 73: 11–31.

Modrego, F., E. Ramírez, A. Tartakowsky, and E. Jara. 2016. "La heterogeneidad territorial del desarrollo en la década de oro de la economía Chilena." In *Los dilemas territoriales del desarrollo en América Latina*, edited by F. Modrego Benito and J. A. Berdegué. Bogotá: Ediciones Uniandes.

Naritomi, J., R. Soares, and J. Assunção. 2007. "Rent Seeking and the Unveiling of 'De Facto' Institutions: Development and Colonial Heritage within Brazil." NBER Working Paper 13545, National Bureau of Economic Research, Cambridge, MA.

Olfert, R., M. Partridge, J. Berdegué, J. Escobal, B. Jara, and F. Modrego. 2014. "Places for Place-Based Policies." *Development Policy Review* 32 (1): 5–32.

Ponczek, V., and G. Ulyssea. 2022. "Enforcement of Labour Regulation and Labour Market Effects of Trade: Evidence from Brazil." *Economic Journal* 132 (641): 361–90.

Quintero, L., and M. Roberts. 2018. "Explaining Spatial Variations in Productivity: Evidence from Latin America and the Caribbean." Policy Research Working Paper 8560, World Bank, Washington, DC.

Rodríguez, J. 2011. "Migración interna y sistema de ciudades en América Latina: Intensidad, patrones, efectos y potenciales determinantes, censos de la década de 2000" (Internal Migration and the Latin American System of Cities: Intensity, Patterns, Impacts and Potential Determinants 2000 Census Round). *Serie población y desarrollo n° 105 (LC/L.3351)*. Santiago: United Nations Economic Commission for Latin America and the Caribbean.

Romero, W., and P. Zapil Ajxup. 2009. "Dinámica territorial del consume, la pobreza y la desigualdad en Guatemala, 1998–2006." Rural Territorial Dynamics Program, Latin American Center for Rural Development (RIMISP), Santiago, Chile.

Rowe, F. 2014. "The Effects of Economic Liberalisation on Inter-Regional Labour Migration in a Transition Economy, Chile." Conference paper, 2014 Tinbergen Workshop: Real People in Virtual Space, Amsterdam.

Sánchez-Reaza, J., and A. Rodríguez-Pose. 2002. "The Impact of Trade Liberalization on Regional Disparities in Mexico." *Growth and Change* 33 (1): 72–90.

Serra, M., M. Pazmino, G. Lindow, B. Sutton, and G. Ramírez. 2006. "Regional Convergence in Latin America." IMF Working Paper WP/06/125, International Monetary Fund, Washington, DC.

Skoufias, E., and G. López-Acevedo. 2009. *Determinants of Regional Welfare Disparities within Latin American Countries*, Vol. 1, *Synthesis*. Washington, DC: World Bank.

Sotelo, S. 2020. "Domestic Trade Frictions and Agriculture." *Journal of Political Economy* 128 (7): 2690–738.

Venables, A. 2017. "Breaking into Tradables: Urban Form and Urban Function in a Developing City." *Journal of Urban Economics* 98 (C): 88–97.

Yúnez Naude, A., J. Arellano González, and J. Méndez Navarro. 2016. "Dinámica del consumo, pobreza y desigualdad municipal en México: 1990–2005." In *Los dilemas territoriales del desarrollo en América Latina*, edited by Modrego Benito and J. A. Berdegué. Bogotá: Ediciones Uniandes.

Productivity Differences with Leading Metropolitan Areas

3

During the Golden Decade (2003–13), the strong demand for commodities increased investments and employment in geographically dispersed rural and mining areas throughout Latin America (Rodríguez 2011; Rowe 2014). By the early 2000s, secondary cities had replaced rural areas as the primary source of migrants to the largest metropolitan areas (Rodríguez 2011). But moving to a larger city did not guarantee success because well-paid formal manufacturing jobs had become scarcer due to deindustrialization (Beylis et al. 2020; Jedwab, Ianchovichina, and Haslop 2022). This chapter analyzes the size and sources of income differences with the largest metropolitan areas in 14 countries in Latin America and the Caribbean (LAC) and the potential for socioeconomic groups to benefit from migration to these cities.

Territorial inequality and migration

In a comprehensive study based on household surveys from the early 2000s, Skoufias and López-Acevedo (2009) document the spatial differences in welfare and their determinants within and across geographic regions above the first administrative level in eight LAC countries.[1] They find that in any given geographic region rural areas were poorer than urban areas, mostly because of differences in education and not differences in returns to education, signaling that in the early 2000s the potential for spatial arbitrage[2] was relatively small in the geographic regions considered in the eight countries. By contrast, differences in returns to education accounted for a larger share of the welfare gap between geographic regions, pointing to greater opportunities for improving welfare from migration over longer distances.

Skoufias and López-Acevedo (2009) also examine the profile of domestic migrants, their incentives to migrate, and the characteristics of sending and receiving regions. Their examination suggests that migrants in the early 2000s were typically young, well-educated, and relatively well-off individuals who moved to their countries' main leading metropolitan areas, mostly in search of better job opportunities, but also to gain access to better amenities, services, or safety in cases of conflict or natural disasters (such as in Colombia). By the early 2000s, secondary cities had become the primary sources of migrants to large urban centers (Rodríguez 2011) in line with the high degree of urbanization in Latin America (United Nations 2016) and the growth of tradable services in larger cities (Jedwab, Ianchovichina, and Haslop 2022), which increased the employment opportunities for those with education and skills.

Evidence from Indonesia presented in Bryan and Morten (2019) also points to sizable within-country productivity gaps. Using microdata spanning 40 years, they find that people tend to migrate to places closer to their homes because of the higher cost of migrating over longer distances,[3] and that amenities matter to workers in choosing a location. However, Bryan and Morten (2019) caution that policies aimed at lowering the barriers to migration may not result in aggregate productivity gains as large as those suggested by the within-country productivity gaps because sorting or selection can give rise to *unexploitable* productivity gaps. If leading metropolitan areas are more productive places because more productive people choose to live in them, then potential migrants will not be as productive as current residents in the leading areas, and encouraging them to move there will not boost incomes in a country. By contrast, a productivity gap is *exploitable through migration* if potential migrants could earn higher returns in another location but are deterred by high migration costs. These costs could arise from high travel costs, discrimination, cultural differences, low social capital, and the absence of networks that can provide migrants with information about affordable accommodations and job opportunities in destination cities. Poor conditions in locations where migrants could potentially earn higher income could also deter some migrants. These conditions could include pollution, crime, high rents, lack of amenities, and low-quality or insufficient public services.

Although they do not determine the extent to which spatial productivity gaps in Indonesia are exploitable, Bryan and Morten (2019) assess the output effects of two types of policies that reduce barriers to migration. Their assessment relies on a static general equilibrium model of costly migration in which workers sort into locations with heterogeneous amenities and productivities based on their comparative advantage. The first group of policies aims to lower the cost of migration through, for example, migration subsidies (Bryan, Chowdhury, and Mobarak 2014), migration centers, language training, and road building (Asher and Novosad 2020; Morten and Oliveira 2018). The second group of policies aims to lower the spatial dispersion of amenities by building housing in high-demand locations (Harari 2020; Hsieh and Moretti 2019), reducing pollution in large cities, or providing equitable access to health and education facilities. They find that economic output increases by 7.1 percent from reducing the migration costs to those in the United States and by 12.7 percent from equalizing amenities. The combined effect of the two policies is only slightly smaller than the sum of their separate effects, which suggests that the two policies are very weak substitutes. However, the aggregate effect hides substantial heterogeneity across origin populations, with real income change from reducing the migration costs to those in the United States of between −5 and 25 percent.

Why focus on leading metropolitan areas?

The leading metropolitan areas deserve special attention because they typically are countries' largest business centers and often their national capitals. In about one-third of countries in South America, two-fifths of the population lives in these primate cities, which are magnets for internal migrants, especially the skilled. As shown in figure 2.2 in chapter 2, the leading metropolitan areas are among the top 25 percent of the most productive localities in their respective countries, and in a few, place productivity is close to the maximum of the productivity distribution.

Map 2.1 in chapter 2 displays the leading metropolitan areas highlighted in this report. Because of its large size, Brazil's leading metropolitan area refers to three of its largest urban agglomerations: Belo Horizonte, Rio de Janeiro, and São Paulo. In all other countries except Ecuador and Panama, the largest city is the leading metropolitan area. In Ecuador, the country's capital, Quito, was chosen for that role. In Panama, urban Panamá Province is the leading metropolitan area; it includes Panama City.

Several questions guide the investigation described in this chapter. How much have the income gaps between the leading metropolitan areas and other areas of the countries changed since the early 2000s? To what extent do differences in endowments (or selection) explain the average income gaps and the endowments that contribute the most to these differences? To what extent are income differences exploitable through migration? How much does selection matter for different socioeconomic groups? This chapter draws on work by D'Aoust, Galdo, and Ianchovichina (2023) to answer these questions. It employs information on per capita household labor income from the Socio-Economic Database for Latin America and the Caribbean (SEDLAC) household surveys, pooled together into two periods (the early 2000s and the late 2000s) that align with the two periods used in the analysis of productivity premia and trends in chapter 2. Details on the survey years in the two periods and sample size in the pooled cross-sectional data appear in annex table 3A.1.

Income differences with leading metropolitan areas

The income differences with the leading Latin American metropolitan areas were large in many LAC countries in the early 2000s (figure 3.1). The difference was especially large in Peru, where the average per capita household labor income in Lima was almost three times the corresponding income in other parts of the country. The gaps were also large in Bolivia, Panama, and Paraguay.

FIGURE 3.1   Average labor income gap between the leading metropolitan area and the rest of a country's localities and its decomposition by country and period, LAC region

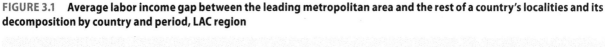

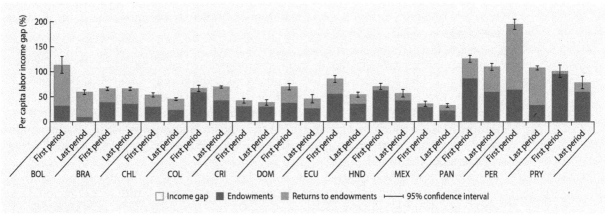

Source: D'Aoust, Galdo, and Ianchovichina 2023.
Note: The income gap is decomposed into an endowment component, capturing differences between the nongeographic household characteristics, such as education, demographics, and employment, in the leading metropolitan and other areas, and a returns-to-endowments component, capturing differences between the returns to these characteristics in the leading and other areas. The figure also shows the 95% confidence interval. To ensure comparability within and across countries, the per capita household labor earnings are deflated to adjust incomes for cost-of-living differences across space and time. Argentina and Uruguay are not included in the figure because the surveys in these countries cover only and mostly urban areas, respectively. The leading metropolitan areas and the respective first and last periods are as follows: Bolivia (BOL): Santa Cruz, 2001–02, 2015–19; Brazil (BRA): Belo Horizonte, Rio de Janeiro, and São Paulo, 2012–14, 2017–19; Chile (CHL): Santiago, 2000 and 2003; 2015 and 2017; Colombia (COL): Bogotá, 2001–03, 2017–19; Costa Rica (CRI): urban Central Valley region (includes San José and other main cities), 2001–03, 2008–09; the Dominican Republic (DOM): city of Santo Domingo, 2000–2002, 2014–16; Ecuador (ECU): Quito (urban Pichincha), 2003–04, 2017–19; Honduras (HND): urban Tegucigalpa (Francisco Morazán), 2004–06, 2017–19; Mexico (MEX): Mexico City metropolitan area, 2000, 2002, and 2004; 2016 and 2018; Panama (PAN): urban Panamá Province, 2001–03, 2017–19; Paraguay (PRY): Asunción, 2002–04, 2017–19; Peru (PER): Lima, 2000–2003, 2017–19.

Over the last two decades, absolute income convergence narrowed to different degrees the income differences with the leading metropolitan areas of countries. And yet by the end of the 2010s, sizable differences with the leading cities were observed in all countries. The gaps remained especially high in Panama, Paraguay, and Peru (figure 3.1). In Panama, without much improvement over the last two decades, the average income level in urban Panamá Province remained at twice the income level in the rest of the country. In Peru, despite a substantial decline in the income gap between the early 2000s and the late 2010s, the average per capita household labor income in Lima was about twice the corresponding income in the rest of the country.

Small income gaps that can be exploited through migration to leading cities

The gaps due to differences in the returns to endowments also declined, except in Brazil, Colombia, Honduras, Mexico, Panama, and Paraguay (figure 3.1). These results are consistent with the decrease in the difference between the location premium in the leading metropolitan area (γ) and the median location premium (γ_{I50}) in Colombia, Honduras, and Panama, as shown in annex table 3B.1.[4] In theory, these gaps—measured by the estimated difference in returns to portable endowments in the leading metropolitan and other areas (see annex box 3B.1 for details)—capture the static effects of any barriers to migration. However, the differences in returns may also reflect differences arising from measurement errors in the nongeographic characteristics, which could bias the estimated differences in returns and therefore affect the interpretation of the results for policy purposes. For example, because the quality of education in lagging regions or secondary cities is likely lower than the quality in the leading metropolitan area, the returns to education in the lagging region or secondary city will appear lower than the returns to education in the leading area, although the returns to the quality-adjusted years of education may be the same.[5] Furthermore, the differences in returns do not capture the dynamic productivity gains from migration to the leading cities, which have been shown by De La Roca and Puga (2017) to be lasting and sizable. Nevertheless, the findings of declining and relatively small income gaps that can be exploited through migration in most LAC countries are consistent with those in Conte and Ianchovichina (2022) of a relatively small dispersion in entry migration barriers across locations within LAC countries, as reported in chapter 4.

By the late 2010s, the income gaps with the leading metropolitan areas were explained mostly by differences in returns to endowments only in Bolivia and Peru (figure 3.1). The large exploitable income gaps suggest that the typical household in these two countries may be able to increase its welfare by migrating to the leading agglomerations. In Brazil, Chile, and Panama, both differences in endowments and returns to these endowments explain the average income gaps, while in all other countries, differences in endowments explain most of the income gaps with leading metropolitan areas (figure 3.1).

Thus in most LAC countries the typical household may not be able to substantially increase its income by migrating to the leading cities. Instead, differences in education explain the majority of the average income gaps with the leading agglomerations (table 3.1). This explanation is consistent with the fact that the leading metropolitan areas in the region attract the educated and those with skills (Ferreyra and Roberts 2018), whereas differences in household demographics and the type of employment in which the household head is engaged play a much smaller role. The next sections explore the heterogeneity of the income gaps across population groups and the extent to which they might be able to benefit from moving to the leading metropolitan area.

TABLE 3.1   Income gaps and the role of endowment differences: LAC region, end of the 2010s

| Country | Per capita labor income (US$, PPP) | | Income gap (%) | Potential increase in income if equal endowments (%) | Endowment (%) | | |
	Leading metropolitan area	Rest of country			Education	Employment	Demographics
Argentina	596.6	341.8	75	43	67	4	30
Bolivia	336.4	211.5	59	8	64	40	−4
Brazil	306.2	184.7	66	32	88	−2	14
Chile	552.8	381.0	45	21	96	3	*1*
Colombia	392.3	231.7	69	38	64	11	25
Costa Rica	455.4	328.9	38	29	81	*1*	18
Dominican Republic	371.3	255.0	46	25	96	*4*	*0*
Ecuador	316.4	205.4	54	33	55	10	36
Honduras	233.6	149.1	57	40	77	*3*	20
Mexico	212.4	160.1	33	22	65	*−1*	36
Panama	608.4	290.2	110	50	59	18	23
Paraguay	532.1	298.3	78	56	66	15	19
Peru	354.2	170.6	108	26	67	12	21
Uruguay	589.7	388.5	52	30	79	7	13

Source: D'Aoust, Galdo, and Ianchovichina 2023.
Note: Results in italics are not significant. Only urban households are included in the samples for Argentina and Uruguay. The last period for most countries is 2017–19, except Chile, 2015 and 2017; Costa Rica, 2008–09; the Dominican Republic, 2014–16; and Mexico, 2016 and 2018. Countries and their leading metropolitan areas are Argentina, Buenos Aires; Bolivia, Santa Cruz; Brazil, Belo Horizonte, Rio de Janeiro, and São Paulo; Chile, Santiago; Colombia, Bogotá; Costa Rica, San José; the Dominican Republic, Santo Domingo; Ecuador, Quito (urban Pichincha); Honduras, urban Tegucigalpa (Francisco Morazán); Mexico, Mexico City; Panama, urban Panamá Province; Paraguay, Asunción; Peru, Lima-Callao region; Uruguay, Montevideo. PPP = purchasing power parity.

High migration barriers for residents of the poorest remote regions

When decomposed by first-level administrative region, the income gaps vary considerably in size within countries, as shown in map 3.1. They are largest for the residents of some of the poorest regions in, for example, remote parts of Argentina's and Brazil's northeast, Colombia's peripheral regions, Mexico's south, and Peru's north and northeast. The variation in income gaps across regions mostly reflects variations in returns to endowments rather than variations in the endowment differences with the leading city (figure 3.2).

Thus although, on average, barriers to migration are not particularly high, they tend to grow with distance and are highest for the residents of the poorest and most remote regions in line with empirical evidence in Skoufias and López-Acevedo (2009) and Bryan and Morten (2019). Distance matters for at least two reasons. First, the cost of travel between migrants' new location and their place of origin rises with distance. It is especially high in the large Latin American countries, where traveling by air is often the only way to access many remote parts in these countries because of the vast distances and the sparseness of national road and rail networks. Migrants' social capital also tends to decline with distance. The strength of migrant networks, which provide migrants with information, job opportunities, and even housing upon arrival in the destination city, tend to diminish with distance from the location of the migrant. The support of social networks is particularly important for the poorest residents, who have limited budgets and information. Location preferences and discrimination may also serve as barriers to migration. D'Aoust, Galdo, and Ianchovichina (2023) find that Afro-descendants and indigenous people in Brazil's north and northeast are significantly less likely to migrate out of their states than white residents with similar levels of education (figure 3.3).

MAP 3.1 Average labor income gaps by administrative region, largest Latin American economies

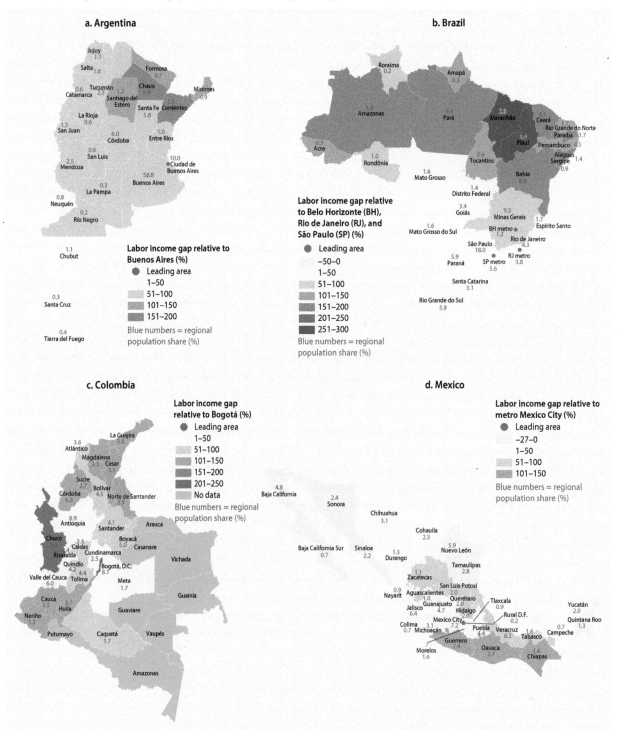

(Continued on next page)

MAP 3.1   Average labor income gaps by administrative region, largest Latin American economies *(continued)*

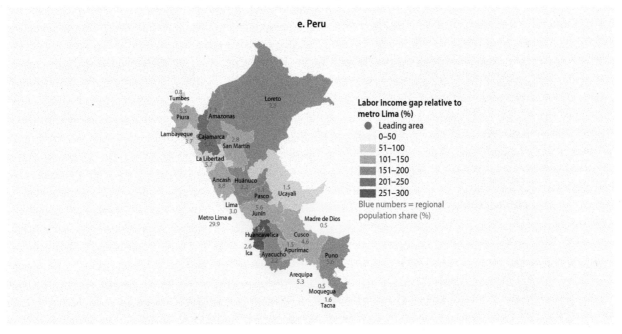

e. Peru

Labor income gap relative to
metro Lima (%)
- Leading area
- 0–50
- 51–100
- 101–150
- 151–200
- 201–250
- 251–300

Blue numbers = regional
population share (%)

Source: D'Aoust, Galdo, and Ianchovichina 2023.
Note: BH = Belo Horizonte; metro = metropolitan; RJ = Rio de Janeiro; rural D.F. = rural Mexico City; SP = São Paulo.

FIGURE 3.2   Decomposition of the average labor income gaps by administrative region, largest Latin American economies

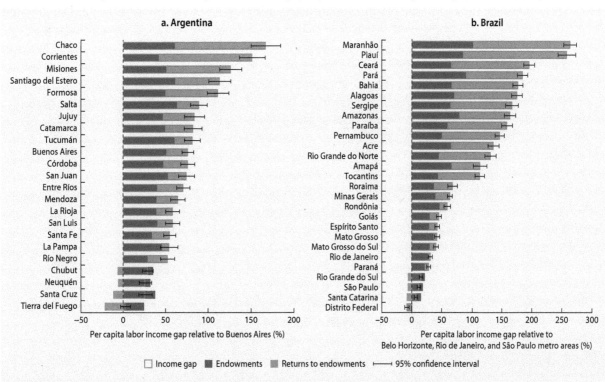

a. Argentina

b. Brazil

☐ Income gap   ■ Endowments   ■ Returns to endowments   ⊢———⊣ 95% confidence interval

(Continued on next page)

FIGURE 3.2   **Decomposition of the average labor income gaps by administrative region, largest Latin American economies**
(continued)

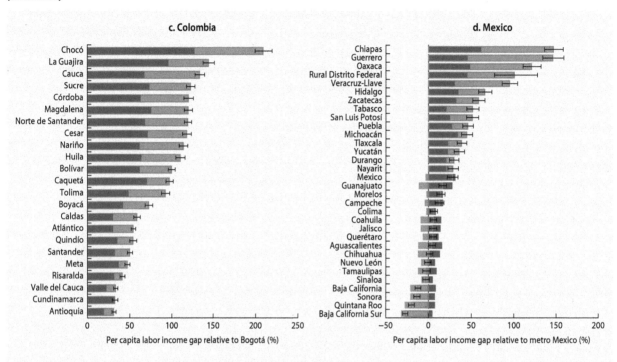

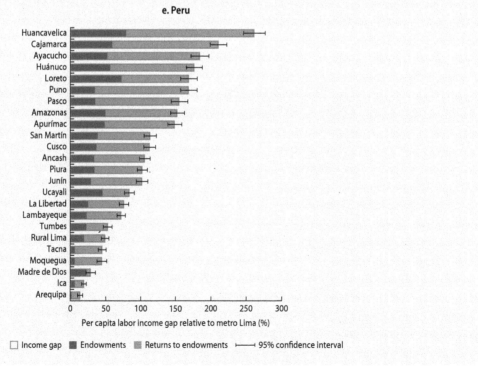

Source: D'Aoust, Galdo, and Ianchovichina 2023.
Note: Metro = metropolitan.

FIGURE 3.3   **Probability of adults leaving Brazil's most lagging states by race and level of education**

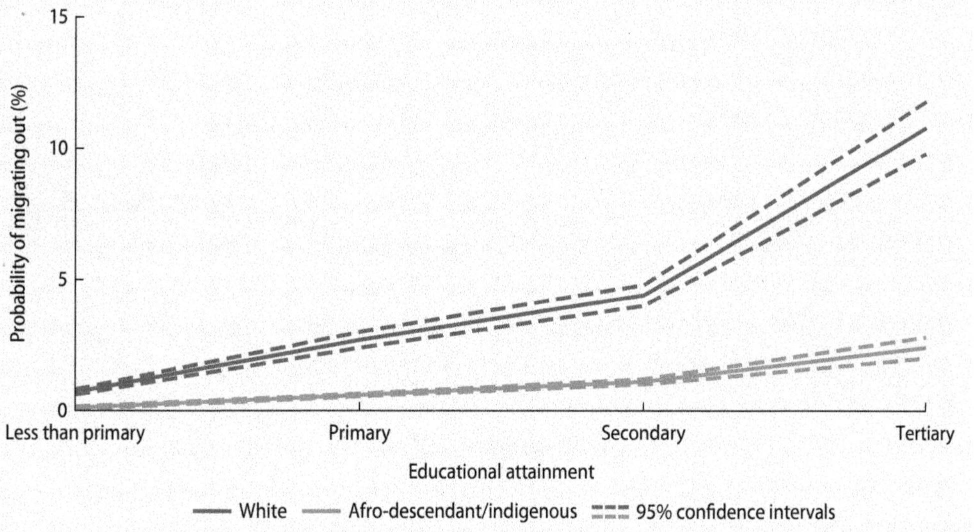

Source: D'Aoust, Galdo, and Ianchovichina 2023.
Note: Lagging states have an income gap of at least 50 percent. They are Acre, Alagoas, Amapá, Amazonas, Bahia, Ceará, Maranhão, Minas Gerais, Pará, Paraíba, Pernambuco, Piauí, Rio Grande do Norte, Rondônia, Roraima, Sergipe, and Tocantins.

Income differences with leading metropolitan areas vary across socioeconomic groups

Income differences with the leading metropolitan areas are generally smaller among urban residents (figure 3.4, panel a) than all households (figure 3.1), in line with the smaller differences in education between the leading metropolitan and secondary cities than between the leading metropolitan areas and the rest of the country, including rural areas. The urban income gaps are smallest (less than 25 percent) in Bolivia, Costa Rica, Honduras, and Mexico, whereas in the rest of the countries they are close to or above 50 percent because the typical urban household in the leading area is, on average, better educated and more productive than similarly endowed households in other urban localities in the country. In Argentina, Brazil, Ecuador, Paraguay, and Uruguay, the urban income gaps mostly reflect endowment deficits, whereas in Chile, Colombia, Panama, and Peru they mostly reflect differences in the returns to these endowments, indicating potentially greater welfare gains for urbanites migrating to the leading areas of these countries.

The income gaps among skilled households[6] are similar or smaller than those among urban households (figure 3.4, panels a and b). In the countries with small urban gaps, including Bolivia, Costa Rica, Ecuador, Honduras, and Mexico, the skilled income gaps

FIGURE 3.4   Average labor income gaps with the leading metropolitan areas and their decomposition by type of household, country, and period, LAC region

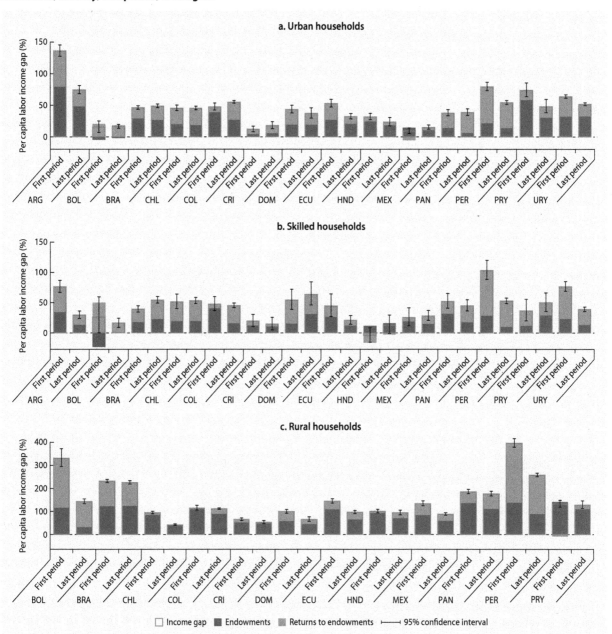

(Continued on next page)

FIGURE 3.4 **Average labor income gaps with the leading metropolitan areas and their decomposition by type of household, country, and period, LAC region** *(continued)*

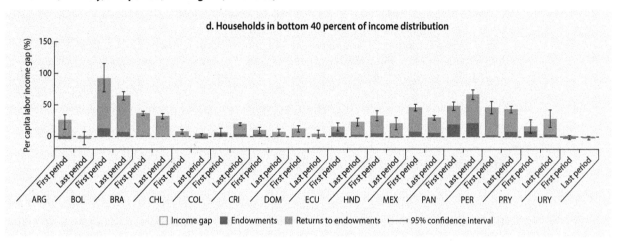

Source: D'Aoust, Galdo, and Ianchovichina 2023.

Note: The income gap is decomposed into an endowment component, capturing differences between the nongeographic household characteristics, such as education, demographics, and employment, in the leading and other areas, and a returns-to-endowments component, capturing differences between the returns to these characteristics in the leading and other areas. The figure also shows the 95% confidence interval. To ensure comparability within and across countries, the per capita household labor earnings are deflated to adjust incomes for cost-of-living differences across space and time. Argentina and Uruguay are not included in panel c because the surveys in these countries cover only and mostly urban areas, respectively. The leading metropolitan areas and the respective first and last periods are as follows: Argentina (ARG): city of Buenos Aires, 2003–05, 2017–19; Bolivia (BOL): Santa Cruz, 2001–02, 2015–19; Brazil (BRA): Belo Horizonte, Rio de Janeiro, and São Paulo, 2012–14, 2017–19; Chile (CHL): Santiago, 2000 and 2003; 2015 and 2017; Colombia (COL): Bogotá, 2001–03, 2017–19; Costa Rica (CRI): urban Central Valley region (includes San José and other main cities), 2001–03, 2008–09; the Dominican Republic (DOM): city of Santo Domingo, 2000–2002, 2014–16; Ecuador (ECU): Quito (urban Pichincha), 2003–04, 2017–19; Honduras (HND): urban Tegucigalpa (Francisco Morazán), 2004–06, 2017–19; Mexico (MEX): Mexico City metropolitan area, 2000, 2002, and 2004; 2016 and 2018; Panama (PAN): urban Panamá Province, 2001–03, 2017–19; Paraguay (PRY): Asunción, 2002–04, 2017–19; Peru (PER): Lima, 2000–2003, 2017–19; Uruguay (URY): Montevideo, 2000–2002, 2017–19.

are also low (around or below 25 percent). In Argentina and Uruguay, the skilled income gaps are smaller than the urban income gaps. The relatively large skilled income gaps (around 50 percent) in Brazil, Chile, Colombia, the Dominican Republic, Panama, and Peru can be attributed mainly to differences in returns to endowments, possibly reflecting barriers to migration due to deficits in the supply of affordable formal housing in these countries' leading cities. According to Bastos (2017), the growing shortage of affordable formal housing in Brazil may act as a deterrent, particularly of skilled workers, who might be more reluctant than the unskilled to live in informal housing of poor quality. Only in Paraguay can the skilled income gaps be attributed to differences in the endowments of the skilled households in the leading metropolitan area and the rest of the country.

The rural income gaps with leading metropolitan areas (figure 3.4, panel c) are much larger than the average income gaps for all households (figure 3.1) and the urban income gaps (figure 3.4, panel a). In most countries, as expected, these gaps can be primarily explained by deficits in education. Only in Bolivia and Peru do the rural gaps mainly reflect differences in the returns to endowments rather than differences in nongeographic household characteristics because both countries are less urbanized than other LAC countries and still have relatively large rural populations in remote, lagging regions. In Brazil, the gaps are large and can be explained both by differences in endowments and by differences in the returns to these endowments. Consequently, in these three countries there is still scope for lifting incomes through policies that reduce the barriers to rural-urban migration.

Migration to the leading metropolitan areas is unlikely to lift the incomes of those in the bottom 40 percent of the income distribution. In most Latin American countries, the income gaps with the leading areas are insignificant or very small among the bottom 40 percent households (figure 3.4, panel d).[7] The gaps are negligible in Argentina, Chile, Costa Rica, the Dominican Republic, and Uruguay. They are also close to or below 25 percent in Colombia, Ecuador, Honduras, Mexico, and Paraguay. Only in Bolivia, Brazil, Panama, and Peru are the income gaps among the bottom 40 percent around 50 percent. They can be explained mostly by differences in returns to endowments, not differences in endowments, suggesting that the bottom 40 percent in these countries might benefit from migration to their leading metropolitan areas.

Growing gender disparities in income gaps with leading metropolitan areas

One way to identify any systematic differences between genders in income gaps with the leading areas is to compare the female and male income gaps at the individual level.[8] Differences between female and male urban labor income gaps were relatively muted in the early 2000s (figure 3.5, panel a), except in Brazil, Mexico, and Uruguay. By the late 2010s, female urban income gaps had widened in Bolivia, Colombia, Ecuador, Peru, and Paraguay. However, only in Colombia had the female urban income gap deteriorated relative to the early 2000s.

The growing gender disparities in the income gaps with the leading metropolitan areas cannot be explained with growing gender disparities among skilled workers. In all countries except Colombia, there were no significant differences in the female and male skilled income gaps (figure 3.5, panel b). Among the bottom 40 percent, female income gaps became significantly larger than male income gaps only in Colombia, Mexico, and Uruguay (figure 3.5, panel d). In Colombia and Mexico, where information on rural residents is available, this development can be attributed to the increase in the female rural income gap. Such gaps also opened in Paraguay and grew in Ecuador, Mexico, Panama, and Peru.

The results presented in this chapter are consistent with the evidence in the migration literature, which documents no change in the preferences of young migrants for large cities (Rodríguez and Busso 2009; Rowe 2013), but indicates a shift in the gender and education composition of domestic migrants to Latin America's largest cities (Rodríguez 2004). This chapter shows that income gaps with leading areas have diminished in most countries since the early 2000s and that they are considerably smaller among the bottom 40 percent than the general population. The differences between the average income in the leading metropolitan areas and the average income in rural areas have declined as well, but in most countries they remain significantly larger than the average income gaps. Although sizable income gaps were observed in all countries except Mexico, these differences in most countries reflected mainly differences in endowments, especially education. Only in Bolivia and Peru, and to a lesser extent Brazil, Chile, and Panama, did sufficiently large income gaps due to differences in the returns to endowments indicate a potential to improve welfare by migrating to leading areas. Barriers to migration also remain high for the residents of the poor, remote regions, particularly in the largest Latin American economies. What are the aggregate growth and welfare implications of migration frictions in the LAC region? The analysis in the next chapter answers this question.

FIGURE 3.5 Average labor income gaps with the leading metropolitan areas by type of individual, gender, country, and period, LAC region

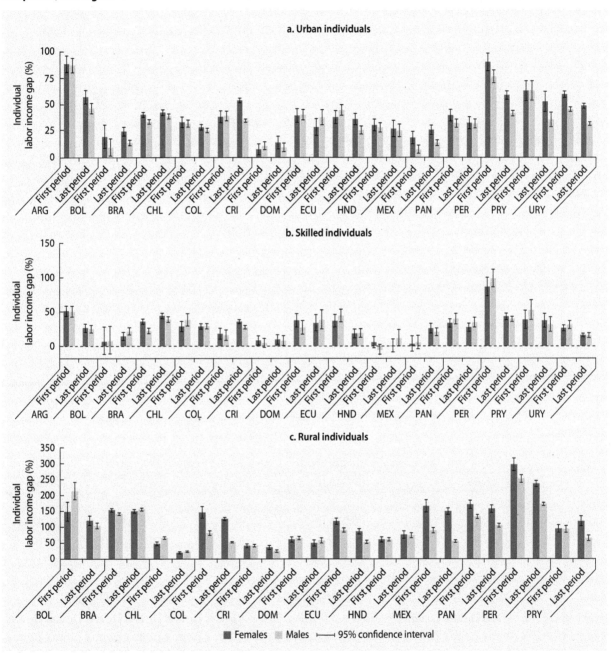

(Continued on next page)

FIGURE 3.5 **Average labor income gaps with the leading metropolitan areas by type of individual, gender, country, and period, LAC region** *(continued)*

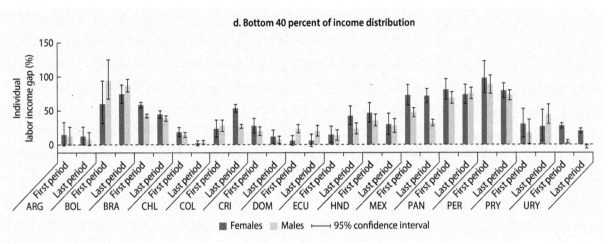

d. Bottom 40 percent of income distribution

■ Females   ▨ Males   ├──┤ 95% confidence interval

Source: D'Aoust, Galdo, and Ianchovichina 2023.
Note: The leading metropolitan areas and the respective first and last periods are as follows: Argentina (ARG): Buenos Aires, 2003–05, 2017–19; Bolivia (BOL): Santa Cruz, 2001–02, 2015–19; Brazil (BRA): Belo Horizonte, Rio de Janeiro, and São Paulo, 2012–14, 2017–19; Chile (CHL): Santiago, 2000 and 2003, 2015 and 2017; Colombia (COL): Bogotá, 2001–03, 2017–19; Costa Rica (CRI): urban Central Valley region (includes San José and other main cities), 2001–03, 2008–09; the Dominican Republic (DOM): city of Santo Domingo, 2000–2002, 2014–16; Ecuador (ECU): Quito (urban Pichincha), 2003–04, 2017–19; Honduras (HND): urban Tegucigalpa (Francisco Morazán), 2004–06, 2017–19; Mexico (MEX): Mexico City metropolitan area, 2000, 2002, and 2004; 2016 and 2018; Panama (PAN): urban Panamá Province, 2001–03, 2017–19; Paraguay (PRY): Asunción, 2002–04, 2017–19; Peru (PER): Lima, 2000–2003, 2017–19; Uruguay (URY): Montevideo, 2000–2002, 2017–19.

Annex 3A Data details on survey years and sample sizes

TABLE 3A.1 **Years and sample size of income gap analysis by period, LAC region**

Country	First period	Sample	Last period	Sample
Argentina	2003, 2004, 2005	49,684	2017, 2018, 2019	61,061
Bolivia	2001, 2002	9,014	2017, 2018, 2019	24,552
Brazil	2012, 2013, 2014	256,293	2017, 2018, 2019	243,827
Chile	2000, 2003	84,428	2015, 2017	91,397
Colombia	2001, 2002, 2003	64,975	2017, 2018, 2019	433,130
Costa Rica	2001, 2002, 2003	20,323	2008, 2009	16,948
Dominican Republic	2000, 2001, 2002	11,415	2014, 2015, 2016	14,771
Ecuador	2003, 2004	43,875	2017, 2018, 2019	45,635
Honduras	2004, 2005, 2006	26,311	2017, 2018, 2019	12,323
Mexico	2000, 2002, 2004	37,672	2016, 2018	103,081
Panama	2001, 2002, 2003	27,020	2017, 2018, 2019	21,983
Paraguay	2002, 2003, 2004	16,160	2017, 2018, 2019	13,799
Peru	2000, 2001, 2002, 2003	40,766	2017, 2018, 2019	80,318
Uruguay	2000, 2001, 2002	48,579	2017, 2018, 2019	61,752

Source: D'Aoust, Galdo, and Ianchovichina 2023.

Annex 3B Decomposition of income gaps

BOX 3B.1 **Decomposition of income gaps: Endowments versus returns to endowments**

D'Aoust, Galdo, and Ianchovichina (2023) decompose the income gaps into an endowment component and a returns-to-endowment component using the following approach. They first estimate per capita labor income as a linear function of a household's portable endowment characteristics[a] in period t in the leading metropolitan area, A, and the rest of the country, R, respectively, so that

$$ln(y_{h,A,t}) = X_{h,A,t}'\psi_{A,t} + \varepsilon_{h,A,t} \tag{B3B.1.1}$$

$$ln(y_{h,R,t}) = X_{h,R,t}'\psi_{R,t} + \varepsilon_{h,R,t}. \tag{B3B.1.2}$$

Then, using the geographic analog of the Blinder-Oaxaca decomposition, they decompose the gap between the average logged per capita household labor income in the leading agglomeration (A), $\overline{ln(y_{A,t})}$, and the corresponding one in the rest of the country (R), $\overline{ln(y_{R,t})}$, so that

$$\overline{ln(y_{A,t})} - \overline{ln(y_{R,t})} = (\bar{X}_{A,t} - \bar{X}_{R,t})'\hat{\psi}_{R,t} + \bar{X}_{A,t}'(\hat{\psi}_{A,t} - \hat{\psi}_{R,t}), \tag{B3B.1.3}$$

where $\hat{\psi}_{A,t}$ and $\hat{\psi}_{R,t}$ are, respectively, the estimated returns to the portable characteristics in locations A and R using equations (B3B.1.1) and (B3B.1.2), and $\bar{X}_{A,t}$ and $\bar{X}_{R,t}$ are the portable characteristics of the typical household in locations A and R at period t.

The first component on the right-hand side of decomposition equation (B3B.1.3) is associated with differences in the nongeographic endowments of the household. This component captures the sorting (selection) of people into the leading metropolitan area. The second component of equation (B3B.1.3) is associated with differences in the returns to these endowments and omitted variables, which indicate the extent to which the income gap might be exploitable through migration.

a. The portable characteristics are the same as those included in regression model (2.1) in chapter 2 and listed in annex table 2A.1.

TABLE 3B.1 Dispersion of location premia after sorting around the average/median/leading area location premia by period, LAC region

Argentina[a]	2003/05	2009/11	2017/19	Bolivia[a]	2001/02	2011/13	2017/19
$\%CV(\gamma_t)\vert_{\overline{\gamma}_t}$	5.298	4.587	4.069	$\%CV(\gamma_t)\vert_{\overline{\gamma}_t}$	9.256	5.869	3.585
$\%CV(\gamma_t)\vert_{\gamma^*}$	4.811	4.312	3.915	$\%CV(\gamma_t)\vert_{\gamma^*}$	8.743	5.597	3.429
Avg. $(\gamma^*-\gamma_t)$	0.397	0.305	0.190	Avg. $(\gamma^*-\gamma_t)$	0.245	0.237	0.226
$\gamma^*-\gamma_{i50}$	0.472	0.357	0.217	$\gamma^*-\gamma_{i50}$	0.336	0.205	0.246
$\gamma^*-\gamma_{i25}$	0.534	0.436	0.241	$\gamma^*-\gamma_{i25}$	0.526	0.296	0.265
Growth $(\gamma_{t,t'})$			0.056	Growth $(\gamma_{t,t'})$			0.042

Brazil	2000	2010		Chile	2000/03	2009/11	2015/17
$\%CV(\gamma_t)\vert_{\overline{\gamma}_t}$	8.971	7.685		$\%CV(\gamma_t)\vert_{\overline{\gamma}_t}$	5.303	4.327	3.780
$\%CV(\gamma_t)\vert_{\gamma^*}$	8.241	7.137		$\%CV(\gamma_t)\vert_{\gamma^*}$	5.052	4.202	3.671
Avg. $(\gamma^*-\gamma_t)$	0.390	0.359		Avg. $(\gamma^*-\gamma_t)$	0.223	0.153	0.160
$\gamma^*-\gamma_{i50}$	0.318	0.280		$\gamma^*-\gamma_{i50}$	0.219	0.157	0.178
$\gamma^*-\gamma_{i25}$	0.717	0.694		$\gamma^*-\gamma_{i25}$	0.385	0.295	0.290
Growth $(\gamma_{t,t'})$		0.026		Growth $(\gamma_{t,t'})$			0.051

Colombia[a]	2001/03	2008/10	2017/19	Costa Rica	2001/03	2008/09	
$\%CV(\gamma_t)\vert_{\overline{\gamma}_t}$	3.433	3.127	2.346	$\%CV(\gamma_t)\vert_{\overline{\gamma}_t}$	3.869	3.241	
$\%CV(\gamma_t)\vert_{\gamma^*}$	3.360	2.948	2.241	$\%CV(\gamma_t)\vert_{\gamma^*}$	3.685	3.138	
Avg. $(\gamma^*-\gamma_t)$	0.092	0.270	0.221	Avg. $(\gamma^*-\gamma_t)$	0.252	0.185	
$\gamma^*-\gamma_{i50}$	0.055	0.314	0.227	$\gamma^*-\gamma_{i50}$	0.227	0.177	
$\gamma^*-\gamma_{i25}$	0.166	0.374	0.323	$\gamma^*-\gamma_{i25}$	0.329	0.258	
Growth $(\gamma_{t,t'})$			0.032	Growth $(\gamma_{t,t'})$		0.063	

Dominican Republic	2000/02	2008/10	2014/16	Ecuador	2003/04	2009/11	2017/19
$\%CV(\gamma_t)\vert_{\overline{\gamma}_t}$	5.543	4.531	4.237	$\%CV(\gamma_t)\vert_{\overline{\gamma}_t}$	7.087	5.625	4.474
$\%CV(\gamma_t)\vert_{\gamma^*}$	5.145	4.287	4.048	$\%CV(\gamma_t)\vert_{\gamma^*}$	6.359	5.269	4.237
Avg. $(\gamma^*-\gamma_t)$	0.380	0.280	0.226	Avg. $(\gamma^*-\gamma_t)$	0.441	0.282	0.241
$\gamma^*-\gamma_{i50}$	0.351	0.246	0.175	$\gamma^*-\gamma_{i50}$	0.406	0.263	0.221
$\gamma^*-\gamma_{i25}$	0.549	0.416	0.343	$\gamma^*-\gamma_{i25}$	0.605	0.409	0.347
Growth $(\gamma_{t,t'})$			−0.004	Growth $(\gamma_{t,t'})$			0.029

(Continued on next page)

TABLE 3B.1   Dispersion of location premia after sorting around the average/median/leading area location premia by period, LAC region *(continued)*

Honduras	2004/06	2009/11	2017/19	Mexico	1990	2000	2015
$\%CV(\gamma_t)\big|_{\overline{\gamma_t}}$	9.195	7.835	8.380	$\%CV(\gamma_t)\big|_{\overline{\gamma_t}}$	14.668	10.488	7.615
$\%CV(\gamma_t)\big|_{\gamma^*}$	8.561	7.349	7.899	$\%CV(\gamma_t)\big|_{\gamma^*}$	13.558	9.750	7.142
Avg. $(\gamma^*-\gamma_t)$	0.306	0.286	0.256	Avg. $(\gamma^*-\gamma_t)$	0.349	0.333	0.308
$\gamma^*-\gamma_{t50}$	0.232	0.259	0.252	$\gamma^*-\gamma_{t50}$	0.207	0.294	0.226
$\gamma^*-\gamma_{t25}$	0.577	0.496	0.503	$\gamma^*-\gamma_{t25}$	0.604	0.599	0.462
Growth $(\gamma_{t,t'})$			0.005	Growth $(\gamma_{t,t'})$			0.017

Panama[a]	2001/03	2009/11	2017/19	Peru	2000/03	2008/10	2017/19
$\%CV(\gamma_t)\big|_{\overline{\gamma_t}}$	6.614	7.076	5.865	$\%CV(\gamma_t)\big|_{\overline{\gamma_t}}$	11.244	9.063	6.985
$\%CV(\gamma_t)\big|_{\gamma^*}$	6.272	6.513	5.538	$\%CV(\gamma_t)\big|_{\gamma^*}$	9.371	7.899	6.207
Avg. $(\gamma^*-\gamma_t)$	0.222	0.371	0.272	Avg. $(\gamma^*-\gamma_t)$	0.665	0.527	0.489
$\gamma^*-\gamma_{t50}$	0.152	0.301	0.203	$\gamma^*-\gamma_{t50}$	0.650	0.522	0.513
$\gamma^*-\gamma_{t25}$	0.420	0.524	0.380	$\gamma^*-\gamma_{t25}$	0.913	0.785	0.702
Growth $(\gamma_{t,t'})$			0.030	Growth $(\gamma_{t,t'})$			0.030

Uruguay[a]	2000/02	2008/10	2017/19
$\%CV(\gamma_t)\big|_{\overline{\gamma_t}}$	3.668	2.834	2.783
$\%CV(\gamma_t)\big|_{\gamma^*}$	3.402	2.736	2.664
Avg. $(\gamma^*-\gamma_t)$	0.351	0.153	0.210
$\gamma^*-\gamma_{t50}$	0.389	0.129	0.186
$\gamma^*-\gamma_{t25}$	0.444	0.252	0.346
Growth $(\gamma_{t,t'})$			0.012

Source: D'Aoust, Galdo, and Ianchovichina 2023.
Note: The location premia (after sorting) of leading metropolitan areas correspond to the first-level administrative unit where a leading area is located. The location premia of the multi-municipality leading areas in Brazil, Chile, Mexico, and Peru are the average location premia of the municipalities in the leading metropolitan area. (Annex table 3B.2 shows details on the number of municipalities included in each leading area, their location premia, and type of municipality.) $\%CV(\gamma_t)\big|_{\overline{\gamma_t}}$ and $\%CV(\gamma_t)\big|_{\gamma^*}$ measure the coefficient of variability of the location premium (after sorting) around the mean and the leading metropolitan area, respectively. Avg. $(\gamma^*-\gamma_t)$ measures the average gap in location premium of the leading area γ^* and the other locations (γ_t). $(\gamma^*-\gamma_{t50})$ and $(\gamma^*-\gamma_{t25})$ measure the gap between the location premium of the leading area and the median and bottom quartile location premia, respectively. Growth $(\gamma_{t,t'})$ refers to the annual growth in the location premium over the longest period available. For Mexico, the reported growth is for the period 2000–2015.
a. Analysis conducted at the first administrative level.

BOX 3B.2   Correspondence between the gap in location premia and the gap in returns to endowments between the leading metropolitan area and other areas of a country

Because the leading area A typically includes a small fraction of the country's municipalities, one can assume that the average returns to endowments are approximately equal to the average returns to endowments outside the leading area ($\hat{\psi}_t \approx \psi_{R,t}$). Then, the difference between the estimated location premia after sorting in the leading area and in the rest of the country, using equation (2.1) in chapter 2, is approximately equal to the difference in the returns to endowments in the decomposition (B3B.1.3 in box 3B.1), so that

$$\hat{\gamma}_{A,t}^{as} - \hat{\gamma}_{R,t}^{as} \approx \bar{X}_{A,t}{}' \left(\hat{\psi}_{A,t} - \hat{\psi}_{R,t} \right),$$

(B3B.2.1)

where $\hat{\gamma}_{R,t}^{as}$ is expected to be close to the average estimated location premia after sorting, $\hat{\gamma}_t^{as}$.

Indeed, D'Aoust, Galdo, and Ianchovichina (2023) find that the right-hand side and left-hand side of equation (B3B.2.1) are approximately equal in each country case. The correlation between the right-hand side and the left-hand side for the sample of countries included in this chapter is also high at 0.78 in the first period and 0.73 in the second period.

At the country level, differences between the right-hand side and left-hand side of equation (B3B.2.1) are expected to be larger when (1) the periods are not fully aligned due to survey data availability; (2) some municipalities are omitted from estimation of the location premia after sorting due to missing information on household characteristics; and (3) the households are not evenly distributed across municipalities. For example, if the share of households living in municipalities with below-median location premia is higher than those in municipalities with above-median location premia, then the right-hand side of equation (B3B.2.1) is expected to be higher than its left-hand side. This is the situation in Bolivia, where 62 percent of all households lived in areas with below-median location premia in the last period (see figure B3B.2.1, panel a). The opposite is observed in Honduras, where 59 percent of all households live in areas with above-median location premia (figure B3B.2.1, panel b).

FIGURE B3B.2.1   Location premia by share of households: Bolivia and Honduras, 2017–19

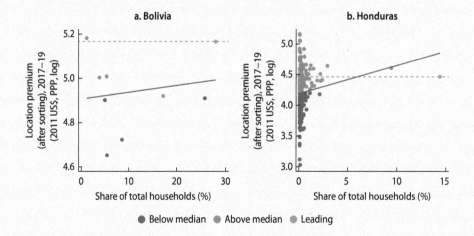

Source: D'Aoust, Galdo, and Ianchovichina 2023.
Note: PPP = purchasing power parity.

TABLE 3B.2 Characteristics of the municipalities included in the leading metropolitan areas, LAC region

Country	Number of municipalities in leading areas	Location premium, latest period				Municipality type					
						Metro		Urban		Rural	
		Mean	Std. dev.	Min.	Max.	Large	Small	Large	Small	Large	Small
Argentina	1	5.01									
Bolivia	1	5.17									
Brazil	3	5.05	0.03	5.03	5.09	3					
Chile	32	5.52	0.26	5.26	6.35			32*			
Colombia	1	4.98									
Costa Rica	1	5.75						1*			
Dominican Republic	1	5.07						1*			
Ecuador	1	4.56						1*			
Honduras	1	4.47						1*			
Mexico	56	4.95	0.13	4.58	5.27	5	2	3	12	3	2
Panama	1	4.89						2			
Peru	2	4.39	0.13	4.29	4.48			2*			
Uruguay	1	4.93									

Source: D'Aoust, Galdo, and Ianchovichina 2023.
Note: Asterisk denotes number of urban municipalities. Max. = maximum; metro = metropolitan; min. = minimum; std. dev. = standard deviation.

Notes

1. The countries are Bolivia, Brazil, Colombia, Ecuador, Guatemala, Mexico, Nicaragua, and Peru.
2. *Spatial arbitrage* refers to the act of moving from an area where demand for labor is low to an area where the demand for labor is high in the hope of being able to find a job that pays a higher wage.
3. Distance erodes migrants' social capital and increases the cost of home visits.
4. For Brazil and Mexico, the periods shown in annex table 3B.1 do not align with the periods shown for the two countries in figure 3.1 because the table reflects information from the IPUMS census data presented in chapter 2, whereas the figure shows information based on data from the SEDLAC household surveys.
5. Annex box 3B.2 shows that the difference between the estimated location premia in the leading metropolitan area and the average location premium in the country, $\gamma^* - \overline{\gamma}_l$, shown in annex table 3B.1, is approximately equal to the difference in the returns to endowments in the decomposition equation (B3B.1.3) in annex box 3B.1, shown in figure 3.1 in light blue.
6. Skilled households are those in which the household head has at least some tertiary education and households in which the highest education attainment is beyond secondary education.
7. The methodology for estimating the income gaps among the bottom 40 percent first identifies the bottom 40 percent in the entire sample and then assigns them to the leading metropolitan location or the rest of the country.
8. The SEDLAC data are representative only at the household level, but it is possible to conduct the analysis at the individual level to compare the income gaps by gender.

References

Asher, S., and P. Novosad. 2020. "Rural Roads and Local Economic Development." *American Economic Review* 110 (3): 797–823.

Bastos, P. 2017. "Spatial Misallocation of Labor in Brazil." Unpublished manuscript, World Bank, Washington, DC.

Beylis, G., R. Fattal-Jaef, R. Sinha, M. Morris, and A. Sebastian. 2020. *Going Viral: COVID-19 and the Accelerated Transformation of Jobs in Latin America and the Caribbean.* World Bank Latin American and Caribbean Studies. Washington, DC: World Bank.

Bryan, G., S. Chowdhury, and A. Mobarak. 2014. "Underinvestment in a Profitable Technology: The Case of Seasonal Migration in Bangladesh." *Econometrica* 82 (5): 1671–1748.

Bryan, G., and M. Morten. 2019. "The Aggregate Productivity Effects of Internal Migration: Evidence from Indonesia." *Journal of Political Economy* 127 (5): 2229–68.

Conte, B., and E. Ianchovichina. 2022. "Spatial Development and Mobility Frictions in Latin America: Theory-Based Empirical Evidence." Policy Research Working Paper 10071, World Bank, Washington, DC.

D'Aoust, O., V. Galdo, and E. Ianchovichina. 2023. "Territorial Productivity Differences and Dynamics within Latin American Countries." Policy Research Working Paper 10480, World Bank, Washington, DC.

De La Roca, J., and D. Puga. 2017. "Learning by Working in Big Cities." *Review of Economic Studies* 84: 106–42.

Ferreyra, M. M., and M. Roberts, eds. 2018. *Raising the Bar for Productive Cities in Latin America and the Caribbean.* Washington, DC: World Bank.

Harari, M. 2020. "Cities in Bad Shape: Urban Geometry in India." *American Economic Review* 110 (8): 2377–2421.

Hsieh, C.-T., and E. Moretti. 2019. "Housing Constraints and Spatial Misallocation." *American Economic Journal: Macroeconomics* 11 (2): 1–39.

Jedwab, R., E. Ianchovichina, and F. Haslop. 2022. "Consumption Cities versus Production Cities: New Considerations and Evidence." Policy Research Working Paper 10105, World Bank, Washington, DC.

Morten, M., and J. Oliveira. 2018. "The Effects of Roads on Trade and Migration: Evidence from a Planned Capital City." NBER Working Paper 22158, National Bureau of Economic Research, Cambridge, MA.

Rodríguez, J. 2004. "Internal Migration in Latin America and the Caribbean: Regional Study, Period 1980–2000." *Serie población y desarrollo no. 50 (LC/L.2059–P).* Santiago: United Nations Economic Commission for Latin America and the Caribbean.

Rodríguez, J. 2011. "Migración interna y sistema de ciudades en América Latina: Intensidad, patrones, efectos y potenciales determinantes, censos de la década de 2000" (Internal Migration and the Latin American System of Cities: Intensity, Patterns, Impacts and Potential Determinants, 2000 Census Round). *Serie población y desarrollo no. 105 (LC/L.3351).* Santiago: United Nations Economic Commission for Latin America and the Caribbean.

Rodríguez, J., and G. Busso. 2009. *Internal Migration and Development in Latin America between 1980 and 2005: A Comparative Study with a Regional Focus based on Seven Countries.* Santiago: United Nations Economic Commission for Latin America and the Caribbean.

Rowe, F. 2013. "Spatial Labour Mobility in a Transition Economy: Migration and Commuting in Chile." PhD thesis, University of Queensland, Australia.

Rowe, F. 2014. "The Effects of Economic Liberalisation on Inter-regional Labour Migration in a Transition Economy, Chile." Conference paper, 2014 Tinbergen Workshop: Real People in Virtual Space, Amsterdam.

Skoufias, E., and G. López-Acevedo. 2009. *Determinants of Regional Welfare Disparities within Latin American Countries*, Vol. 1: *Synthesis.* Washington, DC: World Bank.

United Nations. 2016. *The World Cities Data Booklet.* New York: United Nations.

PART

II

Mobility Frictions and Spatial Misallocation

obility frictions in the form of trade and migration barriers play an important role in understanding spatial differences in labor income because they affect the distribution of economic activity and people and thus productivity differences in and across countries. An inaccessible terrain; sparse, narrow, or poorly maintained roads; limited modes of transportation; and expensive transportation services erect barriers to both trade *and* migration. A host of other factors can also keep people in place. Limited information on economic opportunities, an insufficient supply of land, unaffordable formal housing and consumer amenities, legal migration restrictions, discriminatory practices, and social or cultural factors can also deter, to different degrees, the mobility of socioeconomic groups (Bryan and Morten 2019). High trade costs have negative implications for aggregate economic efficiency because costly and deficient transportation services limit market access and the ability of firms to trade. The dispersion of productivity across cities is minimized and cities' contribution to aggregate productivity is maximized (Selod and Soumahoro 2018) when intercity transport costs are low because firms in smaller, secondary cities can specialize and gain from economies of scale. High entry barriers in productive places are also highly distortionary because they make it difficult for workers to migrate to these locations, generating misallocation and constraining long-run growth (Hsieh and Moretti 2019).

Chapter 4 is organized around three main questions: How large are mobility frictions in the LAC countries? Which type of mobility frictions—entry barriers or transport costs—are more harmful to economic growth and welfare in the region? What policies can reduce mobility frictions and raise long-run economic growth and welfare?

References

Bryan, G., and M. Morten. 2019. "The Aggregate Productivity Effects of Internal Migration: Evidence from Indonesia." *Journal of Political Economy* 127 (5): 2229–68.

Hsieh, C.-T., and E. Moretti. 2019. "Housing Constraints and Spatial Misallocation." *American Economic Journal: Macroeconomics* 11 (2): 1–39.

Selod, H., and S. Soumahoro. 2018. "Transport Infrastructure and Agglomeration in Cities." In *Raising the Bar for Productive Cities in Latin America and the Caribbean*, edited by M. M. Ferreyra and M. Roberts. Washington, DC: World Bank.

Barriers to Trade and Labor Mobility and Their Aggregate Effects

4

This chapter presents estimates of granular entry migration costs and bilateral transport costs in Latin America and the Caribbean (LAC) and the policy effects of cuts in these costs on aggregate economic growth and welfare. Entry migration costs by location are estimated using the approach of Desmet, Nagy, and Rossi-Hansberg (2018), which is modified to reflect the territorial differences in initial welfare[1] in the LAC countries. These differences can be substantial, as shown by Burger, Hendriks, and Ianchovichina (2022), who proxy welfare with self-reported well-being data from the Gallup World Poll (GWP) in Colombia, and by Gollin, Kirchberger, and Lagakos (2017), who proxy utility in low- and middle-income countries with differences in per capita consumption. Transport costs between any pair of locations are estimated at a finely disaggregated geospatial level using the least-cost route approach in Allen and Arkolakis (2014), factoring in the geography of and the distance between locations, the availability of different types of connectivity infrastructure, and the relative costs of different modes of transportation.

Entry migration costs

Entry migration costs, estimated at a finely disaggregated geospatial scale circa 2000,[2] are displayed in map 4.1. These are average location-specific entry migration costs because Desmet, Nagy, and Rossi-Hansberg (2018) study the local change in population, not where migrants come from. The costs can be higher or lower than the average for different groups coming from different places and belonging to different socioeconomic groups. The entry migration costs capture the total cost of entering a location, including the cost of overcoming immigration restrictions, the cost of travel to the location, information and psychological costs, restrictions stemming from land regulations, and housing supply constraints. The estimated entry migration costs vary by location within and across the LAC countries. As expected, entry migration costs are lowest in the low-income

MAP 4.1   Calibrated entry migration costs by finely disaggregated locations: LAC region, circa 2000

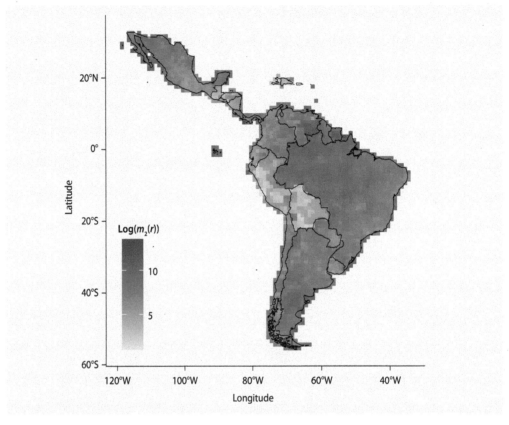

Source: Conte and Ianchovichina 2022.
Note: Conte and Ianchovichina (2022) calibrate the entry migration costs using the dynamic spatial general equilibrium model of Desmet, Nagy, and Rossi-Hansberg (2018); geocoded data from Latinobarómetro and the Gallup World Poll; and finely disaggregated data on population and value added by grid cell (typically 1-arc degree cell) from G-Econ data for 2000 (Nordhaus et al. 2006). Desmet, Nagy, and Rossi-Hansberg (2018) assume that the cost of migration from location s to r, m(s,r), is the product of the entry migration cost at the origin, $m_1(s)$, and the entry migration cost at the destination, r, $m_2(r)$. There is no cost to staying in the same location, whereas a migrant who leaves a location will receive a benefit (or pay a cost), which is the inverse of the cost (or benefit) of entering the location. The LAC region includes Mexico, all countries in Central and South America, and the Dominican Republic and Haiti in the Caribbean.

countries of Central America and in Bolivia and Peru, and highest in the higher-income countries such as Argentina, Brazil, Costa Rica, and Mexico (figure 4.1). In all cases, however, entry migration costs in the region are lower than those in the United States and the European Union (see figure 4.1).

Entry migration costs are also high in remote areas, where living conditions are harsh, such as in the difficult-to-reach areas of the Amazon basin, the mountainous areas and the extreme south of Argentina and Chile, and some of the high-density urban areas, which tend to struggle with agglomeration costs, especially traffic congestion, unaffordable formal housing, and an inadequate supply of quality basic services and infrastructure, some of which may deter potential migrants. Roberts (2018) finds that traffic congestion rises much more rapidly with population density in Latin America than in the rest of the world. Congestion in the formal housing market—manifested in the existence of large informal settlements—is another potential barrier. Although the population living in informal

FIGURE 4.1 Average estimated migration barriers in the LAC region, Southeast Asia, and the European Union relative to those in the United States, circa 2000

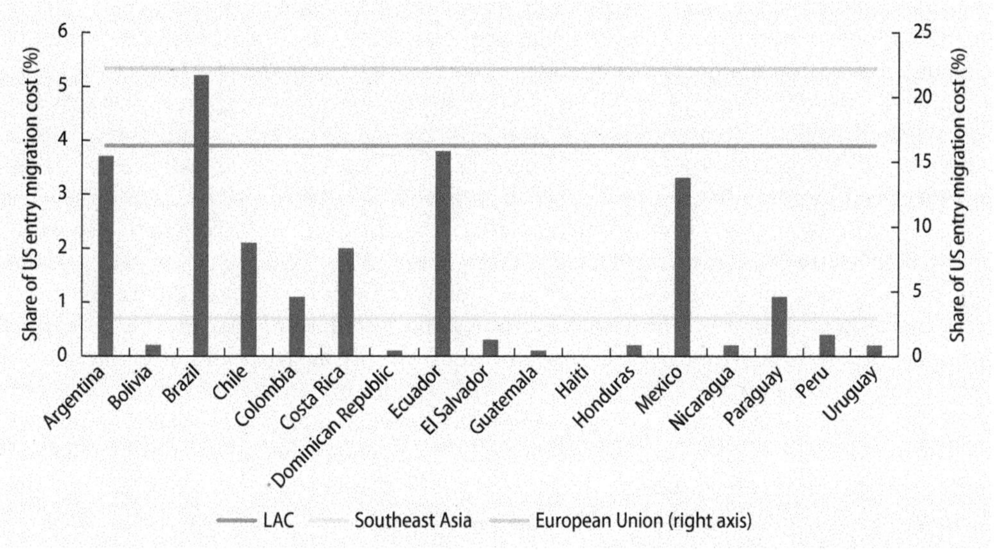

— LAC —— Southeast Asia —— European Union (right axis)

Source: Conte and Ianchovichina 2022.
Note: Conte and Ianchovichina (2022) calibrate the entry migration costs using the dynamic spatial general equilibrium model in Desmet, Nagy, and Rossi-Hansberg (2018), a spatially differentiated initial utility, and finely disaggregated data on population and value added by grid cell (typically a 1-arc degree cell) from G-Econ data for 2000 (Nordhaus et al. 2006).

settlements declined from 35 percent of all urban residents in 1990 to 20 percent in 2014, progress has been slow. Because of the high urbanization rate, slightly more than 100 million Latin Americans still live in substandard urban conditions in informal urban settlements throughout the region.

Interregional and intercity transport costs

Interregional transport costs are higher in Latin America than in other emerging markets because many South American countries have vast territories and challenging terrains. Transport costs also reflect the condition and availability of national and cross-country infrastructure networks for different modes of transportation. The road density in Latin America is lower than that in all other regions except Sub-Saharan Africa (World Bank 2009), and the railway networks are similarly underdeveloped (Fay et al. 2017). Only 22 percent of land freight is transported by rail in Latin America, compared with 35–45 percent in North America, Europe, and East Asia (Ferreyra and Roberts 2018). In Brazil, Chile, Colombia, Mexico, and Peru—countries that together account for more than two-thirds of the LAC region's exports—80 percent of the cargo was transported by trucks in the early 2010s (Mesquita Moreira et al. 2013). In addition, issues such as government regulations,[3] inefficiencies,[4] imperfect competition,[5] backhaul problems, congestion delays, and information frictions raise the prices of transport services.

Typically, sparse transport networks are a pressing issue in the initial stages of development when the share of spatially dispersed rural residents is still relatively high. In Latin America, high transport costs may not be as problematic for two reasons. First, almost

80 percent of the population lives in dense urban areas located along the coast, in highly productive commodity-growing areas, or in areas with historical significance.[6] Second, exports are concentrated in a relatively few populous municipalities along the coasts of Brazil, Colombia, and Peru (Mesquita Moreira et al. 2013). In Brazil, only 20 percent of all municipalities reported exporting any products in 2010, and the top 10 municipalities accounted for more than half of all exports. In 2006, Colombia's exports were spatially concentrated in just 269 municipalities located in the country's north and representing a quarter of all municipalities. In Peru, 45 percent of its exports came mostly from coastal provinces and some landlocked resource-rich areas in 2009. The overlap between the most populous and exporting areas is much smaller in Chile and Mexico, where exporting municipalities are concentrated in the northern areas of the two countries, whereas the population is concentrated in and around the capital cities in the countries' core areas.

In the context of highly concentrated exports and population, sparser, less developed transport networks may not be a serious problem if exporting areas and more productive and populous areas are well connected. The findings by Mesquita Moreira et al. (2013) suggest that transport costs to ports are generally lower for the larger exporting municipalities in the five countries included in their study. However, the question of whether the more populous and most productive areas—the *top locations*—are well connected remains unanswered. It is also unclear how the domestic transport costs between such locations compare with those in other emerging economies.

Conte and Ianchovichina (2022) provide some answers. They define *top locations* in a country or the region as the areas with a gross domestic product (GDP) per capita in the top quartile of the within-country or within-region distribution and population above the median in the country or region. Map 4.2, panel a, shows the top locations in the European Union, Latin America, and Southeast Asia, and map 4.2, panel b, shows the top locations in the largest economies in the Americas and East Asia—Brazil, China, and the United States. A focus on the transport costs between top locations, which also include the leading metropolitan areas discussed in chapter 3, is warranted for improving welfare, productivity, and opportunities for increased specialization in the manufacturing sector as trade patterns evolve over time or adjust to shocks such as climate change.

Figure 4.2, panel a, compares the transport costs between pairs of top urban locations in the European Union, Latin America, and Southeast Asia. The thicker right tail of the LAC distribution suggests that it is much costlier to transport goods between top locations in Latin America than between similar locations in the European Union or Southeast Asia. Even after controlling for distance, there are many more equidistant top location pairs with higher transport costs in Latin America than in the European Union or Southeast Asia (figure 4.2, panel a). Although shipments between top locations in the United States are costlier than those in Brazil or China, where activity is clustered along their east coasts (figure 4.2, panel b), there are many more pairs of equidistant locations with relatively high transport costs in Brazil than in either China or the United States (figure 4.2, panel b).

The high intercity transport costs present a problem. Good intercity connectivity is essential for reducing the within-country dispersion in city productivity and improving the ability of firms to specialize and gain from economies of scale in smaller, well-connected cities.[7] Secondary urban areas have the potential to become "competitive" cities that create jobs, raise productivity, and increase incomes (Kilroy et al. 2015; Rodríguez-Pose and Griffiths 2021),[8] but in the LAC region, in addition to connectivity issues, smaller cities struggle with the provision of infrastructure, basic consumer amenities, and local public goods and services.

MAP 4.2 **Top locations within regions or countries**

a. European Union, Latin America and the Caribbean, and Southeast Asia

- ■ Top location
- ■ Other locations
- □ No data

IBRD 47567 |
OCTOBER 2023

b. Brazil, China, and the United States

- ■ Top location
- ■ Other locations
- □ No data

IBRD 47568 |
OCTOBER 2023

Source: Conte and Ianchovichina 2022.
Note: In the maps, the top locations (dark blue grid cells) belong to the top quartile of the within-region or within-country per capita gross domestic product (GDP) distribution, and their population exceeds the median population of the country or region. Data are missing for territories and countries in gray. GDP per capita at the grid cell level is from the G-Econ database (Nordhaus et al. 2006).

FIGURE 4.2 **Distribution of transport costs between pairs of top urban locations by region and country**

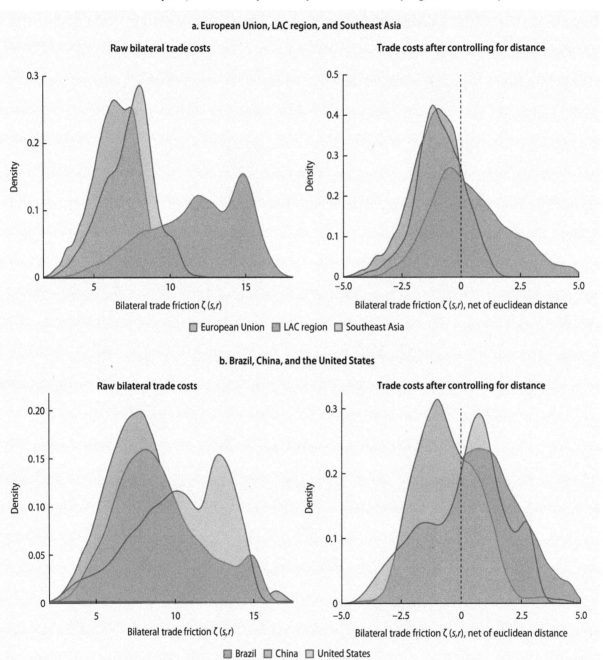

a. European Union, LAC region, and Southeast Asia

Raw bilateral trade costs

Trade costs after controlling for distance

■ European Union   ■ LAC region   ■ Southeast Asia

b. Brazil, China, and the United States

Raw bilateral trade costs

Trade costs after controlling for distance

■ Brazil   ■ China   ■ United States

Source: Conte and Ianchovichina (2022), based on the least-cost route approach in Allen and Arkolakis (2014) and the methodology in Desmet, Nagy, and Rossi-Hansberg (2018).
Note: The cost between any pair of locations, ζ (s,r), reflects the geography of and the distance between the locations, the availability of different types of connectivity infrastructure, and the relative costs of using different modes of ground transportation. The graphs compare the raw trade costs between pairs of top locations and the trade costs between equidistant pairs of top locations—that is, the cost net of euclidean distance in each region or country. Top urban locations in a country or a region are its more populous and most productive locations whose population and productivity are higher than the median and top quartile, respectively.

Underinvestment in intercity road network improvements

One reason for the high intercity transport costs is the insufficient and misallocated investment in domestic road networks in Latin America.[9] Since 1990, the region has spent about 3 percent of its GDP on public investments, or far less than East Asia and most other developing regions. Gorton and Ianchovichina (2021), who estimate the inefficiencies in the road networks of 16 Latin American countries using the state-of-the-art spatial general equilibrium model with endogenous transport costs in Fajgelbaum and Schaal (2020), show that many countries have misallocated the little investment undertaken in their domestic road networks.

Like other models aimed at solving an optimal transport problem (Alder 2019; Allen and Arkolakis 2019), the Fajgelbaum and Schaal (2020) model requires choosing least-cost routes across pairs of locations while offering two distinct advantages over other methodologies. First, road congestion allows reductions in the search space and substantial savings in computation time,[10] which is essential because of the large size of the road networks in many countries in South America. In this case, consumption and production in each location are not fixed but respond to general equilibrium forces. By contrast, without congestion, which is typical in other studies and a special case in Fajgelbaum and Schaal (2020), the optimal transport problem can be solved independently from the general equilibrium outcomes by mapping sources with a fixed supply to destinations with a fixed demand. In this special case, the solution in Fajgelbaum and Schaal (2020) matches closely the least-cost route optimization solutions found in the literature. Second, the model can be easily calibrated so that each grid cell's per capita value added and population match those observed in the data and can easily capture the existing road network in each country in a discretized form.[11]

Box 4B.1 in annex 4B presents the Fajgelbaum and Schaal model, which prioritizes aggregate outcomes over equity concerns and identifies road inefficiencies by maximizing aggregate welfare (see annex 4B for a discussion of the data and annex 4C for details on the calibration of parameters).[12] Although external trade is not explicitly considered in the model, connectivity to many major ports is nevertheless given priority because many of the centers producing differentiated domestically traded goods are densely populated areas near major ports, and the roads linking ports to the interior of the country are also used for shipments of commodity exports. Gorton and Ianchovichina (2021) also find that the needs for domestic road improvements[13] align to a large extent with the needs for transnational road improvements within MERCOSUR and the Andean Community.[14]

The model captures the spatial misallocations in Latin America's road networks with the wedge between the optimal and actual levels of infrastructure along each link (map 4.3). The results suggest that, in general, countries have underinvested in roads connecting their major (leading) cities to other populous secondary urban areas and overinvested in the less densely populated parts of their countries. In Chile, the results indicate overinvestment in roads in the north and underinvestment in the central parts of the country. In Argentina, underinvestment is detected along links radiating from Buenos Aires toward urban centers in Entre Ríos and Santa Fe, poorer areas in the northeast, and provinces to the west of the province of Buenos Aires, whereas overinvestment is observed in the country's south. In Peru, there is underinvestment in roads along the coast and roads connecting populous urban areas in the mountainous regions to coastal cities, whereas investments in the country's southeast are considered to be higher than optimal. There is underinvestment in roads along the coast of Brazil, including roads connecting Belo Horizonte, Rio de Janeiro, and

MAP 4.3   **Overinvestment and underinvestment in roads, selected countries, Latin America**

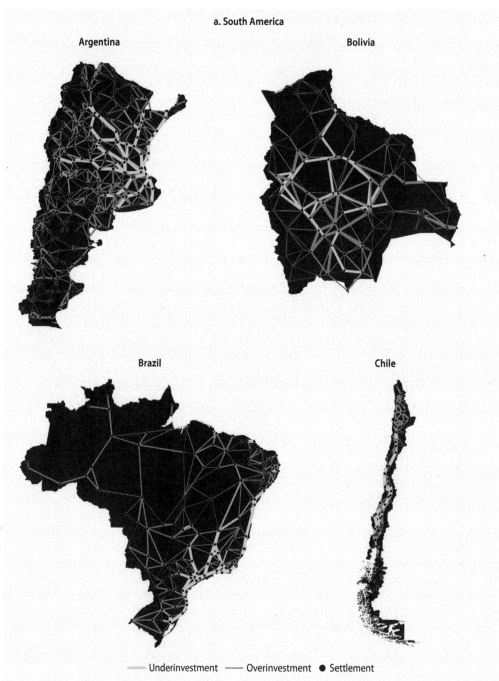

a. South America

Argentina

Bolivia

Brazil

Chile

—— Underinvestment   —— Overinvestment   ● Settlement

(Continued on next page)

MAP 4.3   Overinvestment and underinvestment in roads, selected countries, Latin America
(continued)

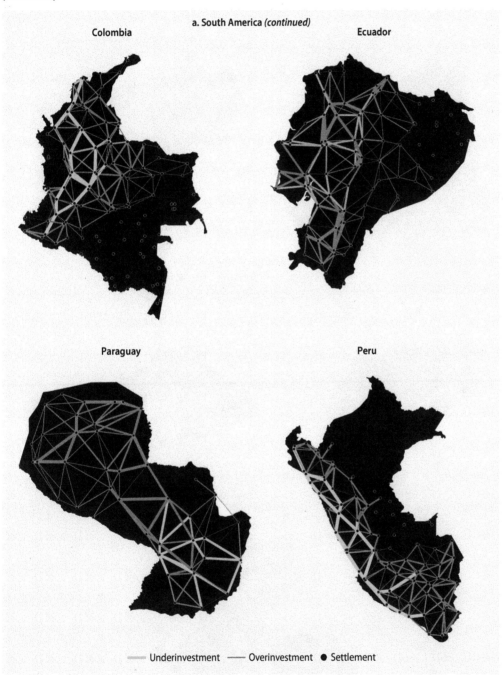

a. South America *(continued)*

Colombia

Ecuador

Paraguay

Peru

——— Underinvestment   ——— Overinvestment   ● Settlement

(Continued on next page)

MAP 4.3 **Overinvestment and underinvestment in roads, selected countries, Latin America**
(continued)

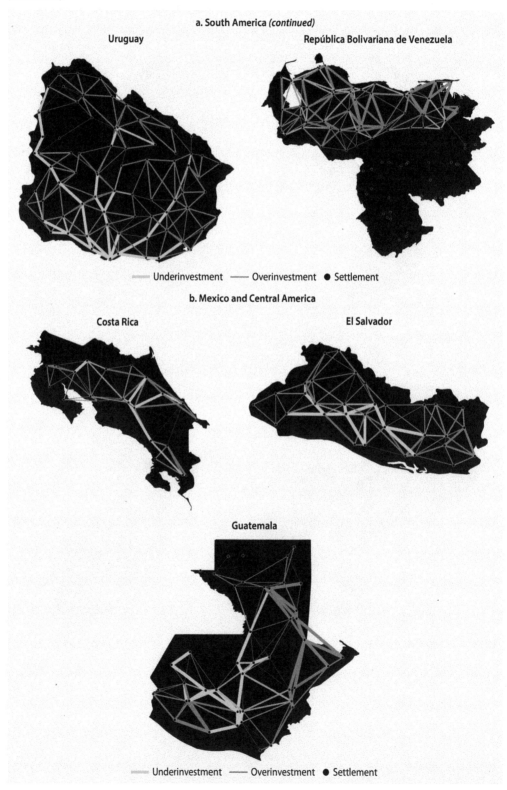

a. South America *(continued)*

Uruguay

República Bolivariana de Venezuela

—— Underinvestment —— Overinvestment ● Settlement

b. Mexico and Central America

Costa Rica

El Salvador

Guatemala

—— Underinvestment —— Overinvestment ● Settlement

(Continued on next page)

MAP 4.3 **Overinvestment and underinvestment in roads, selected countries, Latin America** *(continued)*

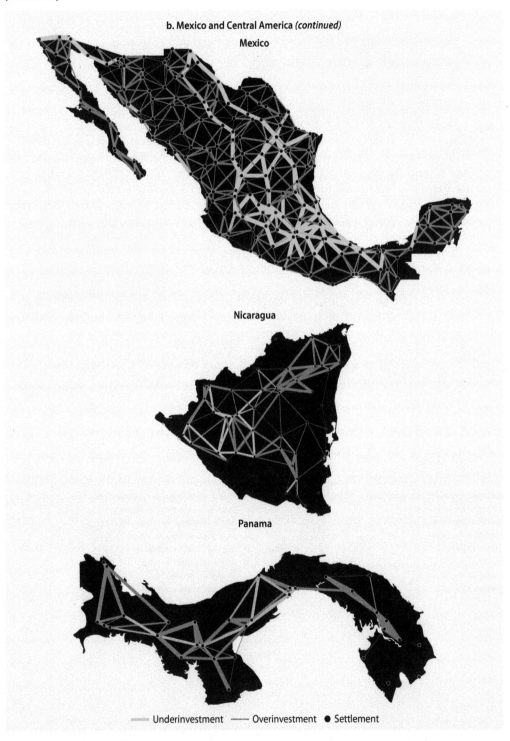

b. Mexico and Central America *(continued)*

Mexico

Nicaragua

Panama

——— Underinvestment ——— Overinvestment ● Settlement

Source: Gorton and Ianchovichina 2021.
Note: Green indicates underinvestment, whereas red indicates overinvestment. Thicker segments represent links with larger deviations from the efficient levels of investment. The nodes represent settlements.

São Paolo to cities in the northeast. In Colombia, underinvestment is observed in roads connecting Bogotá with cities in the north, northwest, and southwest. For Mexico, the model suggests overinvestment in the trunk road infrastructure in the western parts of the country and the Yucatán Peninsula and underinvestment in eastern Mexico, starting at the border city of Cuidad Juárez and extending to Monterrey and the densely populated core at the center of which is Mexico City.

Welfare effects of misplaced road investments

The spatial inefficiencies in road networks have welfare implications through their effects on transport costs, which alter the patterns of trade flows and travel, as well as production and consumption in each locality. Transport costs influence, by means of general equilibrium forces, the prices at which goods are shipped and the incentives for specialization. They are shaped by two opposing forces. Transport costs decline after improvements in the road infrastructure connecting a pair of locations, but as shipments between these locations increase, congestion increases along the link, and trade costs adjust upward. The overinvestment in rural roads reflects perhaps the need to transport agricultural and resource commodities produced in remote regions. However, it may indicate that infrastructure investments are based on equity considerations[15] or political priorities rather than efficiency.

The static annual welfare losses from road infrastructure inefficiencies are estimated at 2.4 percent in Argentina and at 2.1 percent in Brazil (figure 4.3, panel a). The efficiency losses are smallest in the Central American countries and Uruguay, where 40 percent of the population lives in the capital city of Montevideo, and more than 95 percent of the population lives in urban areas, many of them along the coast and around the capital.

FIGURE 4.3   **Welfare effects of domestic road inefficiencies and improvements, selected Latin American countries**

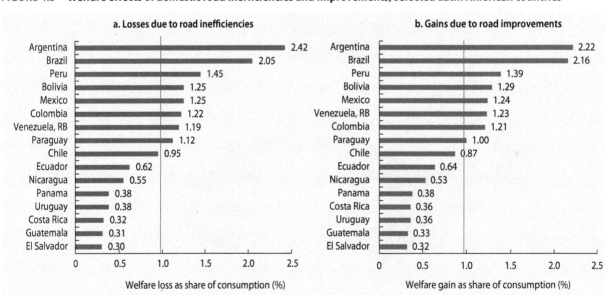

Source: Gorton and Ianchovichina (2021), using the spatial general equilibrium model of Fajgelbaum and Schaal (2020).
Note: The welfare loss from misallocated roads is equivalent to the welfare gain from optimal reallocation. The vertical line in each panel indicates the regional loss (or gain) as a simple average.

On average, the regional welfare loss from inefficiencies in Latin America's domestic road networks is estimated at 1.6 percent of regional consumption (as a weighted average) or about 1 percent of consumption (as a simple average). This loss is comparable to the one in Europe reported in Fajgelbaum and Schaal (2020). Although European national road networks are more developed than those in Latin America, Europe's population is also more spatially dispersed within countries. In Latin America, more than 70 percent of urban areas have population densities above the global median, while in Europe this share is less than 20 percent (Roberts 2018). These welfare losses are conservative estimates for two reasons.[16] First, Gorton and Ianchovichina (2021) assume that congestion increases on roads that receive additional investments. Without congestion, which is the standard assumption in the literature, the welfare effects of optimal road improvements would approximately double.[17] Second, Gorton and Ianchovichina (2021) use a static model in which trade frictions do not affect agglomeration forces and there are no spatial productivity spillovers from firms' investments. Such productivity effects would amplify the welfare losses from spatial inefficiencies and the gains from optimal improvements in the domestic road networks, as shown later in this chapter.

Additional, optimally positioned improvements[18] can correct for the observed inefficiencies in the domestic road networks of Latin American countries (Gorton and Ianchovichina 2021). Therefore, their spatial pattern, shown in green in map 4.4, is closely aligned with the spatial pattern of road underinvestments, shown in green in map 4.3. The welfare gains from these optimal road improvements are similar in size to the welfare losses from the observed inefficiencies (figure 4.3, panel b), but these gross estimates do not factor in the financing costs of increasing the road construction budget. If resources are sought by raising taxes or pulling resources from other public investments, the welfare gains would be smaller. Nevertheless, these results are useful because they are indicative of the optimal spatial allocation of road infrastructure projects. Reducing the size of a budget by 80 percent reduces the welfare gains from the investments by 44 percent and affects quantitively, but not qualitatively, the placement of road investments.

Welfare effects of road improvements and their spatial variation

In the short run the areas that gain the most from the additional optimal investments in intercity road networks (map 4.4) are often not the leading areas where most of the improvements are made, but instead are poorly connected, lagging areas located in the periphery of these expansions, as illustrated by Argentina, Brazil, and Mexico in map 4.5. The optimal cuts in transport costs reduce spatial inequality by increasing relatively more the consumption in locations with initially low levels of consumption.[19] Evidence from India suggests that these improvements can stimulate economic development in districts along the highway, especially those with better access to education and stronger initial financial development (Das et al. 2019; Ghani, Grover, and Kerr 2013). In Argentina, such complementary investments have been shown to increase the welfare effects of road investments along the corridors linking Buenos Aires with the northwest by an estimated 45 percent and with Mesopotamia by an estimated 65 percent (World Bank 2020).

MAP 4.4 **Additional optimal road improvements, selected Latin American countries**

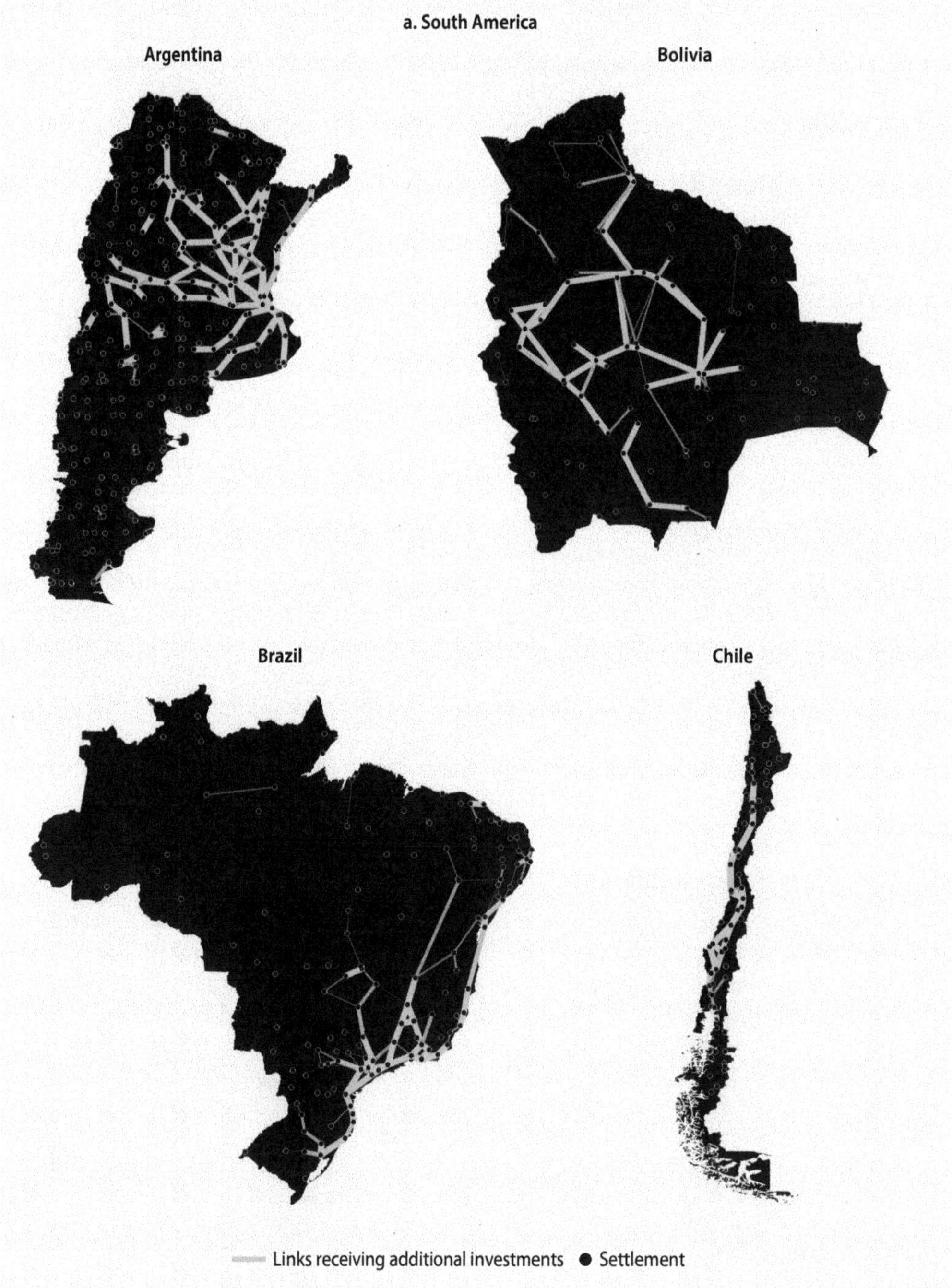

a. South America

Argentina

Bolivia

Brazil

Chile

Links receiving additional investments ● Settlement

(Continued on next page)

MAP 4.4   **Additional optimal road improvements, selected Latin American countries** *(continued)*

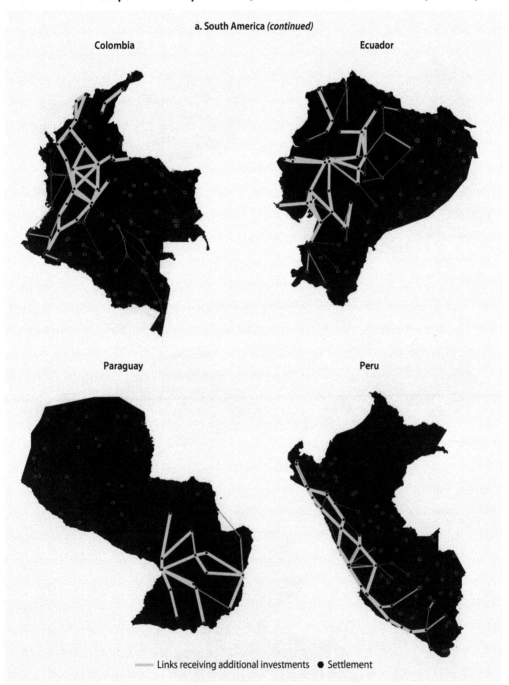

a. South America *(continued)*

Colombia   Ecuador

Paraguay   Peru

Links receiving additional investments   ● Settlement

(Continued on next page)

MAP 4.4 **Additional optimal road improvements, selected Latin American countries** *(continued)*

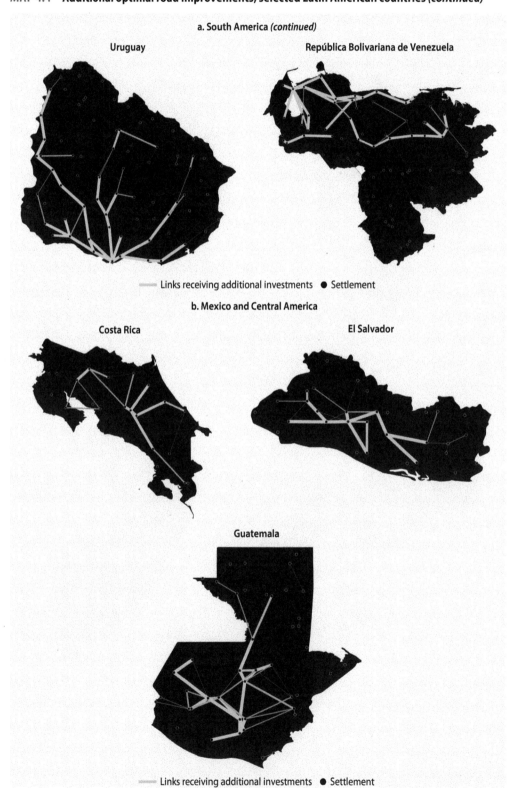

a. South America *(continued)*

Uruguay

República Bolivariana de Venezuela

——— Links receiving additional investments   ● Settlement

b. Mexico and Central America

Costa Rica

El Salvador

Guatemala

——— Links receiving additional investments   ● Settlement

(Continued on next page)

MAP 4.4   Additional optimal road improvements, selected Latin American countries *(continued)*

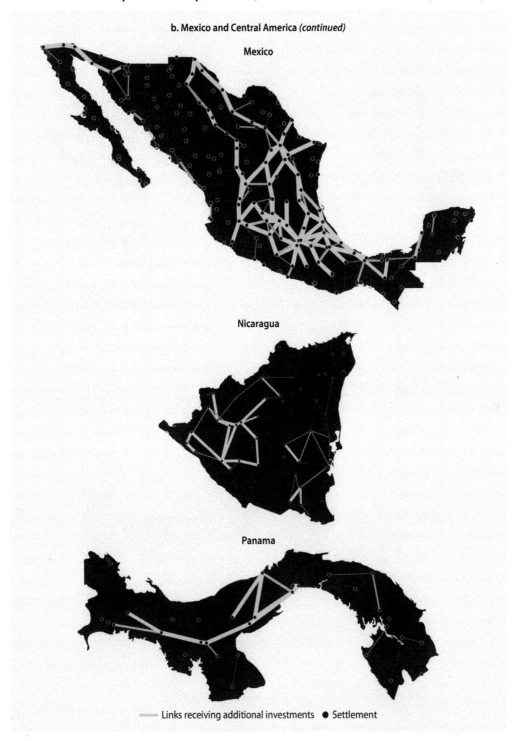

b. Mexico and Central America *(continued)*

Mexico

Nicaragua

Panama

——— Links receiving additional investments   ● Settlement

Source: Gorton and Ianchovichina 2021.
Note: The links receiving additional road investments are green. The additional road investments correspond to a 50 percent increase in the infrastructure network. Thicker segments represent links with larger investments. The nodes represent settlements.

MAP 4.5   Spatial distribution of welfare effects from optimal road improvements, Argentina, Brazil, and Mexico

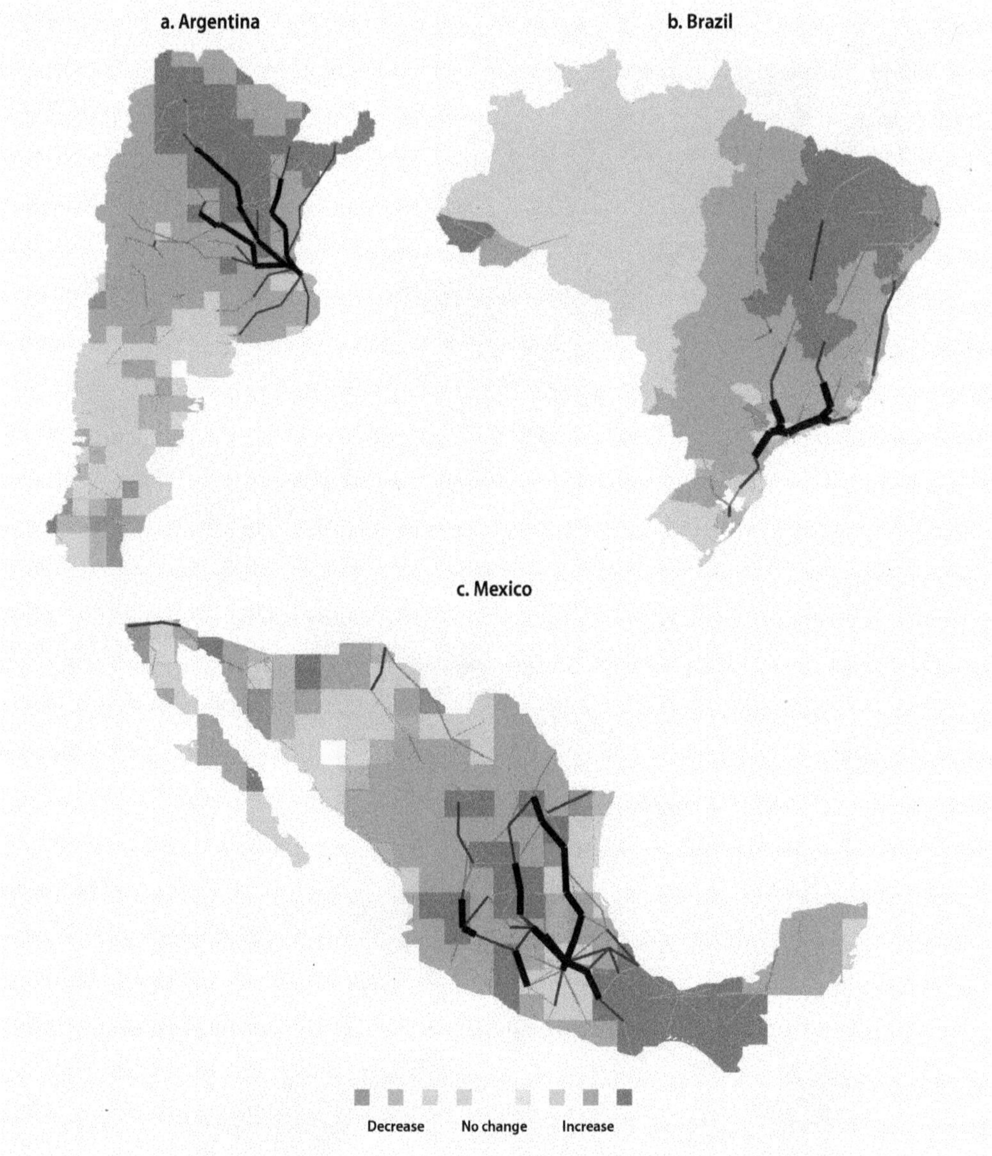

a. Argentina

b. Brazil

c. Mexico

Decrease   No change   Increase

Source: Gorton and Ianchovichina 2021.
Note: Green shades identify the cells with welfare increases, whereas orange shades identify the cells with welfare declines. The darker the shade, the larger is the increase or decline. Black and gray lines identify road links that receive additional infrastructure investments for road improvements. The darker and thicker the line, the larger are the investments.

Which type of mobility friction creates larger economic inefficiencies?

The advanced stage of urbanization and the chronically low public investment rates in the LAC region may signal that migration barriers are not the main source of spatial inefficiency in the region (figure 4.4). Yet in highly urbanized economies there may be barriers that prevent the mobility of labor across predominantly urban areas, especially

FIGURE 4.4   Public investment rates by region, 1990s, 2000s, and 2010s

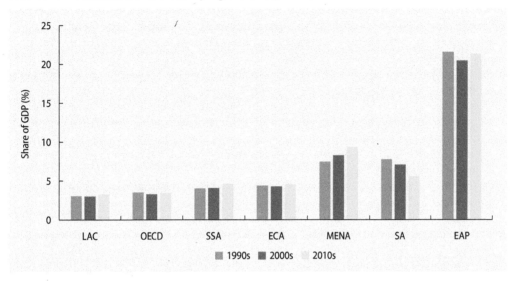

Source: World Bank, based on data from the International Financial Statistics, International Monetary Fund (https://data.imf.org/?sk=4c514d48-b6ba
-49ed-8ab9-52b0c1a0179b).
Note: Regional aggregates are weighted averages. EAP = East Asia and Pacific; ECA = Europe and Central Asia; LAC = Latin America and the
Caribbean; MENA = Middle East and North Africa; OECD = Organisation for Economic Co-operation and Development; SA = South Asia;
SSA = Sub-Saharan Africa; GDP = gross domestic product.

movement between secondary cities and primary urban centers. Furthermore, as
described in the previous section, in some countries the static aggregate welfare effects of
underinvestment in road networks may not be substantial. In such economies, migration
barriers may present a bigger cost from an aggregate growth or welfare perspective.

Conte and Ianchovichina (2022) explore the relative importance of migration frictions by comparing the effects of reduced trade and migration costs on long-run spatial
development in Latin America. They use fine-grained spatial data, including on initial
utility, which varies across subnational regions within LAC countries (see annex 4A for
details), and the state-of-the-art dynamic global spatial general equilibrium model of
Desmet, Nagy, and Rossi-Hansberg (2018), whose technical features are summarized
in box 4A.1. Several properties of the model stand out. First, it captures all locations
on Earth, and each location is unique because of its relative position to other locations,
which determines its transport costs, amenities, and initial utility. Second, national bor-
ders restrict migration across countries, but migration frictions also exist within countries. Third, labor productivity in each location evolves over time because firms have
incentives to improve their local technology in response to changes in the size of the
market for their products.[20] However, firms also benefit from the diffusion of innova-
tions developed in other locations. And, fourth, agglomeration forces affect a location's
productivity and its amenities because higher population density promotes innovation,
but also results in greater congestion costs.

The baseline scenario shows the expected spatial evolution of Latin America over the
next century in the absence of any changes to mobility frictions. Two counterfactuals are
then compared against the baseline. In the first counterfactual, trade costs are reduced in
an optimal way along the segments identified to receive additional investments by Gorton

and Ianchovichina (2021), as shown in map 4.4. This way, Conte and Ianchovichina (2022) simulate the long-term effects of additional optimal road investments aimed at addressing the spatial inefficiencies in the road networks of the Latin American countries. As discussed earlier, these inefficiencies are more pronounced along road segments that link more productive and populous locations, which include some of the top urban locations in the Latin American countries. The costs of shipping goods between such locations are also higher in Latin America than in the United States, the European Union, China, and Southeast Asia (figure 4.2). In the second counterfactual, the entry migration costs in the top locations are reduced to those in the bottom quartile of the domestic distribution of entry migration costs. The focus on entry barriers in top locations is warranted because Hsieh and Moretti (2019) show that aggregate efficiency losses are significant when entry costs in top locations are high.

In the long run (circa 2100), dynamic gains generate much stronger growth effects from optimal reductions in transport costs than the short-run gains presented in the previous section. The estimated increase relative to the baseline in the present discounted values of the regional real per capita income is assessed at 15 percent and of welfare at 54 percent (table 4.1). Although they expose lagging areas to competition in the longer run, optimal reductions in transport costs also stimulate specialization, innovation, and agglomeration of economic activity in areas with better market access. Meanwhile, technological diffusion fuels growth in neighboring areas (map 4.6) and boosts not only internal trade and migration, but also external trade and international migration.[21] At the end of the century, these interventions are expected to increase the wages and the population in areas along Brazil's coast, especially in the south; in parts of Uruguay, northern Argentina, and Paraguay; in the core of Chile around Santiago; and in the highlands of Bolivia, Ecuador, and Peru (map 4.6). The gains in welfare are higher than the gains in output because migration allows people to relocate to areas with better amenities. In small and relatively low-income countries, in addition to boosting economic activity, these investments enable countries to retain residents who otherwise would migrate to other countries.

By contrast, reductions in the entry migration costs in top locations—whenever they are higher than the bottom quartile entry costs—have a negligible effect on the present discounted value of the region's real per capita income (−0.5 percent) in the long run (2100)—see table 4.1. The small growth effect reflects the relatively small dispersion in entry migration costs in Latin American economies. The muted effect is further eroded over time by agglomeration diseconomies. However, the welfare gain is projected to be considerably larger (19.1 percent) because the reduction in entry migration costs allows some people to relocate to areas with better amenities and derive higher utility. These results suggest that high transport costs, not high entry migration costs, are the key constraint to long-run economic growth in Latin America.

TABLE 4.1   Change in the present discounted values of output and welfare under two alternative scenarios relative to baseline, 2000–2100

	Variable	
Scenario	Real per capita GDP (% change)	Welfare (% change)
Optimal reductions in trade costs	15.05	53.64
Reduction in entry migration costs in top locations	−0.53	19.10

Source: Conte and Ianchovichina 2022.

MAP 4.6 Effects of cuts in intercity transport costs in 2100 by location, LAC region

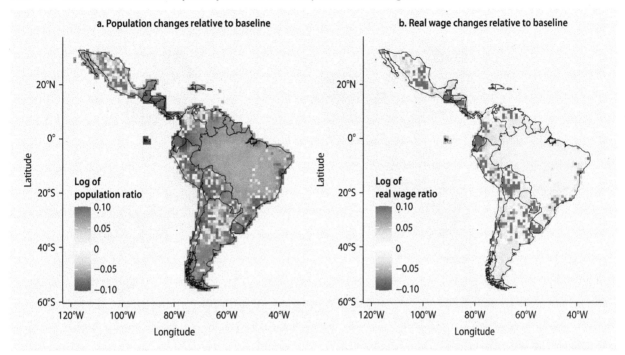

Source: Conte and Ianchovichina (2022), using the dynamic spatial general equilibrium model of Desmet, Nagy, and Rossi-Hansberg (2018) and the optimal reductions in trade costs from Gorton and Ianchovichina (2021).
Note: The maps show the log ratio between the grid cell level of population (or real wages) in the simulation with optimal cuts in trade costs and the baseline with no cuts. Values larger than zero indicate higher outcomes, and values smaller than zero indicate lower outcomes in the simulation with lower trade frictions.

Welfare effects of additional optimal investments in transnational road networks

Gorton and Ianchovichina (2021) show that the high transport costs among major cities in Latin America reflect in part misallocated and insufficient investment in transnational road networks. Within MERCOSUR, optimal road investments are needed to improve road connectivity between the largest cities of each member country and thus lower the cost of trade among members of the bloc (map 4.7, panel a). The need for additional optimal road investments is greatest in Brazil, which accounts for 71 percent of the total additional investment in the bloc, followed by Argentina (22 percent), Paraguay (7 percent), and Uruguay (7 percent).

Within the Andean Community, additional optimal investments are needed to improve road connectivity from La Paz in Bolivia, along the coast of Peru to Lima, and then through Quito to Medellín. Half of the infrastructure growth needs to occur in Colombia, a quarter in Peru, slightly less than a quarter in Ecuador, and the remaining tiny portion in Bolivia. Fortunately, in the countries expected to make the bulk of the additional investments in transnational roads—Brazil, Colombia, and Peru—many of the links receiving optimal transnational investments are also those receiving optimal domestic investments. Thus there is an alignment between the domestic and regional needs for improved road connectivity.

The estimated welfare gains from additional optimal investments in improved international road connectivity in MERCOSUR and the Andean Community are largest for Paraguay and Bolivia, the landlocked and less developed members of their respective trade

MAP 4.7   Optimal improvements in transnational road networks, MERCOSUR and Andean Community

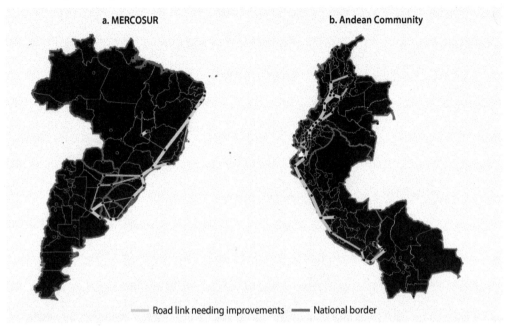

a. MERCOSUR   b. Andean Community

━━━ Road link needing improvements   ━━━ National border

Source: Gorton and Ianchovichina (2021), using the spatial general equilibrium model of Fajgelbaum and Schaal (2020).
Note: MERCOSUR is a South American trade bloc. Its full members are Argentina, Brazil, Paraguay, and Uruguay. The Andean Community is a free trade area that includes Bolivia, Colombia, Ecuador, and Peru. Road network segments identified in green need improvements. The thicker and brighter the line, the larger are the investments.

FIGURE 4.5   Welfare effects of optimal improvements of transnational road networks, MERCOSUR and Andean Community

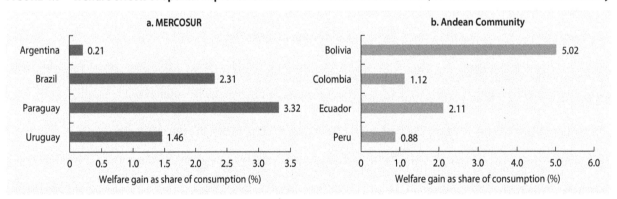

a. MERCOSUR

Argentina	0.21
Brazil	2.31
Paraguay	3.32
Uruguay	1.46

Welfare gain as share of consumption (%)

b. Andean Community

Bolivia	5.02
Colombia	1.12
Ecuador	2.11
Peru	0.88

Welfare gain as share of consumption (%)

Source: Gorton and Ianchovichina (2021), using the spatial general equilibrium model of Fajgelbaum and Schaal (2020).
Note: MERCOSUR is a South American trade bloc. Its full members are Argentina, Brazil, Paraguay, and Uruguay. The Andean Community is a free trade area that includes Bolivia, Colombia, Ecuador, and Peru.

blocs (figure 4.5). In all member countries except Argentina and Peru, these gains are comparable or bigger than those associated with additional investments in domestic road networks.

Overcoming the curse of distance through digital technologies

During the COVID-19 pandemic, many countries coped with restrictions on movements by switching to home-based work. The availability of high-speed internet and digital technologies for data sharing and collaboration made it possible to perform virtually many jobs that had required face-to-face interactions, in turn reducing dramatically the need for business travel and daily commuting. Similarly, the digital delivery of services—for example, virtual appointments with doctors, lawyers, accountants, teachers, and other service providers—reduced the need for customers to visit service providers and travel during the day. By reducing the need to travel to work, digital technologies can also attenuate congestion and urban pollution.[22]

An international comparison of people's ability to telecommute to work by Montañés et al. (2021) suggests that Latin America is behind other emerging markets and member countries of the Organisation for Economic Co-operation and Development (OECD). Unlike most OECD economies, where in the late 2010s between 15 and 38 percent of workers had jobs suitable for home-based work (figure 4.6), in Argentina, Brazil, Chile, and Uruguay these rates ranged between 10 and 14 percent; in all other Latin American countries they were 10 percent or below (figure 4.7).

Generally, the share of workers with jobs suitable for telecommuting increases with the country's level of economic development, the quality and cost of its digital and information and communication technology (ICT) infrastructure services, and the share of good quality (formal) jobs in the economy. Although most countries had registered growth in jobs suitable for telecommuting during the 2010s, this growth was weak in many countries, including Brazil, Colombia, El Salvador, Mexico, Panama, and Peru, and in Bolivia and Ecuador it was negative. Thus there is heterogeneity in the ability of countries to take advantage of telecommuting possibilities.

Across socioeconomic groups, there are large differences between the shares of workers who can telecommute to work (figure 4.8). Younger (ages 25–34), more skilled and educated workers, women, urbanites, and the affluent are more likely to have jobs that allow them to switch to telecommuting than older, less skilled workers, men, rural residents, and the poor, respectively. Formal employees of large firms and public

FIGURE 4.6 **Share of workers who have jobs suitable for telecommuting by country**

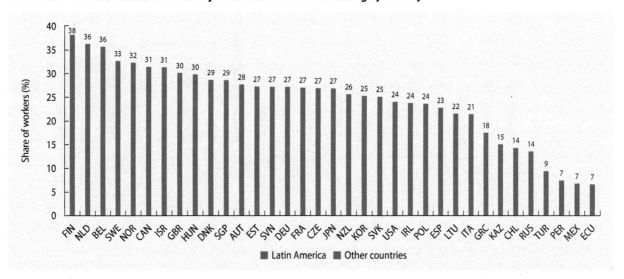

Source: Montañés et al. (2021), based on Hatayama, Viollaz, and Winkler (2020) and surveys from the Programme for the International Assessment of Adult Competencies (PIAAC, https://www.oecd.org/skills/piaac/).
Note: The vertical axis shows the share of workers who can work from home. The reference year varies by country groups: 2011–12: Austria, Belgium (Flanders), Canada, the Czech Republic, Denmark, Estonia, Finland, France, Germany, Ireland, Italy, Japan, the Republic of Korea, the Netherlands, Norway, Poland, the Russian Federation, the Slovak Republic, Spain, Sweden, and the United Kingdom (England and Northern Ireland); 2014–15: Chile, Greece, Israel, Lithuania, New Zealand, Singapore, Slovenia, and Türkiye; 2017: Ecuador, Hungary, Kazakhstan, Mexico, Peru, and the United States. For country abbreviations, see International Organization for Standardization (ISO), https://www.iso.org/obp/ui/#search.

FIGURE 4.7   **Trends in the share of workers with jobs amenable to home-based work, LAC region**

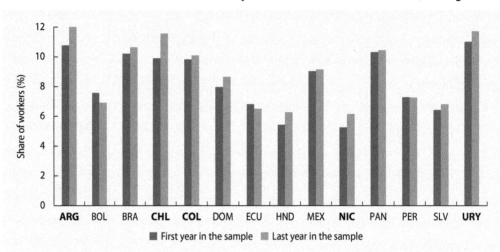

Source: Montañés et al. (2021), based on harmonized data from the Socio-Economic Database for Latin America and the Caribbean (SEDLAC, https://www.cedlas.econo.unlp.edu.ar/wp/en/estadisticas/sedlac/) at the two-digit ISCO-08 level in the International Standard Classification of Occupations.
Note: The vertical axis shows the share of workers who can work from home. Countries in bold are those with at least an eight-year gap between the first and last year available in the sample. For country abbreviations, see International Organization for Standardization (ISO), https://www.iso.org/obp/ui/#search.

FIGURE 4.8   **Average share of workers able to telecommute by socioeconomic group, LAC region**

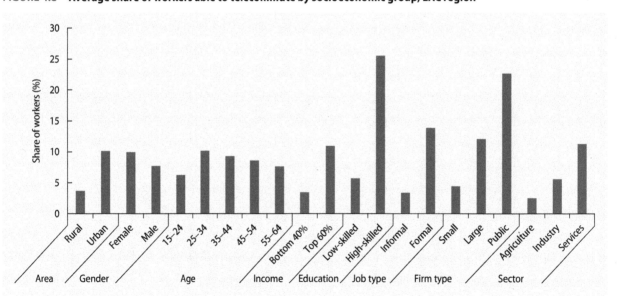

Source: Montañés et al. (2021), based on harmonized data from the Socio-Economic Database for Latin America and the Caribbean (CEDLAC and World Bank, https://www.cedlas.econo.unlp.edu.ar/wp/en/estadisticas/sedlac/) at the two-digit ISCO-08 level in the International Standard Classification of Occupations.
Note: The vertical axis shows for the most recent year in the sample the share of workers who can work from home averaged across all LAC countries in the sample. High-skilled workers are those who completed a tertiary education; low-skilled workers are the rest. Job formality is defined using the productive definition in which formal workers include salaried workers in a large private firm or the public sector, the self-employed with a college education, and employers.

companies and those working in professional services have jobs that are most suitable for telecommuting.

Montañés et al. (2021) find that education and job formality status are the strongest predictors of workers' telecommuting abilities, while age, gender, and location explain only a small share of the observed differences in telecommuting rates.[23] When indicators for economic sector and home access to the internet are included in the analysis, the estimations suggest that the jobs least suitable for telecommuting are those in the hospitality industry, commerce, agriculture, and construction, while the most suitable are those in public administration, finance, business, education, and health services. The jobs most suitable for telecommuting also tend to pay significantly higher wages.

Although at the individual level the rural-urban gap plays a minimal role in explaining observable differences in workers' ability to telecommute, in most countries there are significant cross-country differences between the rural and urban deficits in internet access for workers with jobs suitable for telecommuting, as well as significant regional disparities beyond the urban-rural dimension. In Brazil, Chile, and Uruguay, all workers with jobs suitable for home-based work have access to the internet at home (figure 4.9). In other countries, the deficits are larger in rural areas, where fewer people have jobs suitable for telecommuting. For example, in Mexico's rural areas 73 percent of workers in jobs suitable for telecommuting do not have internet access at home versus 24 percent in urban areas. In Colombia, the respective shares are 82 percent in rural areas versus 35 percent in urban areas. In Guatemala, Nicaragua, and Peru, most if not all rural workers with jobs suitable for telecommuting do not have home internet access.

However, internet access is only one of several factors enabling telecommuting. Most of the subnational differences in the amenability of jobs to home-based work stem from differences in the availability of jobs that could be performed from home (proxied with the size of the public sector) and differences in skills and education levels (figure 4.8).

FIGURE 4.9 **Rural and urban workers with jobs suitable for telecommuting but who have no internet access at home, LAC region**

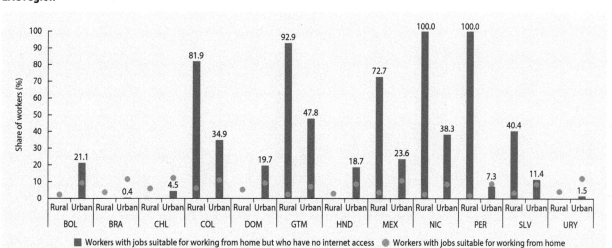

Source: Montañés et al. (2021), based on Socio-Economic Database for Latin America and the Caribbean (CEDLAS and the World Bank, https://www.cedlas.econo.unlp.edu.ar/wp/en/estadisticas/sedlac/) household survey data.
Note: For Bolivia, the Dominican Republic, and Honduras, the zeros in terms of the percentage of workers with jobs suitable for working from home (WFH) but who have no internet access at home indicate the absence of individuals with jobs suitable for telecommuting. For Brazil, Chile, and Uruguay, the zeros indicate that all workers with WFH-amenable jobs have internet access at home. For country abbreviations, see International Organization for Standardization (ISO), https://www.iso.org/obp/ui/#search.

Nevertheless, internet access is a necessary condition for telecommuting and further development of the digital economy, and access to fast, reliable, and affordable internet services is key to this strategy.

The cost of broadband services varies both across and within countries. The average subscription cost is highest in the Central American countries (figure 4.10, panel a). Affordability, measured as the ratio between the average national subscription cost and the regional income per capita, also varies widely. Internet services are most unaffordable for the poorest residents of the LAC region (figure 4.10, panel b), especially those in rural areas (figure 4.10, panel c). In Honduras, which is an extreme case, the cost of a fixed broadband subscription accounts for nearly 90 percent of the average income of those in

FIGURE 4.10   Internet affordability and internet access by region and welfare group

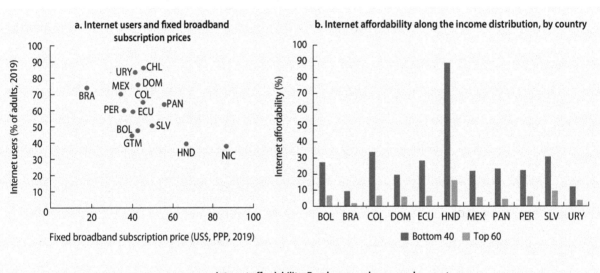

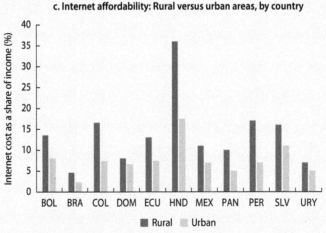

Source: Montañés et al. (2021), based on data from the Socio-Economic Database for Latin America and the Caribbean (CEDLAS and the World Bank, https://www.cedlas.econo.unlp .edu.ar/wp/en/estadisticas/sedlac/) and the International Telecommunication Union (ITU, https://www.itu.int/en/Pages/default.aspx).
Note: Price data correspond to the monthly price for a fixed broadband 5-gigabyte (GB) plan (expressed in 2011 international dollars adjusted for purchasing power parity, PPP). Internet price data from the ITU are at the country level and refer to 2019 (panel a). Internet affordability is calculated as the ratio between the monthly price for a fixed broadband 5 GB plan and the regional average monthly income per capita (both variables expressed in 2011 PPP international dollars). Bottom 40 refers to individuals in the bottom 40 percent of the income distribution; top 60 refers to all other individuals. For country abbreviations, see International Organization for Standardization (ISO), https://www.iso.org/obp /ui/#search.

the bottom 40 percent of the income distribution, compared with 16 percent for those in the top 60 percent of households. In all other countries, this cost varies between 9 and 34 percent of the average income of the bottom 40 percent.

The evidence presented in this chapter suggests that high transport costs between top urban locations, not high entry migration barriers in these locations, constrain long-run economic growth in the LAC region. The high within-country and cross-country intercity transport costs reflect, in part, underinvestment in national and transnational intercity road networks. These results are consistent with the findings by Quintero and Roberts (2018) and Blankespoor et al. (2017). In the short run, additional optimal road investments can reduce both high intercity transport costs *and* territorial inequality. In the long run, while exposing some lagging areas to more competition, optimal reductions in transport costs are expected to stimulate the specialization, innovation, and agglomeration of economic activity in urban areas with better market access. Digital technologies could help countries overcome the curse of distance, but recent data suggest that in most LAC countries the share of people with jobs suitable for telecommuting is lower than that in OECD countries and emerging Europe. The development of alternative modes of transport, such as river and rail, along routes that in the past received insufficient investments in road infrastructure improvements may also be warranted in the context of climate and mass transit priorities. The next chapter turns to the nature of economic activity and employment in Latin America's urban areas and other factors shaping urban productivity.

Annex 4A Endogenous growth model, data, and calibration of entry migration costs

This annex presents in box 4A.1 the model of Desmet, Nagy, and Rossi-Hansberg (2018). A description of both the data required to implement the model and the calibration of entry migration costs follows.

BOX 4A.1   Global endogenous growth model with spatial heterogeneity

In the model of Desmet, Nagy, and Rossi-Hansberg (2018), the world is represented by a two-dimensional space S consisting of a continuum of locations. Each location r has land density $H(r) > 0$ and an initial population of workers $\overline{L_0}(r)$. Consumers decide how much to consume and where to live. In each period t, consumers derive utility from local amenities $a_t(r)$, the consumption y_t of a representative good, modeled as a constant elasticity of substitution (CES) aggregate of differentiated varieties. Consumers have homogeneous preferences and cannot borrow or save, and so in each period they consume all their income, which is derived from wages and land rents. Thus the utility of a consumer i who chooses to live in location r in period t is given by

$$u_t^i(\overline{r},r) = a_t(r) \times y_t(r) \times \varepsilon_t^i(r) \times \overline{m}(\overline{r},r)^{-1}, \qquad (B4A.1.1)$$

where $\overline{r} = (r_0,...,r_{t-1})$ denotes the history of locations where the consumer lived prior to period t, and $\overline{m}(\overline{r},r) = \Pi_{s=1}^t m(r_{s-1},r_s)$ is the migration cost cumulatively incurred based on all past choices $\overline{r}$ and the current location r. The local amenities of location r, $a_t(r) = \overline{a}(r)\overline{L_t}(r)^{-\lambda}$, depend on the fundamental and exogenous level of amenities in r, $\overline{a}(r)$, and the parameter driving the negative externalities to population density, $\lambda > 0$.

(Continued on next page)

BOX 4A.1   Global endogenous growth model with spatial heterogeneity (continued)

When choosing where to live, consumers are guided by the stochastic taste shock $\varepsilon_t^i(r)$, distributed according to a Fréchet distribution, which depends on parameter Ω. This parameter determines the heterogeneity of agents' preference on where to live and the intensity of congestion forces in the economy. The higher Ω, the higher are the frictions to the mobility of consumers across S. Finally, in the absence of migration frictions within a location, only the destination-specific entry barriers $m_2(r)$ in the current period matter for the optimal location choice. Then, the total population in location r at time t has the closed-form solution

$$H(r)\overline{L_t}(r) = \frac{u_t(r)^{1/\Omega} m_2(r)^{-1/\Omega}}{\int_S u_t(v)^{1/\Omega} m_2(v)^{-1/\Omega} dv} \overline{L}, \qquad \text{(B4A.1.2)}$$

where $u_t(r) = a_t(r)y_t(r)$.

In each location r, firms produce a good $\omega \in [0,1]$, using land and labor so that production per unit of land of good ω in location r at period t takes the form of

$$q_t^\omega(r) = \phi_t^\omega(r)^{\gamma_1} z_t^\omega(r) L_t^\omega(r)^\mu. \qquad \text{(B4A.1.3)}$$

The firm's productivity depends on a local, variety-specific productivity parameter, $z_t^\omega(r)$, as well as an innovation parameter, $\phi_t^\omega(r)$, drawn from a Fréchet distribution so that local productivity at any point in time is partially driven by agglomeration economies, local innovation, and the diffusion of innovation to nearby locations. In each unit of land, a continuum of firms competes in prices. Because the firms are similar over small units of land, locally firms face perfect competition. The solution to the static profit maximization of a firm is such that the shipping price of variety ω produced in r and consumed in s is proportional to the marginal cost of production, $mc_t(r)$, at r and the trade costs between the two locations, $\zeta(s,r)$. In the absence of credit markets, trade is balanced location by location, so that local nominal income in r equals total expenditure from all locations s on goods produced in location r. This implies that

$$w_t(r)H_t(r)\overline{L_t}(r) = \int_S \left[\frac{T_t(r)\left[mc_t(r)\zeta(s,r)\right]^{-\theta}}{\int_S T_t(u)\left[mc_t(u)\zeta(s,u)\right]^{-\theta} du} \right] w_t(s)H_t(s)\overline{L_t}(s)ds, \qquad \text{(B4A.1.4)}$$

where $w_t(r)$ denotes nominal ages, and $w_t(r)H_t(r)\overline{L_t}(r)$ denotes income. A dynamic equilibrium of the economy exists and is a sequence of static equilibria where, in each period t, markets for goods and labor clear. That requires both (B4A.1.2) and (B4A.1.4) to simultaneously hold in each period.

In Desmet, Nagy, and Rossi-Hansberg (2018) and Conte and Ianchovichina (2022), the Earth's surface is divided into about 17,000 1° × 1° grid cells. The destination-specific entry migration costs, $m_2(r)$, are quantified for each location r using a calibration strategy, which starts with estimation of the fundamental amenities $(\overline{a}(r))$ to the initial level of utility $(u_0(r))$ ratio, $(\overline{a}(r) / u_0(r))$, for each location r of the model in a way that allows the model-implied economic activity and population to match exactly the spatial distribution of the economic activity and population worldwide for the year 2000. The main source for these data is the G-Econ data set (Nordhaus et al. 2006), which provides global gridded GDP and population data.

Conte and Ianchovichina (2022) proxy initial utility in the Latin American countries with geocoded data on subjective well-being from several survey rounds of the Latinobarómetro covering the period 1997–2000. The Latinobarómetro provides much finer geographical coverage of the LAC region than the Gallup World Poll (GWP); it is representative of the subnational level, whereas the GWP is representative of the national level. To increase the spatial coverage of subjective well-being within countries for which the information from Latinobarómetro was insufficient, Conte and Ianchovichina (2022) also use the individual-level data from the GWP for Argentina, Brazil, Colombia, Ecuador, Mexico, and Paraguay for the period 2000–2015. In this way, they obtain information on subjective well-being for about 100 additional coordinates that are then matched to the Desmet, Nagy, and Rossi-Hansberg (2018) grid. For the rest of the world, they follow Desmet, Nagy, and Rossi-Hansberg (2018) and use the GWP's average subjective well-being (SWB) Cantril Ladder scores circa 2000 to proxy initial utility.

The Cantril Ladder is an ordinal scale indicating how people rate their own lives. The scores range from 0 for the worst possible life to 10 for the best possible life. Although the benchmarks for worst and best possible life may vary across individuals, regions, and countries, Desmet, Nagy, and Rossi-Hansberg (2018) abstract from such potential differences in the benchmarks based on the finding by Deaton and Stone (2013) and Stevenson and Wolfers (2013) of a relationship between subjective well-being and the log of real income that is similar within the United States as well as across countries. To convert the ordinal SWB scores into cardinal values, Desmet, Nagy, and Rossi-Hansberg (2018) estimate a cross-country regression of SWB of an individual i residing in location r on the log of their real income (Deaton and Stone 2013; Kahneman and Deaton 2010).[24]

For compatibility with the 0–10 scale of the Cantril Ladder metric used in the GWP, the recorded answers to the life satisfaction question in the Latinobarómetro—which fall into four categories: "very satisfied," "fairly satisfied," "not very satisfied," and "not at all satisfied"—are set at 10, 7.5, 5.0, and 2.5, respectively. The countries covered in this adjustment are Argentina, Bolivia, Brazil, Chile, Colombia, Costa Rica, Ecuador, El Salvador, Guatemala, Honduras, Mexico, Nicaragua, Panama, Paraguay, Peru, Uruguay, and República Bolivariana de Venezuela. Next, Conte and Ianchovichina (2022) geocode all 536 coordinates of the interview locations in the Latinobarómetro surveys. They then overlay the coordinates at the first administrative level (states) and calculate the average well-being in each of the administrative units. They also normalize the values so that the maximum equals one within each country.[25] Finally, they lay the Desmet, Nagy, and Rossi-Hansberg (2018) grid over the administrative shape of the Latin American countries to obtain the 0–1 scale of within-country well-being and multiply the subjective well-being values used by Desmet, Nagy, and Rossi-Hansberg (2018) by this scale to obtain adjusted heterogeneous values for subjective well-being within the Latin American countries. Using the values for initial utility, the values for initial amenities are determined, and the model is simulated one period forward. The estimated destination-specific entry migration costs, $m_2(r)$, presented in map 4.1, are the values for which the model-implied population distribution in the subsequent year matches the one observed in the data. Table 1 in Conte and Ianchovichina (2022) presents the complete set of all calibrated parameters along with their sources.

Annex 4B Model, data, and representation of road networks

This annex presents in box 4B.1 the model of Fajgelbaum and Schaal (2020) and the general equilibrium effects of optimal road improvements. It then discusses the data required to implement the model and shows the representation of the domestic road network in a selected country.

BOX 4B.1   General equilibrium effects of optimal road improvements

Infrastructure investments have important general equilibrium effects, which are captured in the spatial model of Fajgelbaum and Schaal (2020). An improvement in one link of a road network affects every other location in the economy. It is assumed that a discrete set of 10 tradable goods are produced in the economy's most populous locations. All remaining locations produce a homogeneous nontraded good. The social planner determines the optimal investments in each road link jk (I_{jk}), the gross trade flows along the link of traded good n (Q_{jk}^n), and the optimal allocation of consumption (c_j, h_j) and production (D_j^n) across locations. This is accomplished by maximizing welfare from the consumption of a composite traded good (c_j) and nontraded good (h_j) and *jointly* solving the triple-nested optimization problem

$$\max_{I_{jk}} \max_{Q_{jk}^n} \max_{\left\{c_j, h_j, D_j^n, L_j^n, V_j^n, X_j^n\right\}} \sum_j L_j U\left(c_j, h_j\right), \tag{B4B.1.1}$$

subject to (1) a network building constraint, $\sum_j \sum_{k \in N(j)} \delta_{jk}^I I_{jk} \leq K$, given a preexisting network; (2) a flow constraint ensuring that in each location j the sum of good n's consumption, intermediate use ($X_j^{1n}, \ldots, X_j^{Nn}$), and the quantity shipped out of the location does not exceed the total production and imports of good n in location j; (3) a local factor market clearing constraint for labor and other primary factors, $V_j^n = (V_j^{1n}, \ldots, V_j^{Mn})$; (4) nonnegativity constraints on consumption, domestic trade flows, and factor use; and (5) availability of trade commodities and nontraded goods in each location. A national labor market clearing condition must also be satisfied if labor is mobile.

In contrast with standard models with exogenous transport costs, transport costs (τ_{jk}) are *endogenous* so that

$$\tau_{jk}(Q, I) = \frac{\delta_{jk}^\tau Q^\beta}{I^\gamma}. \tag{B4B.1.2}$$

They depend on how much is invested in each road link (I) and on the quantity of traded goods transported along the link (Q). Transport costs *decline* with increased investments along the link. However, as traffic along the link increases, transport costs *rise* due to congestion reflecting the increased probability of road accidents, road damage, and longer travel times. Therefore, trade flows increase with road quality,[a] decline with congestion, and increase with the price differentials between the two locations. Trade costs also depend on the geographic frictions $\delta_{jk}^\tau = \delta_0^\tau dist_{jk}$. The per kilometer cost of building along each jk link is

$$\ln\left(\frac{\delta_{jk}^I}{dist_{jk}}\right) = \ln\left(\delta_0^I\right) - 0.11 \times 1\left(dist_{jk} > 50km\right) + 0.12 \times \ln\left(ruggedness_{jk}\right), \tag{B4B.1.3}$$

where δ_{jk}^I measures the resources allocated to the jk link, which increase with the ruggedness of the terrain.

a. Road quality is inferred from the road class and pavement type.

The model in Fajgelbaum and Schaal (2020) is implemented by first constructing a grid describing the spatial distribution of economic activity and population in a country and a discretized road network that is a proxy for the country's existing road network. For the grids of relatively small Latin American countries, Gorton and Ianchovichina (2021) use 0.5-arc degree cells or 0.25-arc degree cells. However, in most cases they use 1-arc degree cells because many Latin American countries have large territories. For Brazil, even 1-arc degree cells are too small and result in a country grid with more than 800 cells. Because the computational issues become intense when the number of grid cells exceeds approximately 300, Gorton and Ianchovichina (2021) use as grid cells Brazil's mesoregions, which are administrative subdivisions of the Brazilian states. Table 4B.1 lists the main characteristics of the countries' grid and road networks.

Following Fajgelbaum and Schaal (2020), Gorton and Ianchovichina (2021) obtain population data from NASA's Socioeconomic Data and Applications Center (SEDAC) Gridded Population of the World (GPW), version 4, and value-added data from Yale University's G-Econ 4.0 (Nordhaus et al. 2006). Because it is important to use population and value-added data for the same year, both data sets refer to 2005, which is the latest year for which G-Econ data are available.[26] For Brazil, Instituto Brasileiro de Geografia e Estatística provides population and GDP data by mesoregion.

Gorton and Ianchovichina (2021) adjust the country grids of Chile, Nicaragua, and Peru to accommodate unique geographies that pose challenges to roadbuilding. In Peru, Iquitos is surrounded by a natural reserve area, and many other areas of the country are covered by forests, where roadbuilding is environmentally undesirable. Using the University of Maryland's global tree cover data set and considering grid cells to be unbuildable if at least 80 percent of a cell is covered by tree canopy, they exclude northeastern Peru from the grid. Taking these geographies into account matters for devising policy-relevant optimal road networks. Without this restriction, the optimal road network connects Iquitos to Lima and other surrounding cities. At the same time, the model does not consider it optimal to build roads in the Amazon region of Brazil. Therefore, Gorton and Ianchovichina (2021) need not impose additional restrictions on building in Brazil's Amazon region. In the case of Chile, they exclude the southern portion of the country based on the distribution of reserve areas as measured by the Chilean government.[27] In Nicaragua, a large lake prevents roadbuilding in its southeast. The grid is therefore restricted to cells that are not majority water, based on data on the locations of inland bodies of water from the International Steering Committee for Global Mapping, accessed via New York University.

Gorton and Ianchovichina (2021) measure the extent and quality of each country's existing road network using the World Bank's Global Roads Inventory Project (GRIP), and they supplement these data with information from OpenStreetMap. They convert each actual road network into a discretized network, which is a graph composed of nodes and edges. For each country, they measure infrastructure quality along each link of the network (that is, the edge of the graph) based on the information from GRIP on the type of road (motorway, trunk, primary, secondary, tertiary, local), the type of surface (paved, unpaved, asphalt, ground), and the number of lanes along each road segment. They also measure the "ruggedness" of each link from ETOPO1 Global Relief Model.

Table 4B.1 displays the characteristics of the actual and discretized networks for 16 Latin American countries. For all countries, the discretized network is much shorter in length than the actual road network because the length of the discretized network reflects the shortest path between each set of nodes (population centroids) in the discretized network, while the actual road network comprises thousands of segments connecting thousands of nodes throughout the country. In other words, the discretized network summarizes the actual road network's connections between the population centers of each grid cell (map 4B.1). Average infrastructure, while correlated with the average number of lanes per kilometer, is often lower than the average number of lanes in each country because Gorton and Ianchovichina (2021) adjust the average infrastructure index to reflect whether travel occurs via primary or nonprimary roads. For example, because much of southern Argentina can be traversed only along nonprimary roads, the average infrastructure

TABLE 4B.1   Country grid and road network summary statistics, Latin America

Country	Actual network		Discretized network			
	Length of network (km)	Average number of lanes (per km)	Cell size (arc-degree cells)	Number of cells	Length of network (km)	Average infrastructure index
Argentina	855,713	1.67	1.0	294	118,406	0.73
Bolivia	121,098	1.98	1.0	101	51,248	0.56
Brazil	727,041	2.00	—[a]	137	109,479	1.27
Chile	118,456	1.92	1.0	69	18,226	0.88
Colombia	410,003	1.80	1.0	108	55,227	0.52
Costa Rica	20,254	1.96	0.5	22	4,996	1.41
Ecuador	87,531	1.91	0.5	87	23,216	0.66
El Salvador	30,313	1.93	0.3	32	6,489	1.20
Guatemala	42,981	1.92	0.5	44	10,018	0.83
Mexico	796,553	2.09	1.0	201	102,400	1.36
Nicaragua	26,952	1.95	0.5	47	12,276	0.99
Panama	11,196	1.96	0.5	33	4,255	1.07
Paraguay	49,434	2.01	1.0	42	12,911	0.78
Peru	226,267	2.03	1.0	85	35,269	0.97
Uruguay	81,089	1.97	0.5	75	10,082	1.19
Venezuela, RB	123,567	1.67	1.0	84	42,280	0.63

Source: Gorton and Ianchovichina 2021.
Note: The average infrastructure index is the distance-weighted, road type–weighted average number of lanes connecting two grid cells. A discretized network is a graph composed of nodes and edges. km = kilometers.
a. In Brazil, mesoregions are used as grid cells.

MAP 4B.1   Actual and discretized road network, Argentina

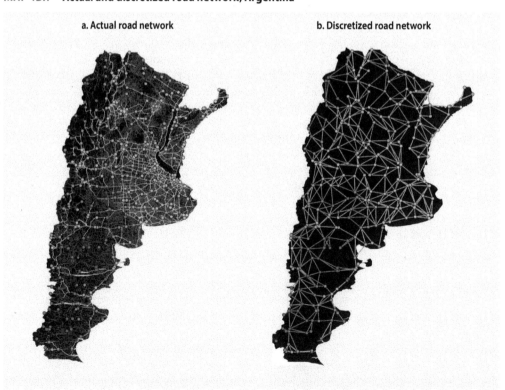

a. Actual road network   b. Discretized road network

Source: Gorton and Ianchovichina 2021.
Note: A discretized network is a graph composed of nodes and edges.

quality across discretized edges in Argentina is considerably lower than the average number of lanes, since travel between a considerable number of nodes involves travel along nonprimary roads. Because the grid cells are neither square nor uniform in size, in the case of Brazil an edge exists between two population centroids if they share a border and are within 800 kilometers of each other. NASA's SEDAC Gridded Population of the World is the source on population centers in Brazil.

Annex 4C Calibration details

In the absence of internal trade data and parameter estimates from existing studies, Gorton and Ianchovichina (2021) rely on the parameters governing congestion, returns to infrastructure, preferences, and the sensitivity of transport costs to distance from Fajgelbaum and Schaal (2020). They calibrate the latter using domestic trade data from Spain, a highly urbanized country whose population is concentrated in the capital and cities along its coasts. In line with results for other developed countries such as the United States, Fajgelbaum and Schaal (2020) find that Spain's internal trade is highly sensitive to distance. In a regression of the log of the observed territorial import shares on the log of distance, the coefficient on distance is –1.368 with a standard error of 0.058.[28] Thus a 10 percent increase in distance results in a 13.7 percent decline in trade, while in the United States a 10 percent increase in distance leads to a 14 percent decline in trade (Duranton 2015). However, the model-predicted response is much more muted and in line with empirical estimates from Colombia. With the calibrated model, Fajgelbaum and Schaal (2020) find that a 10 percent increase in distance results in a 9 percent decline in trade. This is close to the result in Duranton (2015), who estimates that in Colombia a similar increase in distance results in a 6 percent decline in trade flows. He explains the significantly lower sensitivity of internal trade in Colombia to distance by pointing to the larger share of agricultural goods and natural resources, which are typically traded over longer distances. Thus the choice to rely on the parameterization in Fajgelbaum and Schaal (2020) is adequate for a typical Latin American country.

Notes

1. Welfare or utility refers to the standard of living of people in a given area.
2. Annex 4A provides information on the data used to proxy initial utility and calibrate the entry migration costs, and box 4A.1 discusses the technical features of the model.
3. In Colombia, the government requires shippers in most sectors other than agriculture and beer to contract trucking companies through intermediaries. It also sets minimum prices for trucking services along the country's most important routes, which are binding along some of them as shown in Cantillo and Hernández (2022).
4. Except in Brazil and Mexico, the firms providing these services are low-productivity, small-scale establishments with aging fleets (World Bank 2021).
5. Allen et al. (2022) and Osborne, Pachón, and Araya (2014) provide evidence of imperfect competition in Colombia and Central America, respectively.
6. Using the approach of Maloney and Caicedo (2016), Restrepo Cadavid and Cineas (2018) find that 40 percent of the variation in subnational population densities in the region can be explained by location fundamentals, such as proximity to large bodies of water, fertile land, and a terrain that offers a strategic advantage. The remaining variation could be explained by other unmeasured fundamentals such as natural resources or historical "accidents." However, the strong persistence of subnational population density varies across countries (Maloney and Caicedo 2016). It is higher than average in Colombia and Mexico and lower than average in Argentina and Uruguay (Restrepo Cadavid and Cineas 2018).

7. Reductions in transport costs have been shown to increase the spatial concentration of firms (Ghani, Goswami, and Kerr 2016), firm birth (Holl 2004), employment (Mesquita Moreira et al. 2013), and firm efficiency (Datta 2012).

8. In Brazil, as many people moved out as moved into metropolitan areas, and those who moved out relocated in intermediate (secondary) cities, increasing their real wages. Only low-skilled domestic migrants lost in nominal terms (Egger 2021).

9. This study focuses on roads because it is the dominant mode of transport in Latin America. Development of alternative modes of transport, such as river and rail, along routes that have received insufficient investments in road infrastructure improvements may be warranted based on other priorities, such as climate and mass transit.

10. Such savings are possible because optimal infrastructure investments can be represented as functions of optimal prices, avoiding a direct search in the network space.

11. The model abstracts from smaller roads connecting to the major roadways. A discretized network is a graph composed of nodes and edges.

12. Agglomeration forces minimize the bias in the results due to the time lag in the initial economic and population data.

13. The model does not distinguish between road maintenance and new infrastructure investments. Within the model, over- and underinvestment are relative concepts. Thus in countries that chronically underinvest in their roads, it is possible that even roadways identified as links where overinvestment occurred may have received insufficiently high infrastructure investments.

14. MERCOSUR is a South American trade bloc established by the Treaty of Asunción in 1991. Its full members are Argentina, Brazil, Paraguay, and Uruguay. República Bolivariana de Venezuela has been suspended indefinitely since December 2016. The Andean Community is a free trade area that includes Bolivia, Colombia, Ecuador, and Peru.

15. Road transport is the most efficient mode of transport in low-density locations, where people may be reluctant to move elsewhere because of preferences and barriers to migration.

16. The welfare results are robust to changes in the assumption about labor mobility across locations (Gorton and Ianchovichina 2021).

17. For example, the welfare gain increases from 1.2 percent to about 2.5 percent in Colombia (Gorton and Ianchovichina 2021).

18. The model does not distinguish between different types of road improvements, including rehabilitation and maintenance projects, projects that improve the road surface (such as upgrades of dirt roads to paved ones or the resurfacing of degraded paved roads), projects that broaden existing roads by adding new lanes, or projects that improve the flow of traffic, such as bridges and interchanges.

19. This finding is consistent with the idea that the infrastructure investments made to reduce trade costs in an optimal way equalize the marginal utility of consumption across locations (Fajgelbaum and Schaal 2020).

20. The size of the market depends on transport costs and the location's geography relative to other locations.

21. Because investments in transportation infrastructure are made in an optimal way, the gains of locations that become denser and more productive outweigh any congestion costs and the losses of locations that experience outmigration.

22. There are, however, exceptions. Stokenberga, Ivarsson, and Fulponi (2023) find that e-commerce worsened congestion in Bogotá and Buenos Aires because of the increase in the number of freight vehicle trips, which were not offset by the very small reduction in the number of private vehicle trips.

23. Montañés et al. (2021) determine the contribution of each of the factors to the probability of telecommuting by estimating individual-level regressions, which control for individual and job characteristics and country fixed effects.

24. The regression includes a location fixed effect to address endogeneity concerns that a location with a higher utility attracts more people and affects the amenity levels in the location.

25. If an administrative unit does not have data on well-being from the Latinobarómetro, they assign to it the minimum for the country.

26. Gorton and Ianchovichina (2021) report that their results are robust to the use of population data from WorldPop. They do not use nighttime lights data to measure economic activity in each grid cell because such data may underestimate the size of output in rural areas. High value-added rural areas producing commodities are common in Latin America.
27. For details, please see http://areasprotegidas.mma.gob.cl/areas-protegidas/.
28. These results are presented in figure 4, panel a, of Fajgelbaum and Schaal (2020).

References

Alder, S. 2019. "Chinese Roads in India: The Effect of Transport Infrastructure on Economic Development." Unpublished manuscript, University of North Carolina, Chapel Hill.

Allen, T., and C. Arkolakis. 2014. "Trade and the Topography of the Spatial Economy." *Quarterly Journal of Economics* 129 (3): 1085–1140.

Allen, T., and C. Arkolakis. 2019. "The Welfare Effects of Transportation Infrastructure Improvements." NBER Working Paper 25487, National Bureau of Economic Research, Cambridge, MA.

Allen, T., D. Atkin, S. C. Cantillo, and C. Hernández. 2022. "Trucks." https://sites.google.com/site/treballen/research.

Blankespoor, B., T. Bougna, R. Garduno-Rivera, and H. Selod. 2017. "Roads and the Geography of Economic Activities in Mexico." Policy Research Working Paper 8226, World Bank, Washington, DC.

Burger, M., M. Hendriks, and E. Ianchovichina. 2022. "Happy but Unequal: Differences in Subjective Well-Being across Individuals and Space." *Applied Research in Quality of Life* 17 (3): 1343–87.

Cantillo, S. C., and C. Hernández. 2022. "A Toolkit for Setting and Evaluating Price Floors." Social Science Research Network. https://doi.org/10.2139/ssrn.4207884.

Conte, B., and E. Ianchovichina. 2022. "Spatial Development and Mobility Frictions in Latin America: Theory-Based Empirical Evidence." Policy Research Working Paper 10071, World Bank, Washington, DC.

Das, A., E. Ghani, A. Grover, W. Kerr, and R. Nanda. 2019. "Infrastructure and Finance: Evidence from India's GQ Highway Network." Working Paper No. 19-121, Harvard Business School, Boston, MA.

Datta, S. 2012. "The Impact of Improved Highways on Indian Firms." *Journal of Development Economics* 99 (1): 46–57.

Deaton, A., and A. Stone. 2013. "Two Happiness Puzzles." *American Economic Review* 103 (3): 591–97.

Desmet, K., D. Nagy, and E. Rossi-Hansberg. 2018. "The Geography of Development." *Journal of Political Economy* 126 (3): 903–83.

Duranton, G. 2015. "Roads and Trade in Colombia." *Economics of Transportation* 4 (1): 16–36.

Egger, E.-M. 2021. "Migrating Out of Mega-cities: Evidence from Brazil." *IZA Journal of Development and Migration* 12 (1): 1–35.

Fajgelbaum, P., and E. Schaal. 2020. "Optimal Transport Networks in Spatial Equilibrium." *Econometrica* 88 (4): 1411–52.

Fay, M., L. Andres, C. Fox, U. Narloch, S. Straub, and M. Slawson. 2017. *Rethinking Infrastructure in Latin America and the Caribbean: Spending Better to Achieve More.* Washington, DC: World Bank.

Ferreyra, M. M., and M. Roberts, eds. 2018. *Raising the Bar for Productive Cities in Latin America and the Caribbean.* Washington, DC: World Bank.

Ghani, E., A. Goswami, and W. Kerr. 2016. "Highway to Success: The Impact of the Golden Quadrilateral Project for the Location and Performance of Indian Manufacturing." *Economic Journal* 126 (591): 317–57.

Ghani, E., A. Grover, and W. Kerr. 2013. "Highway to Success in India: The Impact of the Golden Quadrilateral Project for the Location and Performance of Manufacturing." Policy Research Working Paper 6320, World Bank, Washington, DC.

Gollin, D., M. Kirchberger, and D. Lagakos. 2017. "In Search of a Spatial Equilibrium in the Developing World." NBER Working Paper 23916, National Bureau of Economic Research, Cambridge, MA.

Gorton, N., and E. Ianchovichina. 2021. "Trade Networks in Latin America: Spatial Inefficiencies and Optimal Expansions." Policy Research Working Paper 9843, World Bank, Washington, DC.

Hatayama, M., M. Viollaz, and H. Winkler. 2020. "Jobs' Amenability to Working from Home." Policy Research Working Paper 9241, World Bank, Washington, DC.

Holl, A. 2004. "Transport Infrastructure, Agglomeration Economies, and Firm Birth: Empirical Evidence from Portugal." *Journal of Regional Science* 44 (4): 693–712.

Hsieh, C.-T., and E. Moretti. 2019. "Housing Constraints and Spatial Misallocation." *American Economic Journal: Macroeconomics* 11 (2): 1–39.

Kahneman, D., and A. Deaton. 2010. "High Income Improves Evaluation of Life but Not Emotional Well-Being." *Proceedings of the National Academy of Sciences* 107 (38): 16489–93.

Kilroy, A., L. Francis, M. Mukim, and S. Negri. 2015. *Competitive Cities for Jobs and Growth: What, Who, and How*. Washington, DC: World Bank.

Maloney, W., and F. V. Caicedo. 2016. "The Persistence of (Subnational) Fortune." *Economic Journal* 126 (598): 2363–401.

Mesquita Moreira, M., J. Blyde, C. Volpe, and D. Molina. 2013. *Too Far to Export: Domestic Transport Costs and Regional Export Disparities in Latin America and the Caribbean*. Washington, DC: Inter-American Development Bank.

Montañés, R., J. Barreto, C. Bonilla, D. Sánchez, and H. Winkler. 2021. "Working from Home in Latin America and the Caribbean: Enabling Factors and Inequality Implications." Background paper prepared for this report, World Bank, Washington, DC.

Nordhaus, W., A. Azam, D. Novoa, K. Hood, N. Victor, M. Mohammed, A. Miltner, et al. 2006. "The G-Econ Database on Gridded Output: Methods and Data." Working paper, Yale University, New Haven, CT.

Osborne, T., M. Pachón, and G. Araya. 2014. "What Drives the High Price of Road Freight Transport in Central America?" Policy Research Working Paper 6844, World Bank, Washington, DC.

Quintero, L., and M. Roberts. 2018. "Explaining Spatial Variations in Productivity: Evidence from Latin America and the Caribbean." Policy Research Working Paper 8560, World Bank, Washington, DC.

Restrepo Cadavid, P., and G. Cineas. 2018. "Urbanization, Economic Development, and Structural Transformation." In *Raising the Bar for Productive Cities in Latin America and the Caribbean*, edited by M. M. Ferreyra and M. Roberts. Washington, DC: World Bank.

Roberts, M. 2018. "The Many Dimensions of Urbanization and the Productivity of Cities in Latin America and the Caribbean." In *Raising the Bar for Productive Cities in Latin America and the Caribbean*, edited by M. M. Ferreyra and M. Roberts. Washington, DC: World Bank.

Rodríguez-Pose, A., and J. Griffiths. 2021. "Developing Intermediate Cities." *Regional Science Policy and Practice* 13 (3): 441–56.

Stevenson, B., and J. Wolfers. 2013. "Subjective Well-Being and Income: Is There Any Evidence of Satiation?" *American Economic Review* 103 (3): 598–604.

Stokenberga, A., E. Ivarsson, and J. Fulponi. 2023. "A Net Cure or Curse? Tracking the Impact of E-Commerce on Urban Freight Transport Intensity in Bogotá and Buenos Aires." Policy Research Working Paper 10485, World Bank, Washington, DC.

World Bank. 2009. *World Development Report 2009: Reshaping Economic Geography*. Washington, DC: World Bank.

World Bank. 2020. *Territorial Development in Argentina: Diagnosing Key Bottlenecks as the First Step toward Effective Policy*. Washington, DC: World Bank.

World Bank. 2021. "Regulation and Performance of Logistics Services Markets in Latin America." Background paper, *Productive Competition in Latin America and the Caribbean*. World Bank, Washington, DC.

PART

III

Urban Productivity

Cities in Latin America and the Caribbean (LAC) are systemically important for aggregate economic growth. Most of the region's workforce is concentrated in large, dense metropolitan areas. In the mid-2010s, the share of Latin Americans living in large cities with 1 million or more residents was close to 40 percent—higher than the corresponding share in Asia, Africa, and Europe (United Nations 2016)—and more than 60 percent of Latin American cities were denser than the global mean (Roberts 2018).

Economic theory suggests that such high spatial concentration can generate significant agglomeration economies that can serve as a powerful boost to urban productivity through both supply-side and demand-side channels. On the supply side, co-location can increase the productivity of firms and workers through sharing, matching, and learning (Duranton and Puga 2004; Puga 2010). Firms and individuals benefit from sharing infrastructure (such as subways and airports) and cultural and educational amenities (such as museums and universities). The presence of a large pool of workers with diverse skills and of many suppliers of intermediate products makes it easier to match workers and inputs to firms, increasing output quality and quantity through specialization (Marshall 1890) and spurring innovation through learning by doing and learning from diversity (Jacobs 1961). These mechanisms for generating supply-side agglomeration externalities are at the core of the agglomeration economics literature. On the demand side, co-location can induce spatial agglomeration benefits (Fujita 1988) because proximity increases the size of markets for firms and consumers by lowering transport costs (Alcácer and Chung 2014) and search costs, and it improves welfare through better access to a greater variety of goods and services.

However, the *net* effect of high density may be small or even negative in the absence of institutional arrangements that can coordinate the provision of public goods and services and address the negative externalities of density associated with traffic and housing congestion, crime, environmental degradation, and disease. Grover, Lall, and Maloney (2022) provide evidence of high agglomeration costs in low- and middle-income countries, where urbanization has created "sterile" agglomeration economies.[1] In most countries in the LAC region, the positive effect of density on wages is completely offset by the higher cost of operating in cities. Examples are the Central American countries (Costa Rica, El Salvador, Guatemala, Honduras, and Nicaragua), Chile, Colombia (Duranton 2016; Quintero and Roberts 2018), and Mexico (Quintero and Roberts 2018). Small but positive net returns to density have been observed only in Brazil (Chauvin et al. 2017; Quintero and Roberts 2018) and Peru (Quintero and Roberts 2018).

Chapter 5 reveals that deindustrialization has led to a decline in urban productivity in the LAC region because it has shifted the employment composition of urban areas, especially the largest ones, toward less dynamic, low-productivity nontradables. Compared with urban tradables, these activities tend to benefit *less* from urban density, and their agglomeration benefits are reduced relatively *more* by congestion, which is a major problem in the region's largest cities.

Note

1. According to Grover, Lall, and Maloney (2022), agglomeration economies are "sterile" when agglomeration costs are so high that they outweigh the *pure* (gross) agglomeration benefits. Using manufacturing censuses for four countries, Grover and Maloney (2022) find that the elasticity of physical total factor productivity with respect to density is negative in Colombia, Ethiopia, and Indonesia and positive only in Chile.

References

Alcácer, J., and W. Chung. 2014. "Location Strategies for Agglomeration Economies." *Strategic Management Journal* 35 (12): 1749–61.

Chauvin, J. P., E. Glaeser, Y. Ma, and K. Tobio. 2017. "What Is Different about Urbanization in Rich and Poor Countries? Cities in Brazil, China, India, and the United States." *Journal of Urban Economics* 98: 17–49.

Duranton, G. 2016. "Agglomeration Effects in Colombia." *Journal of Regional Science* 56 (2): 210–38.

Duranton, G., and D. Puga. 2004. "Micro-foundations of Urban Agglomeration Economies." In *Handbook of Regional and Urban Economics* 4: 2063–117.

Fujita, M. 1988. "A Monopolistic Competition Model of Spatial Agglomeration: Differentiated Product Approach." *Regional Science and Urban Economics* 18 (1): 87–124.

Grover, A., S. Lall, and W. Maloney. 2022. *Place, Productivity, and Prosperity: Revisiting Spatially Targeted Policies for Regional Development.* Washington, DC: World Bank.

Grover, A., and W. F. Maloney. 2022. "Proximity without Productivity: Agglomeration Effects with Plant-Level Output and Price Data." Policy Research Working Paper 9977, World Bank, Washington, DC.

Jacobs, J. 1961. *The Death and Life of Great American Cities.* New York: Vintage Books.

Marshall, A. 1890. *Principles of Economics.* London: Macmillan.

Puga, D. 2010. "The Magnitude and Causes of Agglomeration Economies." *Journal of Regional Science* 50 (1): 203–19.

Quintero, L., and M. Roberts. 2018. "Explaining Spatial Variations in Productivity: Evidence from Latin America and the Caribbean." Policy Research Working Paper 8560, World Bank, Washington, DC.

Roberts, M. 2018. "The Many Dimensions of Urbanization and the Productivity of Cities in Latin America and the Caribbean." In *Raising the Bar for Productive Cities in Latin America and the Caribbean*, edited by M. M. Ferreyra and M. Roberts. Washington, DC: World Bank.

United Nations. 2016. *The World Cities Data Booklet.* New York: United Nations.

Deindustrialization, Agglomeration, and Congestion | 5

Most urbanites in Latin America and the Caribbean (LAC) live in cities that are denser than global norms. Although they benefit from strong, positive, *skill-related* agglomeration externalities, they fail to capture the broader benefits of agglomeration through co-location and market access (Ferreyra and Roberts 2018). Evidence suggests that the net returns to density are insignificant in most LAC countries (Quintero and Roberts 2018) and that urban productivity is behind the urban productivity frontier in advanced economies such as the United States (Restrepo Cadavid and Cineas 2018). Previous studies have suggested that the "sterile" agglomeration economies in the region arise from weak institutional arrangements that cannot effectively address the costs of high density (Ferreyra and Roberts 2018), especially in the largest cities, where local governments also face coordination costs that reduce productivity (Duque et al. 2019).

This chapter looks at structural and spatial factors that may have weakened the benefits of density in the LAC region. It explores how the employment profile of cities differs within and across countries and how these differences in economic activity affect the ability of firms to benefit from agglomeration economies. The chapter argues that the incomes of Latin Americans may be able to catch up more quickly to those in advanced economies if a larger share of Latin America's largely urban workforce is employed in urban tradables. A faster catch-up is possible with tradables because productivity levels in the tradable sectors vary little across countries (Duarte and Restuccia 2010, 2020), and international trade positively affects endogenous innovation and growth through market access, comparative advantage, competition, and knowledge spillovers (Melitz and Redding 2021). Each of these channels has the potential to generate dynamic gains from trade—gains that tend to be much bigger than the static ones. According to Duarte and Restuccia (2010), the productivity catch-up in manufacturing explains about 50 percent of the gains in aggregate productivity across countries, whereas low productivity and lack of catch-up in services explain the slowdown, stagnation, and decline observed across countries. Jedwab, Ianchovichina, and

Haslop (2022) find that wages are higher in urban tradables than in nontradables. Furthermore, in countries where the share of workers with jobs in urban tradables is low, human capital is employed in less productive sectors, and the returns to experience in urban areas are overall lower.

Agglomeration economies may also be larger in countries where the share of employment in urban tradables is disproportionately high. Firms in the tradable sectors tend to benefit more from co-location than firms in the nontradable sectors (Burger, Ianchovichina, and Akbar 2022; Venables 2017a). The benefits are especially large for firms relying more heavily on skilled workers because cities offer abundant opportunities for sharing, matching, and learning. By contrast, these benefits tend to be relatively small for firms in the nontradable sectors, such as retail, personal services, and construction, because they employ relatively low-skilled labor, account for a large share of activity in the economy, and are unlikely to exhibit increasing returns to scale if they were to agglomerate (Venables 2017a). Smaller firms in the nontradable sector are also exposed to intense competition in the larger and denser urban markets. Indeed, according to Burger, Ianchovichina, and Akbar (2022), returns to urban density are heterogeneous and higher for formal establishments supplying urban tradables, especially export and foreign-owned enterprises, than for firms supplying services in the local market. The latter firms are often smaller, less experienced, and informal.

Congestion may also be more harmful to firms in the nontradable sectors because they depend on access to local markets. Although these markets are potentially larger in bigger and denser cities, traffic congestion and intensive competition can considerably reduce their size. Burger, Ianchovichina, and Akbar (2022) find that congestion reduces the agglomeration benefits of all firms, but this effect is stronger for services[1] than for manufacturing and for smaller, less experienced, domestically owned firms that serve the domestic market (figure 5.1).

FIGURE 5.1   The moderating effect of congestion on the "pure" returns to urban density by sector and firm type

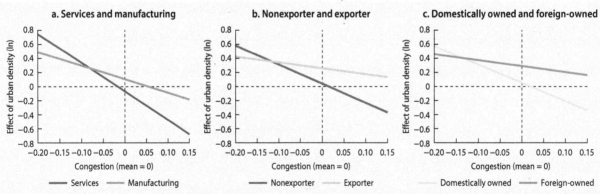

a. Services and manufacturing
b. Nonexporter and exporter
c. Domestically owned and foreign-owned

Source: Burger, Ianchovichina, and Akbar (2022), using geocoded, firm-level data on 38,526 formal establishments in 356 metropolitan areas in 80 developing economies from the World Bank's Enterprise Surveys (https://www.enterprisesurveys.org/en/enterprisesurveys) and a new global database on city-level mobility and congestion (Akbar et al. 2022). *Note:* The difference in the slope indicates the difference in the speed with which increases in congestion reduce the returns to density for the respective types of firms. The returns to urban density are the pure agglomeration economies, which capture both demand-side, market-size externalities and the supply-side learning externalities, net of any quality effects due to sorting and any potential effects of productivity on density (reverse causality).

Urban employment profiles

Venables (2020) provides some intuition about the differences in the employment composition along a country's urban hierarchy by emphasizing the importance of agglomeration economies, which capture the benefits firms reap from the presence of other firms in the same area. With development, such agglomeration forces allow production cities, which have a disproportionately high share of employment in tradables, to grow and assume global importance. Yet the same agglomeration forces that allow production cities to become quite large make it difficult to start new tradable activities elsewhere. Meanwhile, an adjustment to shocks (positive or negative) increases the number of consumption cities, which have a disproportionately low share of employment in tradables. Still, it is unclear to what extent cities with the same population size located in countries with similar income levels differ in terms of the size of their employment shares in urban tradables and nontradables and what types of cities dominate the urban hierarchy in different countries.

Jedwab, Ianchovichina, and Haslop (2022) answer these questions by obtaining the sectoral employment composition of 6,865 functional urban areas (FUAs) worldwide, using newly available microdata for 74 countries for 1960–2015. These urban areas are home to 3 billion people and account for three-quarters of the world's urban population. Jedwab, Ianchovichina, and Haslop (2022) classify each urban area into three city types: production, consumption, and neutral. A *production city* has a disproportionately high employment share of urban tradables; a *consumption city* has a disproportionately low employment share of urban tradables; and a *neutral city* has a share of employment in tradables that is neither too low nor too high. Box 5.1 provides details on the data and methodology used to classify cities based on their employment composition, and map 1.1 in chapter 1 shows the global distribution of production (blue), consumption (red), and neutral (gray) cities circa 2000. Production cities are located mostly in Europe, China, and India, whereas consumption cities are common in resource-rich countries throughout Sub-Saharan Africa, parts of Southeast Asia, and the Middle East. The remarkable feature of China's "production urbanization" is that it is supported by the whole urban system (Jedwab, Ianchovichina, and Haslop 2022). In India, there is a mix of specialized production and consumption cities (map 1.1).

In South America, cities are mainly consumption and neutral types. Cities in Colombia, Haiti, Peru, and República Bolivariana de Venezuela are mainly consumption ones. Cities in Argentina, Bolivia, Ecuador, and Chile are a mix of consumption and neutral types (map 5.1). Brazil, Mexico, and the countries in Central America have a mix of consumption, production, and neutral cities. However, the production cities in these countries are small in size. Of the top 25 megacities whose population exceeds 10 million, four are in Latin America, but none is a large, globally significant production city (table 5.1). The largest globally significant production cities are in China, India, Viet Nam, and Europe, and the largest consumption cities are in Brazil and Indonesia. Of the 25 largest cities in Latin America, only two are production cities (Guatemala City and San Salvador), seven are consumption cities (Rio de Janeiro, Bogotá, Belo Horizonte, Recife, Fortaleza, Salvador, and Guayaquil), and the rest are neutral (table 5.2).

BOX 5.1   Data and methodology for classifying cities based on their employment composition

For their classification, Jedwab, Ianchovichina, and Haslop (2022) use Integrated Public Use Microdata Series (IPUMS) census microdata for 76 countries and 191 country-years (1960–2015). The microdata include information on the administrative unit in which the respondent lives, the respondent's sector, and whether the respondent lives in an urban area. The data are processed by first selecting urban observations and obtaining observations on the resident's second-level administrative unit. Residents employed in urban tradables, which include manufacturing and tradable services (finance, insurance, and real estate, FIRE), are identified in each administrative unit, and this information is then used to calculate the labor shares for each functional urban area (FUA). Because censuses are conducted only every 10–15 years, the closest observation to 2000 (within the 1990–2015 period) is used for each country-FUA pair. In this way, Jedwab, Ianchovichina, and Haslop obtain data on employment shares in 6,865 FUAs. The data on the population size of these FUAs (circa 2000) are retrieved from the Global Human Settlement Layer (GHSL) database.

The 3 billion people in the 6,865 FUAs account for 75 percent of the world's urban population. Kolmogorov–Smirnov tests confirm that the global distribution of city sizes is not significantly different from the one in their sample. However, data on a few large, advanced economies (such as Japan) are not available in IPUMS. To increase the sample's representativeness, Jedwab, Ianchovichina, and Haslop (2022) divide all countries worldwide into 10 deciles based on their log per capita gross domestic product (in purchasing power parity) circa 2000. Based on the differences between the shares of each decile in the world's urban population and in their sample, they create weights oversampling high-income countries.

With the goal of identifying which cities have high employment shares in tradables relative to other cities of the same size and for a given level of urban economic development, Jedwab, Ianchovichina, and Haslop (2022) sort the FUAs into 10 deciles. Based on a range of log population from 10.8 (50,000) to 17.2 (30 million), the resulting thresholds are 95,000, 180,000, 341,000, 648,000, 1,227,000, 2,306,000, 4,377,000, 8,351,000, and 15,570,000. Because the top two bins have few FUAs (22 and 13, respectively), they are aggregated. Using this sample and the population of each FUA as weights, Jedwab, Ianchovichina, and Haslop regress the FUA's employment share in manufacturing and FIRE (MFGFIRE) circa 2000 on eight size category (CAT) dummies (omitting the lowest size category of 50,000–95,000) and their interactions with the 2000 urban share (URB) of the FUA's country, as well as a dummy identifying whether the FUA is the capital city (CAP). For FUA a in country c and population category p, the model is

$$\text{MFGFIRE}_{a,c,2000} = \alpha + \sum_{p=2}^{9} \beta_p 1\left(\text{CAT}_\alpha = p\right) + \sum_{p=2}^{9} \gamma_p 1\left(\text{CAT}_\alpha = p\right) * \text{URB}_c \\ + \delta \text{URB}_c + \xi \text{CAP}_\alpha + \mu_a.$$

(B5.1.1)

(Continued on next page)

BOX 5.1   Data and methodology for classifying cities based on their employment composition *(continued)*

The regression residual μ measures to what extent the FUA has a high or low employment share in tradables given its size and its country's level of economic development. In the classification of Jedwab, Ianchovichina, and Haslop (2022), a production city is any FUA with a residual value above five. This definition further distinguishes production cities with a low (5–10), medium (10–15), or high (>15) value. A consumption city is any FUA with a residual value below –5, also distinguishing consumption cities with a low (–5, –10), medium (–10, –15), or high (>–15) value. Cities in the (–5, 5) range are classified as neutral.

MAP 5.1   Distribution of production, consumption, and neutral cities in the Americas, circa 2000

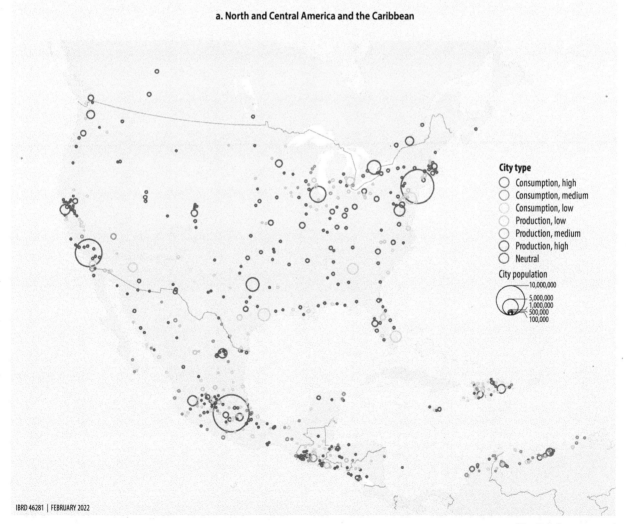

a. North and Central America and the Caribbean

City type
○ Consumption, high
○ Consumption, medium
○ Consumption, low
○ Production, low
○ Production, medium
○ Production, high
○ Neutral

City population
—10,000,000
5,000,000
1,000,000
500,000
100,000

IBRD 46281 | FEBRUARY 2022

(Continued on next page)

MAP 5.1 **Distribution of production, consumption, and neutral cities in the Americas, circa 2000** *(continued)*

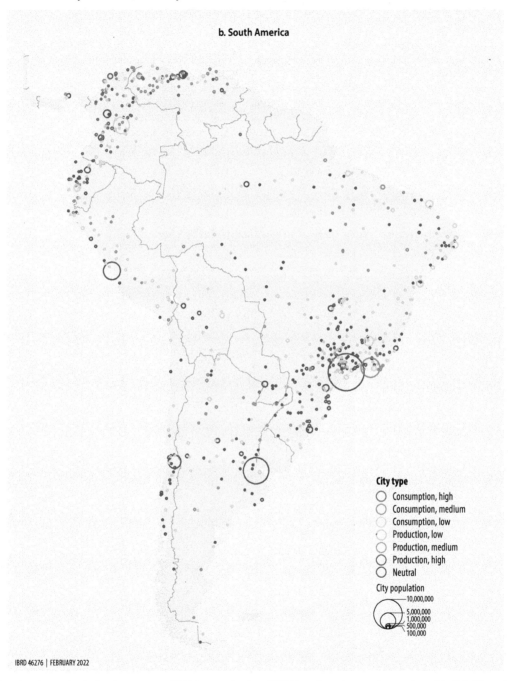

b. South America

City type

○ Consumption, high
○ Consumption, medium
○ Consumption, low
○ Production, low
○ Production, medium
○ Production, high
○ Neutral

City population

10,000,000
5,000,000
1,000,000
500,000
100,000

IBRD 46276 | FEBRUARY 2022

Source: Jedwab, Ianchovichina, and Haslop (2022), using Integrated Public Use Microdata Series (IPUMS, https://www.ipums.org/) census data and the Global Human Settlement Layer database (https://ghsl.jrc.ec.europa.eu/download.php).
Note: Paler shades of each color indicate lower values for the extent to which a city can be classified as each specific type.

TABLE 5.1 **Employment profile of global megacities with population of over 10 million based on the classification in box 5.1, circa 2000**

Ranking	City	Country	Category	Residual (%)	Population, 2000s (millions)
1	Delhi	India	Neutral	−1.7	30.1
2	Jakarta	Indonesia	Consumption, low	−5.3	29.8
3	Shanghai	China	Production, medium	10.2	26.9
4	Manila	Philippines	Neutral	1.6	25.0
5	Cairo	Egypt, Arab Rep.	Neutral	−0.8	23.5
6	Kolkata	India	Consumption, low	−5.8	23.1
7	Mumbai	India	Neutral	−2.1	22.3
8	**São Paulo**	**Brazil**	**Neutral**	**0.5**	**21.7**
9	**Mexico City**	**Mexico**	**Neutral**	**1.6**	**21.4**
10	Beijing	China	Neutral	3.0	21.3
11	New York	United States	Neutral	−4.4	19.5
12	Guangzhou	China	Production, high	15.7	16.7
13	Bangkok	Thailand	Neutral	1.3	16.3
14	Los Angeles	United States	Neutral	−2.5	15.7
15	**Buenos Aires**	**Argentina**	**Neutral**	**0.3**	**15.0**
16	Istanbul	Türkiye	Production, low	6.3	14.8
17	Tehran	Iran, Islamic Rep.	Neutral	1.2	13.4
18	Ho Chi Minh	Viet Nam	Production, low	6.6	12.8
19	Jieyang	China	Neutral	−3.1	12.7
20	Lagos	Nigeria	Consumption, high	−18.1	12.3
21	Bangalore	India	Production, low	5.3	11.9
22	Chengdu	China	Consumption, low	−6.7	11.7
23	Suzhou	China	Production, low	9.9	11.4
24	Paris	France	Production, low	7.7	11.2
25	**Rio de Janeiro**	**Brazil**	**Consumption, medium**	**−10.2**	**10.8**
26	Surabaya	Indonesia	Consumption, medium	−11.7	10.8
27	Chennai	India	Consumption, low	−8.8	10.6

Source: Jedwab, Ianchovichina, and Haslop 2022.

TABLE 5.2 Employment profile of largest LAC cities based on the classification in box 5.1, circa 2000

City	Country	Category	Residual (%)	Population, 2000s (millions)
São Paulo	Brazil	Neutral	0.5	21.7
Mexico City	Mexico	Neutral	1.6	21.4
Buenos Aires	Argentina	Neutral	0.3	15.0
Rio de Janeiro	Brazil	Consumption, medium	−10.2	10.8
Lima	Peru	Neutral	−1.9	9.7
Bogotá	Colombia	Consumption, low	−8.5	9.1
Santiago	Chile	Neutral	2.2	7.1
Guadalajara	Mexico	Neutral	1.3	5.2
Belo Horizonte	Brazil	Consumption, low	−9.2	5.0
Monterrey	Mexico	Neutral	4.8	4.5
Santo Domingo	Dominican Republic	Neutral	−1.3	4.2
Recife	Brazil	Consumption, low	−9.1	3.7
Fortaleza	Brazil	Consumption, low	−5.3	3.6
Medellín	Colombia	Neutral	0.3	3.6
Caracas	Venezuela, RB	Neutral	0	3.6
Guatemala City	Guatemala	Production, medium	11.3	3.5
Puebla	Mexico	Neutral	3.7	3.4
Salvador	Brazil	Consumption, low	−9.5	3.3
Curitiba	Brazil	Neutral	−0.8	3.0
Guayaquil	Ecuador	Consumption, low	−8.5	2.9
Porto Alegre	Brazil	Neutral	−2.8	2.9
Port-au-Prince	Haiti	Neutral	−4.7	2.8
Quito	Ecuador	Neutral	−2.0	2.7
San Salvador	El Salvador	Production, low	6.5	2.8
Campinas	Brazil	Neutral	2.8	2.5

Source: Jedwab, Ianchovichina, and Haslop 2022.

The deindustrialization of Latin America's cities

The employment share of urban tradables in Latin America and the Caribbean has been in decline since the 1980s, especially in the region's largest cities (figure 1.1 in chapter 1). The steep drop in manufacturing employment (figure 2.4, panel a, in chapter 2) could not be compensated by the increase in employment in urban tradable services (figure 2.4, panel b). The deindustrialization of the LAC region's urban areas, observed at the regional level (figure 1.1), occurred in all large Latin American economies, but to different degrees (figure 5.2). The employment share of tradables declined the most in the largest cities of Brazil. In the 1980s, this share was about 45 percent, but by the 2010s it had fallen to 30 percent. A similar development was observed in Mexico, where the largest city, Mexico City, lost tradable jobs, and the employment share of tradables declined from about 40 percent to less than 30 percent. In the 2000s, the employment share of tradables increased in smaller Mexican urban areas, reflecting the boost to manufacturing in border regions in the north after the North American Free Trade Agreement (NAFTA) came into effect in 1994.

FIGURE 5.2   Evolution of share of employment in tradables by city size and decade, LAC region

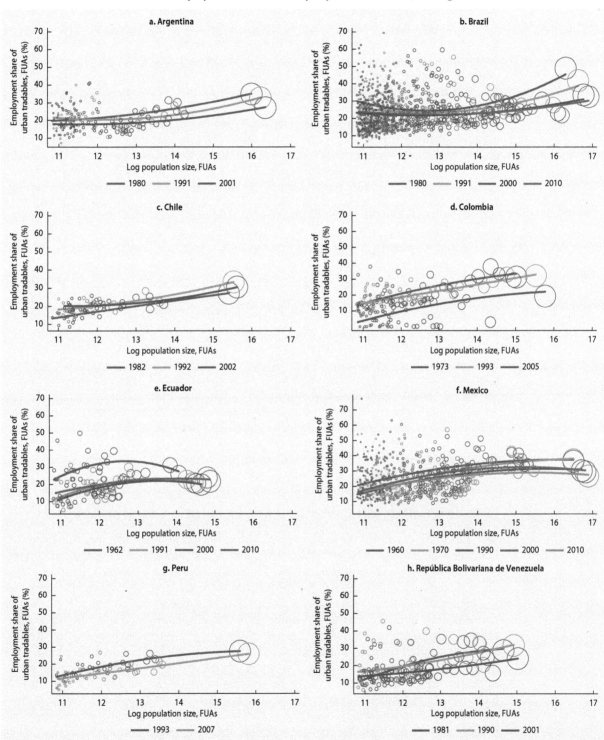

Source: Jedwab, Ianchovichina, and Haslop (2022), using Integrated Public Use Microdata Series (IPUMS, https://www.ipums.org/) census data and the Global Human Settlement Layer database (https://ghsl.jrc.ec.europa.eu/download.php).
Note: The graphs show the downward shift over time in the trend line, linking the employment share of tradables, which include manufacturing and tradable services such as finance, insurance, and real estate services, and the size of functional urban areas (FUAs), proxied with the log of the number of inhabitants of the FUA.

In Argentina and República Bolivariana de Venezuela, the decline in manufacturing was steepest in the largest cities and least pronounced in the smallest urban areas. In Peru, the decline in tradable jobs was most pronounced in midsize urban areas, while in Colombia and Ecuador cities of all sizes lost jobs in manufacturing (figure 5.2). In Colombia, the deindustrialization occurred relatively quickly between the mid-1990s and the mid-2000s, while in Ecuador most of it unfolded in the 1970s and 1980s. Only Chile was able to defy this trend until the early 1990s. After that, the employment share in manufacturing declined in the larger Chilean cities.

Latin America began deindustrializing after abandoning efforts to industrialize through import substitution policies (Beylis et al. 2020).[2] Deindustrialization was pronounced in the largest Latin American cities (figure 5.2). In Brazil, the largest cities—Belo Horizonte, Rio de Janeiro, and São Paulo—experienced steeper declines in formal employment and earnings because they were exposed to larger tariff cuts during the period of liberalization (Dix-Carneiro and Kovak 2017). Workers who lost their manufacturing jobs did not migrate to rural areas; instead, they switched to informal, lower-quality jobs in the nontradable sector (Dix-Carneiro and Kovak 2017). Thus the employment structure of the largest cities in the region shifted toward urban nontradables.

Another major development was the commodity boom from the early 2000s to the mid-2010s. As the largest exporter of agricultural products to the rest of the world and the third-largest exporter of fuel and mining exports (after Sub-Saharan Africa and the Middle East and North Africa), Latin America benefited from the increase in resource rents for both capital-intensive and labor-intensive commodity exports (Jedwab, Ianchovichina, and Haslop 2022). Because fuels, mineral products, and a few high-rent cash crops require little labor, the increase in resource export earnings raised incomes and spending on imported goods and services and the demand for urban nontradables, shifting employment toward this sector (Gollin, Jedwab, and Vollrath 2016). In line with the efficient nature of Latin America's agribusiness sector, the commodity boom did not increase the rural population in the LAC region, but it did slow the pace of rural-to-urban migration (Rodríguez-Vignoli and Rowe 2018). Steep competition, especially from China after it acceded to the World Trade Organization in 2001, along with accelerated adoption of labor-saving technologies, also depressed manufacturing employment after the early 2000s.

Deindustrialization weakened agglomeration economies

The shift in the composition of urban employment toward nontradables not only depressed labor productivity growth in urban areas, but it also weakened the potential of LAC countries to benefit from agglomeration economies. Based on geocoded, firm-level data on 38,526 formal establishments in 356 metropolitan areas in 80 developing economies, Burger, Ianchovichina, and Akbar (2022) show that the so-called "pure"[3] returns to urban density in terms of labor productivity are insignificant and lower for firms delivering services[4] than for manufacturing establishments (figure 5.3). These returns are also lower for smaller, younger, less experienced domestically owned firms and are highest for foreign-owned establishments and exporters (figure 5.3). Stated differently, the "pure" agglomeration economies tend to be higher in cities where there are many established manufacturing export firms. Unfortunately, the evidence that in many large Latin American cities the share of urban tradables is disproportionately low suggests that many urban enterprises in the region are domestically oriented establishments providing nontradable services. They are also less likely to become exporters (Lederman et al. 2014) and to participate in global value chains than are firms in other regions (Rocha and Ruta 2022).

The results in Burger, Ianchovichina, and Akbar (2022) are in line with the predictions of urban economic theory. Venables (2017a) argues that the supply-side benefits

FIGURE 5.3   Heterogeneous "pure" agglomeration economies

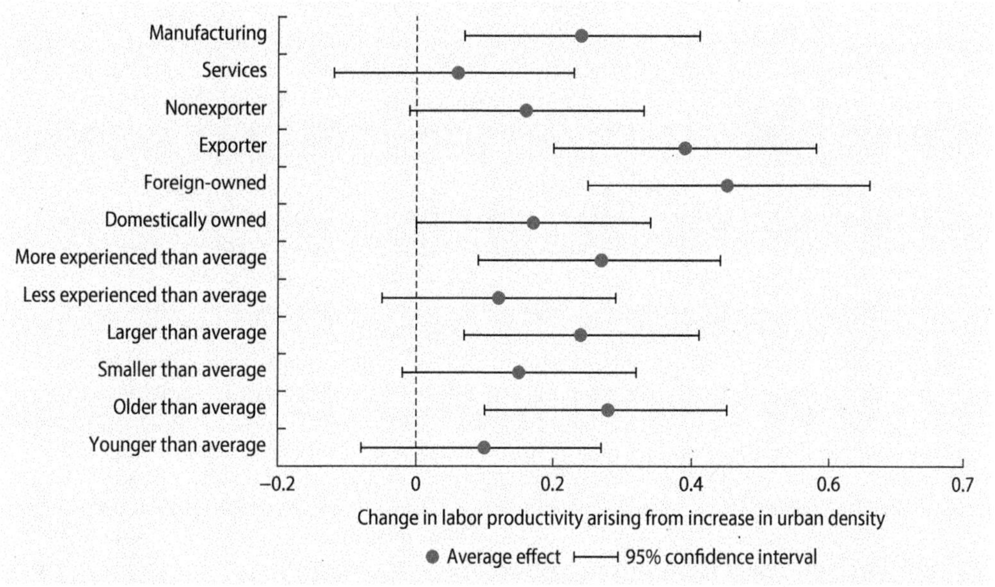

Source: Burger, Ianchovichina, and Akbar 2022.
Note: The figure shows "pure" agglomeration effects by type of firm—that is, the estimated change in labor productivity, measured as the natural logarithm of sales per worker arising from an increase in urban density after controlling for firm characteristics, firm-level and metropolitan-level agglomeration diseconomies, metropolitan-level averages of firm-level variables, and industry, country, and year fixed effects—based on geocoded, firm-level data on 38,526 establishments in 356 metropolitan areas in 80 developing economies. A coefficient of 0.1 means that if urban density doubles, labor productivity increases by 10 percent. Services include firms involved in either tradable or nontradable activities.

of co-location are relatively small for firms in the nontradable sectors such as retail, personal services, construction, government, and property management. By contrast, these benefits are relatively large for firms in the tradable sector, especially those using more skill-intensive labor (Andersson, Klaesson, and Larsson 2014; Bacolod, Blum, and Strange 2009; Matano, Obaco, and Royuela 2020; Stavropoulos, van Oort, and Burger 2020; Venables 2017a). Cognitive skills that help people better absorb and process information and knowledge are more valuable in more concentrated markets. Such skills enhance the benefits from matching (Behrens and Robert-Nicoud 2015) and the knowledge spillovers between firms (Caragliu and Nijkamp 2012).

Mobility issues and agglomeration economies

Traffic congestion and poor urban mobility are well-known costs of agglomeration. Recent research on urban mobility by Akbar et al. (2022) reveals that road traffic is generally much slower in low- and middle-income countries, mostly because of infrastructure deficiencies in fast-growing developing metropolitan areas. Congestion is a bigger problem in relatively developed economies. For a better understanding of the nature of urban mobility issues in the LAC region, this section draws on the work of Akbar et al. (2022), who estimate indexes of urban mobility and congestion in 1,228 cities worldwide, including 195 in the LAC region. Box 5.2 describes the estimation details, and annex 5A provides additional information on how Akbar et al. delineate cities and sample trip instances. The indexes are then used to study the link between density and mobility or congestion, conditional on the level of development in a country for the world sample of cities and for cities in Latin America and the Caribbean.

BOX 5.2   City-level mobility indexes and congestion

The estimation of indexes of urban mobility and congestion[a] by Akbar et al. (2022) relies on a set of roughly 538 million trip instances queried on Google Maps between June and October 2019. Each trip instance is one of 20 million randomly selected pairs of origins and destinations queried at one of roughly 21 randomly selected times of day and days of the week. In each case, Akbar et al. (2022) record Google's estimate of the duration and distance of the most recommended and fastest routes and obtain measures of real-time speed with and without traffic. They then regress trip speed on trip distance and distance to the city center, including controls for the city time of day, day of the week, weather, and, at times, the class of road being taken. The estimated city fixed effects are the baseline indexes of city mobility, which are comparable across cities. Using a comparable basket of trips in each city, they compute constant elasticity of substitution (CES) city-specific mobility indexes, which are directly analogous to price indexes. Then, because Akbar et al. (2022) observe the same trips at different times of the day, they conduct analogous estimations and compute city-level mobility indexes without traffic. The difference between this index and the baseline index is the index of congestion. Accordingly, the overall mobility index decomposes exactly into the congestion index and the uncongested mobility index, and each index can be related to city characteristics for cross-city comparisons.

The mobility data of Akbar et al. (2022) offer several advantages over alternative sources, such as INRIX and TomTom data, which have been used in previous studies on this topic in the LAC region (see, for example, Selod and Soumahoro 2018). First, the mobility indexes are based on millions of trips on Google Maps, simulated over the same period of time using the same trip sampling strategy for cities worldwide. This simulation was done precisely to facilitate cross-country analysis of the kind undertaken here. Second, Akbar et al. (2022) show that their mobility indexes are robust to various alternative trip sampling strategies, such as different weights on trip destinations, directions of travel, or time of day. The indexes also condition out the effect of trip characteristics that may vary systematically across cities and would bias any speed estimates based on actual trips. Third, using data for India, Akbar et al. (2018) show that the predicted speeds of the simulated trips are still comparable to those of actual trips in cities, including relatively small cities where one might worry more about poor data quality.

a. Mobility index and speed index are used interchangeably.

The results suggest that, as expected, in all countries urban mobility declines with urban density, mainly due to low uncongested mobility, not congestion (figure 5.4). Even without congestion, dense buildup leads to slower mobility stemming from narrower roads and more intersections, but also shortens trips, improving market access. Nevertheless, in the LAC region cities of all sizes have lower uncongested mobility than comparable cities in the rest of the world (figure 5.5). Unlike the United States, where 87 of the 100 cities with best mobility can be found in the data set of Akbar et al. (2022), the LAC region simply does not have cities with good mobility. The cities with the best mobility in the region are typically small, and none is among the cities with best mobility worldwide (annex table 5A.1). Meanwhile, uncongested mobility declines much faster with density in the LAC region than in the rest of the world (figure 5.4), pointing to urban planning and infrastructure issues along the whole urban hierarchy.

The systematic comparison of urban traffic patterns by city size in the LAC region and the rest of the world[5] also suggests that some of the most congested cities in the world are large Latin American cities (figure 5.5). Bogotá leads the ranking as the most congested

FIGURE 5.4   How urban mobility, congestion, and uncongested mobility change with density, world and LAC region

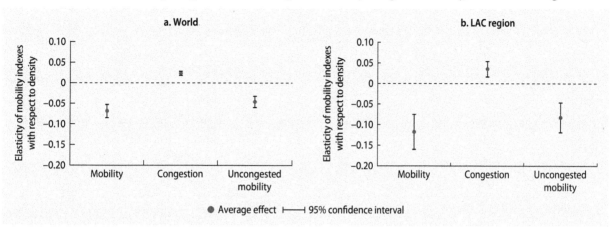

Source: Akbar (2022), based on data from Akbar et al. (2022).
Note: The figures show the average effect of density on mobility, as well as the 95% confidence interval. Construction of mobility indexes allows derivation of the elasticity of mobility with respect to density by subtracting the elasticity of congestion from the elasticity of uncongested mobility. This approach reveals that the bulk of the density effects on mobility are driven by their effects on uncongested mobility rather than congestion. The Latin America and the Caribbean (LAC) region includes Argentina, Bolivia, Brazil, Colombia, Costa Rica, the Dominican Republic, Ecuador, El Salvador, Guatemala, Honduras, Jamaica, Mexico, Nicaragua, Paraguay, Peru, Trinidad and Tobago, Uruguay, and República Bolivariana de Venezuela.

FIGURE 5.5   Distribution of uncongested mobility and congestion indexes by city size, LAC region and rest of the world

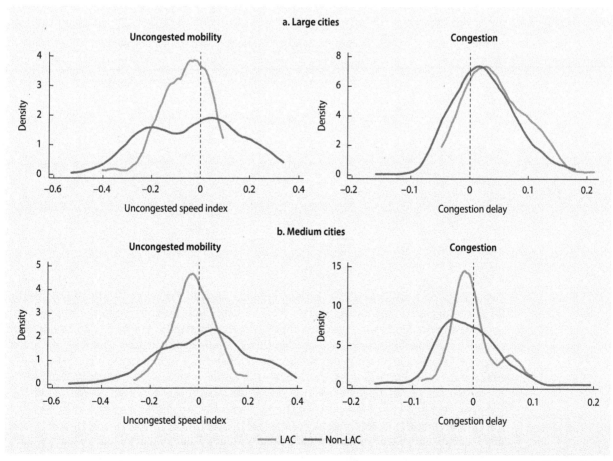

(Continued on next page)

FIGURE 5.5   **Distribution of uncongested mobility and congestion indexes by city size, LAC region and rest of the world *(continued)***

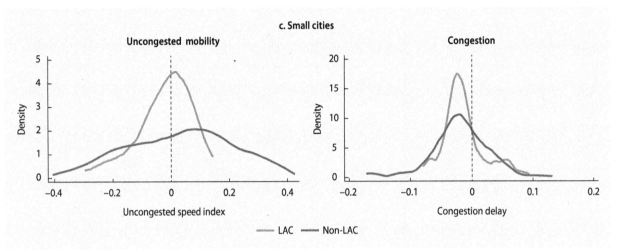

Source: Akbar (2022), based on data from Akbar et al. (2022).

TABLE 5.3   **World ranking: 10 slowest and 10 most congested cities in the LAC region**

	Slowest				Most congested		
World ranking	City	Country	Index	World ranking	City	Country	Index
19	Lima	Peru	−0.41	1	Bogotá	Colombia	0.21
25	Bogotá	Colombia	−0.40	10	Mexico City	Mexico	0.15
33	Mexico City	Mexico	−0.36	15	Guatemala City	Guatemala	0.14
38	La Paz	Bolivia	−0.36	19	Panama City	Panama	0.13
63	São Paulo	Brazil	−0.30	22	Santo Domingo	Dominican Republic	0.13
67	Huancayo	Peru	−0.30	24	Medellín	Colombia	0.12
69	Guatemala City	Guatemala	−0.29	25	Rio de Janeiro	Brazil	0.12
73	Cusco	Peru	−0.29	32	São Paulo	Brazil	0.12
75	Oaxaca de Juárez	Mexico	−0.28	38	San José	Costa Rica	0.11
85	Medellín	Colombia	−0.27	41	Recife	Brazil	0.11

Source: Akbar (2022), using data from Akbar et al. (2022).

city in the world, while Mexico City, Guatemala City, and Panama City are among the top 20 most congested cities worldwide (table 5.3). Although Lima is not in the top 10 most congested Latin American cities, it is the 15th most congested Latin American city and the city with the slowest uncongested speed in the region. It is also striking that four of the five largest LAC cities are among the 10 slowest cities in the region and are also slow relative to the rest of the world. Bogotá and Mexico City—the largest cities and capitals of two of Latin America's most developed economies and members of the Organisation for Economic Co-operation and Development (OECD)—are not only among the slowest LAC cities, but also are among the most congested (table 5.3). Other large cities with both congestion and mobility issues are Guatemala City, Medellín, and São Paulo. The full ranking of LAC cities is available in annex table 5A.1.

FIGURE 5.6 **The moderating effect of urban mobility and congestion on the return to density, LAC region**

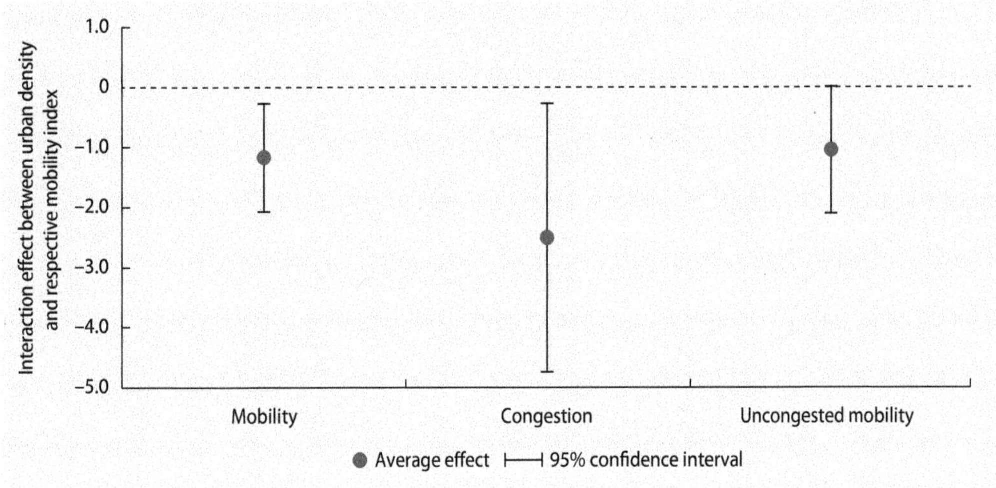

Source: Burger, Ianchovichina, and Akbar 2022.
Note: The figure shows the point estimates together with the 95% confidence intervals.

Burger, Ianchovichina, and Akbar (2022) use the new database of mobility indexes of Akbar et al. (2022) presented in this section to examine how firm-specific returns to density vary with urban uncongested mobility and congestion. Their results suggest that agglomeration economies are lost mainly through congestion (figure 5.6), which limits the ability of firms to benefit from external economies of scale (also see Collier and Venables 2016; Gerritse and Arribas-Bel 2018; Venables 2017b) and is a particularly serious problem in the LAC region's largest cities (figure 5.5, panel a). Congestion is especially harmful to agglomeration economies in mega *consumption* cities, where nontradable services play a disproportionately large role. Although markets for nontradable services are potentially larger in bigger and denser cities, traffic congestion and competition can considerably reduce their size because these services are often provided face to face during peak business hours. Manufacturing firms can better cope with congestion by using storage and transporting inputs and final goods during off-peak traffic hours. Indeed, this report shows that although traffic congestion reduces the agglomeration benefits of all firms, this effect is much stronger for firms in services and for smaller, less experienced, domestically owned firms that serve the domestic market (figure 5.1).

Apart from their effects on agglomeration economies, intracity connectivity issues affect productivity through diverse channels. These issues have been shown to matter for US employment (Duranton and Turner 2012), US domestic trade (Duranton, Morrow, and Turner 2014), and household purchases of durable goods in Mexico through their effect on property values and access to credit (Gonzalez-Navarro and Quintana-Domeque 2016). Congestion also has far-reaching effects. It not only hurts the productivity of the urban economy, especially nontradable services, but it also lowers the quality of life in a city by increasing pollution and limiting market access. According to TomTom, residents of Bogotá, the world's most congested city, lose 9.6 days a year sitting in traffic. This is double the time spent in traffic in Madrid. In Lima residents are stuck in traffic for about 8.7 days a year.

Finally, a comparison of mobility indexes across different types of trips in LAC cities suggests that there is little variation in the speeds in the middle of the night across different

FIGURE 5.7 **Urban speeds throughout the day, LAC region**

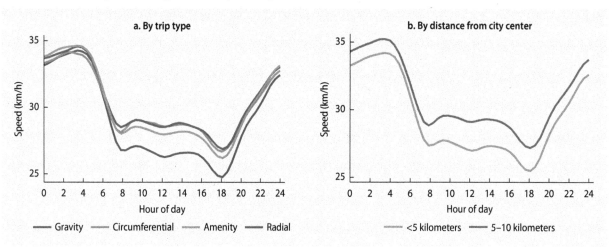

Source: Akbar (2022), based on data from Akbar et al. (2022).
Note: A *radial trip* connects a random location close to the city center to a more distant random location on the periphery of the city. A *circumferential trip* joins a random location that is at least 2 kilometers from the city center to a destination at the same distance from the city center but approximately 30 angular degrees apart. A *gravity trip* joins a random pair of locations whose distance from each other is drawn from a distribution that mimics the distribution of distances observed in many travel surveys. An *amenity trip* joins a random location in the city with the location of various highly visited amenities (such as schools and cultural centers). In panel a, all trips are limited to between 5 and 10 kilometers in length. km/h = kilometers per hour.

trip types (figure 5.7). During the day, the trips most vulnerable to congestion are the radial ones to and from the city center, which is expected in LAC cities because of their monocentric nature. Trips closer to the city center occur at lower daytime speeds than trips farther away. They are also slower during the night, suggesting that the difference can be attributed not only to inner-city congestion during peak daytime hours, but also to differences in travel infrastructure between the core and the periphery of these cities as well as accessibility issues.

This chapter argues that the absence of large production cities in the LAC region limits the region's potential to catch up to the standards of living in advanced economies and may even explain why some LAC countries are stuck in a middle-income trap. Deindustrialization and the rise of the resource economy have depressed labor productivity growth in urban areas by shifting the composition of urban employment toward low-productivity urban nontradables. Nontradables offer lower returns to experience, benefit less from density, and have a much more limited potential for catch-up through dynamic productivity gains than urban tradables. The ability of firms in the nontradable sectors to benefit from urban density is also hampered relatively more by traffic congestion, which is an especially serious problem in the densest and largest LAC consumption cities, such as Bogotá, Guayaquil, and Rio de Janeiro.[6] Chapter 6 takes a closer look at some of the larger LAC cities for a better understanding of the within-city spatial factors that limit urban productivity.

Annex 5A Data for the construction of city-level mobility indexes and ranking of LAC cities based on these indexes

Akbar et al. (2022) cover 1,228 cities that either had an estimated population of at least 300,000 in 2018 or are country capitals. They exclude cities in China and the

Republic of Korea, where Google Maps is restricted, and a few other cities that are missing credible variation in real-time travel data. City locations are obtained from the United Nations, and the spatial extent of each city is defined as the surrounding contiguous 1-kilometer urban grid cells in the Settlement Model of the Global Human Settlement Layer (GHSL).[7] In some cases, multiple urban polygons are combined into one city, or an urban polygon is split into multiple cities. The city extents are typically much smaller than metropolitan areas and functional urban areas (FUAs)—see Moreno-Monroy, Schiavina, and Veneri (2021). This approach is suitable for the purpose of measuring speeds and congestion in areas with high traffic.

To sample trip origins and destinations within cities, Akbar et al. (2022) further restrict the areas to only the built-up 38-meter pixels from the GHSL's built-up layer (Corbane et al. 2020). They define a *trip* as an ordered pair of points (origin and destination) that are at least 1 kilometer apart in a straight-line distance and a *trip instance* as a trip taken at a specific time on a specific day. The number of trips in each city is proportional to the square root of the city's population. To identify trip origins and destinations, they use various sampling strategies, each reflecting different types of urban travel (for example, radial trips to and from city centers or trips to amenities such as school or recreational areas), and verify that they lead to similar outcomes. Each trip is queried at multiple times of the day and days of the week so that the aggregate distribution of departure times across trip instances mimics the distribution of departure times in the US National Household Travel Survey. They oversample sparse late-night departure times to make sure most trips have at least one instance during quiet times, which is important for accurate measurement of congestion. Table 5A.1 shows the ranking of cities in Latin America and the Caribbean (LAC) based on the city-level mobility indexes.

TABLE 5A.1 Ranking of LAC cities based on speed and congestion (showing most congested/slowest first)

Slowest				Most congested			
Ranking	City	Country	Speed index	Ranking	City	Country	Congestion index
19	Lima	Peru	−0.41	1	Bogotá	Colombia	0.21
25	Bogotá	Colombia	−0.40	10	Mexico City	Mexico	0.15
33	Mexico City	Mexico	−0.36	15	Guatemala City	Guatemala	0.14
38	La Paz	Bolivia	−0.36	19	Panama City	Panama	0.13
63	São Paulo	Brazil	−0.30	22	Santo Domingo	Dominican Republic	0.13
67	Huancayo	Peru	−0.30	24	Medellín	Colombia	0.12
69	Guatemala City	Guatemala	−0.29	25	Rio de Janeiro	Brazil	0.12
73	Cusco	Peru	−0.29	32	São Paulo	Brazil	0.12
75	Oaxaca de Juárez	Mexico	−0.28	38	San José	Costa Rica	0.11
85	Medellín	Colombia	−0.27	41	Recife	Brazil	0.11
94	Belém	Brazil	−0.26	43	Cali	Colombia	0.11
96	Pasto	Colombia	−0.26	45	Santiago	Chile	0.10
97	Recife	Brazil	−0.26	50	Maceió	Brazil	0.10
98	Buenos Aires	Argentina	−0.26	53	Port of Spain	Trinidad and Tobago	0.10
106	Rio de Janeiro	Brazil	−0.25	56	Lima	Peru	0.10
107	Santos	Brazil	−0.25	60	Pereira	Colombia	0.09

(Continued on next page)

TABLE 5A.1   Ranking of LAC cities based on speed and congestion (showing most congested/slowest first) *(continued)*

	Slowest				Most congested		
Ranking	City	Country	Speed index	Ranking	City	Country	Congestion index
116	Arequipa	Peru	−0.23	61	Pasto	Colombia	0.09
122	Asunción	Paraguay	−0.23	71	Quito	Ecuador	0.09
123	Santo Domingo	Dominican Republic	−0.23	75	Buenos Aires	Argentina	0.09
128	Barranquilla	Colombia	−0.22	80	San Salvador	El Salvador	0.08
129	Cali	Colombia	−0.22	81	Salvador	Brazil	0.08
133	Cuernavaca	Mexico	−0.22	94	Santiago	Dominican Republic	0.08
152	Oruro	Bolivia	−0.20	103	Cuenca	Ecuador	0.07
157	Quito	Ecuador	−0.20	110	Manaus	Brazil	0.07
161	Puebla	Mexico	−0.19	111	Belém	Brazil	0.07
164	San José	Costa Rica	−0.19	117	Porto Alegre	Brazil	0.07
182	Grande São Luis	Brazil	−0.18	122	Villavicencio	Colombia	0.07
194	Maceió	Brazil	−0.17	126	Arequipa	Peru	0.07
196	Trujillo	Peru	−0.17	128	Cartagena	Colombia	0.07
200	Puerto Vallarta	Mexico	−0.17	129	Temuco	Chile	0.06
202	Cartagena	Colombia	−0.17	137	Barranquilla	Colombia	0.06
210	Acapulco de Juárez	Mexico	−0.17	139	Ibagué	Colombia	0.06
213	Salvador	Brazil	−0.17	141	Valparaíso	Chile	0.06
214	Xalapa	Mexico	−0.17	150	Grande São Luis	Brazil	0.06
219	San Salvador	El Salvador	−0.16	154	Kingston	Jamaica	0.06
225	Uruapan	Mexico	−0.16	158	Alajuela	Costa Rica	0.06
230	Fortaleza	Brazil	−0.16	160	Belo Horizonte	Brazil	0.06
232	Pereira	Colombia	−0.15	167	Tijuana	Mexico	0.06
235	Guadalajara	Mexico	−0.15	170	Guayaquil	Ecuador	0.06
248	Cuautla Morelos	Mexico	−0.14	178	Florianópolis	Brazil	0.05
252	Cúcuta	Colombia	−0.14	186	Valledupar	Colombia	0.05
260	Cochabamba	Bolivia	−0.14	189	Ciudad del Este	Paraguay	0.05
261	Belo Horizonte	Brazil	−0.14	191	Cusco	Peru	0.05
268	Veracruz	Mexico	−0.13	195	La Serena-Coquimbo	Chile	0.05
269	Santiago	Dominican Republic	−0.13	211	Fortaleza	Brazil	0.05
270	Tehuacán	Mexico	−0.13	213	Concepción	Chile	0.05
272	Iquitos	Peru	−0.13	218	Vitoria	Brazil	0.05
279	Toluca de Lerdo	Mexico	−0.13	222	Heredia	Costa Rica	0.05
288	Bucaramanga	Colombia	−0.13	233	Guadalajara	Mexico	0.04
290	Morelia	Mexico	−0.13	241	Bucaramanga	Colombia	0.04
294	León de los Aldama	Mexico	−0.12	246	Asunción	Paraguay	0.04
297	Ibagué	Colombia	−0.12	264	Monterrey	Mexico	0.04
305	Panama City	Panama	−0.12	276	Caracas	Venezuela, RB	0.03
318	Neiva	Colombia	−0.11	279	Puebla	Mexico	0.03

(Continued on next page)

TABLE 5A.1 Ranking of LAC cities based on speed and congestion (showing most congested/slowest first) *(continued)*

Slowest				Most congested			
Ranking	City	Country	Speed index	Ranking	City	Country	Congestion index
321	Villavicencio	Colombia	−0.11	282	Curitiba	Brazil	0.03
326	Tepic	Mexico	−0.11	284	Toluca de Lerdo	Mexico	0.03
340	Tuxtla Gutierrez	Mexico	−0.10	297	Santa Marta	Colombia	0.03
350	Tijuana	Mexico	−0.10	323	Manizales	Colombia	0.03
352	Santa Marta	Colombia	−0.10	325	Blumenau	Brazil	0.03
359	Vitoria	Brazil	−0.09	342	León de los Aldama	Mexico	0.02
360	Santiago	Chile	−0.09	347	Posadas	Argentina	0.02
368	Matamoros	Mexico	−0.09	349	Montevideo	Uruguay	0.02
372	Monteria	Colombia	−0.09	352	Goiânia	Brazil	0.02
373	Valparaiso	Chile	−0.09	354	Morelia	Mexico	0.02
374	Tampico	Mexico	−0.09	355	Neiva	Colombia	0.02
375	Juiz de Fora	Brazil	−0.09	363	Tegucigalpa	Honduras	0.02
380	Heredia	Costa Rica	−0.09	365	Brasília	Brazil	0.02
386	Alajuela	Costa Rica	−0.08	372	Santos	Brazil	0.02
392	Manaus	Brazil	−0.08	373	Juiz de Fora	Brazil	0.02
397	Natal	Brazil	−0.08	374	Córdoba	Argentina	0.02
401	Piura	Peru	−0.07	377	Querétaro	Mexico	0.02
402	Corrientes	Argentina	−0.07	391	Ciudad Juárez	Mexico	0.02
407	Orizaba	Mexico	−0.07	405	Oaxaca de Juárez	Mexico	0.02
408	Manizales	Colombia	−0.07	420	San Pedro Sula	Honduras	0.02
409	Port of Spain	Trinidad and Tobago	−0.07	434	Xalapa	Mexico	0.01
411	Buenaventura	Colombia	−0.07	435	San Miguel de Tucumán	Argentina	0.01
416	Porto Alegre	Brazil	−0.07	454	Neuquen	Argentina	0.01
419	Guayaquil	Ecuador	−0.07	464	Joinville	Brazil	0.01
438	Neuquen	Argentina	−0.06	467	Rosario	Argentina	0.01
440	Managua	Nicaragua	−0.06	470	San Luis Potosí	Mexico	0.01
441	Tlaxcala	Mexico	−0.06	483	João Pessoa	Brazil	0.01
448	Ciudad Juárez	Mexico	−0.06	485	Natal	Brazil	0.01
451	Temuco	Chile	−0.06	486	Piura	Peru	0.01
452	Córdoba	Mexico	−0.06	497	Mexicali	Mexico	0.01
457	Ciudad del Este	Paraguay	−0.05	503	La Plata	Argentina	0.01
460	Feira de Santana	Brazil	−0.05	506	Cuiabá	Brazil	0
462	Cuenca	Ecuador	−0.05	507	Mendoza	Argentina	0
463	Ensenada	Mexico	−0.05	512	Los Mochis	Mexico	0
464	Querétaro	Mexico	−0.05	513	Campinas	Brazil	0
470	La Plata	Argentina	−0.05	528	Cúcuta	Colombia	0
472	Juazeiro do Norte	Brazil	−0.05	540	Puerto Vallarta	Mexico	0
479	Teresina	Brazil	−0.05	558	Campos dos Goytacazes	Brazil	0

(Continued on next page)

TABLE 5A.1   Ranking of LAC cities based on speed and congestion (showing most congested/slowest first) *(continued)*

	Slowest				Most congested		
Ranking	City	Country	Speed index	Ranking	City	Country	Congestion index
483	Cancún	Mexico	−0.05	559	Cancún	Mexico	0
488	Valledupar	Colombia	−0.04	562	Feira de Santana	Brazil	0
489	Irapuato	Mexico	−0.04	564	Huancayo	Peru	0
491	Montes Claros	Brazil	−0.04	568	Culiacán	Mexico	0
495	Caracas	Venezuela, RB	−0.04	585	Tehuacán	Mexico	0
497	Poza Rica de Hidalgo	Mexico	−0.04	586	Villahermosa	Mexico	0
499	Curitiba	Brazil	−0.04	591	Managua	Nicaragua	0
509	Caruaru	Brazil	−0.03	592	Teresina	Brazil	0
512	Aracaju	Brazil	−0.03	594	Tepic	Mexico	0
517	Volta Redonda	Brazil	−0.03	598	Tampico	Mexico	0
519	Montevideo	Uruguay	−0.03	611	Resistencia	Argentina	−0.01
522	Monterrey	Mexico	−0.03	614	Montes Claros	Brazil	−0.01
525	La Serena-Coquimbo	Chile	−0.03	616	Veracruz	Mexico	−0.01
530	Mérida	Mexico	−0.03	618	Caruaru	Brazil	−0.01
539	Campina Grande	Brazil	−0.02	624	Santa Cruz	Bolivia	−0.01
545	Rio Branco	Brazil	−0.02	625	Jundiaí	Brazil	−0.01
546	Tegucigalpa	Honduras	−0.02	626	Pelotas	Brazil	−0.01
548	Kingston	Jamaica	−0.02	628	Aracaju	Brazil	−0.01
554	Culiacán	Mexico	−0.02	630	Sorocaba	Brazil	−0.01
556	Santa Cruz	Bolivia	−0.02	643	Cuernavaca	Mexico	−0.01
558	Los Mochis	Mexico	−0.02	650	Aguascalientes	Mexico	−0.01
559	Aguascalientes	Mexico	−0.02	657	Durango	Mexico	−0.01
560	Campos dos Goytacazes	Brazil	−0.02	663	Tacna	Peru	−0.01
562	João Pessoa	Brazil	−0.02	665	Caxias do Sul	Brazil	−0.01
566	Salta	Argentina	−0.01	667	Volta Redonda	Brazil	−0.01
571	San Luis Potosí	Mexico	−0.01	668	São José dos Campos	Brazil	−0.01
575	Colima	Mexico	−0.01	677	Tuxtla Gutierrez	Mexico	−0.01
578	Durango	Mexico	−0.01	682	Santa Fe	Argentina	−0.01
580	San Miguel de Tucumán	Argentina	−0.01	683	San Juan	Argentina	−0.01
582	Pachuca de Soto	Mexico	−0.01	687	Armenia	Colombia	−0.01
600	Sorocaba	Brazil	0	688	Macapá	Brazil	−0.01
601	Córdoba	Argentina	0	690	Mérida	Mexico	−0.01
608	Cuiabá	Brazil	0	698	Corrientes	Argentina	−0.01
610	Coatzacoalcos	Mexico	0	704	Nuevo Laredo	Mexico	−0.02
612	Celaya	Mexico	0	705	Saltillo	Mexico	−0.02
614	Mar del Plata	Argentina	0	716	Maringá	Brazil	−0.02
615	San Pedro Sula	Honduras	0	718	Valencia	Venezuela, RB	−0.02
618	Mazatlán	Mexico	0	723	Porto Velho	Brazil	−0.02

(Continued on next page)

TABLE 5A.1   Ranking of LAC cities based on speed and congestion (showing most congested/slowest first) *(continued)*

	Slowest				Most congested		
Ranking	City	Country	Speed index	Ranking	City	Country	Congestion index
628	Rosario	Argentina	0.01	725	Mar del Plata	Argentina	−0.02
629	Villahermosa	Mexico	0.01	730	Trujillo	Peru	−0.02
634	Armenia	Colombia	0.01	734	Matamoros	Mexico	−0.02
638	Posadas	Argentina	0.01	735	Acapulco de Juárez	Mexico	−0.02
640	Mexicali	Mexico	0.01	738	Salta	Argentina	−0.02
645	Goiânia	Brazil	0.02	745	Zacatecas	Mexico	−0.02
646	Nuevo Laredo	Mexico	0.02	750	São José do Rio Preto	Brazil	−0.02
647	Barcelona-Puerto La Cruz	Venezuela, RB	0.02	759	Boa Vista	Brazil	−0.02
650	Campo Grande	Brazil	0.02	760	Londrina	Brazil	−0.02
659	Santa Fe	Argentina	0.02	761	Campina Grande	Brazil	−0.02
671	Resistencia	Argentina	0.02	765	Ensenada	Mexico	−0.02
679	Reynosa	Mexico	0.03	782	Juazeiro do Norte	Brazil	−0.02
688	Vitória da Conquista	Brazil	0.03	787	Franca	Brazil	−0.02
691	Porto Velho	Brazil	0.03	789	Santiago del Estero	Argentina	−0.02
698	Florianópolis	Brazil	0.03	791	Ribeirão Preto	Brazil	−0.02
707	Ciudad Victoria	Mexico	0.03	792	La Laguna	Mexico	−0.02
710	Concepción	Chile	0.04	807	Cochabamba	Bolivia	−0.02
712	Petrolina	Brazil	0.04	808	Ciudad Obregón	Mexico	−0.02
714	Macapá	Brazil	0.04	810	Petrolina	Brazil	−0.02
720	Zacatecas	Mexico	0.04	811	Anápolis	Brazil	−0.02
724	Valencia	Venezuela, RB	0.04	815	Colima	Mexico	−0.02
745	Maracaibo	Venezuela, RB	0.05	818	Reynosa	Mexico	−0.02
746	Pelotas	Brazil	0.05	819	Campo Grande	Brazil	−0.02
751	Brasília	Brazil	0.05	830	Tlaxcala	Mexico	−0.03
754	Campinas	Brazil	0.05	832	Maracay	Venezuela, RB	−0.03
758	Saltillo	Mexico	0.06	833	Barquisimeto	Venezuela, RB	−0.03
762	São José do Rio Preto	Brazil	0.06	838	Ponta Grossa	Brazil	−0.03
793	Barquisimeto	Venezuela, RB	0.07	840	Uruapan	Mexico	−0.03
798	Maracay	Venezuela, RB	0.07	841	Uberlândia	Brazil	−0.03
800	Uberaba	Brazil	0.07	843	Bahia Blanca	Argentina	−0.03
801	São José dos Campos	Brazil	0.07	847	Barcelona-Puerto La Cruz	Venezuela, RB	−0.03
802	Joinville	Brazil	0.07	851	Uberaba	Brazil	−0.03
803	Monclova	Mexico	0.07	867	Monteria	Colombia	−0.03
806	Piracicaba	Brazil	0.07	869	Taubaté	Brazil	−0.03
808	Mendoza	Argentina	0.07	874	Coatzacoalcos	Mexico	−0.03
810	Taubaté	Brazil	0.07	880	Cascavel	Brazil	−0.03
815	Jundiaí	Brazil	0.08	887	Mazatlán	Mexico	−0.03
817	Tacna	Peru	0.08	906	Chihuahua	Mexico	−0.03

(Continued on next page)

TABLE 5A.1 Ranking of LAC cities based on speed and congestion (showing most congested/slowest first) *(continued)*

	Slowest				Most congested		
Ranking	City	Country	Speed index	Ranking	City	Country	Congestion index
819	Bahia Blanca	Argentina	0.08	911	Vitória da Conquista	Brazil	−0.03
821	Santiago del Estero	Argentina	0.08	914	Irapuato	Mexico	−0.03
832	San Salvador de Jujuy	Argentina	0.09	928	Hermosillo	Mexico	−0.04
843	Ciudad Obregón	Mexico	0.09	930	Buenaventura	Colombia	−0.04
852	Bauru	Brazil	0.09	931	Ciudad Guayana	Venezuela, RB	−0.04
854	Boa Vista	Brazil	0.10	940	Celaya	Mexico	−0.04
862	Caxias do Sul	Brazil	0.10	950	Piracicaba	Brazil	−0.04
864	Uberlândia	Brazil	0.10	955	Bauru	Brazil	−0.04
865	Ponta Grossa	Brazil	0.10	956	San Salvador de Jujuy	Argentina	−0.04
869	Maringá	Brazil	0.10	957	Ciudad Victoria	Mexico	−0.04
874	Ribeirão Preto	Brazil	0.10	965	Córdoba	Mexico	−0.04
880	La Laguna	Mexico	0.11	972	Pachuca de Soto	Mexico	−0.04
882	Hermosillo	Mexico	0.11	975	Monclova	Mexico	−0.04
885	Londrina	Brazil	0.11	988	Ipatinga	Brazil	−0.04
899	Blumenau	Brazil	0.12	991	Orizaba	Mexico	−0.04
900	Ipatinga	Brazil	0.12	998	Poza Rica de Hidalgo	Mexico	−0.04
926	Chihuahua	Mexico	0.13	1,012	La Paz	Bolivia	−0.05
933	Guarenas-Guatire	Venezuela, RB	0.13	1,023	Maracaibo	Venezuela, RB	−0.05
968	Anápolis	Brazil	0.15	1,079	Barinas	Venezuela, RB	−0.06
969	Cabimas	Venezuela, RB	0.15	1,090	Cuautla Morelos	Mexico	−0.06
970	Cascavel	Brazil	0.15	1,102	Maturín	Venezuela, RB	−0.06
980	Barinas	Venezuela, RB	0.16	1,117	Guarenas-Guatire	Venezuela, RB	−0.06
990	Acarigua-Araure	Venezuela, RB	0.17	1,124	Acarigua-Araure	Venezuela, RB	−0.07
991	Franca	Brazil	0.17	1,147	Rio Branco	Brazil	−0.07
999	Maturín	Venezuela, RB	0.17	1,150	Iquitos	Peru	−0.07
1,025	San Juan	Argentina	0.20	1,167	Oruro	Bolivia	−0.08
1,071	Ciudad Guayana	Venezuela, RB	0.23	1,171	Cabimas	Venezuela, RB	−0.08

Source: Akbar et al. 2022.
Note: The speed index is measured by the estimated city fixed effect and is centered around its mean. The congestion factor is measured from a similar regression using log trip duration minus log trip duration in the absence of traffic as the dependent variable and is also centered around its mean.

Notes

1. This finding applies to nontradable services because services include nontradables, and the share of nontradables in services is large (Burger, Ianchovichina, and Akbar 2022).
2. With the adoption of labor-saving technologies and the growth of knowledge-intensive services, many developed countries also experienced deindustrialization. In the LAC region, deindustrialization occurred prematurely at a much lower level of development (Beylis et al. 2020) and was not accompanied by a large expansion of tradable services (Jedwab, Ianchovichina, and Haslop 2022).

3. The "pure" agglomeration economies capture both the demand-side market-size externalities and the supply-side learning externalities, net of any quality effects due to sorting and any potential effects of productivity on density (reverse causality). These benefits can be substantially reduced and even completely offset by agglomeration diseconomies or congestion costs. Thus the net agglomeration economies can be much smaller than the "pure" agglomeration benefits.
4. The data do not allow Burger, Ianchovichina, and Akbar (2022) to differentiate between tradable and nontradable services.
5. Such a comparison cannot be made for intraurban market access because there are no data sources on urban accessibility in a large set of developing country cities.
6. Akbar and Duranton (2017) find that in Bogotá the welfare loss from congestion is small, but they also recognize that more work is needed to explore the determinants of uncongested speed (and congestion) and how they correlate with other urban features, such as the composition of the road network, terrain elevation, and nightlight density.
7. M. Pesaresi and S. Freire, GHS-SMOD R2016A—GHS Settlement Grid, Following the REGIO Model 2014 in Application to GHSL Landsat and CIESIN GPW v4-Multitemporal (1975-1990-2000-2015), Joint Research Centre (JRC), European Commission, Brussels, 2016.

References

Akbar, P. A. 2022. "Mobility and Congestion in Urban Areas in Latin America and the Caribbean." Background paper prepared for this report, World Bank, Washington, DC.

Akbar, P. A., V. Couture, G. Duranton, and A. Storeygard. 2018. "Mobility and Congestion in Urban India." NBER Working Paper 25218, National Bureau of Economic Research, Cambridge, MA.

Akbar, P. A., V. Couture, G. Duranton, and A. Storeygard. 2022. "The Fast, the Slow, and the Congested: Urban Transportation in Rich and Poor Countries." CEPR Press Discussion Paper No. 18401, Centre for Economic Policy Research, London. https://cepr.org/publications/dp18401.

Akbar, P. A., and G. Duranton. 2017. "Measuring the Cost of Congestion in a Highly Congested City: Bogotá." University of Pennsylvania, Philadelphia.

Andersson, M., J. Klaesson, and J. P. Larsson. 2014. "The Sources of the Urban Wage Premium by Worker Skills: Spatial Sorting or Agglomeration Economies?" *Papers in Regional Science* 93 (4): 727–47.

Bacolod, M., B. S. Blum, and W. C. Strange. 2009. "Skills in the City." *Journal of Urban Economics* 65 (2): 136–53.

Behrens, K., and F. Robert-Nicoud. 2015. "Agglomeration Theory with Heterogeneous Agents." *Handbook of Regional and Urban Economics* 5: 171–245.

Beylis, G., R. Fattal-Jaef, R. Sinha, M. Morris, and A. Sebastian. 2020. *Going Viral: COVID-19 and the Accelerated Transformation of Jobs in Latin America and the Caribbean.* World Bank Latin American and Caribbean Studies. Washington, DC: World Bank.

Burger, M., E. Ianchovichina, and P. Akbar. 2022. "Heterogenous Agglomeration Economies in the Developing Countries: The Roles of Firm Characteristics, Sector Tradability, and Urban Mobility." Policy Research Working Paper 9954, World Bank, Washington, DC.

Caragliu, A., and P. Nijkamp. 2012. "The Impact of Regional Absorptive Capacity on Spatial Knowledge Spillovers: The Cohen and Levinthal Model Revisited." *Applied Economics* 44 (11): 1363–74.

Collier, P., and A. J. Venables. 2016. "Urban Infrastructure for Development." *Oxford Review of Economic Policy* 32 (3): 391–409.

Corbane, C., M. Pesaresi, P. Politis, A. Florczyk, M. Melchiorri, S. Freire, M. Schiavina, et al. 2020. "The Grey-Green Divide: Multi-temporal Analysis of Greenness across 10,000 Urban Centres Derived from the Global Human Settlement Layer (GHSL)." *International Journal of Digital Earth* 13 (1): 101–18.

Dix-Carneiro, R., and B. Kovak. 2017. "Trade Liberalization and Regional Dynamics." 107 (10): 2908–46.

Duarte, M., and D. Restuccia. 2010. "The Role of the Structural Transformation in Aggregate Productivity." *Quarterly Journal of Economics* 125 (1): 129–73.

Duarte, M., and D. Restuccia. 2020. "Relative Prices and Sectoral Productivity." *Journal of the European Economic Association* 18 (3): 1400–43.

Duque, J. C., N. Lozano-Gracia, J. Patiño, and P. Restrepo. 2019. "Institutional Fragmentation and Metropolitan Coordination in Latin American Cities: What Consequences for Productivity and Growth?" Policy Research Working Paper 8696, World Bank, Washington, DC.

Duranton, G., P. Morrow, and M. Turner. 2014. "Roads and Trade: Evidence from the US." *Review of Economic Studies* 81 (2): 681–724.

Duranton, G., and M. Turner. 2012. "Urban Growth and Transportation." *Review of Economic Studies* 79 (4): 1407–40.

Ferreyra, M. M., and M. Roberts, eds. 2018. *Raising the Bar for Productive Cities in Latin America and the Caribbean.* Washington, DC: World Bank.

Gerritse, M., and D. Arribas-Bel. 2018. "Concrete Agglomeration Benefits: Do Roads Improve Urban Connections or Just Attract More People?" *Regional Studies* 52 (8): 1134–49.

Gollin, D., R. Jedwab, and D. Vollrath. 2016. "Urbanization with and without Industrialization." *Journal of Economic Growth* 21 (1): 35–70.

Gonzalez-Navarro, M., and C. Quintana-Domeque. 2016. "Paving Streets for the Poor: Experimental Analysis of Infrastructure Effects." *Review of Economics and Statistics* 98 (2): 254–67.

Jedwab, R., E. Ianchovichina, and F. Haslop. 2022. "Consumption Cities versus Production Cities: New Considerations and Evidence." Policy Research Working Paper 10105, World Bank, Washington, DC.

Lederman, D., J. Messina, S. Pienknagura, and R. Jamele. 2014. *Latin American Entrepreneurs: Many Firms but Little Innovation.* World Bank Latin American and Caribbean Studies. Washington, DC: World Bank.

Matano, A., M. Obaco, and V. Royuela. 2020. "What Drives the Spatial Wage Premium in Formal and Informal Labor Markets? The Case of Ecuador." *Journal of Regional Science* 60 (4): 823–47.

Melitz, M., and S. Redding. 2021. "Trade and Innovation." NBER Working Paper 28945, National Bureau of Economic Research, Cambridge, MA.

Moreno-Monroy, A., M. Schiavina, and P. Veneri. 2021. "Metropolitan Areas in the World: Delineation and Population Trends." *Journal of Urban Economics* 125: 103242.

Quintero, L., and M. Roberts. 2018. "Explaining Spatial Variations in Productivity: Evidence from Latin America and the Caribbean." Policy Research Working Paper 8560, World Bank, Washington, DC.

Restrepo Cadavid, P., and G. Cineas. 2018. "Urbanization, Economic Development, and Structural Transformation." In *Raising the Bar for Productive Cities in Latin America and the Caribbean*, edited by M. M. Ferreyra and M. Roberts. Washington, DC: World Bank.

Rocha, N., and M. Ruta. 2022. *Deep Trade Agreements: Anchoring Global Value Chains in Latin America and the Caribbean.* Washington, DC: World Bank.

Rodríguez-Vignoli, J., and F. Rowe. 2018. "How Is Internal Migration Reshaping Metropolitan Populations in Latin America? A New Method and New Evidence." *Population Studies* 72 (2): 253–73.

Selod, H., and S. Soumahoro. 2018. "Transport Infrastructure and Agglomeration in Cities." In *Raising the Bar for Productive Cities in Latin America and the Caribbean*, edited by M. M. Ferreyra and M. Roberts. Washington, DC: World Bank.

Stavropoulos, S., F. G. van Oort, and M. J. Burger. 2020. "Heterogeneous Relatedness and Firm Productivity." *Annals of Regional Science* 65: 403–37.

Venables, A. 2017a. "Breaking into Tradables: Urban Form and Urban Function in a Developing City." *Journal of Urban Economics* 98 (C): 88–97.

Venables, A. 2017b. "Expanding Cities and Connecting Cities: Appraising the Effects of Transport Improvements." *Journal of Transport Economics and Policy (JTEP)* 51 (1): 1–19.

Venables, A. 2020. "Winners and Losers in the Urban System." In *Urban Empires: Cities as Global Rulers in the New Urban World*, edited by E. Glaeser, K. Kourtit, and P. Nijkamp. New York: Routledge.

PART
IV
Segregation and Informality

Urban inequality has been a feature of cities since antiquity. Using data on house sizes from 63 different settlements spanning four continents and 110 centuries, a team of archeologists calculated Gini indexes of urban inequality (Kohler et al. 2017). Their estimates suggest that inequality increased as hunters and gatherers transitioned to agricultural life, and that for the first 25 centuries this increase was similar in the Americas and Eurasia. Inequality then stagnated in the Americas, but continued to rise in Eurasia, reflecting the ability of Eurasians to cultivate much bigger plots of land using large farm animals, unlike in the Americas, where land cultivation by hand remained the practice. The uneven distribution of large animals within settlements eventually translated into the uneven distribution of farm surpluses and growing inequality. With time, inequality rose not only in Europe but also in the colonies established by Europeans in other parts of the world, including the Americas. By 1784, inequality was high in cities in Nueva España, which included the territories of today's Mexico, Central America, Cuba, and parts of the United States, as indicated by a Gini index estimated at 0.63. In 1872, about a hundred years later, the Gini index in Brazil was 0.43 (Milanovic, Lindert, and Williamson 2011).

Income inequality continues to be an urban phenomenon in Latin America and the Caribbean (LAC). Differences in income within municipalities explain 80 percent of income inequality in the region (Acemoglu and Dell 2010). Income inequality also rises faster with city size in Latin America than in the United States (Ferreyra and Roberts 2018). An increase of 10 percent in city population is associated with a 0.29 percent increase in income inequality in Latin America, while the corresponding increase in US cities is just 0.12 percent (Ferreyra and Roberts 2018).

Highly unequal cities are often segregated cities, divided into spatially distant poor and affluent parts. Indeed, evidence from high-income countries suggests that income inequality and segregation go hand in hand. Both increased in the United States in the 1980s and 1990s (Reardon and Bischoff 2011) and in Europe in the 2000s (Musterd et al. 2016).

Residential segregation, which reflects the distribution of residents by income across city neighborhoods, may indicate people's preferences for living close to those with a similar socioeconomic status or for accessing housing and amenities in central parts of the city. However, if public services and jobs are of poor quality or are missing altogether from low-income neighborhoods, residential segregation can hurt the poor and vulnerable through its negative effect on schooling (Baum-Snow and Lutz 2011; Katz, Kling, and Liebman 2001), health (Acevedo-García et al. 2003; Alexander and Currie 2017), and intergenerational mobility (Chetty, Hendren, and Katz 2016). Segregation may also hurt the welfare of residents because of unequal access to opportunities (OECD 2018) and limited social capital (Chetty et al. 2022; Granovetter 1973). Having strong ties with friends and neighbors is of little use if there are no resources to share or if no one has access to good-quality jobs (Granovetter 1973), whereas having strong ties with a diverse set of friends can help improve the adult socioeconomic status of poor children (Chetty et al. 2022). Such friendships are unlikely to develop in a divided city. Chapter 6 explores the spatial dimensions of urban inequality and informality and their implications for productivity and economic growth in some of Latin America's largest cities.

References

Acemoglu, D., and M. Dell. 2010. "Productivity Differences between and within Countries." *American Economic Journal: Macroeconomics* 2 (1): 169–88.

Acevedo-García, D., K. Lochner, T. Osypuk, and S. Subramanian. 2003. "Future Directions in Residential Segregation and Health Research: A Multilevel Approach." *American Journal of Public Health* 93 (2): 215–21.

Alexander, D., and J. Currie. 2017. "Is It Who You Are or Where You Live? Residential Segregation and Racial Gaps in Childhood Asthma." *Journal of Health Economics* 55: 186–200.

Baum-Snow, N., and B. Lutz. 2011. "School Desegregation, School Choice, and Changes in Residential Location Patterns by Race." *American Economic Review* 101: 3019–46.

Chetty, R., N. Hendren, and L. F. Katz. 2016. "The Effects of Exposure to Better Neighborhoods on Children: New Evidence from the Moving to Opportunity Experiment." *American Economic Review* 106 (4): 855–902.

Chetty, R., M. Jackson, T. Kuchler, J. Stroebel, N. Hendren, R. Fluegge, S. Gong, et al. 2022. "Social Capital I: Measurement and Associations with Economic Mobility." *Nature* 608: 108–21.

Ferreyra, M. M., and M. Roberts. 2018. *Raising the Bar for Productive Cities in Latin America and the Caribbean.* Washington, DC: World Bank.

Granovetter, M. 1973. "The Strength of Weak Ties Theory." *American Journal of Sociology* 78 (6): 1360–80.

Katz, L., J. Kling, and J. Liebman. 2001. "Moving to Opportunities in Boston: Early Results of a Randomized Mobility Experiment." *Quarterly Journal of Economics* 116 (2): 607–54.

Kohler, T., M. Smith, A. Bogaard, G. Feinman, C. Peterson, A. Betzenhauser, M. Pailes, et al. 2017. "Greater Post-Neolithic Wealth Disparities in Eurasia than in North America and Mesoamerica." *Nature* 551 (7682): 619–22.

Milanovic, B., P. Lindert, and J. Williamson. 2011. "Pre-industrial Inequality." *Economic Journal* 121 (551): 255–72.

Musterd, S., S. Marcinczak, M. van Ham, and T. Tammaru. 2016. "Socioeconomic Segregation in European Capital Cities: Increasing Separation between Poor and Rich." *Urban Geography* 38 (7): 1062–83.

OECD (Organisation for Economic Co-operation and Development). 2018. *Divided Cities: Understanding Intra-urban Inequalities.* Paris: OECD.

Reardon, S., and K. Bischoff. 2011. "Income Inequality and Income Segregation." *American Journal of Sociology* 116: 1092–153.

Urban Inequality, Segregation, and Informality Traps

6

Is there a link between income segregation—the spatial dimension of intraurban income inequality—and urban productivity? Using newly available data from population and city surveys, this chapter sheds some light on this question by first documenting socioeconomic inequality and segregation in the largest metropolitan areas of Brazil, Colombia, and Mexico. It then examines the links between residential segregation and urban productivity in Bogotá and the efficiency losses associated with residential labor market segregation and informality in Mexico City.

The literature on the leading causes and consequences of urban income segregation has mainly focused on the United States. Schelling (1969) demonstrated that preferences for worker composition within a neighborhood can lead to urban segregation, even in an integrated city. More recent theoretical papers show that when households have preferences about the composition of their neighborhoods, segregation can arise and affect welfare through the consumption of public goods (Bayer, McMillan, and Rueben 2005; Becker and Murphy 2000). Caetano and Macartney (2021), Caetano and Maheshri (2017), and Card, Mas, and Rothstein (2008) provide evidence on Schelling's "tipping point"—that is, when the minority share of residents in a neighborhood grows to such a point that all majority residents leave (Schelling 1969).

Divisions within Latin American cities

Relatively little work has been undertaken on income segregation in Latin America. The Organisation for Economic Co-operation and Development (OECD) has featured work on Brazil by Moreno-Monroy (2018), and Peters and Skop (2007) have focused on sociospatial segregation in Lima, Peru. The biggest challenge in documenting income segregation is obtaining representative data below the municipal level in metropolitan areas. The smallest areas for which the census data are representative are "neighborhoods," which comprise several adjacent census tracts. This chapter relies on population census data for Brazil in 2010, Colombia in 2018, and Mexico in 2010 and 2020 to characterize the intraurban dispersion in poverty rates in the largest cities in Brazil and the socioeconomic vulnerabilities in the largest cities of Colombia and Mexico. Annex 6A provides details on the definition of *socioeconomic vulnerability indexes* and the methodology for estimating them.

The poverty incidence shown in map 6.1 reveals that in Brazil, Brasilia, Rio de Janeiro, and São Paulo are segregated cities. This segregation is most apparent in the capital city,

183

Brasilia, where poor residents live mostly outside the city center. In São Paulo, the poor reside primarily in the city's south and, to a lesser extent, in other parts of the urban periphery. Rio de Janeiro appears slightly less segregated. The affluent are found mostly in the western neighborhoods of the city, while the poor are concentrated in the center north and dispersed throughout the city's eastern neighborhoods. The spatial patterns of socio-economic vulnerability in the largest metropolitan areas in Colombia and Mexico similarly suggest that these are segregated metropolitan areas (map 6.2). Although the patterns differ across cities, in all cases they show that some parts of these cities have a higher prevalence of residents who struggle along multiple socioeconomic dimensions. In Colombia, the incidence of the most vulnerable people—those belonging to clusters 1–3 in map 6.2—is highest in the largest cities and lowest in the smallest ones (figure 6.1). In Mexico, the percentage of vulnerable people is highest in Mexico's large metropolitan areas, with a

MAP 6.1   Intraurban poverty incidence at the neighborhood level in the largest metropolitan areas, Brazil, 2010

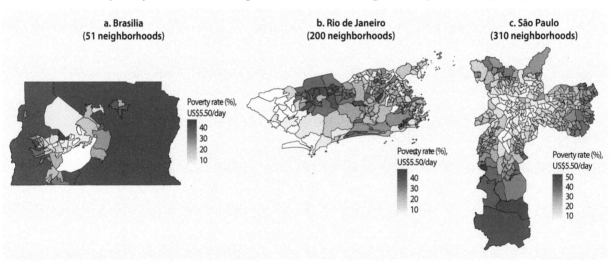

Source: Van der Weide, Ferreira de Souza, and Barbosa 2020.

MAP 6.2   Socioeconomic vulnerability at the neighborhood level in the largest metropolitan areas, Colombia and Mexico

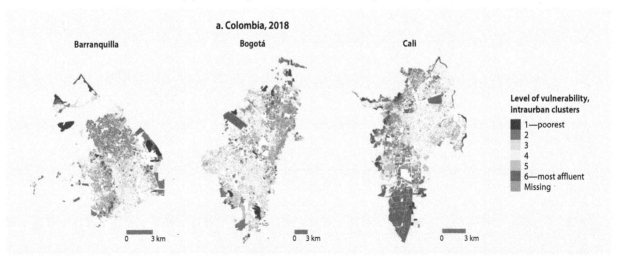

(Continued on next page)

MAP 6.2   **Socioeconomic vulnerability at the neighborhood level in the largest metropolitan areas: Colombia and Mexico** *(continued)*

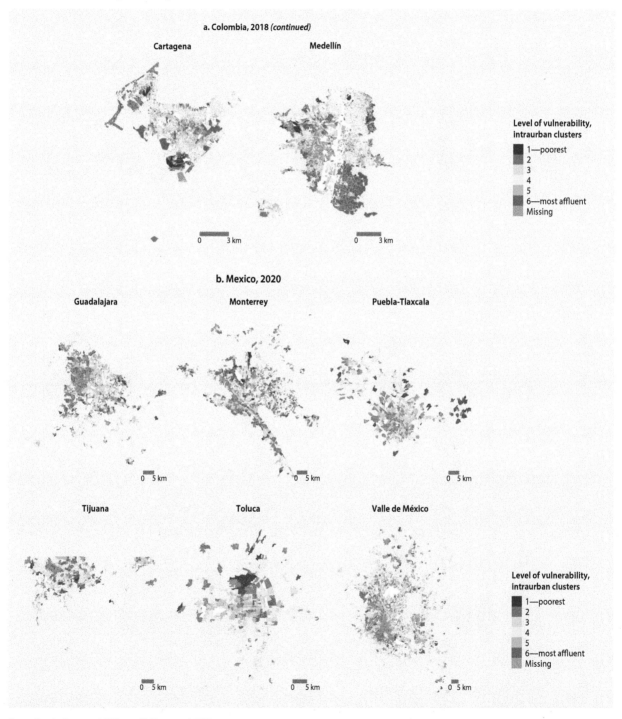

a. Colombia, 2018 *(continued)*

Cartagena   Medellín

Level of vulnerability, intraurban clusters
1—poorest
2
3
4
5
6—most affluent
Missing

0   3 km   0   3 km

b. Mexico, 2020

Guadalajara   Monterrey   Puebla-Tlaxcala

0 5 km   0 5 km   0 5 km

Tijuana   Toluca   Valle de México

Level of vulnerability, intraurban clusters
1—poorest
2
3
4
5
6—most affluent
Missing

0 5 km   0 5 km   0 5 km

Sources: Panel a: Duque et al. 2021; panel b: Duque et al. 2022.
Note: Data are for the most recent year available. In the legends, 1 identifies areas with the highest vulnerability, and 6 identifies those with the lowest vulnerability.

FIGURE 6.1   **Population share by socioeconomic vulnerability cluster and city size, Colombia and Mexico**

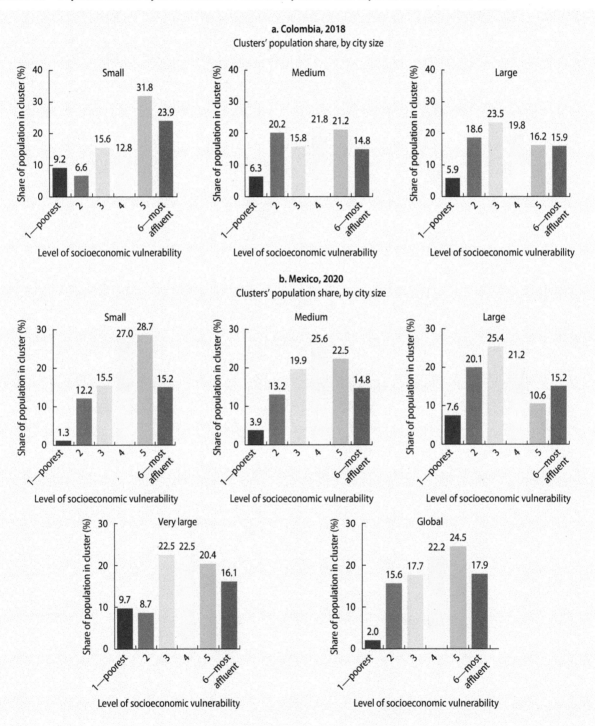

Sources: Panel a: Duque et al. 2021; panel b: Duque et al. 2022.
Note: On the x-axis, 1 identifies areas with the highest level of socioeconomic vulnerability, and 6 identifies areas with the lowest level of socioeconomic vulnerability. City sizes by population in Colombia: small = <100,000; medium = 100,000–1 million; large = >1 million. City sizes by population in Mexico: small = <500,000; medium = 500,000–900,000; large = 900,000–2 million; very large = 2 million–10 million; and global (only Mexico City metropolitan area) = 21.2 million.

population of between 900,000 and 2 million and not its megacities, with a population of more than 2 million (figure 6.1).

Although it declined in the 2010s, the prevalence of urban socioeconomic vulnerability was higher at the end of the 2020s in Mexico than in Colombia in 2018 (figure 6.2). Unlike Colombia, where vulnerability has been highest in the north and lowest in the largest cities in the country's core (figure 6.2, panel a), in Mexico vulnerability has been higher in the capital, Mexico City, and in cities in the center and the south than in the country's north (figure 6.2, panel b). Poor access to decent housing is the main source of socioeconomic vulnerability in both Colombia and Mexico. Inadequate education services in Colombia and poor labor market conditions in Mexico are the other major sources of vulnerability (Duque et al. 2021, 2022).

The spatial patterns reveal overlapping vulnerabilities in the major cities in Colombia and Mexico (map 6.3). For example, in Bogotá households vulnerable in terms of education, housing, and labor market conditions are concentrated in the city's south, whereas those with low vulnerability live in the city's north (map 6.3, panel a). High vulnerability along multiple dimensions is noticeable in Medellín's northeast, Barranquilla's southwest and southeast, Cali's peripheral regions, and Cartagena's north and south (map 6.3, panel a). In Mexico's major cities, socioeconomic vulnerability is typically low along all dimensions in the city's core and high in the city's periphery (map 6.3, panel b).[1]

FIGURE 6.2 **Histograms and country maps of composite vulnerability scores at the metropolitan-area level, Colombia and Mexico**

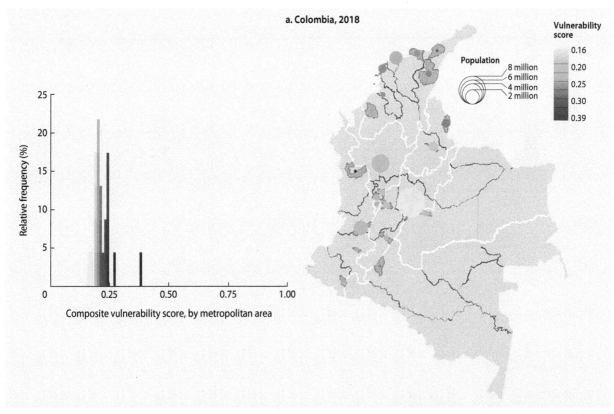

(Continued on next page)

FIGURE 6.2   **Histograms and country maps of composite vulnerability scores at the metropolitan-area level, Colombia and Mexico** *(continued)*

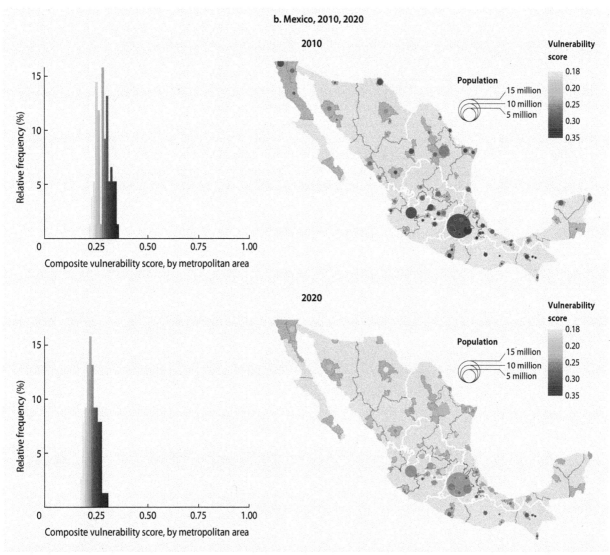

b. Mexico, 2010, 2020

Sources: Panel a: Duque et al. 2021; panel b: Duque et al. 2022.
Note: The composite vulnerability score is the average of the five vulnerability scores by dimension in Mexico and the four vulnerability scores by dimension in Colombia. See table 6A.1 in annex 6A for details on the vulnerability dimensions.

MAP 6.3   LISA clusters by vulnerability dimension and city, Colombia and Mexico

a. Colombia

Barranquilla

Demographics   Education   Housing   Labor

Bogotá

Demographics   Education   Housing   Labor

Cali

Demographics   Education   Housing   Labor

Vulnerability
High-high
High-low
Low-high
Low-low
Not significant

(Continued on next page)

MAP 6.3   LISA clusters by vulnerability dimension and city, Colombia and Mexico *(continued)*

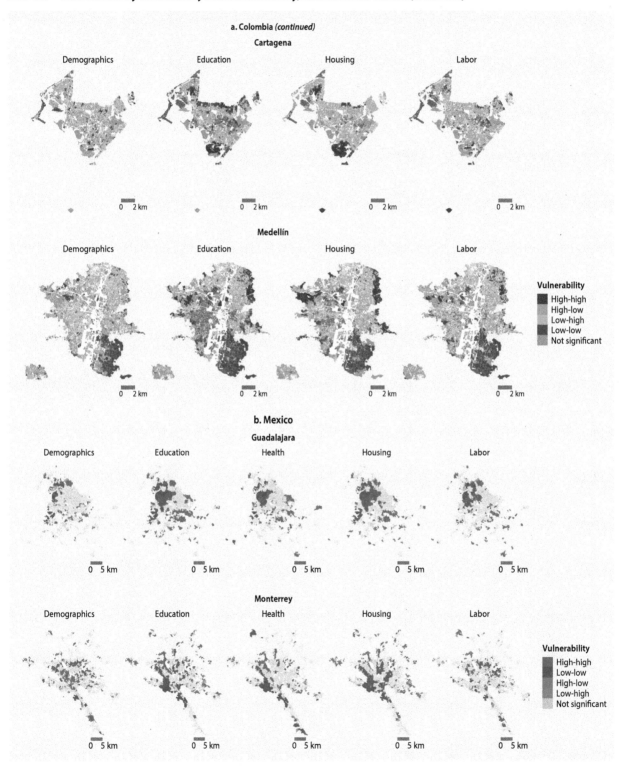

(Continued on next page)

MAP 6.3 **LISA clusters by vulnerability dimension and city, Colombia and Mexico** *(continued)*

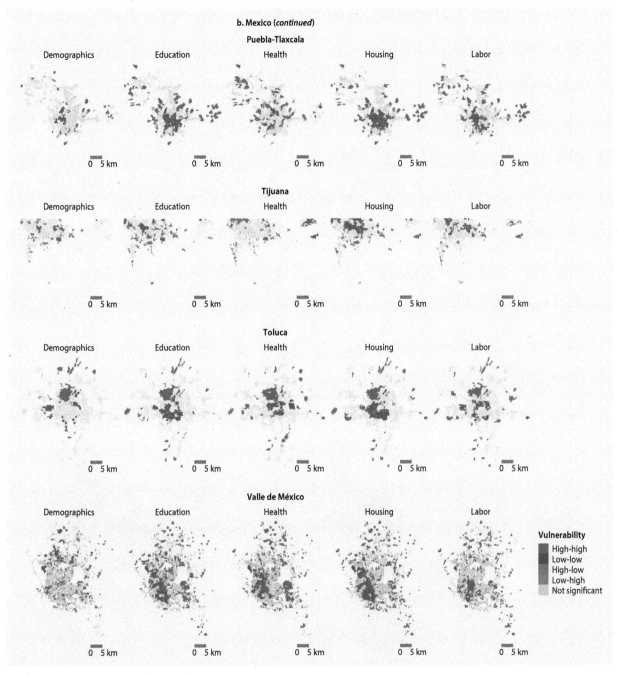

b. Mexico *(continued)*

Puebla-Tlaxcala

Tijuana

Toluca

Valle de México

Vulnerability
High-high
Low-low
High-low
Low-high
Not significant

Sources: Panel a: Duque et al. 2021; panel b: Duque et al. 2022.
Note: These local indicators of spatial association (LISA) maps provide an indication of the extent of significant spatial clustering of similar values of vulnerability in the respective
dimension around each observation (Anselin 1995). High-high = statistically significant cluster of high vulnerability; low-low = statistically significant cluster of low vulnerability;
high-low = outlier of high vulnerability surrounded mostly by low-vulnerability areas; low-high = outlier of low vulnerability surrounded mostly by high-vulnerability areas.

Neighborhood productivity and segregation in Bogotá

Bogotá—a case of special interest—is a city with relatively high levels of income and housing wealth inequality. Although the Gini coefficient nationwide was 0.5 in 2018, in Bogotá it was 0.55 in 2017, according to Heil, Ianchovichina, and Quintero (2022), who use data from a unique multipurpose city survey and housing prices from Bogotá's cadaster. The spatial divisions in terms of socioeconomic conditions (maps 6.2 and 6.3) are indicative of residential segregation (map 6.4). The poorest 20 percent of urban residents tend to be concentrated in the city's south, although poor residents also reside in many other parts of the city (map 6.4, panel a). By contrast, the most affluent 20 percent of Bogotá's residents live largely in the city's affluent north (map 6.4, panel a). The distribution of housing wealth is similar with differences at its low end. Properties in the top 10 percent of the housing price distribution can be found mostly in the city's north (map 6.4, panel b), while the least expensive ones are located only in the city's south and in small sections along the eastern periphery (map 6.4, panel b).

Indexes of income and housing wealth segregation, presented in box 6.1, confirm that income segregation is substantially lower than housing segregation. At the end of the decade, income segregation was highest among residents in the top 20 percent of the income distribution and lowest among those in the bottom 20 percent of the income distribution (figure 6.3, panel a). By contrast, housing wealth segregation was highest among

MAP 6.4 **Spatial distribution of low- and high-income residents and least and most expensive housing, Bogotá**

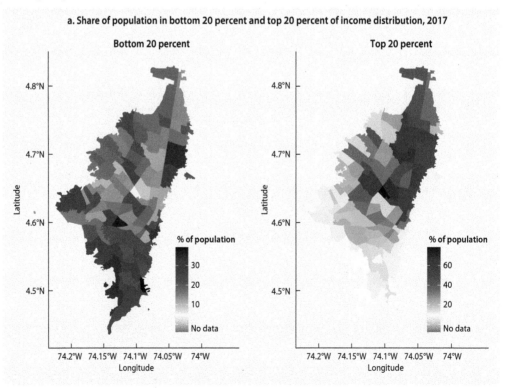

a. Share of population in bottom 20 percent and top 20 percent of income distribution, 2017

(Continued on next page)

MAP 6.4   Spatial distribution of low- and high-income residents and least and most expensive housing, Bogotá *(continued)*

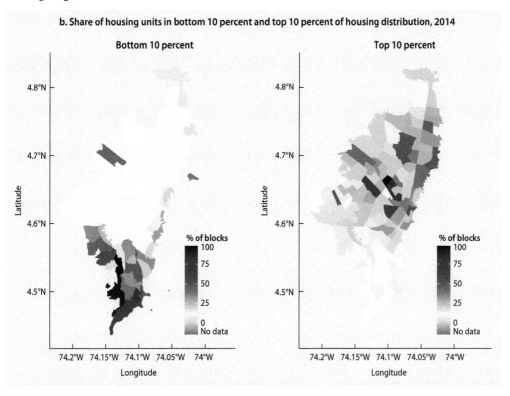

b. Share of housing units in bottom 10 percent and top 10 percent of housing distribution, 2014

Source: Heil, Ianchovichina, and Quintero 2022.
Note: The income used is the total monthly income from a 2017 multipurpose survey (Encuesta Multipropósito, EM) produced jointly by the Secretaría Distrital de Planeación de la Alcaldía Mayor de Bogotá and the Departamento Administrativo Nacional de Estadística (DANE). No information is available for the gray area in each map.

BOX 6.1   Segregation index

Heil, Ianchovichina, and Quintero (2022) use the Information Theory Index, $H(p)$, at different income percentile ranks p of the income distribution. Because only a few percentiles are observed, the function $H(p)$ is approximated using polynomial interpolation from the observed p (see Bischoff and Reardon 2014). The index, also known as the Theil Index (Theil 1972), is given as

$$H(p) = 1 - \sum_{j \in J} \frac{t_j E_j(p)}{TE(p)}, \qquad (B6.1.1)$$

where T is the population of the metropolitan area; t_j is the population of neighborhood j; E_j is the value of the entropy in unit j; and $E(p)$ denotes the citywide entropy of the population when divided into these two groups,

$$E(p) = p\log_2 \frac{1}{p} + (1-p)\log_2 \frac{1}{1-p}. \qquad (B6.1.2)$$

FIGURE 6.3   **Income and housing wealth segregation along the distribution**

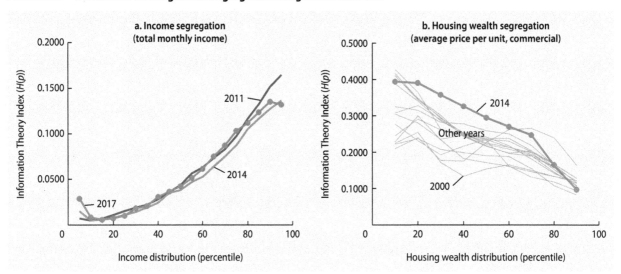

Source: Heil, Ianchovichina, and Quintero (2022), using the Information Theory Index defined with equation B6.1.1 in box 6.1.
Note: Panel a shows that higher-income residents segregated more from the rest in the urban space, while panel b shows that people living in more expensive houses segregated less from the rest in the urban space.

residents in the bottom 20 percent of the housing wealth distribution and lowest among those in the top 20 percent (figure 6.3, panel b). Thus income segregation in Bogotá is a segregation of affluence, while housing segregation is a segregation of poverty. Over time, income segregation stagnated and declined mostly among residents in the top 20 percent between 2011 and 2017, but housing segregation substantially increased between 2000 and 2014.

Heil, Ianchovichina, and Quintero (2022) link segregation and urban productivity by showing that in Bogotá residential location affects access to good jobs and the potential for building housing wealth. First, they document that location premia vary substantially across city neighborhoods. They find that only central neighborhoods offer positive location wage premia, whereas other locations—mostly in the northern parts of the city—offer positive house price premia (map 6.5). In the city's south, both wage and house price premia are negative. Second, they test whether density, education externalities, and connectivity can explain intraurban spatial variations in income and housing wealth at the neighborhood level. Their results suggest that long commuting times are negatively associated with neighborhood wage premia, while education externalities at the neighborhood level and distance to amenities matter for house price premia and ultimately for building housing wealth.

The residents of the city's south are therefore doubly disadvantaged over residents in the city's north. They live in poorly connected parts of the city and are far away from firms offering the best-quality jobs (map 6.6). The TransMilenio bus rapid transit system has eased congestion since 2000, but Bogotá remains the most congested city in the world and the second-slowest city in the region (Akbar 2022). Residents in the south are also unable to build housing wealth because of negative neighborhood education externalities and poor access to consumer amenities and public services (map 6.6). In summary, residential segregation lowers urban productivity by limiting the geographic span of agglomeration economies.

MAP 6.5   Neighborhood productivity and house price premia, Bogotá

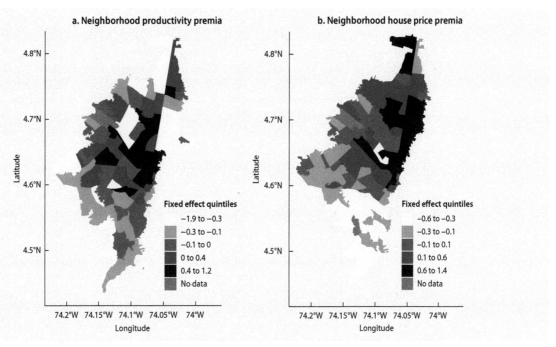

Source: Heil, Ianchovichina, and Quintero (2022), based on the 2017 Encuesta Multipropósito (EM) Generalities Multipurpose Survey (https://www.sdp.gov.co/gestion-estudios-estrategicos/estudios-macro/encuesta-multiproposito).
Note: In panel a, the neighborhood wage premia are the fraction of hourly wages (in 2017 local currency units, log) that cannot be accounted for by observable, nongeographic (portable) individual characteristics. They are the estimated fixed effects in a regression of logged hourly wages of individual *i* in neighborhood (Unidad de Planeamiento Zonal, UPZ) *j* on a set of worker characteristics, including years of education, age, age squared, gender, marital status, and worker's status as a domestic or migrant worker. In panel b, the neighborhood house price premia are the fixed effects in a regression of logged house prices (in 2014 local currency units per square meter) in block (*manzana*) *m* on a set of housing characteristics in the manzana, including density of housing units, population density, average number of rooms per person, and share of residents with electricity, internet, sewerage, and running water connections.

MAP 6.6   Education externalities and distance to amenities, Bogotá

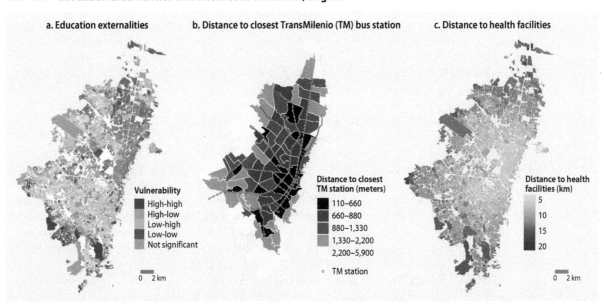

Sources: Panels a and c: Duque et al. 2021; panel b: Heil, Ianchovichina, and Quintero 2022.
Note: In panel a, the local indicators of spatial association (LISA) map indicates the extent of significant spatial clustering of similar values of vulnerability in education around each observation (Anselin 1995). High-high = statistically significant cluster of high vulnerability; high-low = outlier of high vulnerability surrounded mostly by low-vulnerability areas; low-high = outlier of low vulnerability surrounded mostly by high vulnerability areas; low-low = statistically significant cluster of low vulnerability; km = kilometers.

Residential labor market segregation and informality traps in Mexico City

Residential labor market *segmentation*—defined in terms of the extent to which urbanites have access to good-quality formal jobs at a reasonable commuting time (less than 60 minutes) and cost—is linked to but is distinctly different from residential labor market *segregation*. A city has a spatially segmented labor market when a large percentage of its workforce can access only a fraction of all jobs in the city within a reasonable commuting time and cost. If the commuter market access of all socioeconomic groups is comparable, a city may be spatially *segmented*, but not *segregated*—in other words, it may have an accessibility, but not a segregation, problem.

Segmentation and segregation weaken agglomeration economies because there are fewer opportunities for sharing, matching, and learning in segmented or segregated cities. Residential labor market segregation may also give rise to a dual urban economy in which the relatively poor and vulnerable are trapped in poverty and informality. Poor market access and the limited availability of high-quality services and skilled labor in the low-income parts of a city imply that the local firms serving these areas are often informal. Because commuting cost constitutes a big share of the income of relatively unskilled residents, they may often work informally in proximity to their homes (Suárez, Murata, and Campos 2015) and purchase most of their goods and services from local informal firms (Bachas, Gadenne, and Jensen 2020). If a sizable fraction of the labor force in a city has poor access to formal jobs relative to informal ones, residential labor market segregation may lead to the spatial misallocation noted by Hsieh and Klenow (2009) because the informal economy on the periphery of the city does not pay taxes and is less productive than the formal one.

Ianchovichina and Zárate (2021) find evidence of residential labor market segregation and an urban economy dual in nature in Mexico City, based on information from a variety of sources presented in annex 6B. They distinguish between three income groups based on the sociodemographic status of the individual, which is a proxy for household income. *Sociodemographic status* is defined as a part of the survey stratification (*estrato sociodemographico*) at the level of the primary sampling unit (*manzana*). The three income groups are (1) residents with low- and lower-middle sociodemographic status,[2] accounting for 59 percent of the population of Mexico City; (2) residents with upper-middle sociodemographic status, representing 30 percent of the population; and (3) residents with upper sociodemographic status, accounting for 11 percent of the population. As expected, a greater share of the upper sociodemographic group has a tertiary education, owns a car, and relies on private transportation than those in the upper-middle, lower-middle, and low socioeconomic groups (figure 6.4).

Low-income workers tend to live, work, and shop mostly in the periphery of Mexico City (map 6.7), where the share of high-skilled workers is low and informality rates are high (map 6.8). By contrast, upper-middle- and high-income workers live, work, and shop mainly in central city locations (map 6.7), where the share of high-skilled workers is high and informality rates are low (map 6.8). Because most high-skilled workers sort into central city locations with better amenities (figure 6.5) and higher housing prices, differences between high- and low-income workers are associated with differences in neighborhood choices rather than sensitivity to travel times in the city once the fixed effects of transport modes are included. Ianchovichina and Zárate (2021) document the existence of informality traps, characterized by a spatial overlap of peripheral areas with a high concentration

FIGURE 6.4   Characteristics of sociodemographic groups: Mexico City, 2017

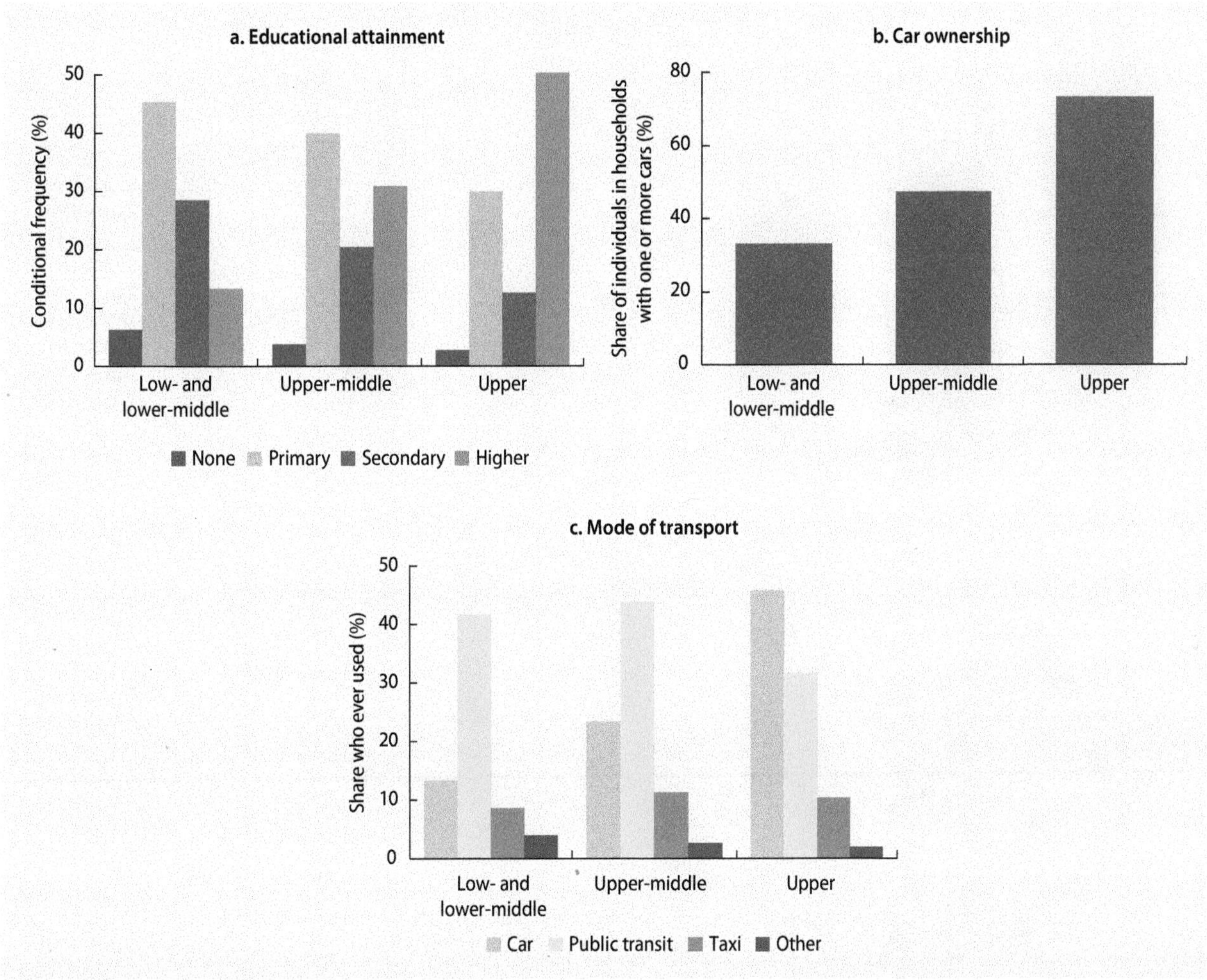

a. Educational attainment

y-axis: Conditional frequency (%) — 0, 10, 20, 30, 40, 50
x-axis: Low- and lower-middle, Upper-middle, Upper

Legend: ■ None   Primary   ■ Secondary   Higher

b. Car ownership

y-axis: Share of individuals in households with one or more cars (%) — 0, 20, 40, 60, 80
x-axis: Low- and lower-middle, Upper-middle, Upper

c. Mode of transport

y-axis: Share who ever used (%) — 0, 10, 20, 30, 40, 50
x-axis: Low- and lower-middle, Upper-middle, Upper

Legend: Car   Public transit   ■ Taxi   ■ Other

Source: Ianchovichina and Zárate 2021.
Note: "Share who ever used" in panel c refers to the share of individuals in each socioeconomic group who used a car, public transit, a taxi, or other mode of transport at least once.

of informal workers, informal workers' residences, and low-skilled workers, which are distant from the urban core where the concentration of formal workers, formal workers' residences, and high-skilled workers is high.

In other large Latin American cities, such as Buenos Aires, Lima, and Santiago, the poor have been relocating to low-income settlements on the outskirts of cities in search of affordable housing. Yet the settlements at the urban periphery often have limited access to affordable public transportation and other services, and there are few sources of formal employment in proximity to people's residences (Negrete and Paquette 2011). Thus the distance between formal work and home has grown for the poor and vulnerable (Kim and Zangerling 2016; Muzzini et al. 2017; Sabatini 1999; Tuiran 2000), implying a rise in residential labor market segregation in Argentina, Chile, and Peru.

MAP 6.7   Trip destinations by income group, Mexico City

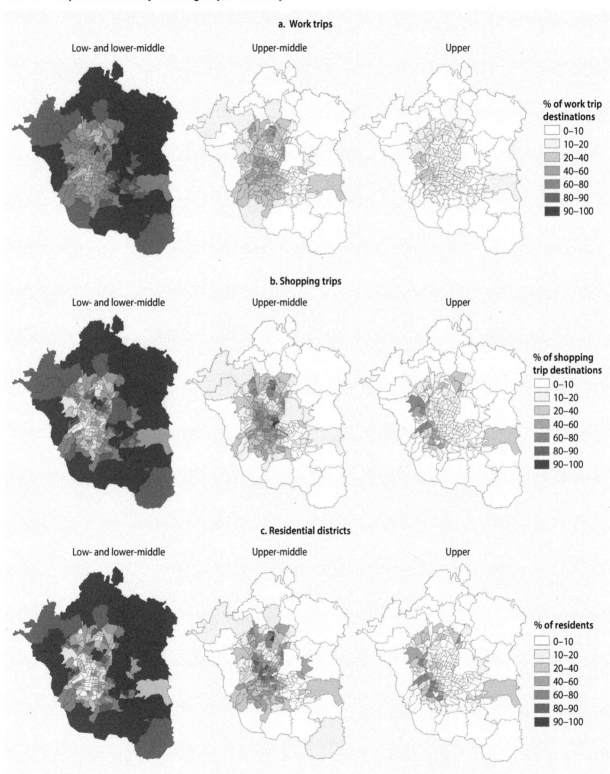

Source: Ianchovichina and Zárate 2021.
Note: Income is proxied with the status of three sociodemographic groups: low- and lower-middle, upper-middle, and upper.

MAP 6.8   Spatial distribution in Mexico City: A modern core and an informal periphery

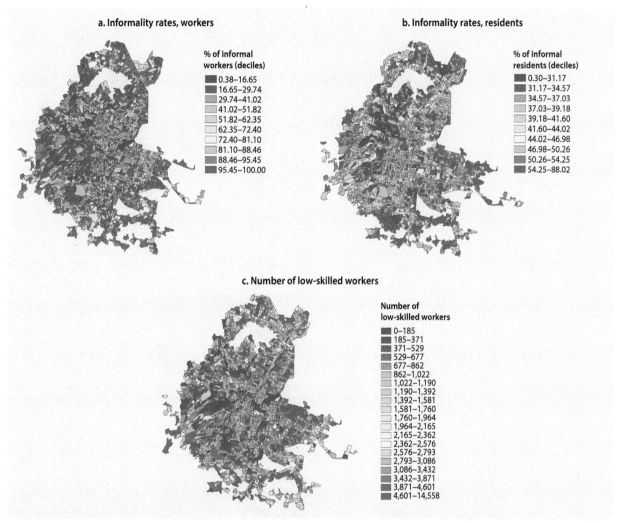

a. Informality rates, workers

% of informal workers (deciles)
- 0.38–16.65
- 16.65–29.74
- 29.74–41.02
- 41.02–51.82
- 51.82–62.35
- 62.35–72.40
- 72.40–81.10
- 81.10–88.46
- 88.46–95.45
- 95.45–100.00

b. Informality rates, residents

% of informal residents (deciles)
- 0.30–31.17
- 31.17–34.57
- 34.57–37.03
- 37.03–39.18
- 39.18–41.60
- 41.60–44.02
- 44.02–46.98
- 46.98–50.26
- 50.26–54.25
- 54.25–88.02

c. Number of low-skilled workers

Number of low-skilled workers
- 0–185
- 185–371
- 371–529
- 529–677
- 677–862
- 862–1,022
- 1,022–1,190
- 1,190–1,392
- 1,392–1,581
- 1,581–1,760
- 1,760–1,964
- 1,964–2,165
- 2,165–2,362
- 2,362–2,576
- 2,576–2,793
- 2,793–3,086
- 3,086–3,432
- 3,432–3,871
- 3,871–4,601
- 4,601–14,558

Sources: Panels a and b: Zárate 2022; panel c: Ianchovichina and Zárate 2021.
Note: The maps show the informality rates of workers and residents and the number of low-skilled workers in each census tract.

Using the spatial general equilibrium model described in annex 6C, Ianchovichina and Zárate (2021) show that such residential labor market segregation—explained by high rents in central locations and high-skilled workers' preferences for better amenities—gives rise to resource misallocation stemming from the informal urban economy. Because informal firms do not pay taxes, there is heterogeneity in the marginal product of labor across establishments located in central versus peripheral city neighborhoods that generates misallocation (Hsieh and Klenow 2009).

FIGURE 6.5   Association between the number of workers in a location and the share of streets with different amenities in the location by skill level, Mexico City

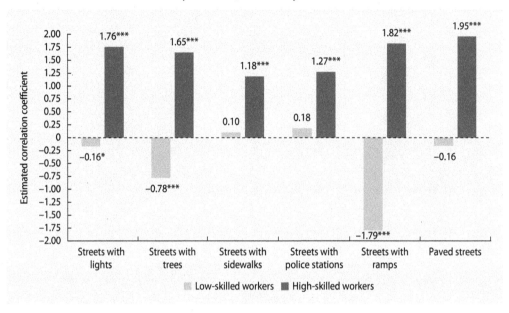

Source: Ianchovichina and Zárate 2021.
Note: The figure shows that the locations where many low-skilled workers live tend to have a low share of streets with amenities, such as lights, trees, and ramps. By contrast, the locations where many high-skilled workers live have a high share of streets with various amenities. The number of workers is calculated at the census level, and the share of streets with a specific amenity is calculated at the borough level.
Significance level: * = 10 percent, *** = 1 percent.

How to reduce the losses associated with residential segregation

The efficiency losses due to residential segregation can be reduced with improved intraurban connectivity in the case of Mexico City. Zárate (2022) shows that adding a new subway line that connects the peripheral neighborhoods with central city locations in Mexico City improves aggregate welfare by 1.3 percent and reduces informality by 4 percentage points in locations benefiting from the new line. The improved connectivity to the low-income areas compensates for any displacement effects that may result from increases in the quality of housing and housing prices and rents in proximity to newly opened metro stations. Pfutze, Rodríguez-Castelan, and Valderrama-Gonzalez (2018) find that such a displacement occurred in Colombia near newly opened bus rapid transit (BRT) stations in Barranquilla, and Tsivanidis (2019) finds the same for the BRT system in Bogotá.[3]

Policies to improve amenities or affordable housing for low-skilled workers in central locations could complement efforts to improve connectivity to low-income neighborhoods. Increasing affordable housing for low-income workers in central city locations by 15 percent is estimated to increase aggregate welfare by around 1.6 percent (without affecting the aggregate utility of high-skilled workers), and to reduce the informality rate by approximately 1 percent (figure 6.6), which is equivalent to a reduction of 1.5 percentage points in aggregate informality. By contrast, gentrification of the periphery has negligible effects on welfare and informality, and it is not an effective way of reducing spatial misallocation and informality in Mexico City (Ianchovichina and Zárate 2021). Thus in Mexico City, improving connectivity to the parts of the city where the poor are trapped in poverty is

FIGURE 6.6   **Effects of improved access to affordable housing for low-skilled workers in central locations in Mexico City**

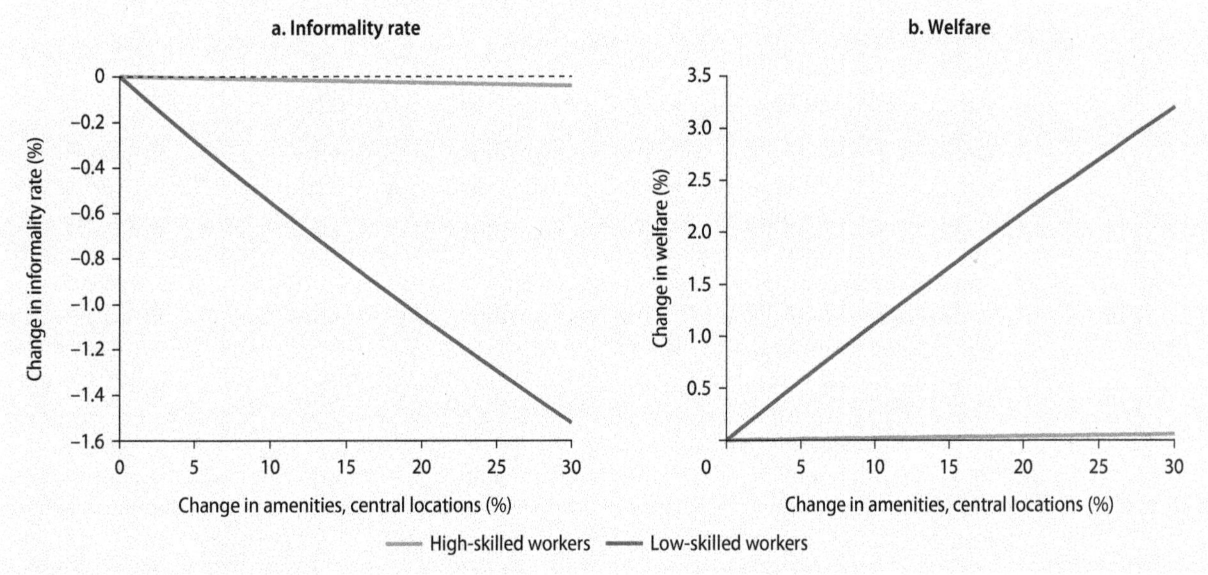

a. Informality rate

b. Welfare

Legend: High-skilled workers — Low-skilled workers

Source: Ianchovichina and Zárate 2021.

the most effective way to reduce spatial misallocation and informality, combined with policies to improve affordable housing for low-skilled residents in or near the central parts of the city.

And yet these measures may be insufficient to address the problem posed by the dual urban economy. Affordable housing projects (such as Bando 2) in Mexico City's central business district have proven difficult to implement. Addressing crime and resolving long-standing deficiencies in and lack of basic infrastructure and public services may also be needed. Furthermore, proximity to jobs may not be sufficient to improve livelihoods. Emerging evidence indicates that labor market intermediation efforts combined with improvements in living standards are needed to help slum residents find better labor market opportunities in Argentina.

This chapter shows that many large cities in Latin America are both unequal and divided into geographically distant poor and affluent parts. Using examples from Colombia and Mexico, the chapter reveals that such divisions weaken agglomeration economies and generate economic inefficiencies. Urban divisions—reinforced by intraurban connectivity issues—lower the returns to density by limiting their geographic scope. In divided cities, the large gains from sharing, matching, and learning are limited to neighborhoods in central business districts where formal firms operate, consumer amenities are abundant, and residents enjoy better-quality basic infrastructure and public services. The opposite is found in low-income neighborhoods, where residents often face multiple deprivations in terms of access to basic infrastructure, public services, and housing. Typically, in the urban periphery firms and workers are mostly informal. The existence of a dual urban economy—a formal, high-productivity one in central business districts and a low-productivity, informal one in low-income neighborhoods—generates spatial misallocation because informal firms do not pay taxes. The occurrence of such misallocation in the region's largest cities undermines aggregate output growth. The next chapter summarizes this study's findings and policy implications.

Annex 6A Socioeconomic vulnerability indexes

Duque et al. (2021, 2022) construct socioeconomic vulnerability indexes capturing vulnerabilities in five different dimensions: housing, demographics, education, labor, and health. Their composite vulnerability index is the average of the five vulnerability scores in each vulnerability dimension. The data used in the computation of the indexes are from the 2010 and 2020 Mexican population censuses, collected by the National Institute of Statistics and Geography (INEGI), and the 2018 Colombian population census, collected by the National Administrative Department of Statistics (DANE). In Mexico, the data cover 75 metropolitan areas at the urban neighborhood (AGEB/block) level, while in Colombia they cover 23 metropolitan areas at the block level.

In most cases, vulnerability is measured as the percentage of households without access to 15 variables of interest (such as electricity, internet, water, sewerage, and health services), the percentage of individuals who do not meet certain benchmarks (such as literacy, school attendance, tertiary education, a job), and the percentage of households vulnerable due to their demographic characteristics (such as headed by a female, speaking an indigenous language, and having a person with disabilities). Table 6A.1 presents the five dimensions of socioeconomic vulnerability. The indexes are standardized to take values of between 0 and 1 so that higher numbers represent higher levels of vulnerability. Local indicators of spatial association (LISA) maps are used to analyze the intraurban spatial patterns of socioeconomic vulnerability and identify the dimensions and the areas in which vulnerability is highest.

TABLE 6A.1   Dimensions of vulnerability, Colombia and Mexico

Dimension	Indicators
Demographics	% of female-headed households % of ethnic population % of disabled Household demographic dependency on minors and elderly
Education	Illiteracy rate among those age 15 years and over School absence rate for youth ages 5–14 % of people over age 18 without a tertiary education % of households with household heads without a higher education (considered only in Colombia)
Health	% of people with no access to health services (only in Mexico)
Housing	% of households without access to electricity % of households without access to internet connection service % of households without access to water % of households without adequate sewerage % of overcrowded households % of households without garbage collection service (only in Colombia) % of households without natural gas service (only in Colombia)
Labor	Unemployment rate % of households with high economic dependency ratio % of child labor among the population ages 10–14 (only in Colombia) % of economically active individuals who worked during the last week and did not receive income (only in Colombia) % of youth who neither study nor work (only in Colombia)

Sources: Duque et al. 2021, 2022.

Duque et al. (2021, 2022) provide details on the methodology for constructing the LISA maps. They use the definition of *metropolitan area* from the Mexican National Council of Population (CONAPO) and DANE, which groups municipalities around the main Colombian cities into 23 metropolitan areas.

Annex 6B Data sources on employment, mobility, and residence in Mexico City

Data on the location of firms and workers are from Mexico's National Institute of Statistics and Geography (INEGI) economic censuses for 1999, 2004, 2009, and 2014 and population censuses for 2000 and 2010. These data are aggregated at the census tract and municipal levels. The social security information in the censuses is used to identify the (in)formal status of workers and establishments.

Information on number of trips and their characteristics is taken from the 2017 travel diary survey. Microcensus data for 2015 are used to construct commuting flows for both the formal and informal sectors by type of skill, allowing Ianchovichina and Zárate (2021) to estimate commuting elasticities that capture how easy it is to substitute formal and informal jobs for low- and high-skilled workers residing in different locations in the city.

Information on housing prices is from vivanuncios.com.mx, Mexico's leading classified website, and a 2014 INEGI survey is the source of information on location characteristics, such as access to transportation, number of streetlights, and access to essential services.

Annex 6C A spatial general equilibrium model of a segregated city with informality

The model in Ianchovichina and Zárate (2021) builds on Zárate (2022) and is closely related to Fajgelbaum et al. (2019), who study how differences in effective tax rates can generate spatial misallocation. It also builds on recent work in the urban quantitative literature (Ahlfeldt et al. 2015; Allen, Arkolakis, and Li 2015; Tsivanidis 2019).

The city is represented in the model as a closed urban economy with a fixed number of workers in each group and land developers who live in the location in which they supply floor space. Each resident in the city derives utility (in the form of a Cobb-Douglas function) from the consumption of a composite good and housing in location i. The resident commutes to location j to work in one of s sectors and belongs to one of g groups of workers.

In each location j and sector s, homogeneous firms produce a differentiated variety v and operate under monopolistic competition. Consumers have constant elasticity of substitution (CES) preferences for the varieties v, and firms use a Cobb-Douglas production function to produce each variety. The inputs of production are labor and commercial floor space, but firms also incur a fixed production cost. Households and firms pay the same price for floor space. With free entry, the number of firms is proportional to the number of workers and commercial floor space in the location, generating agglomeration effects in equilibrium.

Land developers maximize profits and develop floor space using a Cobb-Douglas technology, capital, and land. Because the price of capital is determined in international markets, it is exogenous and fixed at 1. In equilibrium, the profits of land developers are 0; labor supply equals labor demand for each type of worker g; total sales from each location j equal the total expenditures; and government revenue equals the aggregate government expenditure.

Finally, using data on the number of workers, residents, and floor space, as well as key elasticities from Zárate (2022), it is possible to recover the values of the amenity and productivity parameters and compute commuting and trade flows by group and sector. Gravity equations and data from the 2015 Intercensal survey are then used to estimate commuting elasticities.

Notes

1. See Duque et al. (2021, 2022) for information on the spatial concentration of vulnerability characteristics of households in many other cities across Mexico and Colombia.
2. Only 1 percent of the residents in Mexico City have low sociodemographic status. Therefore, this group is merged with the second-lowest group, lower-middle.
3. In this case, high-skilled workers moved into high-amenity, expensive neighborhoods in the north of the city, while low-skilled workers relocated to poor neighborhoods in the south.

References

Ahlfeldt, G. M., S. J. Redding, D. M. Sturm, and N. Wolf. 2015. "The Economics of Density: Evidence from the Berlin Wall." *Econometrica* 83: 2127–89.

Akbar, P. 2022. "Mobility and Congestion in Urban Areas in Latin America and the Caribbean." Background paper prepared for this report, World Bank, Washington, DC.

Allen, T., C. Arkolakis, and X. Li. 2015. "On the Existence and Uniqueness of Trade Equilibria." Working paper, Yale University, New Haven, CT.

Anselin, L. 1995. "Local Indicators of Spatial Association—LISA." *Geographical Analysis* 27 (2): 93–115.

Bachas, P., L. Gadenne, and A. Jensen. 2020. "Informality, Consumption Taxes and Redistribution." Policy Research Working Paper 9267, World Bank, Washington, DC.

Bayer, P., R. McMillan, and K. Rueben. 2005. "Residential Segregation in General Equilibrium." NBER Working Paper 11095, National Bureau of Economic Research, Cambridge, MA.

Becker, G. S., and K. M. Murphy. 2000. *Social Economics: Market Behavior in a Social Environment.* Cambridge, MA: Harvard University Press.

Bischoff, K., and S. Reardon. 2014. "Income Inequality and Income Segregation." *American Journal of Sociology* 116: 1092–1153.

Caetano, G., and H. Macartney. 2021. "What Determines School Segregation? The Crucial Role of Neighborhood Factors." *Journal of Public Economics* 194 (C).

Caetano, G., and V. Maheshri. 2017. "School Segregation and the Identification of Tipping Behavior." *Journal of Public Economics* 148 (C): 115–35.

Card, D., A. Mas, and J. Rothstein. 2008. "Tipping and the Dynamics of Segregation." *Quarterly Journal of Economics* 123 (1): 177–218.

Duque, J. C., N. Lozano-Gracia, G. García, J. Ospina, J. Patiño, and R. Curiel. 2022. "Intraurban Inequality in Mexican Cities." Background paper prepared for this report, Universidad EAFIT, Medellín, Colombia.

Duque, J. C., N. Lozano-Gracia, M. Quiñones, G. García, J. Ospina, J. Patiño, and K. Montoya. 2021. "Intraurban Inequality in Colombian Cities." Unpublished manuscript, Universidad EAFIT, Medellín, Colombia.

Fajgelbaum, P. D., E. Morales, J. C. S. Serrato, and O. Zidar. 2019. "State Taxes and Spatial Misallocation." *Review of Economic Studies* 86 (1): 333–76.

Heil, A., E. Ianchovichina, and L. Quintero. 2022. "Spatial Variations in Income and Wealth in a Segregated City: Evidence from Bogotá." Background paper prepared for this report, World Bank, Washington, DC.

Hsieh, C.-T., and P. Klenow. 2009. "Misallocation and Manufacturing TFP in China and India." *Quarterly Journal of Economics* 124 (4): 1403–48.

Ianchovichina, E., and R. Zárate. 2021. "Segregation, Informality, and Misallocation." Unpublished manuscript, World Bank, Washington, DC.

Kim, Y., and B. Zangerling, eds. 2016. *Mexico Urbanization Review: Managing Spatial Growth for Productive and Livable Cities in Mexico.* Washington, DC: World Bank.

Moreno-Monroy, A. 2018. "Income Segregation in Brazilian Cities: The Role of Vertical Neighborhoods." In *Divided Cities: Understanding Intra-urban Inequalities.* Paris: Organisation for Economic Co-operation and Development.

Muzzini, E., B. Puig, S. Anapolsky, T. Lonnberg, and V. Mora. 2017. *Leveraging the Potential of Argentine Cities: A Framework for Policy Action.* Washington, DC: World Bank.

Negrete, M. E., and C. Paquette. 2011. "La interacción entre transporte público y urbanización en la Zona Metropolitana de la Ciudad de México: Un modelo expansivo que llega a sus límites." *Territorios* (25): 15–33.

Peters, P., and E. Skop. 2007. "Socio-spatial Segregation in Metropolitan Lima, Peru." *Journal of Latin American Geography* 6 (1): 149–71.

Pfutze, T., C. Rodríguez-Castelan, and D. Valderrama-Gonzalez. 2018. "Urban Transport Infrastructure and Household Welfare: Evidence from Colombia." Policy Research Working Paper 8341, World Bank, Washington, DC.

Sabatini, F. 1999. "Tendencias de la segregación residencial urbana en Latinoamérica: Reflexiones a partir del caso de Santiago de Chile." Pontificia Universidad Católica de Chile, Instituto de Estudios Urbanos.

Schelling, T. C. 1969. "Models of Segregation." *American Economic Review* 59 (2): 488–93.

Suárez, M., M. Murata, and J. Campos. 2015. "Why Do the Poor Travel Less? Urban Structure, Commuting and Economic Informality in Mexico City." *Urban Studies* 53 (12): 2548–66.

Theil, H. 1972. *Statistical Decomposition Analysis.* Amsterdam: North-Holland.

Tsivanidis, N. 2019. "Evaluating the Impact of Urban Transit Infrastructure: Evidence from Bogota's TransMilenio." University of California, Berkeley.

Tuiran, R. 2000. "Tendenciasrecientes de la movilidad territorial en algunas zonas metropolitanas de México." *El Mercado de Valores* 60 (3): 47–61.

Van der Weide, R., P. Ferreira de Souza, and R. Barbosa. 2020. "Intergenerational Mobility in Education in Brazil." Unpublished manuscript, World Bank, Washington, DC.

Zárate, R. 2022. "Spatial Misallocation, Informality, and Transit Improvements: Evidence from Mexico City." Policy Research Working Paper 9990, World Bank, Washington, DC.

Leveraging Spatial Development for Faster Inclusive Growth

7

This report identifies three spatial productivity challenges that constrain economic growth in Latin America and the Caribbean (LAC): (1) the deindustrialization of cities, (2) intercity and intracity connectivity issues, and (3) divisions within cities.

Summary of main findings

Five main findings emerge from the empirical analysis presented in this report.

First, a dramatic convergence in labor and place productivity within countries reduced regional inequality between the early 2000s and the late 2010s. However, the lower territorial inequality comes with both good news and bad news. The good news is that relatively poor, predominantly rural regions started catching up due to improvements in agricultural productivity and investments in mining areas. The bad news is the weak growth in urban productivity associated with the deindustrialization of cities in the LAC region.

Second, convergence narrowed the income disparities with leading metropolitan areas, including the gaps that could be exploited by migrating to these top locations— these areas deindustrialized but continued to attract migrants. Among residents in the bottom 40 percent of the income distribution, these gaps have become negligible in most LAC countries, except in Bolivia, Brazil, Panama, and Peru, where regional inequality has remained high.

Third, deindustrialization has shifted urban employment toward less dynamic, low-productivity nontradable activities, such as retail trade, personal services, and construction. These activities offer lower wages and returns to experience, have more limited potential for catch-up through dynamic productivity gains, and benefit less from internal returns to scale than manufacturing and tradable services. This shift constrains the growth in nation-wide productivity because the region's workforce is mostly urban. It also limits urban place productivity because nontradables benefit less from agglomeration economies than urban tradables, and their agglomeration benefits are reduced more rapidly with increases in congestion, which is a major problem in the LAC region's largest metropolitan areas.

Fourth, connectivity issues negatively affect the performance of the LAC region's network of cities by limiting market access, knowledge spillovers, and the ability of firms to specialize and gain from internal economies of scale in smaller urban areas.[1] High intercity transport costs reflect to different degrees in different countries a host of issues, including low and badly allocated investments in road improvements, backhaul problems, imperfect competition, government regulations, and information frictions. Digital technologies can be leveraged to overcome transport infrastructure deficiencies, but the LAC region's progress in expanding access to affordable high-speed internet services, especially among the bottom 40 percent and rural communities, has been slow.

Fifth, reinforced by long and costly commutes, divisions within cities, especially in some of the region's leading metropolitan areas, hurt urban productivity by limiting the geographic span of agglomeration economies to central business districts. Divisions also generate spatial misallocation stemming from the existence of informality traps in low-income neighborhoods, often located in the urban periphery. Moreover, deficiencies in basic infrastructure and public services in these low-income areas reduce the employability, productivity, and resilience of less affluent urbanites through greater exposure to climate shocks, disease, and crime.

Policy priorities

The empirical findings suggest that during the Golden Decade the LAC region's commodity-driven model of development delivered convergence in territorial productivity and living standards but accomplished only a short-lived spirt in economic growth. To accelerate growth in a sustainable, inclusive way and escape the middle-income trap, the region needs to blend its resource-driven model of development with one that better leverages the skills and labor of its urban workers. To develop such a two-pronged development model, countries will have to improve the *productivity and competitiveness* of their urban economy and enhance the efficiency with which they transform natural wealth into *human capital, infrastructure,* and *institutions.* If the region succeeds at these tasks, two engines of growth—urban and rural—will power economic growth beyond the low levels of the past without territorial divergence in living standards. The transition toward a two-pronged model of development depends on whether countries can overcome mutidimensional development challenges that span all geographic scales—national, regional, and local.

Nationwide competitiveness priorities

Countries must tackle economywide competitiveness weaknesses that limit economic growth, particularly that of urban tradables. Their governments must protect macroeconomic stability,[2] improve the quality of and access to public education,[3] address skill gaps,[4] boost nationwide innovation capabilities,[5] and reduce policy and regulatory distortions. Making regulations simpler and more predictable, increasing the transparency of legal frameworks and property protection, strengthening competition policy, improving access to finance, enforcing the rule of law, facilitating trade and investment, and harmonizing behind-the-border regulations will attract foreign investments and stimulate export growth.[6] Improving the state of international connectivity infrastructure and logistics (such as ports) will also help strengthen the competitiveness of the LAC region's exports,[7] allowing its firms to take advantage of global shifts in production, such as those linked to green growth,[8] 3D printing, and the servicification of manufacturing.[9] The weak rise in the share of employment in tradable service sectors over the last three decades suggests that LAC countries also need to implement comprehensive reforms that speed up competition and innovation in these sectors, in addition to closing skill gaps that limit the supply of talent to these sectors.

Progress in these areas should go hand in hand with strengthening the national institutions for managing volatile commodity rents, following the example of Chile, which has developed high-quality institutions for managing resource revenues, delivering social services, and regulating the private sector (Gill et al. 2014). In the context of limited fiscal space and competing priorities, efficient spending of resource rents is crucial to the ability of governments to finance the region's infrastructure needs, estimated at 3.4 percent of the region's gross domestic product (GDP) per year over the period 2015–30 (Rozenberg and Fay 2019).

Improving intergovernmental fiscal systems is another national priority. A report by the Inter-Amercian Development Bank and the Economic Commission for Latin America and the Caribbean (CEPAL) points out that subnational participation in the aggregate public spending of the LAC region doubled between 1985 and 2010, stabilizing at 26 percent in 2019 (IDB and CEPAL 2022). However, subnational governments have limited tax powers and remain highly dependent on central government transfers to fund education, health, transport, security, and many other essential community services. It is therefore essential not only to improve the efficiency of subnational spending and the ability of subnational governments to mobilize their resources, but also to protect subnational public investment and allow subnational governments to responsibly access financial markets.

Regional integration priorities

Optimal improvements of domestic roads connecting the more populous and productive areas of LAC countries can deliver an annual growth dividend estimated at around 1 percent of regional consumption (Gorton and Ianchovichina 2021) and a boost in the present discounted value of regional per capita income of 15 percent by 2100 (Conte and Ianchovichina 2022). Coordinating these domestic optimal road improvements with regional partners in MERCOSUR or the Andean Community could enhance transnational connectivity, generating additional output gains without significantly increasing the costs incurred by individual countries.

Although these are significant benefits, the estimated investment costs associated with improvements in interstate roads are also sizable, averaging between 0.65 and 0.85 percent of regional GDP under various scenarios for the period 2015–30 (Rozenberg and Fay 2019). In many countries, governments will have to complement these investments with other investments, including in environmental services to address, for example, issues associated with road flooding. The average annual cost of flood protection alone is about 0.2 percent of LAC's regional GDP (Rozenberg and Fay 2019).

Because infrastructure projects progress slowly and require financial resources that often are insufficient in the face of competing priorities, governments should abolish regulations that limit competition in the transport sector and raise transport prices along certain routes. They should also combine these infrastructure investments with complementary ones in local public goods and services. In India, the gains in economic activity associated with construction of the Golden Quadrilateral highway have been found to be larger in districts along the highway with better access to education and financial services (Das et al. 2019; Ghani, Grover, and Kerr 2013). In Argentina, such complementary investments have been shown to increase the welfare effects of road investments along the corridors linking Buenos Aires with the northwest by an estimated 45 percent and with Mesopotamia by an estimated 65 percent (World Bank 2020). In addition, authorities should fast-track investments in the information and communication technologies needed for connectivity.

Closing education, knowledge, and information gaps with leading metropolitan areas will contribute to technological diffusion and increase the employability of residents in lagging regions and their potential to benefit from migration to and employment in regional and national urban centers.

Local productivity priorities

How can LAC cities fuel nationwide productivity growth? The relatively small average urban productivity premia in the region (map O.2) and the region's advanced stage of urbanization imply limited national productivity growth from rural–urban migration, except in some of the lower-income LAC countries where agriculture still employs a large segment of the population. To enhance the urban contribution to productivity growth, more LAC urban areas must become "production" cities, whose performance in terms of productivity surpasses their national average. Two examples of US cities that have successfully transformed and raised their productivity over the years are Boston and Pittsburgh. The story of Boston illustrates how different kinds of human capital and a diversified industrial base have helped the city to become more prosperous and resilient over three and a half centuries (Glaeser 2003). The story of Pittsburgh illustrates that deindustrialized cities can come back by shifting into urban tradable services and improving their livability (King and Crommelin 2021).

A World Bank report identifies 750 "competitive" cities that have provided a good environment in which the private sector can create jobs, increase productivity, and raise incomes (Kilroy et al. 2015). In low-, middle-, and upper-middle-income countries, competitive cities are mostly "production" cities specializing in manufacturing and tradable services. Between 2005 and 2010, many competitive cities outperformed their national averages in terms of job growth (73 percent). However, fewer managed to do so in terms of productivity (42 percent) and output growth (50 percent), and a much smaller share of supercompetitive cities surpassed national averages in all three areas (18 percent), pointing to trade-offs in the three areas. No such trade-off was observed between job growth in tradables and in nontradables (Kilroy et al. 2015).[10] Cities in which employment growth in tradables was fastest also recorded high employment growth in nontradables. In less competitive cities, job growth was low in both tradables and nontradables (Kilroy et al. 2015).

Although there is no recipe for becoming a successful competitive city, a set of prerequisites that can help cities reinvent themselves and become competitive has been identified by Kilroy et al. (2015). They include good local institutions, enterprise support and finance, skills and innovation, and infrastructure and access to land. Local governments in competitive cities facilitate and expedite permitting; ensure public safety, law enforcement, and access to essential services such as water, sanitation, feeder roads, and electricity; provide inexpensive land and office space, good logistics services, and skill training; and successfully overcome fragmentation issues that might block progress or increase service provision costs and affect their quality.

Local LAC authorities need to become better at providing infrastructure that improves intraurban mobility and at implementing policies aimed at reducing congestion. Rozenberg and Fay (2019) find that city authorities can meet the demand for urban mobility at a relatively low infrastructure investment cost of about 0.45 percent of the LAC region's GDP through integrated land use and transport planning; greater reliance on integrated public transport systems, including mass transit such as metros and bus rapid transit systems; and policies that increase rail occupancy, discourage private transport,[11] and improve traffic management. The latter policies include congestion pricing; high-occupancy vehicle (HOV) restrictions; parking management; improved access to affordable, fast, and reliable internet infrastructure and digital services; and a reduction in fuel subsidies. Countries could adopt transit-oriented development strategies to ensure that land use, zoning, and building height policies are adjusted proactively to take advantage of the greater accessibility provided by mass transit investment. In this way, population growth and urban development will be channeled to the areas that can be accessed most efficiently.

Local governments must also do more to improve basic urban infrastructure and access to public services, especially in poor neighborhoods where services are deficient or under-provided. Improving the livability of the LAC region's cities will generate growth dividends because cities with skilled workers have higher productivity than other cities, and more livable cities attract talented and skilled workers (Glaeser and Xiong 2017). Investments in consumer amenities related to clean air, public transportation, public education, and health services stimulate innovation in Chinese cities (Zhang, Partridge, and Song 2020), while investments in human capital and public goods and services play an important role in patenting activity across US metropolitan areas, especially in areas with limited natural advantages (Mulligan 2020).

Last but not least, although the entry costs associated with housing do not appear to generate substantial efficiency losses in the LAC region, local governments must improve the supply of affordable quality housing, which is in short supply in low-income neighbor-hoods. As part of this agenda, they need to address long-standing land management issues and put in place flexible institutions that ensure the fluidity of land markets. Michaels et al. (2021) find that dividing land on the outskirts of cities into plots linked to roads and water mains enables the growth of neighborhoods with larger and better laid-out buildings and better-quality housing than similar areas that did not receive basic infrastructure invest-ments. However, the debate about the merits of upgrading and starting anew in existing low-income neighborhoods is ongoing (Duranton and Venables 2020), which suggests that urban land use and management practices in the LAC region remain areas for further exploration.

This report identifies the policy priorities that need attention at the national, regional, and local levels to varying degrees in all LAC countries. Because the number of proposed desirable reforms and investments is large, governments will have to design their own country- or city-specific strategies, factoring in their initial conditions and circumstances. Indeed, this report does not discuss the how and who of these strategies. However, a recent study by Grover, Lall, and Maloney (2022) provides guidance on the steps governments should follow to evaluate the merit of spatially targeted policies and the key stakeholders with whom they must work to make progress and increase the chance that a package of reforms promotes both spatial inclusion and economic transformation. A report by Kilroy et al. (2015) does that at the city level, specifying the stakeholders and the steps local authorities need to take to make cities more competitive.

Notes

1. Internal economies of scale arise from the fixed costs of production internal to a firm.
2. According to the Commission on Growth and Development (2008), macroeconomic stability is a key ingredient of a successful strategy for sustaining high growth rates over more than two decades.
3. The World Bank (2022) offers strategies for closing the learning gaps that opened during the COVID-19 pandemic.

4. Ferreyra et al. (2021) discuss in depth the LAC region's short-cycle programs. These programs offer a way to respond to the needs of the local economy by equipping individuals with skills over a shorter time and at a lower cost than four-year university programs.

5. Ferreyra et al. (2017) document the expansion of higher education in the LAC region and provide policy suggestions for improving its quality.

6. These issues are presented in depth in Rocha and Ruta (2022).

7. Although a discussion of international logistics is beyond the scope of this study, a recent Inter-American Development Bank report by Calatayud and Montes (2021) finds a significant lag in the LAC region's logistics performance relative to that of other regions.

8. A forthcoming World Bank report, tentatively entitled *Opportunities for Latin America and the Caribbean in a Greening World,* explores opportunities for green growth in the region.

9. Nayyar, Hallward-Driemeier, and Davies (2021) discuss the prospects for service-led development.

10. In the LAC region, examples of successful competitive cities that outperformed their national economies in terms of both jobs and output are Bucaramanga in Colombia and Saltillo in Mexico.

11. Some countries have invested in cycling infrastructure to help move away from private motorized modes of transport and have adopted traffic optimization policies to improve transport flows.

References

Calatayud, A., and L. Montes. 2021. *Logistics in Latin America and the Caribbean: Opportunities, Challenges and Courses of Action.* Washington, DC: Inter-American Development Bank.

Commission on Growth and Development. 2008. *The Growth Report: Strategies for Sustained Growth and Inclusive Development.* Washington, DC: World Bank.

Conte, B., and E. Ianchovichina. 2022. "Spatial Development and Mobility Frictions in Latin America: Theory-Based Empirical Evidence." Policy Research Working Paper 10071, World Bank, Washington, DC.

Das, A., E. Ghani, A. Grover, W. Kerr, and R. Nanda. 2019. "Infrastructure and Finance: Evidence from India's GQ Highway Network." Working Paper No. 19-121, Harvard Business School, Boston, MA.

Duranton, G., and A. Venables. 2020. "Place-Based Policies for Development." In *Handbook of Regional Science,* edited by M. Fisher and P. Nijkamp. Berlin: Springer.

Ferreyra, M. M., C. Avitabile, J. Botero Álvarez, F. Haimovich Paz, and S. Urzúa. 2017. *At a Crossroads: Higher Education in Latin America and the Caribbean.* Washington, DC: World Bank.

Ferreyra, M. M., L. Dinarte, S. Urzúa, and M. Bassi. 2021. *The Fast Track to New Skills: Short-Cycle Higher Education Programs in Latin America and the Caribbean.* Washington, DC: World Bank.

Ghani, E., A. Grover, and W. Kerr. 2013. "Highway to Success in India: The Impact of the Golden Quadrilateral Project for the Location and Performance of Manufacturing." Policy Research Working Paper 6320, World Bank, Washington, DC.

Gill, I., I. Izvorski, W. van Eeghen, and D. De Rosa. 2014. *Diversified Development: Making the Most of Natural Resources in Eurasia.* Washington, DC: World Bank.

Glaeser, E. 2003. "Reinventing Boston: 1640–2003." NBER Working Paper 10166, National Bureau of Economic Research, Cambridge, MA.

Glaeser, E., and W. Xiong. 2017. "Urban Productivity in the Developing World." NBER Working Paper 23279, National Bureau of Economic Research, Cambridge, MA.

Gorton, N., and E. Ianchovichina. 2021. "Trade Networks in Latin America: Spatial Inefficiencies and Optimal Expansions." Policy Research Working Paper 9843, World Bank, Washington, DC.

Grover, A., S. Lall, and W. Maloney. 2022. *Place, Productivity, and Prosperity: Revisiting Spatially Targeted Policies for Regional Development.* Washington, DC: World Bank.

IDB (Inter-American Development Bank) and CEPAL (Economic Commission for Latin America and the Caribbean). 2022. "Panorama de las relaciones fiscales entre niveles de gobierno de paises de America Latina y el Caribe." Washington, DC: IDB and CEPAL.

Kilroy, A., L. Francis, M. Mukim, and S. Negri. 2015. *Competitive Cities for Jobs and Growth: What, Who, and How.* Washington, DC: World Bank.

King, C., and L. Crommelin. 2021. "A Different Perspective on Post-industrial Labor Market Restructuring in Detroit and Pittsburgh." *Journal of Urban Affairs* 43 (7): 975–94.

Michaels, G., D. Nigmatulina, F. Rauch, R. Regan, N. Baruah, and A. Dahlstrand. 2021. "Planning Ahead for Better Neighborhoods: Long-Run Evidence from Tanzania." *Journal of Political Economy* 129 (7): 2112–156.

Mulligan, G. 2020. "Revisiting Patent Generation in US Metropolitan Areas: 1990–2015." *Applied Spatial Analysis and Policy* 14: 473–96.

Nayyar, G., M. Hallward-Driemeier, and E. Davies. 2021. *At Your Service? The Promise of Services-Led Development.* Washington, DC: World Bank.

Rocha, N., and M. Ruta, eds. 2022. *Deep Trade Agreements: Anchoring Global Value Chains in Latin America and the Caribbean.* Washington, DC: World Bank.

Rozenberg, J., and M. Fay, eds. 2019. *Beyond the Gap: How Countries Can Afford the Infrastructure They Need while Protecting the Planet.* Sustainable Infrastructure Series. Washington, DC: World Bank.

World Bank. 2020. *Territorial Development in Argentina: Diagnosing Key Bottlenecks as the First Step toward Effective Policy.* Washington, DC: World Bank.

World Bank. 2022. *Two Years After: Saving a Generation.* Washington, DC: World Bank.

Zhang, M., M. Partridge, and H. Song. 2020. "Amenities and the Geography of Innovation: Evidence from Chinese Cities." *Annals of Regional Science* 65: 105–45.